MIGRATIONS IN THE GERMAN LANDS, 1500–2000

SPEKTRUM: *Publications of the German Studies Association*

Series Editor: David M. Luebke, University of Oregon

Published under the auspices of the German Studies Association, *Spektrum* offers current perspectives on culture, society, and political life in the German-speaking lands of central Europe—Austria, Switzerland, and the Federal Republic—from the late Middle Ages to the present day. Its titles and themes reflect the composition of the GSA and the work of its members within and across the disciplines to which they belong—literary criticism, history, cultural studies, political science, and anthropology.

Migrations in the German Lands, 1500–2000

~:~

Edited by

JASON COY, JARED POLEY, AND ALEXANDER SCHUNKA

berghahn
NEW YORK · OXFORD
www.berghahnbooks.com

Published in 2016 by

Berghahn Books

www.berghahnbooks.com

©2016, 2018 Jason Coy, Jared Poley, Alexander Schunka
First paperback edition published in 2018

Library of Congress Cataloging-in-Publication Data

Names: Coy, Jason Philip, 1970– editor of compilation. | Poley, Jared, 1970– editor of
  compilation. | Schunka, Alexander, 1972– editor of compilation.
Title: Migrations in the German lands, 1500–2000 / edited by Jason Coy, Jared Poley, and
  Alexander Schunka.
Description: First edition. | New York : Berghahn Books, 2016. | Series: SPEKTRUM :
  publications of the German Studies Association ; volume 13 | Includes bibliographical
  references and index.
Identifiers: LCCN 2016023122 | ISBN 9781785331442 (hardback) | ISBN
  9781789200799 (paperback) | ISBN 9781785331459 (ebook)
Subjects: LCSH: Germany—Emigration and immigration—History. | Europe,
  German-speaking—Emigration and immigration—History. | Migration,
  Internal—Germany—History. | Migration, Internal—Europe, German-
  speaking—History. | Immigrants—Germany—History. | Immigrants—Europe,
  German-speaking—History.
Classification: LCC JV8020 .M55 2016 | DDC 304.80917/4310903—dc23
LC record available at https://lccn.loc.gov/2016023122

British Library Cataloguing in Publication Data

A catalogue record for this book is available from the British Library

ISBN 978-1-78533-144-2 hardback
ISBN 978-1-78920-079-9 paperback
ISBN 978-1-78533-145-9 ebook

"Wherefore, Lipsius, thou must not forsake thy country, but the affections."

—Justus Lipsius, *De Constantia* (1584)

∽: CONTENTS :∽

∾: TABLES :∾

~: PREFACE :~

JASON COY, JARED POLEY, AND ALEXANDER SCHUNKA

The refugee crisis of 2015–16 in Europe and particularly in Germany has overshadowed the final stages of the preparation of this volume. German politics, society, and media are currently dealing with issues of migration, flight, and asylum in a dimension unknown since the Second World War. Public reactions to the hundreds of thousands of new migrants range from ostentatious expressions of a German *Willkommenskultur* (welcome culture) to massive xenophobia. It is currently unclear to what extent this new influx of migrants from non-European countries—most notably Syria—will change the political, social, and economic landscape of Germany, but it is not far-fetched to believe that it will. The present volume intends to raise an awareness of the historical dimensions of migration to and within Germany, demonstrating that German society and culture is not dealing with such phenomena for the first time.

This volume had its origins in a series of seven panels on migration in German history at the thirty-fifth annual meeting of the German Studies Association in Louisville, Kentucky. The series was intended to bridge the gap between early modern and modern German history, and the program director, Janet Ward, and the entire program committee proved instrumental in these efforts. Mary Lindemann, a member of the German Studies Association Board, and David Luebke, the editor of the Spektrum: Publications of the German Studies Association series, both provided invaluable support when the essay collection was in the planning stages.

The editors would like to thank all of the participants in the migration series in Louisville, the anonymous peer reviewers, as well as the scholars who subsequently stepped in to fill chronological and thematic gaps in the volume. Finally, we would like to thank Zach Bates for his careful attention to the volume's bibliographies.

∽:∼

Migrations in the German Lands:
An Introduction

ALEXANDER SCHUNKA

Overview

The history of human cultures is a history of migrations and movements.[1]
The contours of human mobility are remarkably sensitive to a broader
historical context, and migrations have to a large extent produced and affected
historical realities. Based on the insight that cultures are always shaped by
mobility and exchange, scholars have developed a growing interest in understanding the cross-cultural connections and conflicts that emerge in response
to migration.

Dealing with the history of immigration into Germany during the last
five hundred years, the present volume breaks new ground. For a long time,
immigration *into* Germany was not considered as historically relevant as the
emigrations of Germans to the New World, to Russia, and elsewhere. The
question of whether Germany was predominantly a land of emigration or one
of immigration has become a political issue during the last thirty years, leaving
its imprint on historical research. Migration illustrates a particular tension
between the realities of human movement in German history and the capacity
of the country's social, cultural, and political institutions to absorb its effects.
Indeed, the politics of migration in Germany have helped to produce any
number of frank assertions about the desirability—and in fact the very nature
of—a heterogeneous Germany. The stakes were perhaps never more clear than
in the political statements originating in the 1982 federal coalition agreement
between the West German ruling Christian Democrats (CDU/CSU) and the
liberal Free Democratic Party (FDP): the "Federal Republic of Germany is not
a country of immigration. Therefore all steps acceptable from a humanitarian
point of view need to be taken to prevent the influx of foreigners."[2] In the
years that followed, a number of German conservative politicians, including

chancellor Helmut Kohl, repeatedly stressed that Germany's migratory traditions were outgoing, not incoming, and that Germany was—and presumably always had been—a country of emigration, not immigration.

Yet recently, the contemporary and historic realities of human movement into Germany have been addressed on a larger scale. Likewise, scholars, politicians, and the media have reassessed the political nature of a term like *Einwanderungsland* (immigration country). Gaining ground recently is the idea that Germany boasts a rich history of hosting different immigrant groups, from the descendants of seventeenth-century French Huguenot refugees to those of nineteenth-century *Ruhrpolen* (Polish miners of the Ruhr area), from *Gastarbeiter* ("guest workers" from Southern and Southeast Europe and particularly from Turkey) and *Vertragsarbeiter* (contract workers migrating from several socialist countries in the German Democratic Republic) to *Aussiedler* (ethnic German immigrants from Eastern Europe). As a result, the sense that German society is defined by its historical development as an "immigration society" (*Einwanderungsgesellschaft*) is emerging.[3] In recent years, political experts, influenced by eminent scholars, have explicitly mentioned "both sides of the [German] immigration society."[4] In this respect, the term "immigration society" increasingly includes migrants and non-migrants alike and suggests that the contemporary German *Einwanderungsgesellschaft* evolved from the long history of communication and interaction between migrants and (supposedly native) residents.[5] However idealistic such an implicit revival of the older "melting pot"[6] idea might seem nowadays, its adaptation publicly acknowledges the significance of immigration to German politics, economy, society, and culture. This importance is of course not a new discovery for migration historians.

Contrary to the well-known and well-researched history of the German lands as important areas of emigration and the population there as long-time participants in larger migration systems such as the Atlantic and North Sea Systems,[7] Germany now stands at the crossroads of accepting that it has a long history of immigration as well. This realization is apparent in public memorials and anniversary celebrations such as the fiftieth anniversary of the 1961 German-Turkish *Anwerbeabkommen*[8] (bilateral agreement on labor recruitment) in 2011. Against much historical evidence, *Gastarbeiter* immigration was hailed in this anniversary celebration as the beginning of Turkish immigration into Germany and also of Turkish integration into German society.[9] German media and public memory also recalled the famous arrival in 1964 of the millionth *Gastarbeiter*, a Portuguese worker named Armando Rodrigues de Sá who was awarded a bouquet of flowers and a motorbike at the train station in Cologne.[10] In retrospect, the public memory of immigration into Germany is sometimes presented as a story of German hospitality toward foreigners that neglects the precarious status of the millions of *Gastarbeiter* who not only faced severe difficulties to unite with their families from abroad but who also, as "guests," worked for their host society before they had to return home. In 2013, hardly anyone except a few critical scholars commemorated the fortieth anniversary of the West German *Anwerbestopp* of 1973, the recruitment ban on foreign workers in Germany that preceded similar laws in other European countries, and that set the stage for the starkly anti-immigrant declarations that followed.[11]

Whereas public debates over migration within Germany in the late twentieth century focused on the phenomenon of *Gastarbeiter*, current discussions within German politics and culture increasingly deal with a wide range of migrational and immigrational issues such as poverty migration, specialist migration, "brain drain" (as well as "brain gain"), and the hybrid cultural allegiances of second- and third-generation migrants. At the same time, the longer historic dimensions of migration within, into, and around Germany slowly find their place in scholarship as well as in a public awareness of the historical dimensions of a German "immigration society." Whereas the historiography of certain migrant groups has long existed but mainly lay in the hands of their descendants, as is obvious in the traditional historiography on the French Huguenots, a 2005 double exhibition at the *Deutsches Historisches Museum* in Berlin presented the Huguenots as only one of a wide range of immigrants in the German past, albeit perhaps the most prominent.[12] Apart from late twentieth-century immigrations, migrational issues have long struggled (and struggle still) to gain an adequate place in history textbooks and in overall historical research.[13]

What justifies the present volume is not only its attempt to present state-of-the-art research and to give an overview of this changing situation in the historiography of German migration, but also to provide a diachronic perspective on immigration. The contributions do not claim to present a full range overview of a five-hundred-year-long history of migration into Germany. Taking into account their selective nature (and the obvious thematic gaps necessarily inherent to a collected volume such as the present one), they rather seek to raise the awareness of this important topic among non-German readers and to connect the empiric findings of migration scholars to current discussions in German historiography and culture. Taking into account recent research on the history and culture of migration, this volume provides important insights into the long-neglected history of Germany as a site of immigration as well as into the cultural consequences of this mobility. The essays, written by German and American specialists in the field, examine overarching migrational structures, the development and changes of migrational patterns and regimes from the early modern until the contemporary era, and the individual experiences of migrants over time.[14] Since each essay contains a broader introduction into one particular migrational phenomenon before turning to empirical case studies, the volume also serves as an introductory overview on important aspects of a broad, extremely rich, and sometimes rather messy subject—without attempting to provide a comprehensive, textbook style narrative.

However, a few caveats need to be mentioned that point to the complicated character of the history of migrations more generally. The first is that it often appears difficult to separate between phenomena of immigration as opposed to emigration. Such a seemingly obvious distinction tends to overstress a number of assumptions. One is the notion of clear-cut borders between nation states or territorial entities (including the borders of the European Union or the Mediterranean Sea as a natural frontier between the poorer south and the wealthier north). National and even natural borders are, however, to a great extent, historically constructed and change their meaning and importance over time.[15] Separating emigration from immigration also implies that human movements might be one-dimensional and unidirectional phenomena with a clear point of departure and an equally clear point of destination. However, recent research has pointed out that human mobility is flexible, that it can proceed step-by-step or even in a circular fashion, and that it relies on a number of variable economic, social, political, religious, and legal parameters.

Another equally problematic assumption is the idea that immigrants can always, and more or less intentionally, decide upon their national, ethnic, and emotional allegiances. This is represented in the recent discussions of German politics and media on the *Doppelpass*, the law that native Germans of migrant descent must decide at a certain age which citizenship they accept.[16] Transnational family ties, money transfers, the return of *Gastarbeiter* to their former homelands upon retirement, and the multiple identities of later-generation migrants caught between (at least) two, often conflicting, cultural frameworks shed light upon the problems connected to these shared allegiances between home and host countries.[17] In German popular culture, this comes to the surface not only in discussions about a possible radicalization of third-generation migrants, or about Muslim women in public service wearing headscarves (the *Kopftuchstreit*, or headscarf debate),[18] but also in the evolution of particular immigrant languages (*Kanaksprak*) and literatures that do not seem to fit into binary oppositions between home and host societies.[19] Accepting the evolution of particular migrational "thirdspaces" avoids simple dichotomies and opens up the view on creative practices and the evolution of new, transcultural norms.[20]

In addition, an issue of major importance is the general problem of defining migration. Often migration is considered a change of residence involving the crossing of a (political) border and lasting for a certain period of time.[21] Such a definition is obviously problematic, simply by considering the many different political frontiers that could, as was the case in early modern and modern Germany alike, divide a given city or village. Likewise, forms of regular movement for certain months over many years—as can be found among early modern Austrian or Swiss pastoralists in the upper Rhine era, eighteenth-century traders from Northern Italy, and even twenty-first century harvest hands from Eastern Europe—do not seem to be covered by such a strict definition while they are still seen as temporary work migrations. Similar problems arise when one tries to distinguish forced from voluntary migrations:[22] Is migration to avoid starvation, we could ask, on the forced or on the voluntary side?[23] Is the preemptory decision to emigrate in order to avoid future persecution or even deportation voluntary or forced? What were the opportunities and scope of action of an Ottoman-Turkish prisoner of war in early modern Germany who could otherwise very easily be considered a forced migrant?[24] Is not everyone in some respect a voluntary migrant as long as he or she is able to arrange and pay for a journey to a seemingly better and safer place (depending on age, gender, class, money, knowledge, and other factors)? And what is the amount of migrant agency even within coerced migrations?[25] Only in rare cases during the last five centuries can migrational phenomena into Germany be definitively called forced migration. In the twentieth century, perhaps the most obvious example is the employment of forced laborers under the Nazi regime; in earlier times one might think of prisoners-of-war who sometimes lived under slave-like conditions.[26]

Another distinction occurs between the blurry concepts of immigration/emigration and exile. In early modern Germany, the term emigration had a juridical and/or a political meaning ("immigration" is hardly found at all; "migration" seems to occur for the first time in the early eighteenth century[27]), while exile (*exilium*, a concept originally derived from Roman Law) since the sixteenth century increasingly denoted religiously motivated self-perceptions of someone being temporarily removed from his or her homeland.[28] While in the early modern era the concept of exile is usually a religious one, it gave way to more political connotations only in the later eighteenth century, especially from the French Revolution onward. Nineteenth- and twentieth-century sources often use the term exile as a politically motivated change of place (such as to escape persecution by Nazi Germany) from which a number of intellectuals and other emigrants decided to remigrate back to Germany when persecution and war were over.[29] What both concepts have in common is that being removed from one's place of origin is often considered a temporary, not a permanent, condition.

The blurred concepts as well as the fates of individual migrants (against the backdrop of class, gender, ethnic background, politics, economic situation, travel infrastructures, social ties) might thus justify turning from a structural perspective to the analysis of the lives of individuals. This implies stressing the knowledge, options, and opportunities of migrants rather than applying clear-cut macro-definitions from a bird's eye view of socio-historical scholarship.

Finally, and contrary to what social and economic historians as well as scholars of historical demography have long assumed, migration is not just an issue of exact and quantifiable figures, but sometimes rather one of non-quantifiable perceptions, feelings, and identities. While passenger lists, parish books, police records, and other seemingly exact data might suggest that it would be easy to simply count the number of immigrants and hold them against a presumably exact number of non-immigrant "natives" in order to distill the scope of migration, for most centuries before at least 1850 (and even nowadays with the hardly controllable influx of refugees and "illegal" immigrants), statistical baselines often pretend exactness more than they depict historical realities.

Therefore, and with all these caveats in mind, most essays of the present volume as well as this introduction argue not strictly upon serialized data and sharp definitions but rather try to integrate the contemporary circumstances of human movement while keeping in mind the flaws of the sources. The emphasis on immigration in the present volume is therefore not a strict but a rather heuristic choice, aimed at a better understanding of the other side of German migrations, i.e., the world *in* Germany as opposed to Germans in the *world*. It addresses an English-speaking audience highly aware of their own migrational backgrounds and traditions, which may indeed even connect them to Germany.

Immigration in Germany, 1500–2000

The focus on "Germany," as well as on a period ranging from 1500 to 2000, needs clarification. Both of these limitations are somewhat arbitrary and must be understood loosely. As far as the geographic and political outlook of the book is concerned, there was no "Germany" before 1815 or even before 1871, and there were a number of "Germanies" after that date.[30] Before 1806, the Holy Roman Empire of the German Nation consisted of hundreds of smaller territorial entities, which were largely, but never exclusively, connected to a rather diverse German language and culture. As will be illustrated shortly, there is much evidence that the specific political and confessional heterogeneity of pre-modern Germany had considerable effects on the patterns of migration.

At the same time, one of the eminent characteristics of migration and human movement is that these phenomena transcend and even disrupt seemingly clear-cut boundaries. Still, a certain receptiveness to German languages and cultures was prevalent and necessary for people moving within or into the Empire, at least when migrants got in touch with territorial powers, cultural institutions, churches, or simply with new neighbors. Although French, Czech, and other seemingly "ethnic" immigrant communities existed in eighteenth-century Germany as well as, for instance, Turkish neighborhoods from the later twentieth century onward, their inhabitants were (and are) never fully homogeneous nor completely cut off from their German surroundings.

Considering the common historical periodization of eras such as "early modern" or "modern," it needs to be kept in mind that the history of mobility and migrations does not always fit into larger historical classifications because human movement is often connected to ideas and social practices of a *longue durée* (such as economy and trade, craftsmanship, kinship structures, scholarly exchange, religious ideas) that transgress the boundaries of historical epochs. Yet the legal, political and religious framework of historic Germany and Central Europe, which evolved around 1500, has left its mark on migrations and movements, although perhaps more for sedentary people and the authorities dealing with immigrants than for the migrants themselves. To a certain degree, people on the move had to adapt to the religious, cultural, and political norms of their new host countries when they negotiated with the authorities in order to settle and start making a new living. In this respect, migrants and human movements were affected by processes of state building as manifested in the creation of migrational regimes and citizenship laws, as well as by supranational processes such as an increasing globalization of economies, politics, and communication. This specific framework illustrates why migrations in the early modern and modern eras differ from earlier periods and deserve a closer analysis over a period of the last five hundred years.

Official data issued by the Federal Bureau of Statistics (*Statistisches Bundesamt*) for the year 2013 indicates that about 20 percent of the 80 million inhabitants of Germany had foreign origins.[31] Contrary to such seemingly exact figures, population numbers and immigration rates of earlier times can often be no more than rough guesses: researchers assume that approximately nine million people lived in the Holy Roman Empire around the year 1500, 17 million in 1618, before the Thirty Years War reduced the population to 10 million (1650) after which a general growth set in (22 million in 1800), leading to the population increase of the industrial age (24.8 million in 1815; 40.8 million in 1870; 64.6 million in 1910; 69.8 million in 1940).[32]

Apart from the German emigrations, which amount to approximately 5 million in the nineteenth century, demographers usually consider immigration rates before the twentieth century as rather insignificant in regard to the enormous overall population increase.[33] It has also long been assumed that early modern Germany between 1500 and 1800 in particular consisted of a rather static society characterized by local as well as social stability and dominated by a hierarchic system of estates (*Ständeordnung*) and strong personal and economic ties that bound the population to their overlords and to the land they inhabited. More recent research, however, has shown that early modern societies were highly mobile and that at least one-third of all early modern Germans changed their place of living once in their lives.[34] On an individual level, there were many different reasons why people went on the move, ranging from the pursuit of trade, the wandering of craftsmen, the search for a marriage partner, and the peregrinations of students and scholars, to migrations caused by epidemics, wars, natural disasters, poverty or the wish for economic betterment.[35] In retrospect, individual options often mixed with structural phenomena, making migration history the terrain upon which micro- and macrohistorical forces intersect.[36] While in some cases migrations were part of a life cycle, corresponded with the seasons of the year, or belonged to certain professions, in others they were rather exceptional processes, as in cases of war and confessional persecution.

Considering early modern societies as based on personal presence and interaction (*Anwesenheitsgesellschaft*),[37] immigrations and settlement processes are fascinating frameworks that help analyze the features of communication, connection, and personal interaction in daily life, especially against the backdrop of the administrative, confessional, and cultural plurality within the Holy Roman Empire.[38] Therefore, in a certain sense, the early modern Reich consisted not only of an abundance of semi-independent territories, but also of numerous, albeit different, "immigration societies" (*Einwanderungsgesellschaften*).

Apart from climatic changes and natural disasters, which caused settlement changes in many parts of Europe, the Reformation and its aftermath left perhaps the strongest imprint on central European migration patterns of the early modern era. Confessional strife between Lutherans and Catholics resulted in or contributed to religious conflicts that forced thousands of people to move. In this respect, the Thirty Years War was the most significant, albeit not the only, war in Central Europe that instigated temporary or permanent resettlement.[39] The confessional divisions of Germany also influenced the treatment of vagrant people by sedentary societies because the ideas of the Reformation contributed to a stronger appreciation of local stability and regular work as norms that went along with a growing marginalization of foreign beggars and itinerant groups. This was especially the case in early modern cities, which had always been attractive to people seeking better lives.[40]

Confessional migration is considered one rather distinct type of central European migration between the sixteenth and the eighteenth centuries.[41] Thousands of adherents of the new faith had to change their residence due to religious homogenizations and persecutions, or legitimated their wish to move with their faith. The term *Reformation of the Refugees* has been coined predominantly with respect to Calvinist migrations to underline the creative power of mobility for the transmission of Reformation ideas. This included English and Scottish Presbyterians who fled the anti-Protestant persecutions in England under Mary Tudor and settled for some time in merchant metropolises such as Frankfurt am Main.[42] Dutch Calvinists were an even larger group who left the Netherlands during the Dutch Revolt in the second half of the century. Many of them settled in northwestern Germany and, as Jesse Spohnholz has recently illustrated, managed their daily living among other faiths with a good deal of pragmatic tolerance.[43] A result of the French Wars of Religion of roughly the same period was the first exodus of French Reformed Huguenots, who entered the Rhenish palatinate and its surroundings, founding the first so-called Cities of Exiles (*Exulantenstädte*).[44] In many cases, the evidence shows that immigrant communities were rather fluid and open to others, consisting of ethnically heterogeneous migrant families of different origin, although joint emigrations of families and relatives were also seen. In some cases, these migrant communities seemed to have played an important role as cultural transmitters between home and host societies.

While confessional migrations within the Empire surrounding the important Religious Peace of Augsburg (1555) have not yet been researched comprehensively, other larger emigrations of later decades are well known. These migrations point to the fact that confessional migration was far from a Calvinist phenomenon but rather affected Lutherans and other adherents of the Reformation as well.[45] During the re-catholicization process of the Habsburg lands, thousands of mostly Lutheran Protestants decided to move to the southern and southeastern parts of the Holy Roman Empire where, for instance, Nuremberg became an important cultural center of Austrian Lutheran exiles (*Exulanten*).[46] From the first years of the Thirty Years War, Electoral Saxony had to accommodate large numbers of Protestant exiles from the Habsburg-ruled Bohemian lands who settled at strategic spots close to the border or along the river Elbe and later even founded some Czech church communities where they preserved and sometimes created a common Bohemian heritage.[47] While older research preferred to give exact figures of Austrian or Bohemian migrants based on somewhat mythological statements of contemporaries (for instance, 36,000 Bohemian families), more recent historians try to contextualize these migrations against the backdrop of day-to-day mobility. Still, an influx of probably many more than 100,000 people from the Habsburg lands into southern and central Germany over the seventeenth century seems a reasonable guess.[48]

Only recently, the Roman Catholic dimension of confessional migration is beginning to attract the attention of researchers. However, it seems that due to the number of migrants and accompanying propaganda on the Protestant side, confessionally motivated migrations of Catholics seem to have been rather marginal in Central Europe—apart from military migrations in the Habsburg army or the movements of Dutch and English Catholics to the Southern Netherlands.[49] Sephardic Jews, who settled in Antwerp and elsewhere after their expulsion from the Iberian Peninsula and later came to imperial cities such as Hamburg, have not usually been considered part of the phenomenon of confessional migration.[50]

Emigrations in the name of religion and accompanied by their respective propagandas continued into the late seventeenth and eighteenth centuries, as the famous case of the second *Refuge* of roughly 150,000 to 200,000 Huguenots in the 1680s demonstrates. A number of German rulers competed over attracting Huguenot settlers, although most of the *Refugiés* decided to move to Brandenburg-Prussia, where they settled just as the many Dutch, Swiss, Czech, and other immigrants had done before. Huguenots were particularly successful in creating not only economic and social links to France and the diasporic Huguenot communities in Europe, but also certain myths of migration and religious exile.[51] The famous Salzburg emigrants, who were likewise "invited" by the Prussian King Frederick William I in 1731 to repopulate northeastern Prussia, progressed through the empire in spectacular processions of about 16,000 people altogether. They served as a means for enormous political and religious propaganda.[52] Still the Huguenots and the Salzburgers in Prussia point not only to the longevity of religious exile and confessional migration, but also to the increasing importance of immigration and attracting foreign settlers to support the economies of particular host countries. Together with a refinement of population theory and demographic scholarship among Cameralist politicians,[53] the idea of *Peuplierung* (population increase) was paramount among numerous territories of the Empire, from Brandenburg-Prussia and other territorial states to smaller units such as in the Wetterau where even decidedly heterodox immigrants were allowed to settle in places like Neuwied.[54]

Whereas the larger territories in the eighteenth century actively tried to attract foreigners (such as Brandenburg-Prussia, the Habsburg Empire, where immigrants were meant to populate remote places such as Transylvania, or Russia, which was almost as popular for German emigrants as the Americas), other German states, especially in the southwest of the Empire, tried to prevent the emigration of their population by imposing harsh and threatening fines on potential runaways. All this points to the fact that migrational regimes of German states in the Enlightenment era were changing—not toward more tolerance of refugees, but toward acknowledging their economic potential. Scattered evidence from the perspective of the immigrants, however, indicates that contrary to the official policies, many of the new settlements in Prussia or elsewhere turned out to be unattractive to settlers who either fled from their new homes or never even showed up due to the lack of resources, individual safety, or economic opportunities.

Apart from these larger immigrations, early modern Germany hosted individual expert migrants who would hardly appear in a conventional history of German immigration. Scholars ranged from Reformation theologians of Scottish, Polish, Croatian, or Italian origin (such as John Knox, Matthias Flacius Illyricus, Pier Paolo Vergerio, John a Lasco) to eminent intellectuals such as

Justus Lipsius and Tycho Brahe, from court artisans to alchemists, musicians, theater groups, and soldiers. German armies in the seventeenth century consisted of large networks of British, Irish, and Scottish soldiers, among whom Walter Leslie figures prominently as the assassin of mercenary leader Albrecht von Wallenstein and the founder of a dynasty of soldiers on the continent.[55]

At the same time, the Humanist and Baroque courts of Germany (especially the Imperial Court of Vienna, but also Bavaria, Hesse, and Electoral Saxony) evolved as international centers of scholarship and migrant cultures. Considering the fact that the Holy Roman Empire only indirectly participated in overseas expansion and trade, it is quite remarkable that its numerous courts hosted a wide mix of races and cultures, from former Turkish prisoners captured in the wars against the Ottoman Empire, to Africans, and sometimes even Native Americans. They all had, of course involuntarily, made it to Germany where they were often turned into exotic status symbols of a ruler and his nobility.[56] In the mid-eighteenth century, the Scottish Jacobite immigrant George Keith lived in Potsdam just across from Sanssouci palace as one of the long-time friends of Frederick the Great of Prussia; his private entourage consisted of Kalmyk, Tartar, and African servants, and, as an adopted child, a Turkish Janissary's daughter who ended up marrying a French Huguenot in Berlin.[57]

Court cities such as Vienna and Dresden, with their demand for foreign consumer goods (food and spices, clothing, jewelry), as well as trading centers like Leipzig, Hamburg, and Frankfurt am Main offered opportunities for the development of international merchant infrastructures that often stemmed from a single prominent family. Merchants from certain alpine valleys of northern Italy, especially around Lago di Como, proved influential in building up persisting structures of trade that lasted over many generations and well into the modern era. A striking (but not isolated) example is the Brentano family who started a wine and spice trading business in seventeenth-century Frankfurt and whose later generations ended up as scholars and politicians.[58] A number of well-known German chain stores, some still in business today, have their origins in similar seasonal migrant trade structures of northwest Germany that date back to the seventeenth and eighteenth centuries.[59]

What can be summed up as an early modern means of "brain gain" through migration into Germany relied upon the highly decentralized structures of the Holy Roman Empire. While its numerous territories provided shelter and refuge for suppressed individuals and groups who were expected to enhance the economy, scholarship, and culture of the host countries, the legal structure of the Empire could be detrimental for higher-ranking refugees with particular political goals. Thus, political migrants such as the Bohemian insurgents of 1618 mostly tried not to settle in the Empire but to escape from it for fear of extradition and condemnation, and royal European migrants such as Chris-

tina of Sweden, her successor Charles XII, or the Hungarian Prince Ferenc
Rákóczi II eventually headed for Rome and the Ottoman Empire, respectively,
where they felt far safer than in the heart of Europe. In the course of the
French Revolution of 1789, however, temporary immigrant settlements of
French political refugees evolved in a number of cities along the Rhine, among
which the Koblenz community was perhaps the most remarkable, not only
because of its size but also because of its imitation of French habits abroad.[60]

These immigrations surrounding the French Revolution hint at the important transition into the nineteenth century that, from a migration historian's
point of view appears to be a mixture of continuity and change. While political
and economic factors came to dominate the patterns of migration in what Eric
Hobsbawm has coined the "Dual", i.e., political-cum-industrial, Revolution,
issues of class and gender began to emerge as important factors shaping immigration (especially with regard to migrants from rural peripheries to urban
centers). Whereas in the early modern era, dealing with immigration had often
been an issue of municipal governments and local administrations including
church communities, from the nineteenth century the evolving modern state
and its institutions developed migratory regimes based upon central authorities and upon increasingly refined methods of administering the population.
Undoubtedly, the centralized bureaucracies of the new migratory regimes
perfected their systems of registration, governance, and control as far as the
population, and particularly immigrants, were concerned. At the same time, a
number of rather pre-modern features seem to have remained fairly constant
(such as the meaning of family ties, the structure of communication, the migration cycles of journeymen, traders, and specialists). Furthermore, it needs to be
taken into account that often even the most sophisticated ways of governing
immigrants at least partly failed in practice, leading to the fuzziness of migration, which seems one important characteristic of this phenomenon to this day.

Germany was relatively late in becoming a place of asylum for genuine political refugees. However, in the age of a growing nationalism in the nineteenth
century, political migrants could, under certain conditions, still rely on help
and solidarity. When in the 1830s many Germans financially supported the
refugees of the Grand Emigration from Poland (*Wielka Emigracja*) following
the Polish November Uprising against Russia (1830–31), they probably did
so not only because of a particular antagonism with Russia or because the
refugees had fought for civil liberties, but also because it was obvious that
most of these emigrants would not stay under the authoritative regimes of
the German Confederation (*Deutscher Bund*), but rather would pass through
Germany on their way towards Western Europe.[61]

However, against the backdrop of the large-scale German emigration to
North America, Australia, and other places in the nineteenth century, it
could easily be forgotten that Germany was more than just an emigration

society and that immigration and movements within the country featured prominently. The period of industrialization and abolition of feudal bonds greatly enhanced mobility, even if it did not instigate population movements from rural into metropolitan areas. Movements of journeymen, for instance, continued from early modern times well into the nineteenth century, attracting 140,000 *Gesellen* yearly to a city like Vienna with an overall population of 350,000.[62] Apart from these rather traditional movements, industrialization resulted in a growing need for industrial labor and the immense growth of German cities, which had long been targets of immigration. This increase in migration from the rural peripheries to the centers is particularly obvious in the conglomerate of the Prussian provinces that stretched from the Rhine in the West to Silesia and to partitioned Poland in the east. The movement of Silesians to the capital of Berlin was an impressive phenomenon of the nineteenth century.[63] The migration of *Ruhrpolen* to Prussia's western provinces from the 1870s was even larger and perhaps the biggest population movement in nineteenth-century Germany. It provided a fundamental basis for industrialization (mining, steel mills) in the Ruhr area and affected Prussia, Germany, eastern Europe, and in particular the partitioned Polish nation whose western sections were included in Prussia once after 1792–93 and again after 1848. Technically the migrations of hundreds of thousands of Poles further west (the Polish community comprised approximately 400,000 in 1914) were by and large an internal Prussian migration because many ethnic Poles moved from Prussia's provinces of Posen and Silesia, causing another migration wave of Poles from Russian Poland to fill in the population gaps.[64] As immigrants, *Ruhrpolen* long favored indigenous marriages and crafted a largely closed society. One of the results of this ethnic Polish migration was that, after 1900, the German Empire evolved as the second-biggest importer of workers behind only the United States.[65]

In the Polish-Prussian province of Posen as well as in the Ruhr area and in other parts of Prussia, these migrational dynamics contradicted the Germanization policy of the Prussian state and, at the same time, created strong anti-Polish and anti-Slavic sentiments that lasted well into the twentieth century. In 1885, Germanization policies led to the temporary expulsion of 40,000 non-naturalized Poles and Polish Jews from Prussia. Due to the growing need for laborers, however, a seasonal employment system was introduced in Prussia only a few years later, with three-year contracts for workers from abroad who had to leave the country during the winter months.[66] Such a temporary job rotation preceded similar regulations in the Federal Republic of Germany of the 1950s where *Gastarbeiter* were initially hired only for a fixed number of years.

Up until the early twentieth century, immigration into Germany as well as movements within Germany were legally not a national issue, because they were addressed by the respective territorial authorities. By the nineteenth century, however, debates about immigration and citizenship were closely linked to the evolution of the German nation state and the question of what it means to be German.[67] The Prussian treatment of foreigners after the establishment of the German Empire of 1871 indicates that it was a long way from instituting a concerted German immigration policy that was able to deal with the realities of Central European mobility. Prussian citizenship legislation was based on descent from German parents, and, after the failed revolution of 1848–49, became increasingly influential as an example to other German states. The first overarching, centralized German citizenship law (*Reichs- und Staatsangehörigkeitsgesetz*) from 1913, was again based on German descent.[68] Only upon individual application after a presence of ten years in Germany could immigrants receive naturalization; in case of a long and unauthorized absence abroad, Germans (namely deserters from military service), in turn, could lose their citizenship. What hints at the high priority of German militarization and the responsibility of each male for military service, has at the same time been interpreted as a growing racialization of foreign immigration by German society. Primary victims of this attitude in the German Reich were Russian Poles and East European Jews who rarely achieved naturalization. Legal or economic reasoning served to cover up attitudes of cultural and racial superiority. Not only Jewish newcomers from the east but also assimilated Jews in the later nineteenth and early twentieth centuries were increasingly attributed with a particularly "Asiatic" foreignness, attitudes that helped shape the anti-Semitism of Nazi Germany.[69]

Many features of nineteenth-century immigration, migratory regimes, and attitudes toward foreigners point toward the century to come. The migration regime of the Weimar Republic, as well as the mentality of many Germans toward foreigners from Eastern Europe, retained close continuities with the *Kaiserreich*.[70] In addition, the occupation of the Rhineland by French troops following the treaty of Versailles and largely consisting of soldiers from African colonies triggered off a new anti-colonialist, racist, and sexualized discourse against a *Schwarze Schmach* (black humiliation). Hundreds of children from mixed relationships between French Africans and Germans ended up being sterilized under the Nazis in the 1930s.[71]

Massive changes in immigration policies, albeit not in the overall attitudes vis-à-vis foreigners, occurred only after 1933. In a seeming contradiction to the National Socialist ideology of race, Germanness, and *Volkstum*, the Third Reich period ironically perhaps witnessed the greatest number of foreigners living in Germany. An estimated 13 million forced laborers (*Fremdarbeiter*) from occupied territories all over Europe contributed to the upkeep of the German economy before and during World War II. They often served under slave-like conditions and, in case they survived the breakdown of the Nazi regime in 1945 on German territory, ended up as displaced persons, most of whom, together with Holocaust survivors, went elsewhere as soon as they could.[72] Nazi resettlement policies of the so-called *Volksdeutsche* led to the migrations of millions of allegedly ethnic Germans in Eastern and East Central Europe, who, from 1944 onward, moved farther west.[73]

The reason why Germany's population—numbering almost 70 million in 1940—remained approximately 68 million in 1950 despite the millions lost during the Second World War illustrates that immigration had filled the demographic gaps.[74] Thus, the years around 1945 in Germany and central Europe show probably the greatest extent of mobility ever witnessed in this region. After the end of the Nazi regime, approximately 25 million migrants from abroad (10–12 million displaced persons and around 14 million German refugees from the east), in addition to returned exiles and about 10 million people who had evacuated and thus survived the destruction of German cities, had lost their homes, and were looking for new settlements in a Germany divided into Soviet, American, French, and British sectors.[75] At the same time, up to 700,000 foreign soldiers, stationed in both parts of Germany for the next forty years, were housed in barracks largely separated from the German population, but over time this would not prevent contact and, for instance, mixed relationships and marriages between Allied soldiers and German women.[76] Migration between the sectors of occupied Germany was particularly a phenomenon of East-West movements, with approximately 2.7 million people leaving the newly founded GDR (1949) for the Federal Republic before the building of the Berlin Wall in 1961.[77] In short, Germany in the postwar years consisted of an impressive number of uprooted people, often traumatized by individual experiences of escape and loss in the aftermath of the racist and expansionist actions of Nazi Germany across Europe.

With that said, modern research has still stressed that the postwar Allied reeducation efforts of the German population focused too sparingly on migration and cultural difference, leaving space for continued xenophobia and anti-Semitism in Germany after 1945.[78] The *Grundgesetz* of the Federal Republic explicitly states in Article 116/1 that all "ethnic German" refugees (*Flüchtlinge und Vertriebene*) in Germany were legal German citizens and thus continued the ethnic concept of Germanness well into the postwar period. The integration of these millions of refugees from areas like the Sudetenland (Bohemia), Silesia, East Prussia, and elsewhere, has long been glorified in public memory as an astonishingly smooth process. Only recently have the accompanying individual setbacks, social and economic hardships, and psychological difficulties facing migrants as well as their host communities received more attention.[79]

Continuities in legislation as well as in the attitudes of Germans toward foreigners can indeed be found between the nineteenth and the later twentieth centuries. The large-scale immigration of *Gastarbeiter* during the *Wirtschafts-*

wunder decade of the 1950s in West Germany not only relied on a rotation system resembling earlier Prussian practices (although now it was not so rigidly enforced), but it was also connected from its beginning with, at best, skeptical, and at worst, xenophobic reactions by considerable parts of the population.[80]

Gastarbeiter migration combined the employment needs of Germany, the need for economic and demographic relief of the country of origin, the creation of new markets, the interaction of German firms and foreign countries, and increasingly, the transfer of money from *Gastarbeiter* in Germany to their families in their home countries. The bilateral *Anwerbeabkommen* with Italy in 1955 opened the way for the large-scale employment of Italians in Germany, and similar contracts followed with Spain and Greece (1960), Turkey (1961), Portugal (1964), and socialist but "block free" Yugoslavia (1968). Thus, *Gastarbeiter* policies largely recruited workers from Mediterranean nations experiencing conditions of economic contraction or slow growth (although similar contracts with North African states existed, they did not result in a broader migration).

In a political sense, many of these *Anwerbeabkommen* had their origins in or were heavily influenced by German obligations in international alliances such as the European Community and NATO.[81] A particularly striking example for the effect of global Cold War policies on German immigration is the *Anwerbeabkommen* between Germany and the Republic of Korea in 1963, which, ten years after the Korean War and the political as well as ideological partition of the Korean peninsula, was strongly supported from the South Korean side and brought into Germany several thousand well-trained immigrants, most of them miners and nurses.[82]

At the time of the *Anwerbestopp* in 1973, approximately 3 million foreigners (mostly Turks) lived in West Germany, a country with an overall population of slightly less than 60 million. The joint recruitment ban initiatives of several European countries in the early 1970s used the oil crisis as an excuse to end what was likely to become a permanent mass immigration (although this led to more long-term settlement strategies among the existing immigrant societies, including family reunifications). Trends to collaborate among European countries also illustrate a growing Europeanization of migration patterns and migration regimes from the 1970s.[83]

It should not be overlooked that some of the migrational schemes and contacts from overseas to Germany in the late twentieth century can be traced to earlier times, sometimes dating back to the early modern era or at least the nineteenth or early twentieth centuries. This is obvious in respect to scholarly and student exchanges, but also to industrial labor, craftsmanship, and trade. Here it is possible to gain insight into the actual possibilities of interaction and exchange between foreigners and Germans, which should not be reduced to

German xenophobia. From the early modern era onward, German universities and educational institutions had attracted foreign students, which continued in the fields of natural sciences and engineering, but also the humanities, well into the twentieth century. For instance, the future national author of Pakistan, Muhammad Iqbal, received his doctorate as a British Indian citizen in Munich in 1907; a Japanese student exchange of the 1920s brought some of the first Koreans to Germany, among them poet Mirok Li.[84] Small Italian communities had existed in Germany since the late seventeenth century (such as the court artisans and musicians in the *Italienisches Dörfchen* of Dresden), and temporary Italian migrants like industrial workers or ice cream vendors arrived north of the Alps around the turn of the twentieth century. They fostered the first, albeit small, infrastructure of Italian restaurants in Germany while Germans became increasingly interested in Italian food from the 1910s onwards.[85] The American colony in Dresden around 1900 is another example for such earlier contacts between migrants and Germans.[86]

In Soviet-occupied East Germany after 1945, which became for forty years the German Democratic Republic, organized immigration followed some of the patterns of the West German *Anwerbeabkommen*, even if it started some years later (1973), on a far smaller scale, and with a decidedly more political impetus. Contract workers (*Vertragsarbeiter*) were hired from socialist brother countries (such as postcolonial African states, Vietnam, and Cuba), in order to prepare their home countries for the development of a socialist society and to stress the particular socialist internationalism of the GDR. Foreign workers were segregated from Germans and often employed to do the hardest and most monotonous industry work that Germans would rather avoid. The number of foreigners in the German Democratic Republic, consisting of contract workers, international students, and temporary political asylants, largely from anti-imperialist resistance organizations such as the FLN (Algeria), PLO (Palestine), SWAPO (Namibia), as well as from the Chilean opposition, was small compared to the 4–5 million *Gastarbeiter* and other non-Germans in the Federal Republic in the 1980s. The largest group of non-Germans in the GDR was of course the members of the Soviet army and its civilian administration, with approximately one million people (mostly male) at any given time.[87] Anti-Russian as well as other xenophobic sentiments were widespread among the population, contrary to the official doctrine of friendship with its socialist brother country.

Sometimes the migrational strategies of the GDR were directly opposed to West European immigration schemes, although with limited success (such as in the case of fostering a Yugoslav and North Korean exchange with the GDR).[88] A similarity between West German *Gastarbeiter* and East German *Vertragsarbeiter* was that both populations kept a strong attachment to their countries of origin, leading to the sending of significant amounts of money and goods to their families at home.[89] This was as true for Turks in West Germany as it was for Vietnamese in the eastern part, who, in other respects, differed significantly from Vietnamese immigrants in West Germany. Today, the Vietnamese, who originally came to East Germany as contract workers on a rotation system from the 1980s, still form the largest group of non-European immigrants in the eastern part of unified Germany. Their patterns of immigration completely differ from the fate of the so-called Boat People among whom some 30,000 came to the western part of the country from 1979 as political asylants. Due to the Cold War, Vietnamese immigrants in West Germany had no opportunity to go back to Vietnam. Hence they assimilated rather smoothly into German society, as opposed to the Vietnamese in East Germany, who were separated from Germans and often did not learn German because they expected to return collectively after a few years.[90]

The migrational regime of the GDR vis-à-vis the Federal Republic illustrates that in the latter half of the twentieth century, migration politics became increasingly part of international contexts: economic, social, and political (within the EU, NATO, among Socialist countries, or simply in opposition between the two Germanies). However, West Germany still contained and even revived a nationalist attitude, especially in the era of Chancellor Helmut Kohl, when debates increasingly concentrated on the reduction of the number of foreigners and on a possible misuse of political asylum in Germany. As a reaction, center-left parties as well as trade unions, churches and local initiatives since the early 1980s stressed the benefits of a multicultural (colloq: *Multikulti*) society that, especially in the bigger cities, had started to evolve especially within a socio-economic context (restaurants, ethnic shops, immigrant-German collaboration at work).[91] It was still rarely acknowledged in public that, against the backdrop of frequent polemics toward migrants who seemingly benefited from an overstretched job market and from the German welfare state, their role as tax payers and increasingly as businesspeople made them perhaps less a burden than a benefit to the West German economy.[92] However, the assaults upon migrants in the eastern and western parts of a reunified Germany in the early 1990s as well as the xenophobic attitude among parts of the population toward foreign immigration made clear not only that immigrants often attracted economic fears but also that German politics still had to cope with the country's National Socialist past.

This is obvious in the case of the immigration of "ethnic" Germans from the eastern parts of the European continent. The 1980s and especially the 1990s witnessed an influx of ethnic German *Aussiedler* from east central and eastern Europe and from the states of the former Soviet Union where, due to Stalinist deportation, German communities existed in places as far as Kazakhstan and Siberia where they are nowadays often almost extinct. Such a reverse migration, often based on rather diffuse ideas of German heritage and of ethnic and cultural belonging to a German nation, dates back into the nineteenth century.[93] After the breakdown of Socialism in the early 1990s, the increasing influx of *Aussiedler*, now called *Spätaussiedler*, who were granted a German passport upon arrival because of an alleged German descent, was reduced to certain quotas and connected to a basic knowledge of the German language, which was usually scarce among migrants from the former Soviet Union.

As opposed to the *Aussiedler*, the unclear status of *Gastarbeiter* and the issue of immigration opportunities for foreign workers and their families had been discussed since the 1960s, giving voice to the first statements that West Germany had to face that it was or had become a country of immigration. Still, not only the conservative but also the social democratic governments of the 1960s and 1970s were reluctant to deal with the substantial change in the legislation of foreign immigration, fearing political repercussions with the countries of origin, in addition to economic and social problems in Germany and an increase of xenophobic reactions.[94]

Whereas from the time of the *Anwerbeabkommen* until the 2000s, German legislation had not enforced a strict rotation system of temporary foreign labor, it also did not foster structured immigration policies. Rather, Germany enacted a separation of foreigners from Germans. However, an evolving cultural plurality could no longer be denied, resulting, for instance, in immigrant cultures influenced by their German surroundings (mixed marriages, immigrant pop music, immigrant literature) and vice versa.[95] Even one of the most famous *Gastarbeiter* contributions to German cuisine, the *Döner Kebap*, made its way allegedly from 1970s Berlin to German immigrants and non-immigrants alike.

In recent years, the legal situation for immigrants in Germany has changed. Amendments of laws in 1999 (*Passgesetz*) and 2005 (*Einwanderungsgesetz*), respectively, governed immigration and allowed easier naturalization for migrants and their descendants. Now birth on German soil can serve as the basis for naturalization.[96] As in other countries, such immigration laws nevertheless did not end discussions about the status of immigrants and the ways and means of immigration policies, but it helped to put Germany into an internationally comparable position as an immigrant society with a rich migrational history.

American ketchup, Italian pizza and pasta, Turkish *Döner*, and many other dishes have found their way into seemingly genuine German food habits. However, migrants in Germany today, as in other immigration societies, still face an over-simplification and reduction of their complex and differing cultural backgrounds to certain symbols such as headscarves or to a seemingly monolithic "Islam." Whereas ethnic food has been a long-acknowledged immigrant contribution to German cultural diversity, in other fields Germany now needs to become aware of its historic continuities as an immigrant country in order to understand the contribution of migration for its history and to leave enough space for the growing and vibrant cultural diversity it deserves. In short, even "Germanness" is a far more diverse and complex phenomenon when looked at from a historical perspective than has long been acknowledged.

Outline of This Volume

The case studies presented in this volume explore the long and varied history of migrations in German lands. Although only a small part of the multifaceted story of immigration in Germany can be addressed in more detail, the chapters represent and highlight larger phenomena and structures of migrations in German lands. They cover the large chronological period of the sixteenth to the twentieth centuries from three central thematic angles: religion and exile; flux and the politics of immigration; and cultures of exile and the formation of immigrant identities.

Andrew McKenzie-McHarg, Ulrich Niggemann, and Anna Koch take up questions of how religion and religious identities informed the experience and practice of exile and immigration from the sixteenth to the twentieth centuries. McKenzie-McHarg probes the ways a martyr narrative was used to understand early modern exilic experience. Niggemann takes up the question of Huguenot identities and the ways that assimilation and autonomy were framed by religion. Anna Koch's essay also examines these themes in the context of post-Holocaust "return migration" of Jews to Axis countries by comparing the experiences of returning Italians and Germans. Koch's essay on twentieth-century issues allows us to better see how the themes animating McKenzie-McHarg's and Niggemann's work develop and change across the early modern/modern divide.

The second theme—flux and the politics of immigration—plays out over four essays. Jason Coy and Alexander Schunka provide access to the issues of exile, penal banishment, forced migration, and assimilation in the early modern period. The essays by Roland Gehrke and Jochen Oltmer examine Polish laborers in the *Kaiserreich* and Weimar Republic, and they provide insight not only into the political stakes involved with immigration between 1871 and the Great Depression, but also into the experience of flux that was occasioned by worker and seasonally periodic migrations.

Finally, the historical processes undergirding the formation of "cultures of exile" and of diasporic identities in German-speaking lands that involve aspects of (self-) perception, are taken up by the essays written by Nadine Zimmerli, Christopher Molnar, Jannis Panagiotidis, and Bettina Severin-Barboutie. Zimmerli examines the formation of an expatriate culture in Dresden that was explicitly cultivated by the city leadership; Molnar and Panagiotidis take up the question of how Yugoslav communities experienced life in West Germany. At times explicitly transnational, at times providing a type of ethnic "anchor" for further immigration, these communities not only resisted assimilation but also performed a kind of crafty jujitsu that maximized their power within the asymmetries of the Cold War. Severin-Barboutie concludes this set of essays—and the volume—by considering the ways that (im)migration has been remembered and represented in Germany since the 1970s.

One advantage connected to the kaleidoscopic character of this volume is that it offers a multifaceted approach into different historical phenomena, periods, and methodologies all connected with migration in German lands. The patchwork nature of the volume illustrates that migration research is in some fields still very much in flux (especially in contemporary history), that it is perhaps a better-trodden path for the later twentieth century and increasingly for the early modern era, and, all in all, that migration is in itself a rather messy subject, connected to almost any other possible approach in historiography (politics, society, economy, culture, and gender). If the present volume succeeds in raising a general awareness of the topic especially among non-German readers, the editors are hopeful that future research and publications will fill the existing gaps.

There is, however, no doubt that issues of cultural identity, of religious, political, and economic participation, as well as the fulfillment of certain practical, cultural, and spiritual needs still range broadly among today's migrants, just as among those five hundred years ago. The contributions of this volume document a long process of mutual learning in the daily interactions between migrants and the German host society that was itself formed over centuries on the basis of cultural mobility and demographic change.

Alexander Schunka is Professor of Early Modern History at the Freie Universität Berlin. He received his doctorate in History at the Ludwig-Maximilians-Universität München in 2004 and has since taught early modern history at the universities of Stuttgart and Erfurt. He specializes in the cultural and religious history of early modern Europe with a focus on the history of migrations. His publications include *Soziales Wissen und dörfliche Welt* (2000), *Gäste, die bleiben* (2006), some co-edited volumes, and a number of articles. His forthcoming book will be on the relationship between Protestantism and the birth of German Anglophilia in the eighteenth century.

Notes

1. See Felipe Fernández-Armesto, *Pathfinders: A Global History of Exploration* (Oxford, 2006).
2. "Die Bundesrepublik Deutschland ist kein Einwanderungsland. Es sind daher alle humanitär vertretbaren Maßnahmen zu ergreifen, um den Zuzug von Ausländern zu unterbinden." Neue Bonner Depesche Nr. 10/1982, S. 6, Archiv des Liberalismus IN5-304 (PDF): Retrieved 3 August 2013 from http://www.freiheit.org/files/288/ IN5-304_Koalitionsvereinbarung_1982.pdf.
3. Jan Motte and Rainer Ohliger, "Geschichte und Gedächtnis in der Einwander-ungsgesellschaft. Einführende Betrachtungen," in *Geschichte und Gedächtnis in der Einwanderungsgesellschaft: Migration zwischen historischer Rekonstruktion und Erin-nerungspolitik*, ed. Jan Motte and Rainer Ohliger (Essen, 2004), 7–17.
4. "Sachverständigenrat deutscher Stiftungen für Integration und Migration: Jahres-gutachten 2010," retrieved 8 June 2013 from http://www.svr-migration.de/content/ wp-content/uploads/2010/11/svr_jg_2010.pdf, 6.
5. Ibid., 16.
6. This idea featured prominently in the so-called Chicago School and particularly for the American sociologist Robert Ezra Park, who was influenced by Germans Georg Simmel and Ferdinand Toennies, see Robert Ezra Park, "Human Migration and the Marginal Man," in *American Journal of Sociology* 33, no. 6 (1928): 881–93.
7. Jan Lucassen, *Migrant Labour in Europe, 1600–1900: The Drift to the North Sea* (London, 1984); Peter Marschalck, *Deutsche Überseewanderung im 19. Jahrhundert: Ein Beitrag zur soziologischen Theorie der Bevölkerung* (Stuttgart, 1973).
8. Yasemin Karakaşoğlu, "Turkish Labor Migrants in Western, Central, and Northern Europe since the mid-1950s," in *The Encyclopedia of Migration and Minorities in Europe: From the 17th Century to the Present*, ed. Klaus Bade et al. (Cambridge, 2011), 717–22.
9. "Integration fand durch Arbeit statt" (Armin Laschet), in *Deutschlandradio Kultur*, 28 October 2011, retrieved 10 December 2011 from http://www.dradio.de/dkultur/ sendungen/politischesfeuilleton/1590049/. See also http://www.schleswig-holstein. de/MJGI/DE/ZuwanderungIntegration/Integration/Anwerbeabkommen/ Anwerbeabkommen_node.html, retrieved 10 December 2011.
10. Veit Didczuneit, "Armando Rodrigues de Sá, der millionste Gastarbeiter, das geschenkte Moped und die öffentliche Wirkung. Rekonstruktionen," retrieved 28 January 2014 from http://www.angekommen.com/iberer/Doku/tagung-ditsch.pdf.
11. Marcel Berlinghoff, *Das Ende der "Gastarbeit": Europäische Anwerbestopps 1970–1974* (Paderborn, 2013).
12. Rosemarie Beier-de Haan, ed., *Zuwanderungsland Deutschland: Migrationen 1500–2005, Austellungskatalog* (Berlin, 2005).
13. *Encyclopedia of Migration*, ed. Bade et al.; Oltmer, *Migration*; Sylvia Hahn, *Historische Migrationsforschung*, (Frankfurt am Main and New York, 2012).
14. On the notion of migration regimes see *Europäische Migrationsregime*, ed. Ute Frevert and Jochen Oltmer (Göttingen, 2009: Special Issue of *Geschichte und Gesellschaft*, 35 [2009]).
15. On the historical uses of the concept of space see, from a German perspective, Susanne Rau, *Räume: Konzepte, Wahrnehmungen, Nutzungen* (Frankfurt am Main, 2013).
16. See, for instance, http://www.spiegel.de/politik/deutschland/einwanderung-auslaenderverbaende-kaempfen-fuer-doppelpass-a-933005.html, retrieved 30 December 2013.

17. Nina Glick Schiller, Linda Basch, and Cristina Szanton Blanc, "From Immigrant to Transmigrant: Theorizing Transnational Migration," in *Transnationale Migration,* ed. Ludger Pries (Baden–Baden, 1997), 121–40. Modified in Christiane Harzig and Dirk Hoerder, *What is Migration History?* (Cambridge, 2009), 84–85. Cf. Margrit Pernau, *Transnationale Geschichte* (Göttingen, 2011).
18. See, for instance, Schirin Amir-Moazami, *Politisierte Religion: Der Kopftuchstreit in Deutschland und Frankreich* (Bielefeld, 2007).
19. Most notably in the early work of Feridun Zaimoglu, *Kanak Sprak: 24 Misstöne vom Rande der Gesellschaft* (Hamburg, 1995).
20. On the notion of thirdspace see Edward W. Soja, *Thirdspace: Journeys to Los Angeles and other Real-and-Imagined Places* (Malden, 1996), 56–57, who draws upon, among others, Homi Bhabha, *The Location of Culture* (London et al., 1994).
21. Jochen Oltmer, *Migration im 19. und 20. Jahrhundert* (Munich, 2011), 1; Harald Kleinschmidt, *Menschen in Bewegung: Inhalte und Ziele der historischen Migrationsforschung* (Göttingen, 2002), 20.
22. Recent migration research has stressed that such a distinction can often be blurred, see *Migration, Migration History, History: Old Paradigms and New Perspectives*, eds. Jan and Leo Lucassen, 3rd, rev. ed. (Bern et al., 2005); Oltmer, *Migration*, 63.
23. For an early modern example, see Philip Otterness, *Becoming German: The 1709 Palatine Migration to New York* (Ithaca, NY, 2004).
24. See, for instance, Richard F. Kreutel and Otto Spies, eds., *Leben und Abenteuer des Dolmetschers Osman Ağa: Eine türkische Autobiographie aus der Zeit der großen Kriege gegen Österreich* (Bonn, 1954).
25. On these problems see David Eltis, ed., *Coerced and Free Migration: Global Perspectives* (Stanford, CA, 2002).
26. Ulrich Herbert, *Fremdarbeiter: Politik und Praxis des 'Ausländer-Einsatzes' in der Kriegswirtschaft des Dritten Reiches* (Bonn, 1999); on slavery in a European context from the early modern era onward, see Nicole Priesching, *Sklaverei in der Neuzeit* (Darmstadt, 2014).
27. See Alexander Schunka, "Konfession und Migrationsregime in der Frühen Neuzeit," *Geschichte und Gesellschaft* 35 (2009): 28–63, 31.
28. Alexander Schunka, *Gäste, die bleiben: Zuwanderer in Kursachsen und der Oberlausitz im 17. und frühen 18. Jahrhundert* (Münster, 2006), 130–53.
29. Wolfram Siemann, "Asyl, Exil und Emigration der 1848er," in *Demokratiebewegung und Revolution 1847 bis 1849*, ed. Dieter Langewiesche (Berlin, 1998), 70–91; Marita Krauss, *Heimkehr in ein fremdes Land: Geschichte der Remigration nach 1945* (Munich, 2001).
30. See, for instance, Fritz Stern, *Five Germanys I have Known* (New York, 2006).
31. https://www.destatis.de/DE/ZahlenFakten/GesellschaftStaat/Bevoelkerung/MigrationIntegration/Migrationshintergrund/Tabellen/Migrationshintergrund-Geschlecht.html; jsessionid= ED1E57105F3354AA3A0C17D56AA4BE9E.cae3, retrieved 16 March 2015.
32. Christian Pfister, *Bevölkerungsgeschichte und Historische Demographie, 1500–1800*, 2nd ed. (Munich, 2007), 10; Josef Ehmer, *Bevölkerungsgeschichte und Historische Demographie, 1800–2000* (Munich, 2010), 17f.
33. See, for instance, Ehmer, *Bevölkerungsgeschichte*, 9.
34. Steve Hochstadt, "Migration in Preindustrial Germany," *Central European History* 16 (1983): 195–224.

35. See the overviews by Leslie P. Moch, *Moving Europeans: Migration in Western Europe since 1650*, 2nd ed. (Bloomington, 2003); Dirk Hoerder, *Cultures in Contact: World Migrations in the Second Millennium* (Durham, 2002); *The Encyclopedia of European Migration and Minorities*, ed. Bade et al.; Schunka, "Konfession und Migrationsregime in der Frühen Neuzeit."

36. Hoerder, *Cultures in Contact*, 15–21.

37. Rudolf Schlögl, "Kommunikation und Vergesellschaftung unter Anwesenden: Formen des Sozialen und ihre Transformation in der Frühen Neuzeit," *Geschichte und Gesellschaft* 34 (2008): 155–224.

38. On the interactions among migrants and between migrants and host societies see, among others, Jesse Spohnholz, *The Tactics of Toleration: A Refugee Community in the Age of Religious Wars* (Newark, NJ, 2011); Schunka, *Gäste, die bleiben*; *Migration und kirchliche Praxis: Das religiöse Leben frühneuzeitlicher Glaubensflüchtlinge in alltagsgeschichtlicher Perspektive*, ed. Joachim Bahlcke and Rainer Bendel (Cologne et al., 2008).

39. See, among others, the recent microstudy by Holger Berg, *Military Occupation under the Eyes of the Lord: Studies in Erfurt during the Thirty Years War* (Göttingen, 2010).

40. Martin Rheinheimer, *Arme, Bettler und Vaganten: Überleben in der Not 1450–1850* (Frankfurt am Main, 2000); Jason P. Coy, *Strangers and Misfits: Banishment, Social Control, and Authority in Early Modern Germany* (Leiden, 2008). See Jason Coy's contribution in this volume.

41. Heinz Schilling, "Confessional Migration as a Distinct Type of Old European Long Distance Migration," in *Le migrazioni in Europa, Secc. XIII–XVIII*, ed. Simonetta Cavaciocchi (Prato, 1994), 175–89.

42. Heiko A. Oberman, *John Calvin and the Reformation of the Refugees* (Geneva, 2009); Graeme Murdock, *Beyond Calvin: The Intellectual, Political and Cultural World of Europe's Reformed Churches, c. 1540–1620* (Basingstoke et al., 2004); Christina Garrett, *The Marian Exiles: A Study in the Origins of Elizabethan Puritanism* (Cambridge, 1938).

43. Heinz Schilling, *Niederländische Exulanten im 16. Jahrhundert* (Gütersloh, 1972); Spohnholz, *Tactics of Toleration*.

44. See Raingard Esser, "Exulantenstadt," in *Enzyklopädie der Neuzeit*, ed. Friedrich Jaeger et al. (Stuttgart, 2006), 3:732–33; Martin Papenbrock, *Landschaften des Exils: Gillis van Coninxloo und die Frankenthaler Maler* (Cologne et al., 2001); Myriam Yardeni, *Le refuge protestant* (Paris, 1985).

45. Alexander Schunka, "Lutheran Confessional Migration," *European History Online* (Mainz, 2012), retrieved 7 January 2016 from URL: http://www.ieg-ego.eu/schunkaa-2012-en URN: urn:nbn:de:0159-2012060616.

46. Werner W. Schnabel, *Österreichische Exulanten in oberdeutschen Reichsstädten: Zur Migration von Führungsschichten im 17. Jahrhundert* (Erlangen, 1990).

47. Wulf Wäntig, *Grenzerfahrungen: Böhmische Exulanten im 17. Jahrhundert* (Konstanz, 2007); Schunka, *Gäste, die bleiben*.

48. Schnabel, *Österreichische Exulanten*, 647; Schunka, *Gäste, die bleiben*, 154–56.

49. Bettina Braun, "Katholische Glaubensflüchtlinge: Eine Spurensuche im Europa der Frühen Neuzeit," *Historisches Jahrbuch der Görres-Gesellschaft* 130 (2010): 505–76; Harm Klueting, "Katholische Konfessionsmigration," *European History Online* (Mainz, 2012), retrieved 28 January 2014 from URN: urn:nbn:de:0159-2012091813.

50. Heinz Schilling recently pursued a different approach, Heinz Schilling, "Die früh-neuzeitliche Konfessionsmigration: Calvinisten und sephardische Juden im Vergleich," in *Religion und Mobilität: zum Verhältnis von raumbezogener Mobilität und religiöser Identitätsbildung im frühneuzeitlichen Europa*, eds. Henning P. Jürgens and Thomas Weller (Göttingen, 2010), 113–36; cf. Yosef Kaplan, *An Alternative Path to Modernity: The Sephardi Diaspora in Western Europe* (Leiden et al., 2000), 168–94.

51. Matthias Asche, *Neusiedler im verheerten Land: Kriegsfolgenbewältigung, Migrationssteuerung und Konfessionspolitik im Zeichen des Landeswiederaufbaus: die Mark Brandenburg nach den Kriegen des 17. Jahrhunderts* (Münster, 2006). See the literature quoted in Ulrich Niggemann's contribution in this volume.

52. Mack Walker, *The Salzburg Transaction: Expulsion and Redemption in Eighteenth-Century Germany* (Ithaca, NY, 1992).

53. Justus Nipperdey, *Die Erfindung der Bevölkerungspolitik: Staat, politische Theorie und Population in der Frühen Neuzeit* (Göttingen, 2009).

54. Stefan Volk, "Peuplierung und religiöse Toleranz: Neuwied von der Mitte des 17. bis zur Mitte des 18. Jahrhunderts," *Rheinische Vierteljahresblätter* 55 (1991): 205–31.

55. David Worthington, *British and Irish Emigrants and Exiles in Europe, 1603–1688* (Leiden, 2010); for the relevant courts see, among others, Robert J.W. Evans, *Rudolf II and his World: A Study in Intellectual History, 1576–1612* (Oxford, 1973); Bruce T. Moran, *The Alchemical World of the German Court: Occult Philosophy and Chemical Medicine in the Circle of Moritz of Hesse, 1572–1632* (Stuttgart, 1991); Helen Watanabe-O'Kelly, *Court Culture in Dresden; From Renaissance to Baroque* (Basingstoke et al., 2002).

56. Peter Martin, *Schwarze Teufel, edle Mohren: Afrikaner in Geschichte und Bewusstsein der Deutschen* (Hamburg, 2001); Markus Friedrich, "'Türken' im Alten Reich: zur Aufnahme und Konversion von Muslimen im deutschen Sprachraum (16.–18. Jahrhundert)," *Historische Zeitschrift* 294 (2012): 329–60.

57. On Keith, see Edith E. Cuthell, *The Scottish Friend of Frederic the Great: The Last Earl Marischall*, 2 vols. (London, 1915).

58. Christiane Reves, *Vom Pomeranzengängler zum Großhändler? Netzwerke und Migrationsverhalten der Brentano–Familien im 17. und 18. Jahrhundert* (Paderborn et al., 2012).

59. Chain stores such as "C&A" often originated from the migrational networks of the predominantly Catholic "Tödden", see Hannelore Oberpenning, *Migration und Fernhandel im "Tödden-System": Wanderhändler aus dem nördlichen Münsterland im mittleren und nördlichen Europa des 18. und 19. Jahrhunderts* (Osnabrück, 1996).

60. Daniel Schönpflug, "French Revolutionary Refugees in Europe after 1789: The Example of Germany," in *The Encyclopedia of Migration and Minorities*, ed. Bade et al., 395–97.

61. Roland Gehrke, "Praktische Solidarität als Ausdruck politischer Gesinnung: Die Aktivität der südwestdeutschen 'Polenvereine' von 1831/32," in *Migration als soziale Herausforderung: Historische Formen solidarischen Handelns von der Antike bis zum 20. Jahrhundert*, ed. Joachim Bahlcke, Rainer Leng, and Peter Scholz (Stuttgart, 2011), 273–92; Slawomir Kalembka, *Wielka emigracja 1831–1863* (Toruń, 2003).

62. Oltmer, *Migration*, 16; Annemarie Steidl, *Auf nach Wien! Die Mobilität des mitteleuropäischen Handwerks im 18. und 19. Jahrhundert am Beispiel der Haupt- und Residenzstadt: Regionale Mobilität der städtischen Handwerker* (Vienna, 2003).

63. Martin Düspohl, "Arbeitsmigration nach Berlin im 19. Jahrhundert. Jeder zweite Berliner stammt aus Schlesien," in *"Wach auf, mein Herz, und denke": Zur Geschichte der Beziehungen zwischen Schlesien und Berlin–Brandenburg von 1740 bis heute. "Przebudź się, serce moje, i pomyśl"*, ed. Klaus Bździach (Berlin, 1995), 190–203; Hans-Peter Meister, "Die Berliner Polonia und ihre Verbindung nach Schlesien," in *Wach auf, mein Herz, und denke'*, ed. Bździach, 215–30. On larger patterns of German migrations in the nineteenth century, see Steve Hochstadt, *Mobility and Modernity: Migration in Germany, 1820–1989* (Ann Arbor, MI, 1999).

64. Krystyna Murzynowska, *Die polnischen Erwerbsauswanderer im Ruhrgebiet während der Jahre 1880–1914* (Dortmund, 1979); Christoph Kleßmann, *Polnische Bergarbeiter im Ruhrgebiet 1870–1945: Soziale Integration und nationale Subkultur einer Minderheit in der deutschen Industriegesellschaft* (Göttingen, 1978).

65. Dirk Hoerder, *Geschichte der deutschen Migration vom Mittelalter bis heute* (Munich, 2010), 84.

66. Ulrich Herbert, *Geschichte der Ausländerpolitik in Deutschland: Saisonarbeiter, Zwangsarbeiter, Gastarbeiter, Flüchtlinge* (Munich, 2001), 13–84.

67. Dieter Gosewinkel, *Einbürgern und Ausschließen: Die Nationalisierung der Staatsangehörigkeit vom Deutschen Bund bis zur Bundesrepublik Deutschland* (Göttingen, 2001); Gosewinkel, "Wer ist Deutscher? Deutsche Staatsangehörigkeit im 19. und 20. Jahrhundert," in *Zuwanderungsland Deutschland*, ed. Beier-de Haan, 90–105.

68. Gosewinkel, "Wer ist Deutscher?"; Rogers Brubaker, *Citizenship and Nationhood in France and Germany* (Cambridge et al., 1992). On desertion, from a non-Prussian perspective, see Daniel Kirn, *Soldatenleben in Württemberg 1871–1914: Zur Sozialgeschichte des deutschen Militärs* (Paderborn et al., 2009), 229–45.

69. Cornelia Wilhelm, "Diversity in Germany: A Historical Perspective," in *German Politics and Society* 107, no. 31 (Summer 2013): 13–29.

70. Jochen Oltmer, *Migration und Politik in der Weimarer Republik* (Göttingen, 2005). See his contribution in the present volume.

71. Reiner Pommerin, *'Sterilisierung der Rheinlandbastarde': Das Schicksal einer farbigen deutschen Minderheit, 1918–1937* (Düsseldorf, 1979); Jared Poley, *Decolonization in Germany: Weimar Narratives of Colonial Loss and Foreign Occupation* (Oxford et al., 2007).

72. Frank Caestecker, "Displaced Persons in Europe since the end of World War II," in *The Encyclopedia of Migration and Minorities in Europe*, ed. Bade et al., 314–19; Herbert, *Fremdarbeiter*.

73. Oltmer, *Migration*, 44; Hoerder, *Geschichte der deutschen Migration*, 99–100.

74. Ehmer, *Bevölkerungsgeschichte*, 17–18.

75. I take these figures from Oltmer, *Migration*, 45–47.

76. Christian T. Müller, "Allied Military Personnel in Germany since the End of World War II," in *The Encyclopedia of Migration and Minorities in Europe*, ed. Bade et al., 225–28; Heide Fehrenbach, *Race after Hitler: Black Occupation Children in Postwar Germany and America* (Princeton, NJ, 2005).

77. Oltmer, *Migration*, 45–52; Krauss, *Heimkehr in ein fremdes Land*.

78. Wilhelm, "Diversity in Germany."

79. Mathias Beer, *Flucht und Vertreibung der Deutschen: Voraussetzungen, Verlauf, Folgen* (Munich, 2011), 124–26; Christian Lotz, *Die Deutung des Verlusts: Erinnerungspolitische Kontroversen im geteilten Deutschland um Flucht, Vertreibung und die Ostgebiete*

(1948–1972) (Cologne et al., 2007); Andrew Demshuk, *The Lost German East: Forced Migration and the Politics of Memory, 1945–1970* (Cambridge, 2012).

80. On migration into Germany from the 1950s, see Deniz Göktürk et al., eds., *Germany in Transit: Nation and Migration 1955–2005* (Berkeley et al., 2007); Rita Chin, *The Guest Worker Question in Postwar Germany* (Cambridge et al., 2007); Karen Schönwälder, *Einwanderung und ethnische Pluralität: Politische Entscheidungen und öffentliche Debatten in Großbritannien und der Bundesrepublik von den 1950er bis zu den 1970er Jahren* (Essen, 2002). On the Italians see Roberto Sala, "Vom 'Fremdarbeiter' zum 'Gastarbeiter': Die Anwerbung italienischer Arbeitskräfte für die deutsche Wirtschaft," *Vierteljahrshefte für Zeitgeschichte* 50, no. 1 (2007): 93–120.
81. Karen Schönwälder, "Migration und Ausländerpolitik in der Bundesrepublik Deutschland. Öffentliche Debatten und politische Entscheidungen," in *Zuwanderungsland Deutschland*, ed. Beier-de Haan, 106–19.
82. See the contributions in the exhibition catalogue *Shared. Divided. United*, ed. Nils Sanders et al. (Berlin, 2009).
83. Berlinghoff, *Das Ende der "Gastarbeit"*; Schönwälder, *Einwanderung und ethnische Pluralität*.
84. On Iqbal, see Annemarie Schimmel, *Muhammed Iqbal: Prophetischer Poet und Philosoph* (Munich, 1989); on Li see his autobiography, Mirok Li, *Vom Yalu bis zur Isar* (Sankt Ottilien, 2011). See the contributions in Gerhard Höpp, ed., *Fremde Erfahrungen: Asiaten und Afrikaner in Deutschland, Österreich und der Schweiz bis 1945* (Berlin, 1996).
85. Ulrike Thoms, "From Migrant Food to Lifestyle Cooking: The Career of Italian Cuisine in Europe," in *European History Online* (Mainz, 2011), retrieved 28 January 2014 from http://nbn-resolving.de/urn:nbn:de:0159-2011051250; René Del Fabbro, *Transalpini: Italienische Arbeitswanderung nach Süddeutschland im Kaiserreich 1870–1918* (Osnabrück, 1996).
86. See Nadine Zimmerli's contribution in the present volume.
87. Patrice G. Poutrus, "Die DDR, ein anderer deutscher Weg: Zum Umgang mit Ausländern im SED-Staat," in *Zuwanderungsland Deutschland*, ed. Beier-de Haan, 120–33.
88. Liana Kang-Schmitz, "Nordkoreas Umgang mit Abhängigkeit und Sicherheitsrisiko: Am Beispiel der bilateralen Beziehungen zur DDR" (PhD diss., University of Trier, 2010), esp. part 4, retrieved 2 January 2014 from http://ubt.opus.hbz-nrw.de/volltexte/2011/636/pdf/Nordkorea_DDR.pdf. On "Yugoslav" migrants see the contributions in this volume.
89. Poutrus, "Die DDR"; Klaus J. Bade and Jochen Oltmer, *Normalfall Migration* (Bonn, 2004), 90–96; Felicitas Hillmann, "Riders on the Storm: Vietnamese in Germany's Two Migration Systems," in *Asian Migrants and European Labour Markets: Patterns and Processes of Immigrant Labour Market Insertion in Europe*, ed. Ernst Spaan et al. (London, 2005), 80–100. Patterns of Turkish immigration are covered in Aytaç Eryilmaz and Mathilde Jamin, eds., *Fremde Heimat: Eine Geschichte der Einwanderung aus der Türkei* (Essen, 1998).
90. Hillmann, "Riders on the Storm."
91. Martin Ohlert, *Zwischen "Multikulturalismus" und "Leitkultur": Integrationsleitbild und -politik der im 17. Deutschen Bundestag vertretenen Parteien* (Wiesbaden, 2015), 18–28.

92. Saskia Sassen, "Dienstleistungsökonomien und die Beschäftigung von MigrantInnen in Städten," in *Migration und Stadt: Entwicklungen, Defizite, Potentiale*, ed. Klaus M. Schmals (Opladen, 2000), 87–114; Maria Kontos, "Übergänge von der abhängigen zur selbständigen Arbeit in der Migration: Sozialstrukturelle und biographische Aspekte," in *Arbeitsmigration: WanderarbeiterInnen auf dem Weltmarkt für Arbeitskraft*, ed. Thomas Geisen (Frankfurt, 2005), 217–36.
93. Klaus J. Bade and Jochen Oltmer, eds., *Aussiedler: Deutsche Einwanderer aus Osteuropa* (Osnabrück, 1999); Michael Schönhuth and Daniela Franzke, eds., *Der Einfluss soziokultureller Faktoren auf den Integrationsprozess von Spätaussiedlern* (Saarbrücken, 2003).
94. Schönwälder, "Migration und Ausländerpolitik in der Bundesrepublik Deutschland."
95. Chin, *Guest Worker Question*; Chin, *After the Nazi Racial State: Difference and Democracy in Germany and Europe* (Ann Arbor, MI, 2009), 137ff.
96. Since 1999, German-born people of an immigrant background between the age of eighteen and twenty-three can opt for either German citizenship or the citizenship of their parents: Staatsangehörigkeitsgesetz vom 22.7.1913 in der Fassung vom 15.7.1999, §§ 4, 29; http://www.gesetze-im-internet.de/bundesrecht/rustag/gesamt.pdf, retrieved 30 December 2013.

Bibliography

Amir-Moazami, Schirin. *Politisierte Religion: Der Kopftuchstreit in Deutschland und Frankreich*. Bielefeld, 2007.
Asche, Matthias. *Neusiedler im verheerten Land: Kriegsfolgenbewältigung, Migrationssteuerung und Konfessionspolitik im Zeichen des Landeswiederaufbaus. Die Mark Brandenburg nach den Kriegen des 17. Jahrhunderts*. Münster, 2006.
Bade, Klaus J., and Jochen Oltmer, eds. *Aussiedler: Deutsche Einwanderer aus Osteuropa*. Osnabrück, 1999.
Bahlcke, Joachim, and Rainer Bendel, eds. Migration und kirchliche Praxis: Das religiöse Leben frühneuzeitlicher Glaubensflüchtlinge in alltagsgeschichtlicher Perspektive. Cologne, 2008.
Beer, Mathias. *Flucht und Vertreibung der Deutschen: Voraussetzungen, Verlauf, Folgen*. München, 2011.
Beier-de Haan, Rosemarie, ed. *Zuwanderungsland Deutschland: Migrationen 1500–2005, Austellungskatalog*. Berlin, 2005.
Berg, Holger. *Military Occupation under the Eyes of the Lord: Studies in Erfurt during the Thirty Years War*. Göttingen, 2010.
Berlinghoff, Marcel. *Das Ende der 'Gastarbeit': Europäische Anwerbestopps 1970–1974*. Paderborn, 2013.
Bhabha, Homi. *The Location of Culture*. London, 1994.
Braun, Bettina. "Katholische Glaubensflüchtlinge: Eine Spurensuche im Europa der Frühen Neuzeit." *Historisches Jahrbuch der Görres-Gesellschaft* 130 (2010): 505–76.
Brubaker, Rogers. *Citizenship and Nationhood in France and Germany*. Cambridge, MA, 1992.

Caestecker, Frank. "Displaced Persons in Europe since the End of World War II." In *The Encyclopedia of Migration and Minorities in Europe: From the 17th Century to the Present*, ed. Klaus Bade et al. Cambridge, 2011.

Chin, Rita. *After the Nazi Racial State: Difference and Democracy in Germany and Europe*. Ann Arbor, MI, 2009.

———. *The Guest Worker Question in Postwar Germany*. Cambridge, 2007.

Coy, Jason P. *Strangers and Misfits: Banishment, Social Control, and Authority in Early Modern Germany*. Leiden, 2008.

Cuthell, Edith E. *The Scottish Friend of Frederic the Great: The Last Earl Marischall*. 2 volumes. London, 1915.

Demshuk, Andrew. *The Lost German East: Forced Migration and the Politics of Memory, 1945–1970*. Cambridge, 2012.

Didczuneit, Veit. "Armando Rodrigues de Sá, der millionste Gastarbeiter, das geschenkte Moped und die öffentliche Wirkung. Rekonstruktionen." In http://www.angekommen.com/iberer/Doku/tagung-ditsch.pdf. Retrieved 28 January 2014.

Düspohl, Martin. "Arbeitsmigration nach Berlin im 19. Jahrhundert. Jeder zweite Berliner stammt aus Schlesien." In *'Wach auf, mein Herz, und denke': Zur Geschichte der Beziehungen zwischen Schlesien und Berlin–Brandenburg von 1740 bis heute; "Przebudź się, serce moje, i pomyśl"*, ed. Klaus Bździach. Berlin, 1995.

Ehmer, Josef. *Bevölkerungsgeschichte und Historische Demographie, 1800–2000*. Munich, 2010.

Eltis, David, ed., *Coerced and Free Migration: Global Perspectives*. Palo Alto, CA, 2002.

Eryilmaz, Aytaç, and Mathilde Jamin, eds. *Fremde Heimat: Eine Geschichte der Einwanderung aus der Türkei*. Essen, 1998.

Esser, Raingard. "Exulantenstadt." In *Enzyklopädie der Neuzeit*, ed. Friedrich Jaeger et al., vol. 3. Stuttgart, 2006.

Evans, Robert J.W. *Rudolf II and his World: A Study in Intellectual History, 1576–1612*. Oxford, 1973.

del Fabbro, René. *Transalpini: Italienische Arbeitswanderung nach Süddeutschland im Kaiserreich 1870–1918*. Osnabrück, 1996.

Fehrenbach, Heide. *Race after Hitler: Black Occupation Children in Postwar Germany and America*. Princeton, NJ, 2005.

Fernández-Armesto, Felipe. *Pathfinders: A Global History of Exploration*. Oxford, 2006.

Frevert, Ute, and Jochen Oltmer, eds. Special Issue of *Geschichte und Gesellschaft* 35 (2009).

Friedrich, Markus. "'Türken' im Alten Reich: zur Aufnahme und Konversion von Muslimen im deutschen Sprachraum (16.–18. Jahrhundert)." *Historische Zeitschrift* 294 (2012): 329–60.

Garrett, Christina. *The Marian Exiles: A Study in the Origins of Elizabethan Puritanism*. Cambridge, 1938.

Gehrke, Roland. "Praktische Solidarität als Ausdruck politischer Gesinnung: Die Aktivität der südwestdeutschen 'Polenvereine' von 1831/32." In *Migration als soziale Herausforderung. Historische Formen solidarischen Handelns von der Antike bis zum 20. Jahrhundert*, ed. Joachim Bahlcke et al. Stuttgart, 2011.

Göktürk, Deniz, et al., eds. *Germany in Transit: Nation and Migration 1955–2005.* Berkeley, 2007.

Gosewinkel, Dieter. *Einbürgern und Ausschließen: Die Nationalisierung der Staatsangehörigkeit vom Deutschen Bund bis zur Bundesrepublik Deutschland.* Göttingen, 2001.

———. "Wer ist Deutscher? Deutsche Staatsangehörigkeit im 19. und 20. Jahrhundert." In *Zuwanderungsland Deutschland: Migrationen 1500–2005*, ed. Rosemarie Beier-de Haan. Wolfratshausen, 2005.

Hahn, Sylvia. *Historische Migrationsforschung.* Frankfurt am Main, 2012.

Harzig, Christiane, and Dirk Hoerder. *What is Migration History?* Cambridge, 2009.

Herbert, Ulrich. *Fremdarbeiter: Politik und Praxis des 'Ausländer-Einsatzes' in der Kriegswirtschaft des Dritten Reiches.* Bonn, 1999.

———. *Geschichte der Ausländerpolitik in Deutschland: Saisonarbeiter, Zwangsarbeiter, Gastarbeiter, Flüchtlinge.* Munich, 2001.

Hillmann, Felicitas. "Riders on the Storm: Vietnamese in Germany's Two Migration Systems." In *Asian Migrants and European Labour Markets: Patterns and Processes of Immigrant Labour Market Insertion in Europe*, ed. Ernst Spaan et al. London, 2005.

Hochstadt, Steve. "Migration in Preindustrial Germany." *Central European History* 16 (1983): 195–224.

———. *Mobility and Modernity: Migration in Germany, 1820–1989.* Ann Arbor, MI, 1999.

Hoerder, Dirk. *Cultures in Contact: World Migrations in the Second Millenium.* Durham, 2002.

———. *Geschichte der deutschen Migration vom Mittelalter bis heute.* Munich, 2010.

Höpp, Gerhard, ed. *Fremde Erfahrungen: Asiaten und Afrikaner in Deutschland, Österreich und der Schweiz bis 1945.* Berlin, 1996.

Kalembka, Sławomir. *Wielka Emigracja 1831–1863* [The great emigration 1831–1863]. Toruń, 2003.

Kang-Schmitz, Liana. "Nordkoreas Umgang mit Abhängigkeit und Sicherheitsrisiko: Am Beispiel der bilateralen Beziehungen zur DDR." PhD diss., University of Trier, 2010.

Kaplan, Yosef. *An Alternative Path to Modernity: The Sephardi Diaspora in Western Europe.* Leiden, 2000.

Karakaşoğlu, Yasemin. "Turkish Labor Migrants in Western, Central, and Northern Europe since the mid-1950s." In *The Encyclopedia of Migration and Minorities in Europe: From the 17th Century to the Present*, ed. Klaus Bade et al. Cambridge, 2011.

Kirn, Daniel. *Soldatenleben in Württemberg 1871–1914: Zur Sozialgeschichte des deutschen Militärs.* Paderborn et al., 2009.

Kleinschmidt, Harald. *Menschen in Bewegung: Inhalte und Ziele der historischen Migrationsforschung.* Göttingen, 2002.

Kleßmann, Christoph. *Polnische Bergarbeiter im Ruhrgebiet 1870–1945: Soziale Integration und nationale Subkultur einer Minderheit in der deutschen Industriegesellschaft.* Göttingen, 1978.

Klueting, Harm. "Katholische Konfessionsmigration." In *European History Online* (Mainz, 2012), URN: urn:nbn:de:0159-2012091813. Retrieved 28 January 2014.

Kontos, Maria. "Übergänge von der abhängigen zur selbständigen Arbeit in der Migration: Sozialstrukturelle und biographische Aspekte." In *Arbeitsmigration: WanderarbeiterInnen auf dem Weltmarkt für Arbeitskraft,* ed. Thomas Geisen. Frankfurt, 2005.

Krauss, Marita. *Heimkehr in ein fremdes Land: Geschichte der Remigration nach 1945.* Munich, 2001.

Kreutel, Richard F., and Otto Spies, eds. *Leben und Abenteuer des Dolmetschers Osman Aĝa: Eine türkische Autobiographie aus der Zeit der großen Kriege gegen Österreich.* Bonn, 1954.

Laschet, Armin. "Integration fand durch Arbeit statt." In *Deutschlandradio Kultur* 28 Oct 2011. http://www.dradio.de/dkultur/sendungen/politischesfeuilleton/1590049/. Retrieved 10 December 2011.

Li, Mirok. *Vom Yalu bis zur Isar.* Sankt Ottilien, 2011.

Lotz, Christian. *Die Deutung des Verlusts: Erinnerungspolitische Kontroversen im geteilten Deutschland um Flucht, Vertreibung und die Ostgebiete (1948–1972).* Cologne, 2007.

Lucassen, Jan. *Migrant Labour in Europe, 1600–1900: The Drift to the North Sea.* London, 1984.

Lucassen, Jan, and Leo Lucassen, eds. *Migration, Migration History, History: Old Paradigms and New Perspectives,* 3rd rev. ed. Bern, 2005.

Marschalck, Peter. *Deutsche Überseewanderung im 19. Jahrhundert: Ein Beitrag zur soziologischen Theorie der Bevölkerung.* Stuttgart, 1973.

Martin, Peter. *Schwarze Teufel, edle Mohren: Afrikaner in Geschichte und Bewusstsein der Deutschen.* Hamburg, 2001.

Meister, Hans-Peter, "Die Berliner Polonia und ihre Verbindung nach Schlesien." In *'Wach auf, mein Herz, und denke': Zur Geschichte der Beziehungen zwischen Schlesien und Berlin–Brandenburg von 1740 bis heute. "Przebudź się, serce moje, i pomyśl",* ed. Klaus Bździach. Berlin, 1995.

Müller, Christian T. "Allied Military Personnel in Germany since the End of World War II." In *The Encyclopedia of Migration and Minorities in Europe,* ed. Klaus Bade et al. Cambridge, 2011.

Moch, Leslie Page. *Moving Europeans: Migration in Western Europe since 1650.* 2nd edition. Bloomington, IN, 2003.

Moran, Bruce T. *The Alchemical World of the German Court: Occult Philosophy and Chemical Medicine in the Circle of Moritz of Hesse, 1572–1632.* Stuttgart, 1991.

Motte, Jan, and Rainer Ohliger. "Geschichte und Gedächtnis in der Einwanderungsgesellschaft: Einführende Betrachtungen." In *Geschichte und Gedächtnis in der Einwanderungsgesellschaft: Migration zwischen historischer Rekonstruktion und Erinnerungspolitik,* ed. Jan Motte and Rainer Ohliger. Essen, 2004.

Murdock, Graeme. *Beyond Calvin: The Intellectual, Political and Cultural World of Europe's Reformed Churches, c. 1540–1620.* Basingstoke, 2004.

Murzynowska, Krystyna. *Die polnischen Erwerbsauswanderer im Ruhrgebiet während der Jahre 1880–1914.* Dortmund, 1979.

Nipperdey, Justus. *Die Erfindung der Bevölkerungspolitik: Staat, politische Theorie und Population in der Frühen Neuzeit.* Göttingen, 2012.

Oberman, Heiko A. *John Calvin and the Reformation of the Refugees.* Geneva, 2009.

Oberpenning, Hannelore. *Migration und Fernhandel im "Tödden-System": Wander-händler aus dem nördlichen Münsterland im mittleren und nördlichen Europa des 18. und 19. Jahrhunderts.* Osnabrück, 1996.

Ohlert, Martin. *Zwischen "Multikulturalismus" und "Leitkultur": Integrationsleitbild und—politik der im 17. Deutschen Bundestag vertretenen Parteien.* Wiesbaden, 2015.

Oltmer, Jochen. *Migration im 19. und 20. Jahrhundert.* Munich, 2011.

———. *Migration und Politik in der Weimarer Republik.* Göttingen, 2005.

Otterness, Philip. *Becoming German: The 1709 Palatine Migration to New York.* Ithaca, NY, 2004.

Papenbrock, Martin. *Landschaften des Exils: Gillis van Coninxloo und die Franken-thaler Maler.* Cologne, 2001.

Park, Robert Ezra. "Human Migration and the Marginal Man." In *American Journal of Sociology* 33, no. 6 (1928): 881–93.

Pernau, Margrit. *Transnationale Geschichte.* Göttingen, 2011.

Pfister, Christian. *Bevölkerungsgeschichte und Historische Demographie, 1500–1800.* 2nd ed. Munich, 2007.

Priesching, Nicole. *Sklaverei in der Neuzeit.* Darmstadt, 2014.

Poley, Jared. *Decolonization in Germany: Weimar Narratives of Colonial Loss and For-eign Occupation.* Bern, 2007.

Pommerin, Reiner. *'Sterilisierung der Rheinlandbastarde': Das Schicksal einer farbigen deutschen Minderheit, 1918–1937.* Düsseldorf, 1979.

Poutrus, Patrice G. "Die DDR, ein anderer deutscher Weg: Zum Umgang mit Aus-ländern im SED-Staat." In *Zuwanderungsland Deutschland*, ed. Beier-de Haan, 120–33.

———. "Die DDR." In *Normalfall Migration*, ed. Klaus J. Bade and Jochen Oltmer. Bonn, 2004.

Rau, Susanne. *Räume: Konzepte, Wahrnehmungen, Nutzungen.* Frankfurt am Main, 2013.

Reves, Christiane. *Vom Pomeranzengängler zum Großhändler?: Netzwerke und Migra-tionsverhalten der Brentano–Familien im 17. und 18. Jahrhundert.* Paderborn, 2012.

Rheinheimer, Martin. *Arme, Bettler und Vaganten: Überleben in der Not 1450–1850.* Frankfurt am Main, 2000.

Sala, Roberto. "Vom 'Fremdarbeiter' zum 'Gastarbeiter': Die Anwerbung italienischer Arbeitskräfte für die deutsche Wirtschaft." In *Vierteljahrshefte für Zeitgeschichte* 50, no. 1 (2007): 93–120.

Sanders, Nils et al. *Shared. Divided. United.* Berlin, 2009.

Sassen, Saskia. "Dienstleistungsökonomien und die Beschäftigung von Migrant-Innen in Städten." In *Migration und Stadt: Entwicklungen, Defizite, Potentiale*, ed. Klaus M. Schmals. Opladen, 2000.

Schiller, Nina Glick, Linda Basch and Cristina Szanton Blanc. "From Immigrant to Transmigrant: Theorizing Transnational Migration." In *Transnationale Migration*, ed. Ludger Pries. Baden–Baden, 1997.

Schilling, Heinz. "Confessional Migration as a Distinct Type of Old European Long Distance Migration." In *Le migrazioni in Europa, Secc. XIII–XVIII*, ed. Simonetta Cavaciocchi. Prato, 1994.

———. *Niederländische Exulanten im 16. Jahrhundert*. Gütersloh, 1972.

———. "Die frühneuzeitliche Konfessionsmigration: Calvinisten und sephardische Juden im Vergleich." In *Religion und Mobilität: zum Verhältnis von raumbezogener Mobilität und religiöser Identitätsbildung im frühneuzeitlichen Europa*, ed. Henning P. Jürgens and Thomas Weller. Göttingen, 2010.

Schimmel, Annemarie. *Muhammed Iqbal: Prophetischer Poet und Philosoph*. Munich, 1989.

Schlögl, Rudolf. "Kommunikation und Vergesellschaftung unter Anwesenden: Formen des Sozialen und ihre Transformation in der Frühen Neuzeit." *Geschichte und Gesellschaft* 34 (2008): 155–224.

Schnabel, Werner W. *Österreichische Exulanten in oberdeutschen Reichsstädten: Zur Migration von Führungsschichten im 17. Jahrhundert*. Erlangen, 1990.

Schönhuth, Michael, and Daniela Franzke, eds. *Der Einfluss soziokultureller Faktoren auf den Integrationsprozess von Spätaussiedlern*. Saarbrücken, 2003.

Schönpflug, Daniel. "French Revolutionary Refugees in Europe after 1789: The Example of Germany." In *The Encyclopedia of Migration and Minorities*, ed. Klaus Bade et al. Cambridge, 2011.

Schönwälder, Karen. *Einwanderung und ethnische Pluralität: Politische Entscheidungen und öffentliche Debatten in Großbritannien und der Bundesrepublik von den 1950er bis zu den 1970er Jahren*. Essen, 2002.

———. "Migration und Ausländerpolitik in der Bundesrepublik Deutschland: Öffentliche Debatten und politische Entscheidungen." In *Zuwanderungsland Deutschland*, ed. Rosmarie Beier-de Haan. Wolfratshausen, 2005.

Schunka, Alexander. "Lutheran Confessional Migration." In *European History Online* (Mainz, 2012), URL: http://www.ieg-ego.eu/schunkaa-2012-en URN: urn:nbn:de:0159-2012060616. Retrieved 7 January 2014.

———. "Konfession und Migrationsregime in der Frühen Neuzeit." *Geschichte und Gesellschaft* 35 (January–March 2009): 28–63.

———. *Gäste, die bleiben: Zuwanderer in Kursachsen und der Oberlausitz im 17. und im frühen 18. Jahrhundert*. Hamburg, 2006.

Siemann, Wolfram. "Asyl, Exil und Emigration der 1848er." In *Demokratiebewegung und Revolution 1847 bis 1849*, ed. Dieter Langewiesche. Berlin, 1998.

Soja, Edward W. *Thirdspace: Journeys to Los Angeles and Other Real-and-Imagined Places*. Malden, MA, 1996.

Spohnholz, Jesse. *The Tactics of Toleration: A Refugee Community in the Age of Religious Wars*. Newark, NJ, 2011.

Stern, Fritz. *Five Germanys I Have Known*. New York, 2006.

Steidl, Annemarie. *Auf nach Wien! Die Mobilität des mitteleuropäischen Handwerks im 18. und 19. Jahrhundert am Beispiel der Haupt- und Residenzstadt: Regionale Mobilität der städtischen Handwerker.* Vienna, 2003.

Thoms, Ulrike. "From Migrant Food to Lifestyle Cooking: The Career of Italian Cuisine in Europe." In *European History Online* (Mainz, 2011), http://nbn-resolving.de/urn:nbn:de:0159-2011051250. Retrieved 28 January 2014.

Volk, Stefan. "Peuplierung und religiöse Toleranz: Neuwied von der Mitte des 17. bis zur Mitte des 18. Jahrhunderts." *Rheinische Vierteljahresblätter* 55 (1991): 205–31.

Walker, Mack. *The Salzburg Transaction: Expulsion and Redemption in Eighteenth-Century Germany.* Ithaca, NY, 1992.

Wäntig, Wulf. *Grenzerfahrungen: Böhmische Exulanten im 17. Jahrhundert.* Konstanz, 2007.

Watanabe-O'Kelly, Helen. *Court Culture in Dresden: From Renaissance to Baroque.* Basingstoke et al., 2002.

Wilhelm, Cornelia. "Diversity in Germany: A Historical Perspective." *German Politics and Society* 107, no. 31 (Summer 2013): 13–29.

Worthington, David. *British and Irish Emigrants and Exiles in Europe, 1603–1688.* Leiden, 2010.

Yardeni, Myriam. *Le Refuge protestant.* Paris, 1985.

Zaimoglu, Feridun. *Kanak Sprak: 24 Misstöne vom Rande der Gesellschaft.* Hamburg, 1995.

CHAPTER ONE

~:~

Martyrdom and its Discontents
The Martyr as a Motif of Migration
in Early Modern Europe

ANDREW MCKENZIE-MCHARG

In 1410 the Czech proto-Reformer Jan Hus was excommunicated. One of the letters that he wrote two years later from exile to members of his Prague congregation contains the following passage:

> I have meditated on these evangelic words of our Saviour (John, chap. x.):—
> "The good shepherd giveth his life for the sheep . . ." I have also meditated on
> these words from St. Matthew (chap. x.):—"But when they persecute you in
> one city, flee ye into another." Of these two precepts, so different to each other,
> which ought I to follow? I know not.[1]

The passage thus pits martyrdom against the specific form of migration that I will focus on—namely migration arising from expulsion, or, in short, exile. Hus's predicament was compounded by his ability to adduce scriptural authority for both precepts. The ultimate denouement of this episode is well-known: under an assurance of safe passage, Hus traveled to Constance in 1414 to argue his case and was then arrested and burned the following year as a heretic. His fate seems to serve almost as a harbinger for the efflorescence of martyrdom engendered by the religious differences that in the next century began to etch deep lines of division, mistrust, and conflict throughout Europe. But if Hus's refusal to recant justified his status as a martyr in the eyes of some, was it possible to say that he had embraced a fate opposite to that which had beckoned in the form of exile? The following inquiry seeks to sketch the historical variability in this relationship between forced migration and martyrdom, for as it shall demonstrate, the two precepts were not locked into a diametrical opposition as Hus's letter to his congregation might seem to indicate.

Admittedly, the polarity of migration and martyrdom is affirmed by what can be considered the core definition inhering to the latter term. This definition was articulated by an essay that in 1689 won the prize for eloquence issued by the *Académie Française*: "The title of martyr is awarded to those who die for the sake of religion."[2] By 1689, the early modern resurgence in martyrdom had largely subsided. The recourse to other methods in combating what counted as heresy was exemplified by the policy adopted by the French authorities after Louis XIV had revoked the Edict of Nantes in 1685. No longer would the authorities unwittingly inaugurate cults of martyrdom. Now banishment was the order of the day. The Abbé Raguenet, who penned the essay, refrains from making overt references to the backdrop of renewed Huguenot persecution, but he makes abundantly clear that only those who suffered death for their faith qualified as martyrs in the true sense of the word. A survey of historical documents commenting upon other instances of religious persecution in early modern Europe tends to confirm this finding. Christians were exhorted to accept martyrdom as the option of last resort when flight—or migration—was no longer possible.[3] If martyrdom only applied to those who died for their beliefs, then migration as the alternative was bound to be seen as its opposite. Life or death, migration or martyrdom—the opposition could hardly be more starkly stated.

In the use of the term martyrdom there was, however, scope to stray from this core definition, particularly where an awareness of the originally broader meaning of the term "martyr" had not disappeared. Originally the Greek word simply meant witness.[4] In this sense both the suffering of the martyr who dies on the pyre and the hardship endured by the migrant who takes to the road could be seen as forms of martyrdom.[5] This can be appreciated if we briefly turn our attention to the martyrology produced by the Lutheran theologian Ludwig Rabus bearing the title *Accounts of God's Chosen Witnesses, Confessors, and Martyrs*.[6] The first volume, published in 1552, dealt with ancient Christians whose violent deaths bore witness to their faith, but in subsequent volumes Rabus documented more contemporary cases whose value as testimony to the evangelical truth was not predicated upon a biography ending in homicide. Rabus thus subsumed under the generous canopy of his work martyrs and other witnesses including those who had been expelled and exiled. The narrow definition of "martyr," however, inhibited any direct application of the term to such cases. In the subsequent literature an actual conflation of migrants and martyrs occurs only fleetingly—and when it does it is occasionally qualified, for example, by partnering "martyr" with the term *incruentus* or "unstained by blood."[7] Thus, migrants fleeing religious persecution might merit designation as "martyrs unstained by blood," but this term does not seem to have found wide usage.

Treating migrants as martyrs had a certain consistency with what could be called the general epistemological presumption: that the truth of a doctrine instilled in its adherents the strength to endure pain and suffering. This held true also for those cases where the pain and suffering did not involve blood being shed and did not culminate in death. The following inquiry will examine a number of sources that have been left behind by Lutheran pastors and that reveal various instances when they invoked the motif of martyrdom in an attempt to understand the ordeal of exile and migration.[8] An affinity of sorts obviously existed where migration was the response to religious persecution imposed for reasons of confessional politics.

If it proves possible to demonstrate an initially counter-intuitive alignment of martyrdom and migration, it will nevertheless remain apparent that the appeal to martyrdom in the context of migration was tinged with ambivalence. The specific "discontents" referred to in the title of this essay pertain therefore not so much to martyrdom as the fate endured by real martyrs but rather as the concept referenced by Lutheran pastors in their attempt to understand and dignify their own experience of forced expulsion. From the outbreak of the Reformation until long into the eighteenth century, Lutherans in general and Lutheran pastors in particular were shunted to and fro by the vicissitudes of confessional politics in Germany and the Habsburg territories. Undoubtedly, the numbers of Lutheran pastors who suffered involuntary exile far exceeded those who were executed as martyrs on grounds of confessional allegiance. But even if martyrdom is invoked in the writings of these exiled pastors, it could inadvertently insinuate a rebuke for the religiously fervent—rather than honoring God by acquiescing to a violent death, the migrant had clung to life. In the course of time a preference developed for using an alternative motif to understand the experience of forced migration.[9] As we shall see, this alternative motif was providence.

∗ ∗ ∗ ∗ ∗

It should be emphasized at the outset that the following discussion focuses on only a thin filament of cases extracted from the broader history of migration in early modern Europe. Even relatively cursory investigations reveal a surprisingly high degree of mobility among Europeans in these centuries— large segments of the population were on the move, and this mobility was propelled by diverse motives. Involuntary dislocation was simply a variation on the more general theme of relocation, which, far from being an anomaly, featured in the lives of numerous early modern Europeans. Forced expulsion on religious grounds thus represents only one category in the various typologies that have been devised in an attempt to systematically assess the nature of this mobility.[10] This particular category accommodates those Europeans who were forced to pay the price for the premium that the political authorities placed upon homogeneity of belief and doctrine within their territories. Their displacement thus testifies to the determination that drove the process of confessionalization within Europe. Within the borders of the old Holy Roman Empire, a *Ius Emigrandi* eventually secured for all adherents to the recognized confessions the right to move to territories where the practice of their beliefs was accepted.[11] If Lutherans thus were forced to vacate Catholic territory, the Catholic authorities were forced to accept their departure. This arrangement rendered martyrdom obsolete, but the memory of the martyrs continued to be a source of identity for the confessions and of consolation for those who were forced to take to the road. The focus in what follows will be upon the central European Lutheran experience, but it should not be forgotten that their plight was shared with Huguenots, Mennonites, Jews, and others who were also forced to deal with the ordeal of being uprooted from ancestral lands. In most such cases, no appeal could be made to some *modus operandi* that might give legal sanction to their departure.[12]

We can thus contextualize the movement of a specific group of Lutheran refugees by seeing their particular experience as part of a broader phenomenon of expulsion on religious grounds and then by treating this expulsion in turn as one type within a typology of motivating forces inducing or compelling Europeans to set out in search of a new life. In an attempt to comprehend the inner experience of those Europeans specifically forced to depart their homes for religious reasons, it is worthwhile to attempt another form of contextualization that considers the various responses to the predicament of religious persecution. As the introductory remarks have already intimated, migration was only one option, even if the alternative in the form of martyrdom seems, both now but also then, drastic. There were, however, further options, and if we take account of them it becomes possible to appreciate some of the strategies employed in diluting what at first sight might seem to be the untempered binary opposition of migration and martyrdom. For as quickly becomes apparent, the imposition of religious conformity did admit a series of alternative courses of action.

We can begin with an option whose consequence might seem both drastic and whose mention might seem superfluous in view of its universal condemnation—namely suicide. Whereas the Judeo-Christian proscription placed upon killing others has been amenable to qualifications that have conceded its legitimacy in cases of punishment and war, killing oneself has never merited the serious approbation of any authorities within this cultural and religious tradition. But its enumeration is useful as a limiting case, if for no other reason than the fact that those who had historically acted outside the constraints of this tradition sometimes were considered candidates for the title of martyr.

This was true of Socrates and stoic philosophers such as Seneca who had taken their own lives, even if they had been operating under duress.[13] Furthermore, this consideration could be reworked in other ways that called martyrdom into question. If the authorities were both ruthless and uncompromising, then obstinately rejecting the option of emigrating might seem tantamount to suicide.

If we abstract the use of coercion from all the specifics of a particular situation, then at least three more options are conceivable alongside migration, martyrdom, or suicide.[14] First, one can submit to the authorities and recant. Obviously this course of action was condemned as apostasy and rejected by theologians of all confessions. But the recantation might be undertaken outwardly while a kind of inner emigration allows one to hold on to the condemned beliefs and perhaps even secretly continue to practice them in some form. This option corresponds to Nicodemism, so called after Nicodemus, the Pharisee who in the Gospel of John outwardly remains a devout Jew but who secretly receives instruction from Jesus. While Calvin was uncompromising in his condemnation of Nicodemism, other confessions were less rigid in this regard.[15] Another option was a defiance of authority, which was not secret like Nicodemism or passive like martyrdom. This option of active resistance excited much debate and once more there were confessional differences with the Lutherans in contrast to Calvinists and Catholics expressing the greatest reservations in these matters.[16]

As an example of how the options enumerated above might be paired in other ways than the opposition of martyrdom and migration considered at the outset, it is worth pointing to a tract published in 1528 under the title *Von dem wahrhaftiggen Creutz Christi.*[17] Interesting for present purposes is the playful and paradoxical pseudonym employed by the author of the tract: Nicodemus Martyr. Here the martyr is not opposed to the migrant who remains true to his beliefs by fleeing, but rather to the Nicodemite who hides his beliefs. At the same time, martyr is not meant to be taken literally. In fact, the pseudonym is an interesting comment upon the new communicative possibilities inherent to the medium of print. Print allowed one to be a martyr by giving witness to one's views through an open and public profession. At the same time it was possible to remain hidden in the tradition of Nicodemus by publishing anonymously or under a pseudonym.

By thus opposing the Nicodemite to the martyr this case hints at a strategy for those who were exposed to religious repression and who wished to argue that the migrant and the martyr in actual fact not so different. One could emphasize the commonalities that both martyrdom and migration shared as responses to religious repression by drawing a contrast to other conceivable responses. Neither the migrant nor the martyr recanted like the apostate, nor did they live in public denial of their true beliefs like the Nicodemite. And even though the martyr and the migrant chose forms of passive disobedience, they did not offend Christian humility by actively resisting the worldly authorities, who, as idolatrous as they might be, still enjoyed divine sanction. Thus, the extreme of martyrdom and the more frequent experience of migration could be allied by reference to an alternative response to religious persecution, and this alliance could be consolidated by applying the other strategy alluded to above, namely the appeal to the original broader meaning of the term "martyr." By applying these two strategies, it became in some cases possible to transform a polarity into an affinity.

*   *   *   *   *

The set of alternative responses enumerated above has been derived on a rarefied level of abstraction hovering high above the realities of a specific historical situation. Descending to this level of concrete situations, we find that often certain options simply do not come into contention. The scorn that Luther had reserved for all attempts to employ coercion in combating heresy might have induced an aversion among Lutherans when it came to killing heretics. But more generally, martyrdom relies upon a finely calibrated alignment of people willing to kill and others willing to be killed.[18] Such an alignment did not exist within the Saxon territories in the 1560s when the political authorities clashed with Lutheran pastors who were not willing to accord the writings of Melanchthon the same canonical status as those of Luther. The intricacies of this dispute need not detain us here.[19] Important for present purposes is simply the fact that the authorities, rather than trying and executing recalcitrant theologians, settled on a policy of banishment. In the years 1561–73 over two hundred pastors were dismissed from their offices.

A work published in 1575 bearing the title *De Exiliis* contains passages in which Bartholomäus Gernhard, the author and former preacher at the court in Weimar, insinuates a solidarity between these exiled pastors and martyrs. In part this is achieved by disparaging the Nicodemite option. Gernhard numbers himself to those theologians who profess their beliefs "not secretly, not hidden in a corner, but by suffering and risking life and limb, and who in gratitude to God would not shun death."[20]

The other strategy of generalizing the criterion of martyrdom to include all those who demonstrate resilience in the face of persecution is also employed. Gernhard counsels his fellow exiled theologians: "if you are oppressed by the difficulties and duration of your misery then think that the blame for that lies in the fact that we are as martyrs too sensitive and soft."[21] Then the argument takes a somewhat disingenuous turn, and Gernhard implies that the real martyrs who undergo death are the ones who are overly sensitive. "Who would not prefer," he asks, "to be a genuine martyr who gets everything over and done with in a painful hour?"[22] However, the Lutherans who in the early years of the Reformation actually did experience this "painful hour" find no mention. It is hard to avoid the impression that historical examples too recent and too proximate would have caused the conceit of such arguments to collapse.

At a few points in the tract, constancy (*Beständigkeit*) makes an appearance, but it is not invoked as a hallowed virtue. With the publication in 1584 of Justus Lipsius's *De Constantia*, religious discourse was infused with a powerful dose of Neo-Stoic thought and constancy began to develop a profile that was at the same time distinct and complex.[23] As the Germanist Werner Welzig pointed out, constancy could mean to the seventeenth-century mind either passive resilience or the intrepidness that displays itself in the pursuit of a goal.[24] It was thus a concept that had the range to bridge the divide between migrants and martyrs. This was recognized by those Lutheran pastors who, following the defeat of Protestant forces at the Battle of White Mountain in 1620, were evicted from their parishes as part of a systematic policy of re-catholicization in the Habsburg territories.[25] The sermons they held before their departure exhort their congregations to demonstrate the same constancy in their loyalty to the true word of God as they—their former pastors—demonstrate in taking to the road.[26] The degree to which God might demand constancy of his servants varies and forms a continuum, at one extreme of which lies the ultimate test of martyrdom.

In addition to the virtue of constancy, there were other more symbolic reference points that helped engender a sense of solidarity linking the exiled pastors with the precedent left behind by the martyrs. The first martyr for whom chapters 6 and 7 of the Acts of the Apostles provided scriptural testimony was Saint Stephen. After being tried for blasphemy, the infuriated crowd "cast him out of the city, and stoned him" (Acts 7:58). It is not hard to understand why the pastors would see their fate literally mirrored by the first part of this account and then in the second part more generally reflected to the degree that their expulsion—like Stephen's violent death—also bore witness to God. A sermon printed in 1628 bore the title *Martyrium triumphale* and referenced the repressive religious policy adopted in the Habsburg lands: "When we now preach they storm down upon us and expel us from the town, just like Saint Stephen, that is, one will not tolerate us in these lands, we have to emigrate along with wife and child, and vacate the land."[27]

At the same time, the martyr does not advance to a central motif in these documents. The Old Testament, with its countless stories of the Patriarchs leading their people through the desert, provided a far more accommodating template for migrants attempting to understand their own experiences. Indeed the appropriation of the motif of martyrdom entailed the risk of arousing reproach. This was particularly the case for the pastors. Their predicament was widely discussed in these times.[28] The leading Puritan William Perkins asked in his treatise on cases of conscience, a work that was indeed known to Lutheran theologians: "Whether any man, especially a Minister, may with good conscience flie in persecution?"[29] In the manner of the casuist, Perkins considered all the extenuating circumstances but the judgment was in the end unequivocal: ". . . if the persecution be common to the whole Church, he is not to flie. For it is necessarie at such times especially that those which are strong should support and confirm the weake."[30] The claim that the Lutheran pastors who had vacated their offices qualified as martyrs would presumably have seemed brazen and conceited against the backdrop of a discourse in which such views were being voiced.

The most ambitious attempt to sort out the relationship between martyrdom and migration was provided by Andreas Kesler in 1630. Two years after completing the work to which he gave the title *Patientia Christiania*, his personal library went up in flames as Croatian troops ran rampant though the town of Eisfeld. Whether his exhaustive and exhausting study of persecution in all its forms helped him to process this loss is not known. Interestingly enough, the loss of good books appears as level five of the graduated scale he devised.[31] Just as earthquakes are measured on the Richter Scale, one could measure the intensity of persecution on the "Kesler Scale." Expulsion came after the loss of books as level six, while an ignominious and painful death was one level shy of the ultimate persecution, which Kesler identified as the coercion of conscience.

In addition to thus systematizing and grading the forms of persecution, Kesler provided the reader with insights into the reasons why God permits such wickedness. His inquiry continually returns to the enigma for which Leibniz at the beginning of the next century would coin the term "theodicy." It is interesting to consider how the figure of the martyr does not pose this problem. Indeed, the martyr's triumph derives from the voluntary acceptance of the most abject mortification. The fact that the martyrs, despite their innocence and their loyalty to God, actually acquiesce in a violent death deflates the indignation that otherwise might be aroused by the seemingly perverse mismatch between what the godly deserve and what the godly receive. In describing Luther's theology of martyrdom, Robert Kolb has drawn attention to the reformer's affirmation of its counter-intuitive nature. In effect, Luther devised "a theology of paradox which equated God's wisdom with what seems foolishness to the sinner . . . ."[32] This theology was embedded in an apocalyptic frame that saw in the recent spate of martyrs a sure sign that the Antichrist had stirred from his somnolent state and that the end was nigh.

This situation is very different for the migrant. Migrants fleeing persecution cannot portray what is effectively an involuntary expulsion as an exercise of free will. It is thus not possible for them to integrate an element of volition into their fate without undermining their tragic sense of themselves as victims. On these grounds then, the quandaries of a theodicy announce themselves: Why has God forsaken the very people who are faithful to His word? Why are the godly punished with the loss of their possessions and livelihoods while the material benefits of the abandoned property accrue to the ungodly and the idolatrous?

Gernhard already in the sixteenth century tried to resolve the cognitive dissonance that these paradoxes provoked. He submitted a sequence of observations that enabled the reader to extract some sense and reason from the fate that had befallen God's loyal servants. The first reason is particularly interesting: God imposing a punishment for sinfulness.[33] Admittedly, Gernhard then connects this with the fallen state of humankind, but the generality of this state then drains much of the elucidatory power from his explanation for the misfortune afflicting a particular group. The notion that the adversity has been sent by God to punish wayward sinners reappears on occasions in the documents left behind by the pastors who were expelled from Bohemia.[34] The thought that the harsh fate is self-inflicted is obviously an unpleasant one, but it at least has the effect of correcting the perversity that would otherwise reign in a world where the innocent suffer. Of course, explanations that link the fate of expulsion with sinfulness stand in the way of any appeal to martyrs. A view ascribing the torments of the martyr a punitive character would in essence undermine the very claim to the title of martyr. The martyr must be innocent. Otherwise he or she is less like Christ and more like the two criminals who were crucified on either side of him.[35]

*   *   *   *   *

The definitive answer to the question posed by the discrepancy between merits and deserts was ultimately to be provided not by theological disquisitions but rather by the long-term success eventually enjoyed by Lutherans who fled areas subjected to policies of re-catholicization. The pastors might have articulated for large numbers of their congregation the sense of disorientation that befalls those whose lives are upended for no seemingly just reason. But by the eighteenth century, the Protestant migrants from the Habsburg territories had found not only refuge but also their own place within the society of confessionally more amenable territories. In 1714, Georg Heinrich Goetze published his *Diptycha Exulum, or Register of Migrants*, memorializing those pastors who had fled the persecution in the Habsburg territories. Because their story had in general terms a happy ending, Goetze felt confident in arguing a "reason to feel joy at the sight of a flock of migrants who are guided by God . . . Because constancy and patience come from and are maintained by God, they should be recognized and praised in the migrants."[36] He goes on to proclaim that "constancy is the best" and quotes Matthew 24:13: ". . . he that shall endure unto the end, the same shall be saved."

Being "saved," however, did not just mean transcendental, otherworldly salvation. Goetze's work celebrated how the migrants had triumphed over adversity in this world. The next year Christian Schröter in Bautzen was inspired by Goetze's *Register* to assemble his own account of those constant Lutherans who in being transplanted from hostile to benign environments serve as "witness to God's wondrous guidance."[37] As he writes: "In cases where poor abandoned orphans gain honor and esteem, it is almost possible to feel and touch God's providence with your hands."[38] This providence was manifest not just in the social standing but also in the worldly success of the migrants. As Schröter writes: "Some of the migrants have so enjoyed the sustenance of God's blessings that they bequeathed to their children an inheritance which in its amount was far larger than the houses, fields, and other temporal goods which they possessed before they were forced into exile."[39]

These sentiments mark a fundamental shift when compared to those earlier texts that still betray the spell cast by the early modern cult of martyrdom. Divine truth was no longer seen as manifest in the constancy that it instilled in those who observe and profess it, be they martyrs or migrants. Rather, divine truth is evident in the way migrants and children reap the worldly rewards of their constancy. This fundamental shift took the sting out of forced migration. Viewed retrospectively, it did not seem such a bad option. And when the further passage of time allows us to view these attitudes historically, one thing stands out in particular: martyrdom, as the alternative that Jan Hus had once embraced and that was obviously on the minds of Lutheran pastors throughout the sixteenth and seventeenth century, no longer even merits a mention.

Like any cultural phenomenon, martyrdom experienced its ebb and flow, and by the eighteenth century the forces that sustained either its actual occurrence or its discursive invocation had ebbed away. "Men love life too much and everything around them confirms them in this love."[40] Such is the view expressed in Cesare Beccaria's classic treatise *On Crimes and Punishments*. In actual fact, the view is submitted not as the reason why men shun martyrdom but why they, for the most part, do not commit suicide. It is, however, interesting that Beccaria goes on to compare suicide to emigration—both deplete a state of its citizens. Beccaria's tract, which appeared in 1764, qualifies as a true product of the Enlightenment. True to the general tenor of debate in this period, Beccaria argues on the basis of what he regards as timeless truths. Thus it is "useless" for the state to legislate against emigration, for "how can every point on its borders be sealed?"[41] If one considers the later history of migration in the part of the world on which this paper has concentrated, namely central Europe, then it becomes apparent that in the second half of the twentieth century the political authorities were confident that the borders could indeed be sealed. The implicit denial of a *Ius Emigrandi* such as that which had been instated in the old Empire induced shifts in the range and relative weighting of the alternatives now on offer under the conditions of a divided Cold War Europe—the "Nicodemism" of outward conformity, the "martyrdom" that often was a consequence of defying the state. Admittedly these options had different names and the root causes were ideological in nature rather than religious. But the situations in which many found themselves were variations upon the fundamental and age-old theme of holding onto convictions in a world shaped by constraint and coercion.

Andrew McKenzie-McHarg is a post-doctoral research fellow with the Conspiracy and Democracy Project at CRASSH at the University of Cambridge. Previously he was based at the Forschungszentrum Gotha of the University of Erfurt. His research interests have extended from anti-Jesuit rhetoric in the Early Modern Period to radical streams of thought in late Enlightenment Germany.

Notes

1. I take this translation from the *Letters of John Huss written during his exile and imprisonment*, ed. Émile de Bonnechose (London, 1846), 19. For a discussion of Hus in the context of the general martyrological mentality, see Brad Gregory's magisterial *Salvation at Stake: Christian Martyrdom in Early Modern Europe* (Cambridge, MA, 2001), 63–67.
2. The essay was by the Abbé Raguenet and can be found in *Pieces d'éloquence qui ont remporté le prix de l'academie françoise, depuis 1671 jusqu'en 1748* (Paris, 1740), 1:174.
3. As simply one example of this tendency to see martyrdom as the extreme position, see a tract written by Wittenberg theologians and addressed to the Bohemian Protestants who found themselves as a result of the re-catholicization policy in a state of duress: *Trewhertzige Warnungs-Schrift, Daß man die Päpstische Lehre meyden, und bey der Lutherischen standhafftig bleiben sol: An die Evangelische Christen, so in Böheimb und andern örtern bedrenget werden, aus Christlichem Mitleiden verffasst, und in öffentlichen Druck gegeben / durch die Doctorn und Professorn der Theologischen Facultet zu Wittenberg* (Wittenberg, 1625), 34. For a few comments in the modern literature on this, see Arno Herzig, *Der Zwang zum wahren Glauben: Rekatholisierung vom 16. bis zum 18. Jahrhundert* (Göttingen, 2000), 123–25.
4. For a number of enlightening remarks on the word's etymology, see Léon-E. Halkin, "Hagiographie Protestante," *Analecta Bolianda* LXVIII (1950), 456.
5. What makes this slightly more complex is the fact that martyrdom can also be seen as a metaphor. Thus, Gregory in his study of martyrdom references the spiritual martyrdom of Gregory the Great and quotes the following statement: "Even though we do not bend our bodily neck to the sword, nevertheless with the spiritual sword we slay in our soul carnal desires." (Gregory, *Salvation at Stake*, 50). Here the metaphorical element is apparent, i.e., monks are metaphorically martyrs because the carnal desires are killed by their resolute und unwavering commitment to chastity. My impression

is, however, that martyrdom for migrants is not just a metaphor but rather based on recalling the original broader meaning of the term that in turn allows them to see their tribulations as a genuine form of witness, i.e., martyrdom.

6. Ludwig Rabus, *Der Heyligen ausserwoehlten Gottes Zeugen, Bekennern und Martyrer* (Strasbourg, 1552; subsequent volumes II–VIII, 1554–1558). The best analysis has been provided by Robert Kolb in his *For All the Saints: Changing Perceptions of Martyrdom and Sainthood in the Lutheran Reformation* (Macon, GA, 1987). Gregory notes on page 171 of *Salvation at Stake*: "Rabus's work is fundamentally a compilation of confessors, all of whom were "witnesses" but only some of whom had shed their blood."

7. In a seventeenth-century work, the theologian Andreas Kesler devised general criteria for classifying persecution and named as the fourth criteria the distinction between persecutions *cruentae* and *incruentae*. See Andreas Kesler, *Patientia Christiana: Außführlicher Tractat von der Kirchen Christi Persecution oder Verfolgung bey diesen betrübten Zeiten* (Coburg, 1630), 143. In a further work to which we will turn our attention at a later point, Georg Heinrich Goetze in his *Dipytcha Exulum, Oder Exulanten-Register* (Altenburg, 1714) uses the term once on page 68 to describe one of his exiled pastors.

8. The focus upon pastors is justified by the prominent role that they played in these migratory movements. See Alexander Schunka, "Migrationen evangelischer Geistlicher als Motor frühneuzeitlicher Wanderungsbewegungen," in *Konfession, Migration und Elitenbildung: Studien zur Theologenausbildung des 16. Jahrhunderts*, ed. Herman J. Selderhuis and Markus Wriedt (Leiden, 2007), 3.

9. In general one can say that when compared to the other Calvinist and Anglican confessions martyrdom—both as real experience and as motif—featured less in Lutheranism. Various reasons have been put forward to explain this. See Robert Kolb, *For All the Saints*, 85–102. See also David Baghi, "Luther and the Problem of Martyrdom," in *Martyrs and Martyrologies*, ed. Diana Wood (Oxford, 1993), 209–21.

10. See Thomas Klingebiel, "Migration im frühneuzeitlichen Europa: Anmerkungen und Überlegungen zur Typologiediskussion," in *Réfugiés und Emigrés: Migration zwischen Frankreich und Deutschland im 18. Jahrhundert*, ed. Thomas Höpel and Katharina Middell (Comparaitiv 1997 Heft 5/6) (Leipzig, 1997), 7–38.

11. See Stefan Ehrenpreis, "Ius reformandi—Ius emigrandi: Reichsrecht, Konfession und Ehre in Religionsstreitigkeiten des späten 16. Jahrhunderts," in *Individualisierung, Rationalisierung, Säkularisierung: Neue Wege der Religionsgeschichte*, ed. Michael Weinzierl (Vienna, 1997), 67–95.

12. For an overview of confessional migration, see Heinz Schilling, "Die frühneuzeitliche Konfessionsmigration," in *Migration in der europäischen Geschichte seit dem späten Mittelalter*, ed. Klaus J. Bade (Osnabrück, 2002), 67–90.

13. For the treatment of the philosophers of the Stoa as early martyrs, see Alexandre Tarrête, "Les héros stoïcens, des martyrs païens?" in *Martyrs et Martyrologes*, ed. Frank Lestringant and Pierre-François Moreau (Lille, 2003), 87–110.

14. For a similar discussion of the various responses to religious coercion see the "Kommentar" provided by Werner Wilhelm Schnabel in the volume *Staatsmacht und Seelenheil: Gegenreformation und Geheimprotestantismus in der Habsburgermonarchie*, ed. Rudolf Leeb, Susanne Claudine Pils, and Thomas Winkelbauer (Vienna, 2007), 263. This chapter sees itself as a small contribution to the much larger research program that has been outlined by Schunka, "Glaubensflucht als Migrationsoption," *Geschichte in Wissenschaft und Unterricht* 10 (2005): 547–64.

15. See Perez Zagorin, *Ways of Lying: Dissimulation, Persecution and Conformity in Early Modern Europe* (Cambridge, MA, 1990). See also Gregory, *Salvation at Stake*, 159.

16. For some interesting comments on the various options considered by Calvin in the face of religious persecution, see Ernst Wolf, "Das Problem des Widerstandrechts bei Calvin," in *Widerstandsrecht*, ed. Arthur Kaufmann (Darmstadt, 1972), 152–69, see esp. 154 and 158.

17. Ulman Weiß has persuasively argued that the pseudonym can be plausibly attributed to Sebastian Franck. See Ulman Weiß, "Nicodemus Martyr—ein unbekanntes Pseudonym Sebastian Francks?" *Archiv für Reformationsgeschichte* 85 (1994): 163–79.

18. David Nicholls has pointed out this for the Huguenot context in his essay "The Theatre of Martyrdom in the French Reformation," *Past & Present* 121 (November 1988): 49–73. But even the metaphor of "theatre" fails to do justice to the element of two competing narratives being played out—obviously those who are being killed play the role of martyrs, while those doing the killing do not see their victims in the role of martyrs but rather as heretics or criminals.

19. The complexities of this episode are recounted by Vera von der Osten-Sacken, "Erzwungenes und selbstgewähltes Exil im Luthertum: Bartholomäus Gernhards Schrift *De Exiliis* (1575)," in *Religion und Mobilität: Zum Verhältnis von raumbezogener Mobilität und religiöser Identitäsbildung im frühneuzeitlichen Europa*, ed. Henning P. Jürgens and Thomas Weller (Göttingen, 2010), 41–58.

20. Bartholomäus Gernhard, *De Exiliis, Christliche Erinnerungen aus Gottes Wort. In etlichen furnemen Artickeln zu Ende der Vorrede verzeichnet. An die Enturlaubten und Vertriebenen Prediger aus Düringen / Francken / und Meissen / der unmündigen Herzogen zu Sachsen und Fürstenthumb. bey Ausspendung der contribuirten Stewer gehalten.* (Eisleben, 1575), 9v–r.

21. Ibid., 31r.

22. If we consider an assertion made by David Baghi, such a statement might not have been without precedent—referring to Luther's lecture series on the Book of Genesis, Baghi writes: "Again and again in these lectures we find him [Luther] applauding the long trials of the patriarchs at the expense of the sharper but shorter pains of the martyrs." See David Baghi, "Luther and the Problem of Martyrdom," in *Martyrs and Martyrologies*, ed. Diana Wood (Oxford, 1993), 215.

23. See Alexander Schunka, "Constantia im Martyrium: Zur Exilliteratur des 17. Jahrhunderts zwischen Humanismus und Barock," in *Frühneuzeitliche Konfessionskultur* (Heidelberg, 2008), 175–200. See also Schunka's chapter "Constantia als Ziel und integratives Moment" in his *Gäste, die bleiben: Zuwanderer in Kursachsen und der Oberlausitz im 17. und im frühen 18. Jahrhundert* (Hamburg, 2006), 133–42.

24. Werner Welzig, "Constantia und Barocke Beständigkeit," *Deutsche Vierteljahrschrift für Literaturwissenschaft und Geistesgeschichte*, 35:3 (1961), 418.

25. For an account of this policy see Herzig, *Der Zwang zum wahren Glauben*, 68–80. Howard Louthan has recently attempted to acknowledge the cultural achievements of this policy. See his *Converting Bohemia: Force and Persuasion in the Catholic Reformation* (Cambridge, 2009).

26. Indeed, pastors such as Sigismund Scherertz continued to supply their former congregations with literature calculated to steel them in their loyalty to the Lutheran confession. See, for example, his *Constantia Veritatis Evengelicae: Das ist / Christlich Bericht / Von Beständigkeit bey der Göttlichen Wahrheit des Heiligen Evangelii /*

Augspurgischer Confession: An die hinterlassenen Evangelischen Präger / (auff etlicher Begehren) einfeltig gefasset (Lüneburg, 1623). On Scherertz, Alexander Bitzel, *Anfechtung und Trost bei Sigismund Scherertz: Ein lutherischer Theologe im Dreißigjährige Krieg* (Göttingen, 2002).

27. Valentin Kienast, *Martyrium Triumphale, Märterlicher Triumph Vom Heiligen Märterer Stephano am Heiligen S. Stephans Tag dess 1626 Jahres in Siebenbürgen zu Kysban auff J.F.G. Kupfferhandlung zur Valet-Predigt gehalten* (Leipzig?, 1628)

28. See Bitzel, *Anfechtung und Trost bei Sigismund Scherertz*, 49–56.

29. William Perkins, *The Whole Treatise of the Cases of Conscience* (1628), 215. On Perkins, see James F. Keenan SJ, "William Perkins (1558–1602) and the Birth of British Casuistry," in *The Context of Casuistry*, ed. James F. Keenan SJ and Thomas A. Shannon (Washington, DC, 1995), 105–30.

30. Perkins, *The Whole Treatise*, 219.

31. Andreas Kesler, *Patientia Christiania: Ausführlicher Tractat Von der Kirchen Christi Persecution oder Verfolgung bey diesen betrübten Zeiten* (Coburg, 1630).

32. Robert Kolb, "God's Gift of Martyrdom," *Church History* 64 (1995): 401.

33. Gernhard, 32r–33v.

34. An example of a community who see in their sinfulness the reason why God has deprived them of their pastor can be found in *Das trawrige und schmerzliche Valete M. Wolfgangi Güntheri Pfarrers und Superintendentis der dreyen Herrschaften Friedland / Reichenberg und Seidenbergk . . .* (n.p., 1624), (no pagination—9th page from and including title page).

35. In contradiction to this, Raguenet writes: The martyr "se regarde comme un pécheur qu'a mérité la mort qu'il souffre." Raguenet, *Pieces d'éloquence*, 181. It is highly revealing that in the German translation we find appended to this sentence the following footnote: "Wo bleibt nun das Verdienst, welches der Redner dem Märtyrerthume zueignet, sich aber hier selbst in diesem Stücke, widerspricht?" See M. Johann Michael Uhlichs, *Einleitung in die Lehre der Christen . . .* (Leipzig, 1754), 432.

36. Goetze, *Diptycha Exulum, Oder Exulanten Register* (Altenburg, Göttingen, 1714), 44.

37. Carl Christian Schröter, *Merckwürdige Exulanten-Historie / darinnen besonders um des reinen Evangelii willen Vertriebener Prediger und Schul-Lehrer ihre Lebens-Geschichte enthalten . . .* (Budißin [i.e. Bautzen], 1715), 7.

38. Ibid., 53.

39. Ibid., 8–9.

40. Cesare Beccaria, *On Crimes and Punishments and Other Writings*, ed. Aaron Thomas, trans. Aaron Thomas and Jeremy Parzen (Toronto, 2008), 65.

41. Ibid., 66.

Bibliography

Anonymous. *Das trawrige und schmerzliche Valete M. Wolfgangi Güntheri Pfarrers und Superintendentis der dreyen Herrschaften Friedland / Reichenberg und Seidenbergk . . .* N.P., 1624.

———. *Trewhurtzige Warnungs-Schrift, Daß man die Päpstische Lehre meyden, und bey Lutherischen standhafftig bleiben sol: An die Evangelische Christen, so in Böheimb und andern örtern bedrenget werden, aus Christlichem Mitleiden verffasst, und in öffentlichen Druck gegeben / durch die Doctorn und Professorn der Theologischen Facultet zu Wittenberg.* Wittenberg, 1625.

Baghi, David. "Luther and the Problem of Martyrdom." In *Martyrs and Martyrologies*, ed. Diana Wood. Oxford, 1993.

Beccaria, Cesare. *On Crimes and Punishments and Other Writings*, ed. Aaron Thomas, trans. Aaron Thomas and Jeremy Parzen. Toronto, 2008.

Bitzel, Alexander. *Anfechtung und Trost bei Sigismund Scherertz: Ein lutherischer Theologe im Dreißigjährige Krieg.* Göttingen, 2002.

Ehrenpreis, Stefan. "Ius reformandi—Ius emigrandi. Reichtssrecht, Konfession und Ehre in Religionsstreitigkeiten das späten 16. Jahrhunderts." In *Individualisierung, Rationalisierung, Säkularisierung: Neue Wege der Religionsgeschichte*, ed. Michael Weinzierl. Vienna, 1997.

Gernhard, Bartholomäus. *De Exiliis, Christliche Erinnerungen aus Gottes Wort. In etlichen furnemen Artickeln zu Ende der Vorrede verzeichnet. An die Enturlaubten und Vertriebenen Prediger aus Düringen / Francken / und Meissen / der unmündigen Herzogen zu Sachsen und Fürstenthumb. bey Ausspendung der contribuirten Stewer gehalten.* Eisleben, 1575.

Goetze, Georg Heinrich. *Dipytcha Exulum, Oder Exulanten-Register.* Altenburg, 1714.

Gregory, Brad. *Salvation at Stake: Christian Martyrdom in Early Modern Europe.* Cambridge, MA, 2001.

Halkin, Léon-E. "Hagiographie Protestante." *Analecta Bolianda* 68 (1950): 453–63.

Herzig, Arno. *Der Zwang zum wahren Glauben: Rekatholisierung vom 16. bis zum 18. Jahrundert.* Göttingen, 2000.

Huss, John. *Letters of John Huss Written During his Exile and Imprisonment*, ed. Émile de Bonnechose. London, 1846.

Keenan SJ, James F. "William Perkins (1558–1602) and the Birth of British Casuistry." In *The Context of Casuistry*, ed. James F. Keenan SJ and Thomas A. Shannon. Washington, DC, 1995.

zu Kysban auff J.F.G. Kupfferhandlung zur Valet-Predigt gehalten. Leipzig[?], 1628.

Kesler, Andreas. *Patentia Christiana: Außfürlicher Tractat von der Kirchen Christi Persecution oder Verfolgung bey diesen betrübten Zeiten.* Coburg, 1630.

Kienast, Valentin. *Martyrium Triumphale, Märterlicher Triumph Vom Heiligen Märterer Stephano am Heiligen S. Stephans Tag dess 1626 Jahres in Siebenbürgen*

Klingebiel, Thomas. "Migration im frühneuzeitlichen Europa: Anmerkungen und Überlegungen zur Typologiediskussion." In *Réfugiés und Emigrés: Migration zwischen Frankreich und Deutschland im 18. Jahrhundert*, eds. Thomas Höpel and Katharina Middel. Leipzig, 1997.

Kolb, Robert. *For All the Saints: Changing Perception of Martyrdom and Sainthood in the Lutheran Reformation.* Macon, GA, 1987.

———. "God's Gift of Martyrdom." *Church History* 64 (1995): 399–411.

Louthan, Howard. *Converting Bohemia: Force and Persuasion in the Catholic Reformation.* Cambridge, 2009.

Nicholls, David. "The Theatre of Martyrdom in the French Reformation." *Past & Present* 121 (November 1998): 49–73.

Osten-Sacken, Vera von der. "Erzwungenes und selbstgewähltes Exil im Luthertum. Bartholomäus Gernhards Schrift *De Exiliis* (1575)." In *Religion und Mobilität: Zum Verhältnis von raumbezogener Mobilität und religiöser Identitäsbildung im frühneuzeitlichen Europa*, ed. Henning P. Jürgens and Thomas Weller. Göttingen, 2010.

Perkins, William. *The Whole Treatise of the Cases of Conscience.* 1628.

Rabus, Ludwig. *Der Heyligen ausserwoehlten Gottes Zeugen, Bekennern und Martyrer.* Volume 1. Strasbourg, 1552. Subsequent Volumes 2–8, 1554–1558.

Raguenet, Abbé. "Essay." In *Pieces d'éloquence qui ont remporté le prix de l'academie françoise, depuis 1671 jusqu'en 1748.* Volume 1. Paris, 1740.

Scherertz, Sigismund. *Constantia Veritatis Evengelicae: Das ist / Christlich Bericht / Von Beständigkeit bey der Göttlichen Wahrheit des Heiligen Evangelii / Augspurgischer Confession: An die hinterlassenen Evangelischen Präger / (auff etlicher Begehren) einfeltig gefasset.* Lüneburg, 1623.

Schilling, Heinz. "Die frühneuzeitliche Konfessionsmigration." In *Migration in der europäischen Geschichte seit dem späten Mittelalter*, ed. Klaus J. Bade. Osnabrück, 2002.

Schnabel, Werner Wilhelm. "Kommentar." In *Staatsmacht und Seelenheil: Gegenreformation und Geheimprotestantismus in der Habsburgermonarchie*, ed. Rudolf Leeb, Susanne Claudine Pils, and Thomas Winkelbauer. Vienna, 2007.

Schröter, Carl Christian. *Merckwürdige Exulanten-Historie / darinnen besonders um des reinen Evangelii willen Vertriebener Prediger und Schul-Lehrer ihre Lebens-Geschichte enthalten . . . .* Budißin [i.e. Bautzen], 1715.

Schunka, Alexander. "Glaubensflucht als Migrationsoption." *Geschichte in Wissenschaft und Unterricht* 10 (2005): 547–64.

———. *Gäste, die bleiben. Zuwanderer in Kursachsen und der Oberlausitz im 17. und im frühen 18. Jahrhundert.* Hamburg, 2006.

———. "Migrationen evangelischer Geistlicher als Motor frühneuzeitlicher Wanderungbewegungen." In *Konfession, Migration und Elitenbildung: Studien zur Theologenausbildung des 16. Jahrhunderts*, ed. Herman J. Selderhuis and Markus Wriedt. Leiden, 2007.

Tarrête, Alexandre. "Les héros stoïcens, des martyrs païens?" In *Martyrs et Martyrologes*, ed. Frank Lestringant and Pierre-François Moreau. Lille, 2003.

Uhlichs, M. Johann Michael. *Einleitung in die Lehre der Christen . . . .* Leipzig, 1754.

Weiß, Ulman. "Nicodemus Martyr—ein unbekanntes Pseudonym Sebastian Francks?" *Archiv für Reformationsgeschichte* 85 (1994): 163–79.

Welzig, Werner. "Constantia und Barocke Beständigkeit." *Deutsche Vierteljahrschrift für Literaturwissenschaft und Geistesgeschichte* 35, no. 3 (July 1961): 416–32.

Wolf, Ernst. "Das Problem des Widerstrandrechts bei Calvin." In *Widerstrandsrecht*, ed. Arthur Kaufmann. Darmstadt, 1972.

Zagorin, Perez. *Ways of Lying: Dissimulation, Persecution and Conformity in Early Modern Europe.* Cambridge, MA, 1990.

CHAPTER TWO

~:~

Penal Migration in Early Modern Germany

JASON P. COY

In a perceptive 1988 essay on vagrancy in sixteenth-century Württemberg, Robert Scribner suggested that "any discussion of mobility in early modern Europe should give special attention to the phenomenon of vagrancy."[1] In the decades since Scribner's essay was published, relatively few scholars have taken this advice, and discussions of migration remain largely divorced from discussions of vagrancy and law enforcement. Studies of migration in early modern Germany have approached the subject of mobility from the perspective of either the political and religious changes of the period or the economic factors that drove migrant labor. Studies of the Reformation and its confessional aftermath have usually focused on the mass expulsion of religious exiles associated with the English Reformation, the Peace of Augsburg and the Thirty Years' War in Germany, or the Revocation of the Edict of Nantes by Louis XIV.[2] Most social historians working on early modern Germany, on the other hand, have examined regional migration prompted by economic necessity, as migrant laborers sought work in nearby communities.[3] In a prominent survey of migration in European history, for example, Leslie Page Moch deals extensively with migration prompted by economic and politico-religious factors in the early modern period, but spares only a few pages for vagrancy, which she classifies as "marginal migration." While Moch draws instructive conclusions about the links between rural poverty, regional migration, and vagrancy during economic hard times, she mostly ignores the role of criminal prosecution in these phenomena.[4]

The subject of this chapter is another engine of mobility that has received inadequate attention: penal migration. In the pre-modern era, European magistrates and territorial rulers relegated thousands of convicts to the roads through banishment.[5] In early modern Germany, political fragmentation and recurrent economic and agrarian crises prompted territorial and urban authorities, working to rid their domains of "sturdy beggars," to expel unwanted migrants. These "marginal migrants," charged with petty crimes or labeled vagrants, experienced harsh stigmatization and systematic exclusion.

The policies of territorial princes and urban magistrates, who practiced selective admission of migrants and routinely expelled the unwanted and the unruly, helped shape larger patterns of migration in early modern Germany. While many migrants fled their homelands to escape religious persecution or to pursue economic opportunities, thousands of others were forced onto Germany's roads as convicts banished by local authorities. In early modern Germany, the line dividing impoverished migrants seeking economic opportunity on the road and those unfortunate drifters who local authorities charged with vagrancy was a thin one. Circumstances often pushed migrants into conditions that left them liable to arrest for vagrancy and expulsion by the authorities where they tried to settle, contributing to the levels of mobility created by normal migration patterns. Amid the economic dislocation and rural dispossession of the sixteenth and seventeenth centuries, the troubled period of the Little Ice Age, the European Price Revolution, and the General Crisis of the 1600s, authorities throughout the Holy Roman Empire effectively criminalized the vagrant poor. Exploring penal migration in early modern Germany allows us to reconstruct the links between banishment, vagrancy, and mobility that existed in this troubled era. Official expulsion policies, common until well into the eighteenth century, were a local solution to the economic and social crises that afflicted Germany in the wake of the Thirty Years' War. Given the fragmented political situation in the Holy Roman Empire, it was impossible for local magistrates to force unwanted migrants to return to their native villages and towns, and expulsion merely pushed them into neighboring territories. Consequently, banishment policies, intended to alleviate local pressures, actually served to exacerbate the more widespread problems of vagrancy and dispossession that caused them.

Regulating Migration in Early Modern Germany

Early modern European society was far from static, and migration—whether temporary or permanent—was a normal and necessary aspect of life in the period. The economy of the era, rooted in agriculture and proto-industrial craft production, relied upon a steady supply of cheap, disposable labor in town and country alike. The villages and farms of rural Germany required the labor of itinerate farm workers at harvest time and of household servants and farm hands throughout the year. Landless villagers and impoverished cottagers supplied this largely localized labor, leaving their native hamlets as soon as they were old enough to work, migrating with the seasons in search of wages along routes established by communal tradition. In rural areas, the influx of migrant farm laborers during peak times of the harvest cycle was part of the seasonal rhythm of village life.

The workshops and households of early modern cities and towns also relied upon a continual flow of migrant workers from the countryside, including journeymen, apprentices, and day laborers. The urban settlements of the era, plagued by squalid conditions, periodic outbreaks of epidemic disease, and high infant mortality, required constant in-migration in order to maintain their populations.[6] Extensive population turnover marked early modern urban centers, and a large percentage of the citizenry in German cities and towns during this period had migrated from elsewhere, having purchased citizenship or married into the local social order. Meanwhile, young villagers from poor cottager families also migrated to nearby cities and towns as part of the rural life cycle, using connections from their home region to secure employment. These temporary migrants often lived as resident aliens for a number of years before returning to the countryside, saving their earnings in hopes of being able one day to afford to marry and establish a household in their native village. Females usually sought work as servants in urban households, while males found employment as day laborers or craft workers in workshops. These temporary resident aliens made up a majority of the population in most German towns during this period.[7]

Migration often depended upon individual migrants' relationships to land, village, and family. Landless tenant farmers or poor cottagers, without strong ties to a particular area, were the most likely to migrate in search of wages or alms in tough times. The children of poor families, often viewed as extra mouths to feed, took to the roads at a young age to find work. For impoverished migrants wandering the countryside, cities had the most to offer, but securing steady employment often required some social capital. Employers proved wary about hiring suspicious strangers, and securing a job generally required the social connections afforded by communal and kinship networks that could vouch for the jobseeker.[8] Accordingly, migrants who had been orphaned at a young age or who had left their home village after an unwanted pregnancy or a scrape with the law faced insurmountable difficulties in finding work and risked slipping into the ranks of the unemployed vagabonds on Germany's roadways, struggling for survival through begging, theft, or prostitution.

While rural and urban communities alike relied upon constant in-migration, and the integration of newcomers was a constant feature of early modern life, local authorities worked diligently to regulate migration and sought to bar indigent, unemployed outsiders from settling down. Since the late Middle Ages, authorities had associated the alien, able-bodied poor with disease, disruption, and debauchery, and these attitudes shaped migration policies throughout the Empire. As early as 1495, for example, a mandate in Württemberg ordered ducal officials to arrest idle beggars wandering through their jurisdictions.[9] Reacting to widespread animosity toward wandering beggars, delegates at the 1497 Imperial Diet at Lindau instructed each community to care for its own indigenous poor. Emphasizing the sanctity of work and the secularization of poor relief, the Protestant Reformation both reflected and intensified traditional hostility toward vagrants. Writing in 1528, Martin Luther advised that "every town and village should know and be acquainted with its own poor, listing them in a register so they can help them. But foreign beggars ought not be tolerated without a letter or seal, for there is far too much roguery amongst them."[10] By the time the reformer wrote these words, Wittenberg had already issued a 1521 poor law that outlawed all begging within the city in favor of providing for the "worthy" poor from a community chest. In a revised version issued the following year, the city fathers proclaimed that "no beggars shall be tolerated in our city, rather one shall urge them to work or expel them from the city. But those who because of age or sickness or other misfortune have fallen into poverty shall be provided for from the common chest."[11] Across much of Germany, magistrates adopted similar policies, restricting poor relief to aged or infirm locals and calling for the summary expulsion of vagrants.

Amid the fervor of the early Reformation, the town council in the Swabian city of Ulm issued a comprehensive legal code to deal with foreign beggars. This detailed and highly restrictive legal code, known as the Migrants' Ordinance (*Ordnung der Beywoner halben*), first appeared in 1527 and was reissued verbatim in 1581.[12] In order to protect the solvency of the civic poor chest, the council sought to exclude unemployed migrants, complaining in the preamble of the Migrants' Ordinance that "in lean years, this city, and in particular the honorable council's common citizens, have spent too much on handouts from the civic grain stores, the hospital, the orphanage, and the poorhouse."[13]

Ulm's workshops and storehouses relied upon a steady stream of cheap labor from the countryside, but migrants were permitted to reside in the city only so long as they held stable employment. Accordingly, the central concern of Ulm's sixteenth-century ordinance was the employment status of would-be migrants, presented in terms of strict Lutheran piety:

> according to the word and command of God, no one is to be idle. Therefore, each must earn and win his bread by the sweat of his brow. So must each day laborer, not afflicted with bodily infirmity, and without steady employment, wait on the market each morning for work . . . . Those who do not find work should return after midday and wait again. Those who do not do this, and do not earn wages, but rather appear too many times to be idle, should be expelled from the city and not tolerated here as residents any longer.[14]

Viewing the unemployed as work-shy idlers, Reformation-era authorities sought to distinguish between the "deserving" poor, aged or infirm local paupers eligible for poor relief, and the "undeserving" ones, able-bodied and alien migrants without steady employment, marked for expulsion.

The emphasis on expelling foreign beggars and unemployed migrants apparent in sixteenth-century mandates served to increase the number of rootless wanderers on Germany's roads, and local authorities increasingly viewed the floating population targeted by these policies with suspicion and subjected them to criminal prosecution. These attitudes proved enduring, and amid the turmoil, famine, depression, and disease of the seventeenth century, authorities displayed increasing animosity toward the foreign poor, calling for their summary expulsion.[15] This was true not only of urban magistrates, but also princely authorities, as an edict on vagrancy from seventeenth-century Thuringia demonstrates. In the 1667 revision of his comprehensive *Landesordnung* of 1653, Duke Ernst I of Saxe-Gotha-Altenburg explained that

> [j]ust as every city and village in the territory, according to the ordinance, supports its own poor people, who cannot earn their bread, but does not allow their children, who can earn their bread, to roam about begging, so they absolutely should not tolerate foreign, unworthy beggars and vagabonds in the territory.[16]

The vagrancy problem intensified in the troubled decades of the seventeenth century, as impoverished villagers displaced by the era's chronic military conflicts, economic crises, crop failures, and disease outbreaks took to the roads in a desperate search for stability and sustenance. In response to the perceived threat the wandering poor posed, urban and territorial authorities fostered policies that centered on exclusion and expulsion, impulses that would serve to swell the floating population on Germany's roads in the centuries that followed.

Vagrancy, Exclusion, and Banishment

While early modern Germany was a highly mobile society, the migration regulations we have examined demonstrate tension existed between economic policies encouraging in-migration and ones barring foreign paupers from towns and territories. Animosity toward impoverished outsiders had its origins in the Middle Ages, as paranoia about wandering people (*fahrende Leute*), increasingly associated with disease and disorder, spread. The effort to exclude these threatening outsiders intensified amid the anxiety of the early modern period, as authorities throughout the Empire summarily expelled unemployed outsiders caught begging or squatting in their territories, driving them out without trial or record. In Ulm, for example, an official mandate from the 1420s proclaims the local magistrates' intention to rid their territory of vagabonds, who were characterized as arsonists, thieves, and robbers.[17] Like authorities in other German cities, by the 1490s Ulm's magistrates had declared all unlicensed begging illegal and decreed that foreign beggars were only allowed to remain in the city for a single night. Vagrants, once turned away from the city, would only be readmitted after a month's absence.[18]

By the mid sixteenth century, as the price revolution intensified and rural landlessness increased, impoverished rural folk streamed onto Germany's roads looking for work or alms, and animosity toward these unfortunates intensified. Desperate migrants entered cities, towns, and villages without the economic means to purchase citizenship or the social connections required to secure steady employment, and as outsiders they were barred from poor relief. Alarmed by the rising tide of hungry migrants, civic and territorial magistrates complained in their ordinances about the hordes of vagabonds they encountered. In response, authorities throughout early modern Germany sought to regulate the flow of foreign paupers into their territories by using increasingly stringent regulations and procedures intended to exclude foreign migrants who could not (or would not) work for their daily bread. The brunt of these efforts fell upon the landless poor, the "sturdy beggars" feared throughout Europe since the Middle Ages. Increasingly, local and territorial authorities relied upon expulsion in an effort to deal with impoverished outsiders, migrants labeled "beggars" and characterized as shiftless vagabonds on the roads by choice and owing to their own moral failings.[19] Invariably, these efforts drew a sharp distinction between the local poor, impoverished citizens or subjects who enjoyed the right to reside in the territory, and foreign drifters, who did not.

Increasingly after 1550, authorities sought to deal with the vagrancy problem through banishment. The Bavarian *Landesordnung* issued by Duke Albrecht V in 1553, for example, not only denied foreign vagabonds poor relief, but also ordered their summary expulsion from the territory. Complaining that the "foreign and sturdy beggars" tramping through Bavaria were imposing a heavy burden upon his poor, rural subjects, he proclaimed:

> we command in all seriousness that henceforth all strange, foreign beggars and lepers, who move here and there from one territory to another, upsetting things, are not under any circumstances permitted to beg anymore in our principality, but rather are everywhere to be expelled . . . so that they never come back. They should be turned away at every settlement, pass, bridge, and border and not be allowed to enter, as we have decreed and commanded in several clear mandates.[20]

As confessional conflict and repeated crop failures and outbreaks of epidemic disease brought increasing anxiety and disruption to the Empire after

1550, the punishment of vagrants intensified dramatically. Despite local authorities' increasing determination to rid their domains of vagrants, the number of penniless vagabonds on Germany's roads swelled as fears of famine and economic depression pushed poor cottagers and their children onto the roads. Defying local magistrates' efforts to bar them, impoverished migrants continually drifted throughout the countryside and into nearby urban settlements, as prices rose and poverty spread. Many of these poor migrants found work and settled down as servants or day laborers. Those unable or unwilling to find work, on the other hand, risked being identified as vagrants and expelled by officials charged with driving out the alien poor. Throughout the period, many of these unfortunates were apprehended and driven out without formal sentence during local authorities' periodic round-ups of beggars and street urchins.

The mass expulsion of vagabonds and the banishment of malefactors certainly contributed to the flow of migrants within the Holy Roman Empire, as early modern authorities used banishment in an effort to maintain order in a troubled age. While beadles or watchmen expelled most vagrants and beggars informally without leaving a written record, the criminal archives of a few German cities give a feel for the magnitude of these banishment activities. Augsburg, for example, a city with a population of around 48,000 in the early seventeenth century, banished 274 offenders between 1511 and 1520, another 555 in the decade between 1533 and 1542, and another 701 between 1564 and 1650. Cologne banished 376 offenders in the years 1575–88 alone. Frankfurt banished 859 offenders between 1562 and 1696. Ulm, with a population of around 21,000 in 1600, banished 1,033 offenders over the course of the sixteenth century.[21] Even these considerable banishment rates were a mere fraction of total expulsions, since periodic roundups of anonymous beggars and squatters took place continually in each of these cities, expulsion efforts that are largely absent from the archival record. While the mundane expulsions recorded in the archives of German cities and towns, part of the everyday rhythms of the era's law enforcement, are not as dramatic as the mass deportations of religious exiles during the period, they show that banishment and the forced migration it entailed helped drive mobility in Germany throughout the early modern period.

Those expelled from one territory often faced insurmountable obstacles in their attempts to settle elsewhere. One reason for this was the prevalence of shaming punishments and mutilation—including disfiguring penalties like ear-boring or branding—in early modern jurisprudence that served to render convicts dishonorable.[22] As a result, most vagrants wandered from place to place after being expelled, risking banishment in each settlement they entered as they wandered in search of sustenance. A case from sixteenth-century Ulm involving a vagrant offender named Matheus Jelin not only demonstrates this pattern of serial expulsion, but it also reveals the extent of the roaming it prompted and the serious difficulties magistrates encountered in their efforts to control the migration of rootless paupers. In the spring of 1571 the Ulm authorities had expelled Jelin, a penniless vagabond, from the city along with several companions for "behaving in a disorderly, suspicious manner." Almost a decade later, in February 1580, Jelin drew the attention of Ulm's council again, when he and a woman he called his wife were arrested in nearby Günzburg along with a pair of accomplices for stealing sheep. Sent to Ulm and imprisoned, the council's inquiries into the vagrant's activities since his last stay in the tower gives an indication of how wide-ranging the movements of banished offenders could be. After being turned out of Ulm in 1571, Jelin had likewise been banished from several towns in Alsace, Swabia, and Bavaria, including Strasbourg, Augsburg, Tübingen, and Dillingen, likely circulating through rural hamlets and urban settlements where he might find temporary refuge or support. From the magistrates in Günzburg, the Ulm authorities learned that the troublesome vagabond's crimes had included arson, a means rural beggars often used to threaten villagers who refused to give alms. He had also seduced several women, and the council recorded that Jelin had "led away single daughters and wives both here and elsewhere." The magistrates banished Jelin's "wife" and his other companions, but having determined that he was an incorrigible repeat offender, they placed him in the *Blockhaus*, a crude wooden cell used for long-term incarceration. After several months of confinement, in May 1580 the authorities banished Jelin yet again, this time warning him that if he broke his pledge again and returned to the territory, he would receive a more serious punishment.[23]

The difficulties Ulm's authorities faced in keeping Matheus Jelin from drifting back into their territory were not uncommon. Throughout early modern Germany, territorial rulers and urban magistrates proved incapable of keeping many of the convicts they expelled from returning illegally. In Ulm, for example, over a quarter of the desperate vagabonds driven from the territory were arrested again later and punished for returning illegally.[24]

The problems early modern rulers encountered in trying to control the mobility of the wandering poor continued throughout the seventeenth century. The 1667 *Landesordnung* of Duke Ernst I of Saxe-Gotha-Altenburg, for example, shows how undermanned rulers sought to rely upon officials in each village to monitor and exclude unwanted outsiders. Ernst, lacking the manpower and money to mount effective patrols of his tiny realm, instructed the *Schultheissen*, prominent villagers charged with administering their communities, to be on the lookout for suspicious outsiders and to remain ready to notify the ducal authorities whenever they appeared:

the Schultheissen should watch diligently for idle beggars and tramps, especially Gypsies, and apprehend them and remove them at once. In addition, when players, dancers, jugglers, magicians, and the like arrive, report them immediately to the ducal officials or magistrates.[25]

The longstanding impulse to expel the alien poor persisted in the region until well into the eighteenth century and also retained its key elements: animosity toward the wandering poor and the effort to exclude and expel them beyond territorial borders. According to a mandate issued by another Ernestine prince, Duke Johann Ernst of Saxe-Coburg-Saalfeld, in January, 1715:

> until now, the ordinance against vagabonds, vagrants, foreign beggars, discharged soldiers, foreign Jews, Gypsies, tramps, and other masterless rogues has borne little fruit, and their number has not diminished, but rather there are entire packs of them that commit all sorts of evil deeds, including burglary, theft, robbery, murder, plundering both in houses and on the street.

Faced with this troubling situation, the authorities proclaimed their renewed efforts to exclude these "dissolute and destructive people" from their territory and ordered a series of violent new measures. They instructed their law enforcement officials to expel all of the aforementioned people found in the territory within fourteen days and authorized the patrolmen to shoot dead any vagrants they encountered who were armed or offered any resistance.[26]

* * * * *

Communities in early modern Germany, facing political and confessional foment as well as economic and demographic crisis, relied upon a steady flow of migrant labor. Fearing the disruptive potential of these outsiders, local authorities carefully selected migrants on the basis of their economic potential. Urban magistrates and territorial authorities classified and monitored prospective migrants, allowing the lucky few who found stable employment to enjoy conditional status as resident aliens. These same magistrates then tried to rid their territories of the remaining migrant laborers, who were presented as vagrants and beggars and excoriated as thieves and parasites. Migrants who proved unwilling or unable to find work faced expulsion, often repeated expulsion, as they struggled to survive on the road.

Lacking the effective bureaucratic machinery necessary to control the movement of vagrants, the reach of early modern authorities exceeded their grasp, as was the case in so many other areas of law enforcement. Unable to prevent expelled convicts from slipping back into their territories, authorities issued increasingly strident edicts that sought to stem the tide of unwanted migration. These mandates, in force until well into the eighteenth century, signal the desperation of rulers and magistrates in their attempts to use expulsion to deal with marginal migrants.

One such ordinance, issued by Duke Ernst Friedrich I of Saxe-Hildburghausen in October 1721, illustrates the increasingly harsh measures being brought to bear against vagrants. The ordinance begins with a frank recognition of the difficulties presented by Germany's fragmented jurisdiction, as the duke complained that the Franconian Circle had recently issued a harsh mandate barring vagrants and beggars, which served to drive them into his tiny principality. In response, he issued a series of detailed instructions intended to drive unwanted migrants from his domain. In order to deter vagrants from lingering in the territory, he relied upon the threat of forced labor and mutilation. Any vagrants his officials apprehended were either to be put to work on the construction of his fortifications at Heldsberg or confined in the *Zuchthaus*. After their release from incarceration, the ducal officials were to expel the vagrants from the territory, but not before branding them with the letters "SH" and threatening them with hanging if they ever returned.[27] Thus, even after the establishment of the workhouse, local authorities in Thuringia still ultimately relied upon the traditional means of dealing with the alien poor: expulsion.[28]

Through regulatory activities based upon the classification and selection of suitably employed migrants, German authorities did not so much identify vagabonds or differentiate between vagrants and migrant workers as "create" them. Migrants who found work and submitted to the authority of the local magistrates were defined as resident aliens and tolerated, those who could not or would not were castigated as vagabonds and expelled. Through their verdicts and public punishment rituals, German authorities actually enacted dramatic changes in social status. By punishing unwanted or unruly migrants and casting them out on the roads, the authorities excluded them from respectable, settled society, relegating them to the ranks of the desperate, rootless wanderers who ranged along the roads of the Empire, drifting in search of refuge. Penniless vagabonds expelled from one community drifted into others, where they risked another expulsion. Like a game of "musical chairs," local authorities' expulsion policies merely forced involuntary migrants to circulate from village to village and town to town. Thus, the official response to the problem of the wandering poor—expulsion—was an intensely local solution to economic and social crises that plagued all of German-speaking Europe, one that ultimately proved inadequate to deal with the flood of penniless migrants.

Jason Coy, a Professor of History at the College of Charleston in Charleston, South Carolina, received his doctorate in History at the University of California, Los Angeles in 2001. He is the author of *Strangers and Misfits: Banishment, Social Control, and Authority in Early Modern Germany* (2008) and co-editor of *The Holy Roman Empire, Reconsidered* (2010) and *Kinship, Community, and Self: Social, Cultural, and Intellectual Histories* (2014). He is currently working on a manuscript that explores popular forms of fortunetelling and the clerical campaign against divination in early modern Germany.

Notes

1. Robert W. Scribner, "Mobility: Voluntary or Enforced? Vagrants in Württemberg in the Sixteenth Century," in *Migration in der Feudalgesellschaft*, ed. Gerhard Jaritz and Albert Müller (Frankfurt, 1988), 65.
2. The migration of religious exiles during the Reformation is a staple in the historical literature on the era. See, for example, C. Scott Dixon, *The Reformation in Germany* (Oxford, 2002), 93, 111–13; Ole Peter Grell, "Exile and Tolerance," in *Tolerance and Intolerance in the European Reformation*, ed. Ole Peter Grell and Bob Scribner (New York, 1996), 164; and Peter G. Wallace, *The Long European Reformation: Religion, Political Conflict, and the Search for Conformity, 1350–1750* (New York, 2004), 116. For more detailed treatment of religious exile, see Mack Walker, *The Salzburg Transaction: Expulsion and Redemption in Eighteenth-Century Germany* (Ithaca, NY, 1992); Joel F. Harrington and Helmut Walser Smith, "Confessionalization, Community, and State Building in Germany, 1555–1870," *Journal of Modern History* 69, no. 1 (March 1997): 77–101; J. Jeffrey Tyler, "Refugees and Reform: Banishment and Exile in Early Modern Augsburg," in *Continuity and Change: The Harvest of Late Medieval and Reformation History, Essays Presented to Heiko A. Oberman on his 70th Birthday*, ed. Robert J. Bast and Andrew C. Gow (Leiden, 2000); Ole Peter Grell, "The Creation of a Transnational, Calvinist Network and its Significance for Calvinist Identity and Interaction in Early Modern Europe," *European Review of History/Revue européenne d'histoire* 16, no. 5 (October 2009): 619–36; and Alexander Schunka, "Konfession und Migrationsregime in der Frühen Neuzeit," *Geschichte und Gesellschaft* 35 (January–March 2009): 28–63.
3. For recent surveys on migration in early modern Europe, see Nicholas Canny, *Europeans on the Move: Studies of European Migration, 1500–1800* (Oxford, 1994) and Leslie Page Moch, *Moving Europeans: Migration in Western Europe since 1650* 2nd ed. (Bloomington, IN, 2003). For early modern Germany, see Jan de Vries, "Population," in *Handbook of European History, 1400–1600*, Vol. I: Structures and Assertions, ed. Thomas A. Brady, Jr., Heiko A. Oberman, and James D. Tracy (Leiden, 1995) and Terence McIntosh, "Urban Demographic Stagnation in Early Modern Germany: A Simulation," *Journal of Interdisciplinary History* 31, no. 4 (Spring 2001): 581–612.
4. While Moch, *Moving Europeans*, 88–93, looks at "marginal migrants" like vagrants, she deals almost exclusively with vagrancy in eighteenth-century France.
5. As H.C. Erik Midelfort points out most "studies [of banishment and exile] treat mainly the problems of learned and elite exiles, not those of the poorer sort." See H.C.

Erik Midelfort, "Witchcraft," in *Reformation and Early Modern Europe: A Guide to Research*, ed. David M. Whitford (Kirksville, MO, 2008), 372n70. One exception is Robert W. Scribner, "Mobility: Voluntary or Enforced? Vagrants in Württemberg in the Sixteenth Century," in *Migration in der Feudalgesellschaft*, ed. Gerhard Jaritz and Albert Müller (Frankfurt, 1988), and another is Ernst Schubert, "Mobilität ohne Chance: die Ausgrenzung des fahrenden Leute," in *Ständische Gesellschaft und soziale Mobilität*, ed. Winfried Schulze (Munich, 1988).

6. For the economic role of migrant workers in early modern Germany, see Christian Pfister, "The Population of Late Medieval and Early Modern Europe," in *Germany: A New Social and Economic History, 1450–1630*, ed. Bob Scribner (London, 1996), 55–58.

7. See Moch, *Moving Europeans*, 31–40.

8. For an interesting treatment of how rural women secured urban employment, see William David Myers, *Death and a Maiden: Infanticide and the Tragical History of Grethe Schmidt* (DeKalb, IL, 2011).

9. See Scribner, "Mobility," 65–66.

10. Martin Luther, Foreword to *Mathias Hütlin's Book of Vagabonds* (Wittenberg, 1528).

11. In Albert Leitzmann and Otto Clemen, eds., *Luthers Werke in Auswahl* (Berlin, 1935), 4–6.

12. Stadtarchiv Ulm A 3785 *Ordnung der Beywoner halben* (1527/1581). For background on this legislation, see Andreas Baisch, "Die Verfassung im Leben der Stadt, 1558–1802" in *Die Ulmer Bürgerschaft auf dem Weg zur Demokratie*, ed. Hans Eugen Specker (Ulm, 1997), 197–203. See also Hans Eugen Specker, *Ulm: Stadtgeschichte* (Ulm, 1977), 64; Carl Mollwo, ed., *Das rote Buch der Stadt Ulm* (Stuttgart, 1905); and Eberhard Naujoks, "Ulm's Sozialpolitik im 16. Jahrhundert," *Ulm und Oberschwaben* 33 (1953): 88–98.

13. Preamble to Stadtarchiv Ulm A 3785 *Ordnung der Beywoner halben* (1527/1581).

14. Stadtarchiv Ulm A 3785 *Ordnung der Beywoner halben* (1527/1581).

15. Gerhard Oestereich's "social discipline" model has been highly influential on the study of early modern disciplinary efforts. See his "Strukturprobleme des europäischen Absolutismus," in *Geist und Gestalt des frühmodernen Staates: Ausgewählte Aufsätze* (Berlin, 1969). For a discussion of Oestreich's statist approach, which tends to overemphasize the effectiveness of early modern law enforcement efforts, see also Winfried Schulze, "Gerhard Oestreichs Begriff 'Sozialdisziplinierung in der frühen Neuzeit'," *Zeitschrift für historische Forschung* 14 (1987): 265–302.

16. *Fürstliche Sächsische abermals verbesserte Landes-Ordnung / Des Durchläuchstigen / Hochgebornen Fürsten und Herrn / Herrn Ernsten / Hertzogen zu Sachsen / Jülich / Cleve und Bergk / Landgraffen in Thüringen / Marggraffen zu Meissen / . . . .* (Gotha, 1667), 215.

17. Mollwo, *Das Rote Buch*.

18. Stadtarchiv Ulm A [2001], fol. 46–53 (1492–93). These laws remained in effect throughout the period and were officially renewed in 1586 and again in 1601. See Stadtarchiv Ulm A [4396] *Hauß Ordnung der Armen Sonder Siechen* (1586/1601). See also Specker, *Ulm: Stadtgeschichte*, 105–6. See also Christoph Sachsse and Florian Tennstedt, *Geschichte der Armenfürsorge in Deutschland: vom Spätmittelalter bis zum Ersten Weltkrieg* (Stuttgart, 1980), 64–66.

19. For a useful survey of the fear of vagrants and "sturdy beggars" in early modern Europe, see Robert Jütte, *Poverty and Deviance in Early Modern Europe* (Cambridge, 1994).

20. *Bairische Lanndtßordnung* (Ingolstadt, 1553). These strict policies were mirrored in other territories, as illustrated by an ordinance issued by Duke Johann Friedrich II of Saxony in 1580. Decrying the depredations of "gypsies, beggars, and rogues," the ordinance instructed the duke's subjects to expel these undesirables from the territory without hesitation. See *Johanns Friedrichen, deß Mittlers, Johanns Wilhelm und Johanns Friderichen d. Jüng. Policey- u. Landsordnung* (n.p., 1580). An almost identical mandate issued at Jena in 1589, calls for the expulsion of "useless . . . gypsies, sturdy beggars, and rogues": *Der . . . Fursten und Herren / Herren Friederich Wilhelms / und Herren Johansen Gebrüdern / Hertzogen zu Sachsen / und Marggraven zu Meiseen / etc. Policey und Landesordnunge / zuwolfart / nutz und besten derselben Unterthanen und Fürstenthumb bedacht und ausgangen* (Jena, 1589).
21. These banishment statistics are drawn from Carl A. Hoffmann, "Der Stadtverweis als Sanktionensmittel in der Reichstadt Augsburg zu Beginn der Neuzeit," in *Neue Wege strafrechtsgeschichtlicher Forschung: Konflikt, Verbrechen und Sanktionen in der Gesellschaft Alteuropas, Symposium und Synthesen*, ed. Hans Schlosser and Dietmar Willoweit (Cologne, 1999), 204–5 (Augsburg); Gerd Schwerhoff, *Köln im Kreuzverhör: Kriminalität, Herrschaft und Gesellschaft in einer frühneuzeitlichen Stadt* (Bonn, 1991), 148–53 (Cologne); Richard van Dülmen, *Theatre of Horror: Crime and Punishment in Early Modern Europe* (Cambridge, 1990), 139 (Frankfurt); and Jason P. Coy, *Strangers and Misfits: Banishment, Social Control, and Authority in Early Modern Germany* (Leiden, 2008), 14 (Ulm).
22. Scribner, "Mobility," 78.
23. Stadtarchiv Ulm A 3530 *Ratsprotokolle* Nr. 32, fol. 128b (31 April 1571; 6 May 1580).
24. These recidivism patterns are explored in more detail in Coy, *Strangers and Misfits*, 39–40.
25. *Fürstliche Sächsische revidirte und vermehrte Landes-Ordnung* (Gotha, 1667), 423. There is extensive literature on Ernst I, but for a useful introduction, see the catalog to a 2001 exhibition at the Forschungsbibliothek Gotha that explored his reign: Roswitha Jacobsen and Hans-Jörg Ruge, eds., *Ernst der Fromme (1601–1675): Staatsmann und Reformer* (Jena, 2002).
26. *Die Hoch. Fürstl. Sächs. zur Gesamt-Regierung anhero verordnete Räthe fügen hiermit zu wissen: Demnach zu vernehmen, daß die bißhero wider die Landstreicher . . . ergangene Verordnungen wenig Frucht gehabt, vielmehr aber, daß deren Anzahl sich nicht mindere . . . Als ist mit Wiederholung der obgedachten vorigen Patenten, hiedurch weiter zu verordnen nöthig ermessenw orden . . . .* (Coburg, 1715).
27. *Von Gottes Gnades Wir Ernst Friedrich, Hertzog zu Sachsen, Jülich, Cleve und Berg . . . Fügen hiermit iedermänniglich zu wissen: Was massen wir Uns, wegen Contiguität Unserer Lande mit dem Fränckischen Creyß, und weiln . . . ohngeachtet derer . . . Verordnungen und . . . Mandaten, iedennoch das Ziegeunerische Jaunerisch-Herren-lose Gesinde und Vaganten überhand nehmen . . . gemüßiget funden, über die bereits . . . erlassene Bettel-Ordnung, Uns . . . mit besagten Fränckischen Creyß-Schluß dergestalt zu confirmiren und zu vereinbahren . . . .* (Hildburghausen, 1721).
28. For the appearance of workhouses in early modern Germany, and their integration into traditional regimes for dealing with the alien poor, see Joel F. Harrington, "Escape from the Great Confinement: The Genealogy of a German Workhouse," *Journal of Modern History* 71, no. 2 (June 1999): 308–45.

Bibliography

Anonymous. *Bairische Lanndtßordnung.* Ingolstadt, 1553.

———. *Der . . . Fursten und Herren / Herren Friederich Wilhelms / und Herren Johansen Gebrüdern / Hertzogen zu Sachsen / und Marggraven zu Meiseen / etc. Policey und Landesordnunge / zuwolfart / nutz und besten derselben Unterthanen und Fürstenthumb bedacht und ausgangen.* Jena, 1589.

———. *Fürstliche Sächsische abermals verbesserte Landes-Ordnung / Des Durchläuchstigen / Hochgebornen Fürsten und Herrn / Herrn Ernsten / Hertzogen zu Sachsen / Jülich / Cleve und Bergk / Landgraffen in Thüringen / Marggraffen zu Meissen / . . . .* Gotha, 1667.

———. *Die Hoch. Fürstl. Sächs. zur Gesamt-Regierung anhero verordnete Räthe fügen hiermit zu wissen: Demnach zu vernehmen, daß die bißhero wider die Landstreicher . . . ergangene Verordnungen wenig Frucht gehabt, vielmehr aber, daß deren Anzahl sich nicht mindere . . . Als ist mit Wiederholung der obgedachten vorigen Patenten, hiedurch weiter zu verordnen nöthig ermessenw orden . . . .* Coburg, 1715.

———. *Johanns Friedrichen, deß Mittlers, Johanns Wilhelm und Johanns Friderichend. Jüng. Policey- u. Landsordnung.* N.P., 1580.

———. *Von Gottes Gnades Wir Ernst Friedrich, Hertzog zu Sachsen, Jülich, Cleve und Berg . . . Fügen hiermit iedermänniglich zu wissen: Was massen wir Uns, wegen Contiguität Unserer Lande mit dem Fränckischen Creyß, und weiln . . . ohngeachtet derer . . . Verordnungen und . . . Mandaten, iedennoch das Ziegeunerische Jaunerisch Herren-lose Gesinde und Vaganten überhand nehmen . . . gemüßiget funden, über die bereits . . . erlasse Bettel-Ordnung, Uns . . . mit besagten Fränckischen Creyß-Schlußdergestalt zu confirmiren und zu vereinbahren . . . .* Hildburghausen, 1721.

Baisch, Andreas. "Die Verfassung im Leben der Stadt, 1558–1802." In *Die Ulmer Bürgerschaft auf dem Weg zur Demokratie,* ed. Hans Eugen Specker. Ulm, 1997.

Canny, Nicholas. *Europeans on the Move: Studies of European Migration, 1500–1800.* Oxford, 1994.

Coy, Jason P. *Strangers and Misfits: Banishment, Social Control, and Authority in Early Modern Germany.* Leiden, 2008.

Dixon, C. Scott. *The Reformation in Germany.* Oxford, 2002.

Dülmen, Richard van. *Theatre of Horror: Crime and Punishment in Early Modern Europe.* Cambridge, 1990.

Grell, Ole Peter. "Exile and Tolerance." In *Tolerance and Intolerance in the European Reformation,* ed. Ole Peter Grell and Bob Scribner. New York, 1996.

———. "The Creation of a Transnational, Calvinist Network and its Significance for Calvinist Identity and Interaction in Early Modern Europe." *European Review of History/Revue européenne d'histoire* 16, no. 5 (October 2009): 619–36.

Harrington, Joel F., and Helmut Walser Smith. "Confessionalization, Community, and State Building in Germany, 1555–1870." *Journal of Modern History* 69, no. 1 (March 1997): 77–101.

———. "Escape from the Great Confinement: The Genealogy of a German Workhouse." *Journal of Modern History* 71, no. 2 (June 1999): 308–45.

Hoffmann, Carl A. "Der Stadtverweis als Sanktionensmittel in der Reichstadt Augsburg zu Beginn der Neuzeit." In *Neue Wege strafrechtsgeschichtlicher Forschung: Konflikt, Verbrechen und Sanktionen in der Gesellschaft Alteuropas, Symposium und Synthesen*, ed. Hans Schlosser and Dietmar Willoweit. Cologne, 1999.

Jütte, Robert. *Poverty and Deviance in Early Modern Europe*. Cambridge, 1994.

Leitzmann, Albert, and Otto Clemen, eds. *Luthers Werke in Auswahl*. Berlin, 1935.

Luther, Martin. Foreword to *Mathias Hütlin's Book of Vagabonds*. Wittenberg, 1528.

McIntosh, Terence. "Urban Demographic Stagnation in Early Modern Germany: A Simulation." *Journal of Interdisciplinary History* 31, no. 4 (Spring 2001): 581–612.

Midelfort, H.C. Erik. "Witchcraft." In *Reformation and Early Modern Europe: A Guide to Research*, ed. David M. Whitford. Kirksville, MO, 2008.

Moch, Leslie Page. *Moving Europeans: Migration in Western Europe since 1650*. 2nd edition. Bloomington, IN, 2003.

Mollwo, Carl, ed. *Das rote Buch der Stadt Ulm*. Stuttgart, 1905.

Myers, William David. *Death and a Maiden: Infanticide and the Tragical History of Grethe Schmidt*. DeKalb, IL, 2011.

Naujoks, Eberhard. "Ulm's Sozialpolitik im 16. Jahrhundert." *Ulm und Oberschwaben* 33 (1953).

Oestereich, Gerhard. "Strukturprobleme des europäischen Absolutismus." In *Geist und Gestalt des frühmodernen Staates: Ausgewählte Aufsätze*. Berlin, 1969.

Pfister, Christian. "The Population of Late Medieval and Early Modern Europe." In *Germany: A New Social and Economic History, 1450–1630*, ed. Bob Scribner. London, 1996.

Sachsse, Christoph, and Florian Tennstedt. *Geschichte der Armenfürsorge in Deutschland: vom Spätmittelalter bis zum Ersten Weltkrieg*. Stuttgart, 1980.

Schubert, Ernst. "Mobilität ohne Chance: die Ausgrenzung des fahrenden Leute." In *Ständische Gesellschaft und soziale Mobilität*, ed. Winfried Schulze. Munich, 1988.

Schulze, Winfried. "Gerhard Oestreichs Begriff 'Sozialdisziplinierung in der frühen Neuzeit'." *Zeitschrift für historische Forschung* 14 (1987): 265–302.

Schunka, Alexander. "Konfession und Migrationsregime in der Frühen Neuzeit." *Geschichte und Gesellechaft* 35 (January–March 2009): 28–63.

Schwerhoff, Gerd. *Köln im Kreuzverhör: Kriminalität, Herrschaft und Gesellschaft in einer frühneuzeitlichen Stadt*. Bonn, 1991.

Scribner, Robert W. "Mobility: Voluntary or Enforced? Vagrants in Württemberg in the Sixteenth Century." In *Migration in der Feudalgesellschaft*, ed. Gerhard Jaritz and Albert Müller. Frankfurt, 1988.

Specker, Hans Eugen. *Ulm: Stadtgeschichte*. Ulm, 1977

Stadtarchiv Ulm. *Ordnung der Beywoner halben* (1527/1581).

———. *Hauß Ordnung der Armen Sonder Siechen* (1586/1601).

Tyler, J. Jeffrey. "Refugees and Reform: Banishment and Exile in Early Modern Augsburg." In *Continuity and Change: The Harvest of Late Medieval and Reformation History, Essays Presented to Heiko A. Oberman on his 70th Birthday*, ed. Robert J. Bast and Andrew C. Gow. Leiden, 2000.

Vries, Jan de. "Population." In *Handbook of European History, 1400–1600*, Vol. I: Structures and Assertions, ed. Thomas A. Brady, Jr., Heiko A. Oberman, and James D. Tracy. Leiden, 1995.

Walker, Mack. *The Salzburg Transaction: Expulsion and Redemption in Eighteenth-Century Germany*. Ithaca, NY, 1992.

Wallace, Peter G. *The Long European Reformation: Religion, Political Conflict, and the Search for Conformity, 1350–1750*. New York, 2004.

CHAPTER THREE

∾:∾

No Return?
Temporary Exile and Permanent Immigration among Confessional Migrants in the Early Modern Era

ALEXANDER SCHUNKA

Research on Confessional Migration

Contrary to most English-language scholarship on early modern migration,[1] German historiography traditionally considers confessional issues
as the preeminent feature of early modern migrations in Central Europe. The
reasons for this interesting gap between German and Anglophone research
are at least twofold. On the one hand, since the early modern period the larger
confessional migrant groups associated with the Holy Roman Empire (such
as the Bohemian Exiles, Huguenot Refugees, or Salzburg Protestants) elabo-
rated distinctive historiographical traditions of their own, often originating
from particular group identities and efforts to elicit support from the political
authorities of their host countries. These historiographical traditions therefore
date back to the time of the migrants themselves and their contemporaries,
and continued, although with certain alterations, well into the twentieth
century.[2] On the other hand, the "Confessionalization" paradigm, which has
dominated academic scholarship on early modern Germany since the 1980s,
accentuated the formation of mono-confessional societies in connection with
issues of social discipline and state building. This analytical framework has
shifted the focus from church history to social history and especially to the
"modernizing" potential of confessional migrants, such as their allegedly special
economic skills. These, according to researchers such as Heinz Schilling, not
only derived from the personal expertise of certain migrants (craftsmen, artists), but also from a position of social (and confessional) segregation within
the host societies.[3]

From an early modern perspective it is, however, difficult to situate a distinct "confessional" migration vis-à-vis other, seemingly clear-cut, types of movement (such as the migrations of apprentices and craftsmen, student migrations, or work-related migrations). Similar problems arise when structural categories are applied such as subsistence, betterment, or career migration, or when "voluntary" migrations are contrasted with "forced" ones. Most movements in early modern Europe contained a certain confessional element, and due to the overall importance of religion in daily life, adherence to a certain faith (up to the eventual decision to abandon one's homeland), was never free from economic, social, as well as infrastructural issues. In this respect, confessional migration is inseparable from a generally high (but often overlooked) geographic mobility (over short, as well as long, distances) in the early modern era. What distinguishes "confessional" migration from other movements and motivations are in part the confessionalist state building efforts of early modern polities, but also, to a large extent, the prominence of confessional arguments and narratives among migrants.

All in all, the history of migration still occupies a rather marginal position within German historiography of the early modern era. Confessional migrations often serve as a welcome exception to the widely accepted notion of early modern immobility, as manifested in the typical pre-modern order of the estates (*Ständeordnung*), which supposedly guaranteed a stable society. Nevertheless, tens of thousands of migrants were almost constantly on the move between the sixteenth and the eighteenth centuries. A typical genealogy of confessional migrations would start with the Reformed Dutch in the late sixteenth century, continue with the emigrations from the Habsburg Lands (Austria, Bohemia, Silesia, Hungary) as well as from France in the seventeenth century, and terminate with the Salzburg expulsions in the "enlightened" eighteenth century, in addition to any number of migrations of a smaller demographic and regional scale.[4] Empirical data combined with traditional narratives seem to point to the fact that Protestants ranged among the foremost groups of Central European migrants. Undoubtedly in a number of territories especially in the seventeenth century, the Protestant (Lutheran, Reformed, Bohemian Brethren) population was affected by Catholic Counter-Reformation policies, which could result in fierce persecution and exile. Although recent research has underlined that such a clear Protestant dominance is not always the case even among seemingly clear-cut migrant groups,[5] the direction of these confessionally motivated movements appears to be quite unilinear. Re-catholicization measures were followed by increasing pressure on the population to convert to Roman Catholicism, culminating in an ensuing expulsion of pastors and schoolmen (combined with subtle techniques by Protestants attempting to evade Catholic rites), and at the same time by the flight of thousands to neighboring Protestant countries.[6] According to the state of research, these confessional immigrants settled and either amalgamated with a Protestant host society after one or two generations or retained a rather marginal position due to their particular religious, linguistic, and cultural traditions or their economic skills.[7] Overall, their settlement processes are usually told as success stories. Researchers focused on issues such as integration, partial segregation, and, eventually, absorption into the new societies, along with the alleged economic achievements and cultural benefits that not only the immigrants, but also the receiving societies could draw. These success stories, however, often had their origins in the contemporary political purposes of the receiving countries or are derived from the self-images of the immigrants. This is particularly obvious in the case of the French refugees in Brandenburg-Prussia. They not only appeared as pious and hardworking as well as intermediaries between French and German culture, but they also created stories of loyalty and successful adaptation to Prussian society. Their own traditions often converge with myths of Prussian state building, manifest in the German *Reichskanzler* Bismarck's famous dictum about the Huguenots being the "Best Germans." Similar narratives apply to other religious migrants as well, stressing their piety, perseverance, loyalty, and industriousness.[8]

In a nutshell, confessional migrations share an alleged Protestant background that seems to have produced thousands of Counter-Reformation victims (or at least generated the respective narratives). Historians have long treated these refugee populations as clear-cut ethnic and confessional groups with obvious religious motives whose migration was a one-dimensional phenomenon. Only rarely has it been asked how all these thousands of refugees in the seventeenth and eighteenth centuries got along in their new settings hundreds of miles away from their native places; how, for instance, peasants from Alpine regions adapted to the different economic and geographic surroundings of Prussian Lithuania, or how Czech-speaking Bohemians made their living in German-speaking Saxony. One can easily imagine that acclimating to new circumstances, overcoming economic and social challenges, or being disconnected from a familiar environment might have posed problems to individuals that are hardly discernible in most contemporary sources such as population lists, citizen registers, and other statistical data. It is equally misleading to derive from stereotypical phrases in semi-official documents like petition letters that immigrants were naturally thankful to their new sovereign who had rescued and sheltered so many of them from persecution.[9] Since research has long assumed that religious migrants left their homes because they valued their faith more than their native countries, this has led to the assumption that home contacts did not matter much to a steadfast and pious refugee. Therefore any mention of Protestant emigrants failing to settle and even returning to their catholicized birth places would have proved disturbing to most contemporaries as well as to later generations and would have questioned the ideals and the disposition of migrants as pious and persevering refugees.

Against the backdrop of existing research it is thus important to note the seemingly trivial fact that from a migrant's point of view, early modern confessional migrations usually included at least the possibility of return. This return option does not necessarily correspond to individual failure on the migrant's side but was one of many migratory options available. This chapter argues that religious migrants of the early modern era often considered their status as exiles a merely temporary phenomenon. Only in retrospect was permanent relocation to a foreign country fashioned into a logical consequence of religious persecution. This will be illustrated first along two biographical case studies. Then, as a second step, the chapter focuses on the theological ideas of religious exile, which normally did not advocate permanent immigration. A particular temporariness, as depicted in the contemporary consolatory and devotional literature, fundamentally influenced the self-images of migrants. The final part of this chapter highlights a number of political and social caesuras that contributed to the evolution of permanent settlement strategies as opposed to return options. What followed was a shift in migrants' attitudes from a status as temporary exiles toward one of permanent immigrants, together with a changing relationship vis-à-vis their host societies.

The Flexibilities of Everyday Life among Confessional Migrants

Early modern sources contain numerous, although scattered, examples of migrants returning home. This reveals that almost no place was generally too distant and remote to prevent return journeys. Remigrations took place for instance between Eastern Prussia and the Salzburg mountains, Berlin and cities in France, Dresden and places in Bohemia, Nuremberg and Upper Austria, and even between Transylvania and Styria in the Habsburg Hereditary Lands.[10] Whenever Protestants arrived in their re-catholicized home territories they were obliged to convert to the Roman Catholic faith, just like the many other inhabitants who had once opted against emigration and had stayed.[11] Apparently, upon their return migrants could often rely on the assistance of relatives who belonged to the Catholic faith or who had decided to convert to Catholicism instead of leaving.[12]

More than proto-statistical data, personal accounts of migrants illuminate the flexibility of early modern religious migrations. A fine example is Wenzeslaus Altwasser, a Silesian pastor who had been born Roman Catholic.[13] When he was still a young man he converted to Protestantism, took up theological studies and worked as a pastor in a small town in southwestern Bohemia until shortly after the Battle of White Mountain (1620), which instigated broad re-catholicization measures in the Bohemian Lands. Like other Protestant pastors he was subsequently expelled from his post and went into exile. Whereas a large number of his colleagues managed to acquire new positions in Saxony or other nearby Lutheran territories, Altwasser spent the following years as a traveling beggar in the Saxon-Bohemian borderlands. As we can see from the fascinating, although incomplete diary he kept during this period, he carefully planned his begging journeys and minutely recorded the places he visited and the money he collected. The diary reveals that even during the first years of re-catholicization Altwasser moved back and forth across the border, which was, after all, not an "Iron Curtain" between Protestantism and Roman Catholicism. His excellent geographical knowledge permitted him to arrive in larger cities on market days or public holidays when the streets were filled with locals and foreign visitors and he could thus hope to collect larger amounts of money than on a usual weekday. The fact that seventeenth-century Saxony and Bohemia followed two separate calendars (Julian and Gregorian, respectively), which differed by eleven days, proved useful for Altwasser as well. He could thus exploit Christian holidays such as Easter or Pentecost twice. Depending upon which side of the border he was on, he neither hesitated to accept money from Catholics nor from Protestants. Often he approached ecclesiastics because charity was usually distributed by church officials. It was common for beggar's diaries such as Altwasser's that donators wrote down the sums of their donations and verified them with their signature. Gifts ranged from a glass of milk to the ten *Gulden* Altwasser received from the wife of the Elector of Saxony—some collections could even yield much more. For a while he seems to have made quite a good living as a begging exile who referred to his status as religious refugee whenever necessary and appropriate.

Altwasser, however, did not want to end his life as a wandering beggar and occasionally attempted to find a place to settle. The pastor once even tried to have his Bohemian belongings restituted but failed, even though his brother-in-law happened to be a Catholic government official. These Catholic family connections might have accounted for the fact that he had left his wife and children in Bohemia alone after he had gone on his begging journeys. Altwasser visited them several times before he finally brought them to Saxony where they seem to have accompanied him on his travels for a while. We are not well informed about his life after the year 1630, but it is quite likely that he eventually settled in the city of Zwickau.[14]

If at first glance, and from the perspective of other, more "official" narratives, Altwasser seems to exemplify the opportunism and the failed integration of the thousands of Bohemian exiles who poured into Saxony and other places during the seventeenth century, a second glance indicates that his decision to stay in the border region was a conscious and strategic move. His personal connections to high-ranking members of church and state, who were at times influential in placing other pastors in new positions, should have permitted him to find a new post. Altwasser's case illustrates the difficulties, but also the opportunities of a migrant who did not commit himself fully to the receiving country. Hopes of return figure as an option throughout his diary, although they are not explicitly addressed. At any rate, his diary points to the mixed nature between the Catholic and the Protestant spheres in everyday life and at the range of individual opportunities under Counter-Reformation circumstances.[15] The few preserved personal accounts such as Altwasser's diary shed light upon an important sphere of social marginality below the larger migrational flows. Experiences such as his might have been more common than is often assumed.[16]

Fifty years later, the expulsion of the Huguenots from France produced a number of personal accounts and autobiographical writings as well. The Calvinist merchant Jacob Etienne from the French city of Metz, for instance, describes his escape and immigration to Germany in a detailed memoir.[17] Like Altwasser's diary, his account provides insight into the everyday life and the meticulous planning and arrangements of mobility under early modern circumstances of confessional and political pressure.

Etienne was not an impoverished pastor-turned-beggar like Altwasser but a rather wealthy merchant. He was thirty years old when he finally left his native city of Metz in the Lorraine region of Western France in 1685 and settled in the Rhenish Palatinate close to the French border. This escape was not a hurried flight but a well-planned enterprise preceded by six years of preparations and by some explorative journeys to the German lands and back. When he left France for good, Etienne's wish was to stay as near as possible to his relatives in Metz who looked after his business even after he had left. When Roman Catholic influence in the Palatinate increased during the Nine Years' War, however, Etienne decided to move more inland to the Landgraviate of Hesse and eventually settled in Kassel. In the following years, a number of his family members left France as well and scattered across Protestant Europe, including his brother who tried to make a living in the Brandenburg-Prussian capital of Berlin like so many other French emigrants. This brother, however, soon left Prussia and eventually joined the Dutch army, whereas Etienne's sister-in-law even gave up her exile completely and returned to her birthplace in re-catholicized France. Etienne, who tried to present himself in his memoir as a pious, honest, and industrious Protestant merchant, treated this case of renunciation from the Protestant faith only in one short sentence. Like many other French refugees he apparently centered his political hopes on the Dutch army, but was not completely disappointed at the conclusion of the Treaty of Rijswijk (1697) when the refugees' hopes to return to France were dashed. Meanwhile, he had become a successful paper merchant and Church Elder in the Hessian capital of Kassel with business contacts all over Europe.[18]

What seems to be and is presented as a typical Huguenot success story nevertheless hints at the temporality and insecurity of religious exile. Etienne's escape was well planned, and he initially stayed as close as he could to his French homeland leaving the border region only as a last resort. His memoirs reveal a number of movement options back and forth even under the hardest restrictions. Even though he made himself and his relatives out to be a good Calvinist merchant family, he had at least one renegade among his closest family members.

The stories of Altwasser and Etienne have been singled out rather haphazardly as two of many telling examples hinting at a much broader phenomenon. They reveal the importance of ongoing mobility (including home contacts) even for so-called religious refugees who, according to traditional narratives, should have been glad and proud to burn all their bridges behind them and settle in a safe place of refuge. The two cases also underline that religious exile was not a one-way option, rather it consisted of many geographical steps and social nuances and could sometimes even result in a circular migration process. Furthermore, the choice of exile and of a place to live was not solely a matter of religious conviction.[19] A particular state of migrational uncertainty in the biographies of Altwasser and Etienne also seems to be typical for many confessional migrants once historians look behind the broader social processes and try to retrieve the historical subjects from their anonymity.[20] Finally, both personal accounts seem to correspond with the contemporary notion that religious exile was largely considered not a permanent life plan but a temporary condition of only the most steadfast of all believers—which, for the less devoted also included the option to move on and, perhaps, to return home.

Stereotypes and Narratives

It has already been pointed out that in the evolving group narratives there was often no adequate place for the actual flexibility of everyday migration and less so for returnees. Such narratives corresponded with or even originated from petition letters, chronicles, immigrant lists, and other official or private documents representing the interactions between the majority of immigrants and the authorities of the host societies. Under certain circumstances it could prove crucial for migrants to maintain that they were not weak-minded characters who had just run away from their former lives but had instead unswervingly followed their faith and convictions up to the point where a change of place was inevitable. The fact that migrants as well as host societies produced a plethora of material on successful immigration and settlement is probably the reason why the issue of onward or return migration has been widely neglected in the early modern history of religious exile. Although in the long run a number of settlements turned out to be failures, such as in Prussia, narratives of a more official and authoritative character often unwaveringly stressed the overall success of early modern migration regimes.[21] In a certain sense, return migrants were an embarrassment to the glorious stories of persecution, peregrination, accommodation, and assimilation. Thus from a perspective of successful immigration it was hard to subsequently integrate the "deserteurs" into general narratives. If these renegades were mentioned at all by contemporaries, then only in a derogatory sense as selfish and unreliable individuals looking for short-term success and exchanging their true faith for worldly commodities such as the "flesh pots of Egypt" (Exodus 16:3) or even "Bohemian dumplings."[22] Accordingly, return migrants appeared to value their material gains more than godly lives. They also provided ammunition for the host authorities to believe in a "typical" unreliability and inconstancy of foreigners, an impression that had to be prevented at any rate by the majority of immigrants.[23]

There is however an interesting gap between the official traditions found among host authorities as well as in migrant historiography on the one hand and the self-images of migrants on the other. These self-images of religious refugees were based on the idea that the notion of exile denoted only a transitional or liminal time span with the objective of permanent settlement in a strange land, in the former homeland (after the true faith had been restored), or eventually in heaven. The Bohemian beggar Altwasser identified his year-long travels with his *exilium*.[24] In chronicles or in the context of burials there is mention of Bohemian immigrants as "former exiles," which indicates that the status of an exile was one that could be overcome eventually.[25] Even the typical early modern German word *Exulant*, indicating the status of a religious refugee, derives from the Latin participle *exulans*, which can roughly be translated as "being temporarily banished" or "living temporarily in a foreign place."[26] This points to the fact that religious migrants considered their own situation as merely transitory.

Such a presumed temporariness corresponds with a more spiritual meaning of exile found in printed sermons and theological or devotional works. Following up on medieval concepts of pilgrimage or *peregrinatio*, the writings of early modern emigrant pastors of a Protestant background described the period of exile as a test in religious constancy and at the same time as a period of hardship imposed on the chosen ones by the Lord.[27] The notion of religious exiles being on a pilgrimage through all the calamities of this world until they finally gain their reward in eternity became an important topos of emigrant theology.[28] As John Amos Comenius puts it, all earthly ties wither under the harsh light of exile: "A wise man makes everywhere his home."[29] The time of exile became a period between a fatherland lost and regained, whether on earth or in heaven. Protestant clerics thus often used examples from the Old Testament, such as the Babylonian exile of the Jews, to add meaning and comfort to a situation that might have otherwise appeared meaningless and disturbing.

In sermons, the idea of exile oscillated between the punishment of the sinners and a reward for the true believers. In some cases, religious exiles were depicted as the chosen ones and as those who had to accept their dire circumstances happily because persecution and exile served as proof of God's mercy toward the strong. But persecution and expulsion could also point to a temporary state of atonement for the sins of an individual or of the community. In this regard, the years of exile implied a waiting status in order to increase purity and godliness.[30] To put it crudely, religious exile could turn out to be a Protestant version of purgatory.

Without a doubt, depicting religious exiles as the chosen people and displaying them as the true believers had a paraenetical and didactic meaning not only for refugees, but also for all other Protestants who had not experienced the hardships of exile themselves.[31] It could also stimulate the locals to give generous donations to impoverished immigrants like Altwasser. Just like everyday practices of migration, immigrants' self-images illustrate that contemporary ideas of religious exile differed from the teleological perspective of later days, which, as will be argued in the final part of this chapter, came into being after actual hopes of return were dashed.

From Exile to Settlement

The above-cited accounts of Wenzeslaus Altwasser and Jacob Etienne relate to the two largest migrational phenomena in seventeenth-century central Europe whose peak periods are roughly separated by sixty years. Most Habsburg Protestants moved in the 1620s and most French Huguenots in the 1680s. These movements differ in many respects, notably in regard to the policies of the German territories involved in accommodating the migrants. While, for instance, politicians in Saxony had hoped that under the circumstances of the Thirty Years' War the influx of strangers from the Habsburg lands would terminate after a short while, the political authorities in Brandenburg-Prussia actively tried to attract Huguenot as well as other settlers for a number of demographic, economic, and confessional reasons.[32] However, what both migrational processes had in common was not only their alleged confessional background but also the fact that in both cases, migrants often waited for a possibility to return home. This is why Brandenburg-Prussia was not the most attractive of all places for French *refugiés* who, like Jacob Etienne, originally tried to stick to regions in close proximity to their former homelands, such as the Palatinate, the Netherlands, or Switzerland. Accordingly, Austrians had preferred to settle in the few Protestant communities of Southern Germany (such as Nuremberg, Ortenburg, the Upper Palatinate) whereas Bohemian emigrants headed for southern Saxony, especially the *Erzgebirge* regions. At this early stage, only a small number of individuals tried to gain citizenship in their new dwelling places, because they either lacked sufficient funds to pay their admittance (*Bürgergeld*) or, more importantly, they did not want to commit themselves fully to their prospective new authorities. This resulted in complaints by locals that immigrants expected shelter and assistance but were reluctant to participate in communal obligations.[33] From the 1620s, certain cities in border areas close to Habsburg territories faced considerable economic and social troubles caused by an uncontrollable influx of foreigners who were unwilling to move anywhere further inland.[34] Sixty years later, the famous Edict of Potsdam of 1685, in which Elector Frederick William I of Brandenburg-Prussia "invited" French refugees to his territories by promising them economic, legal, and religious benefits, was neither merely a reaction to anti-Protestant politics in France nor simply a strategy to meet the demographic needs of the Hohenzollern state. As recent research has underlined, the Edict was also a result of international diplomatic efforts to solve the refugee problems close to the French borders.[35] The Edict of Potsdam is usually considered the initial spark of the famous immigration policy of Brandenburg-Prussia and has long been somewhat mythologized by both Prussian and Huguenot historiography.

The aims of numerous migrants to stay as close as possible to their former homelands had very practical reasons. As many examples illustrate, early modern borders could never be completely closed, which explains why, among many other individuals, both Altwasser and Etienne benefited from multiple border crossings in order to continue their business in spite of Counter-Reformation policies. In the same vein, Protestants from Bohemia often had not sold their estates but had instead leased them so that they could live from the revenues in their places of exile. A good number of these migrants seem to have moved back and forth, although often illegally, bearing the risk of being arrested.[36] When the Protestant Swedish Army under King Gustavus Adolphus together with his allies from Electoral Saxony tried to conquer Bohemia in the year 1631, many Protestant Bohemian emigrants followed the soldiers in order to resettle in their former homelands, with the result of being exiled once more soon after.[37] A very similar case was the so-called *Glorieuse Rentrée* of the Protestant Vaudois from Geneva to their homeland in the Alpine region of Savoy in 1689 from where they were expelled again some years later.[38]

For Habsburg as well as French emigrants, international treaties such as the Peace of Westphalia in 1648 or the peace treaty of Rijswijk in 1697 significantly worsened the chances to return as a group, although some Habsburg and, respectively, French Protestant activists had agitated to influence the peace negotiations in their favor through lobbying and producing print publications.[39] In both cases, the failure to gain significant political support for the emigrants to return home seems to have initiated new migration processes and/or resulted in different attitudes toward their respective host countries as well as toward shaping their own settlements as immigrant communities. Similar phenomena, which hint at the social and symbolic significance of political or military developments for the dynamics of emigration and return migration, can be found among several other Protestant migrant groups as well as among Dutch and British Catholics in the late sixteenth century and Jacobites after 1697 and 1714–15.[40] However, more research combining political caesuras, social processes, and individual migrant experiences is necessary.

There is, however, strong evidence that in the course of such decisive political or military moves, more and more exiles started to cope with a changing situation and began to adjust to their fate as permanent immigrants. This was the case with the Bohemians in Saxony around 1650 as well as with the Huguenot *refugiés* in a number of German territories around 1700. It resulted in the establishment of particular immigrant church services, in an increasing willingness to take oaths of allegiance to their new authorities, and perhaps also, as evidence suggests, in a stronger awareness of particular minority traditions.[41] In their church services in Dresden, for instance, the Bohemians started to particularly promote the Czech language and Czech traditions (even though a number of immigrants were ethnic Germans and had never spoken Czech before). Similarly, the French language among Huguenot refugees in Brandenburg was increasingly reduced to liturgical, educational, or intellectual matters, but slowly vanished from daily use.[42] At the same time, the political journalism accompanying the peace negotiations at Osnabrück as well as at Rijswijk seems to have reinforced immigrant historiography and the shaping of collective traditions as groups of (formerly) persecuted religious refugees.[43] Of course, generational changes among migrants added to this shift from temporary exile to permanent immigration.

Conclusion

Based upon examples taken primarily from the Habsburg and Huguenot migrations into the Holy Roman Empire in the seventeenth century, this chapter has argued that early modern religious migrations almost always included an option of return. This return possibility can be traced in the actions as well as in the ways of accommodation and integration of immigrants, but also in theological and devotional self-images, which ran counter to the more official traditions of immigration narratives. The desire to return to a (real or imaginary) place of origin vanished only slowly, after certain political, military, or generational changes had added to the practical difficulties of going back. These changes were accompanied by the creation of a new immigrant consciousness and different identity politics among groups of former religious refugees.

It could be assumed, then, that there might be a difference in the experiences and self-images within intracontinental and intercontinental migrations of the early modern era. However, there are sufficient examples that similar migrational patterns applied among long-distance migrants, such as between Central Europe and the Russian Empire,[44] as well as among settlers in the Atlantic world. Protestant emigrants from the Bishopric of Salzburg in the 1730s were reluctant to move to the British North American colonies and to settle there because they could be sure this would have cut them off from their former, although re-catholicized, homes. This was why an international Protestant initiative to settle the Salzburgers in Georgia almost failed.[45]

Recent research has made the point that in their post-migrational lives, early modern immigrants, especially religious migrants, tended to be more mobile than other people.[46] However, against the backdrop of widespread early modern mobility, migrants with religious as well as secular motives did not constitute the exception to a presumed rule of early modern stasis and locality. Early modern migrations should therefore not be analyzed as exceptional, unidirectional, or irreversible movements. In some respects mobility meant an option for almost anyone, and it is probably no exaggeration, as Steve Hochstadt has maintained, to say that at least one-third or even half of all early modern Europeans changed their places of residence at least once in their lives.[47] Confessional migration was therefore part of the mobility structures within early modern society, and this mobility almost always included the option to return home. The neglect of onward and return migration patterns points to the fact that a certain individual autonomy of early modern migrants (as well as of the ones in later periods) needs to be taken into account much more than the social history of early modern migrations has acknowledged.

Alexander Schunka is a Professor of Early Modern History at the Freie Universität Berlin. He received his doctorate in History at the Ludwig-Maximilians-Universität München in 2004 and has since taught early modern history at the universities of Stuttgart and Erfurt. He specializes in the cultural and religious history of early modern Europe with a focus on the history of migrations. His publications include *Soziales Wissen und dörfliche Welt* (2000), *Gäste, die bleiben* (2006), some co-edited volumes, and a number of articles. His forthcoming book will be on the relationship between Protestantism and the birth of German Anglophilia in the eighteenth century.

Notes

1. See, for instance, Dirk Hoerder, *Cultures in Contact: World Migrations in the Second Millennium* (Durham and London, 2011); Leslie Page Moch, *Moving Europeans: Migration in Western Europe since 1650*, 2nd ed. (Bloomington, 2003).
2. On the Huguenots, see Ulrich Niggemann, *Hugenotten* (Cologne, 2011), 99–108; on the Bohemians, see Alexander Schunka, "Forgotten Memories—Contested Representations: Early Modern Bohemian Migrants in Saxony," in *Enlarging European Memory: Migration Movements in Historical Perspective*, ed. Mareike König and Rainer Ohliger (Ostfildern, 2006), 35–46.
3. Heinz Schilling, "Confessional Migration as a Distinct Type of Old European Long Distance Migration," in *Le migrazioni in Europa Secc. XIII–XVIII*, ed. Simonetta Cavaciocchi (Florence, 1994), 175–89.
4. Matthias Asche, "Religionskriege und Glaubensflüchtlinge im Europa des 16. und 17. Jahrhunderts—Überlegungen zu einer Typendiskussion," in *Religionskriege im Alten Reich und in Alteuropa: Begriff, Wahrnehmung, Wirkmächtigkeit*, ed. Franz Brendle and Anton Schindling (Munster, 2006), 435–58; Matthias Asche, "Glaubensflüchtlinge und Kulturtransfer—Perspektiven für die Forschung aus der Sicht der sozialhistorischen Migrations- und der vergleichenden Minderheitenforschung," in *Kultureller Austausch: Bilanz und Perspektiven der Frühneuzeitforschung*, ed. Michael North (Cologne et al., 2009), 89–114; Alexander Schunka, "Konfession und Migrationsregime in der Frühen Neuzeit," *Geschichte und Gesellschaft* 35 (2009): 28–63.
5. Bettina Braun, "Katholische Glaubensflüchtlinge—eine Spurensuche im Europa der Frühen Neuzeit," *Historisches Jahrbuch* 130 (2010): 505–76; Geert H. Janssen, "Quo Vadis? Catholic Perceptions of Flight and the Revolt of the Low Countries, 1566–1609," *Renaissance Quarterly* 64 (2011): 472–99; Alexander Schunka, "Konfessionelle Liminalität: Kryptokatholiken im lutherischen Territorialstaat des 17. Jahrhunderts," in *Migration und kirchliche Praxis: Das religiöse Leben frühneuzeitlicher Glaubensflüchtlinge in alltagsgeschichtlicher Perspektive*, ed. Joachim Bahlcke and Rainer Bendel (Cologne et al., 2008), 113–31.
6. On Counter-Reformation measures and strategies of Protestant survival, see Rudolf Leeb, Susanne Claudine Pils, and Thomas Winkelbauer, eds., *Staatsmacht und Seelenheil: Gegenreformation und Geheimprotestantismus in der Habsburgermonarchie* (Vienna and Munich, 2007); Rudolf Leeb, Martin Scheutz, and Dietmar Weikl, eds., *Geheimprotestantismus und evangelische Kirchen in der Habsburgermonarchie und im Erzstift Salzburg, 17./18. Jahrhundert* (Vienna and Munich, 2009).
7. Thomas Klingebiel, "Migrationen im frühneuzeitlichen Europa: Anmerkungen und Überlegungen zur Typologiediskussion," in *Réfugiés und Émigrés: Migration zwischen Frankreich und Deutschland im 18. Jahrhundert*, ed. Thomas Höpel and Katharina Middell (Leipzig, 1997), 23–38; Alexander Schunka, "Lutheran Confessional Migration," in *European History Online (EGO)*, ed. Leibniz Institute of European History (IEG) (Mainz, 2012). Retrieved 5 November 2013 from http://www.ieg-ego.eu/schunkaa-2012-en URN: urn:nbn:de:0159-2012060616.
8. Etienne Francois, "Vom preußischen Patrioten zum besten Deutschen," in *Die Hugenotten 1685–1985*, ed. Rudolf von Thadden and Michelle Magdelaine, 2nd ed. (Munich, 1986), 198–212; see the contribution of Ulrich Niggemann in the present volume, and also Alexander Schunka, "Constantia im Martyrium: Zur Exilliteratur

des 17. Jahrhunderts zwischen Humanismus und Barock," in *Frühneuzeitliche Konfessionskulturen*, ed. Thomas Kaufmann, Anselm Schubert, and Kaspar von Greyerz (Gütersloh, 2008), 175–200.

9. Alexander Schunka, "Immigrant Petition Letters in Early Modern Saxony," in *Letters Across Borders: The Epistolary Practices of International Migrants*, eds. Bruce S. Elliott, David A. Gerber, and Suzanne M. Sinke (New York and Basingstoke, 2006), 271–90.

10. Stephan Steiner, *Reisen ohne Wiederkehr: Die Deportation von Protestanten aus Kärnten 1734–1736* (Vienna and Munich, 2007), 278–80; Rainer Walz, "Die Ansiedlung der Salzburger Emigranten in Ostpreußen," in *Probleme der Migration und Integration im Preussenland vom Mittelalter bis zum Anfang des 20. Jahrhunderts*, ed. Klaus Militzer (Marburg, 2005), 127–29; Werner Wilhelm Schnabel, *Österreichische Exulanten in oberdeutschen Reichsstädten: Zur Migration von Führungsschichten im 17. Jahrhundert* (Munich, 1992), 588–95. On the Bohemians and Huguenots see the literature quoted below. No systematic research has yet been carried out on return migration in a confessional context.

11. Jörg Deventer, "Zu Rom übergehen: Konversion als Entscheidungshandlung und Handlungsstrategie," in *Staatsmacht und Seelenheil*, 168–80; compare the contributions in Leeb et al., eds., *Geheimprotestantismus*. On the place of conversion in the daily life of early modern Germany and on its connections to mobility and migration see Duane Corpis, *Crossing the Boundaries of Belief: Geographies of Religious Conversion in Southern Germany, 1648–1800* (Charlottesville, NC, 2014).

12. E.g. Wulf Wäntig, *Grenzerfahrungen: Böhmische Exulanten im 17. Jahrhundert* (Konstanz, 2007), 320–26. On bi-confessional life in the New Town of Prague following the Battle of White Mountain, see Olga Fejtová, *Rekatolizace na Novém Městě pražském v době pobělohorské: Já pevně věřím a vyznávám . . .* (Prague, 2012).

13. Wenzeslaus Altwasser's diary is preserved in Ratsschulbibliothek Zwickau: Sig. 12.6.10; see Georg Buchwald, "Wenzeslaus Altwasser: Evangelischer Pfarrer in Bergreichenstein, dann in Schüttenhofen, vertrieben im Jahre 1622," *Jahrbuch der Gesellschaft für die Geschichte des Protestantismus in Österreich* 12 (1891): 55–71; Alexander Schunka, "Exulanten, Konvertiten, Arme und Fremde: Zuwanderer aus der Habsburgermonarchie in Kursachsen im 17. Jahrhundert," *Frühneuzeit-Info* 14 (2003): 66–78.

14. See his correspondence in Ratsschulbibliothek Zwickau: Nachlass Christian Daum, Br. 3.1/3.2.

15. On early modern religious pluralism see Dagmar Freist et al., eds., *Living with Religious Diversity in Early Modern Europe* (Farnham, 2009).

16. The significance of social marginality among migrants is evident from sources relating to the distribution of charity, see Alexander Schunka, *Gäste, die bleiben: Zuwanderer in Kursachsen und der Oberlausitz im 17. und frühen 18. Jahrhundert* (Hamburg, 2006), 270–351. Next to Altwasser's, another fascinating personal account of a confessional migrant would be, for instance, Volkmar Wirth, ed., *Bartholomäus Dietwar: Leben eines evangelischen Pfarrers im früheren markgräflichen Amte Kitzingen von 1592–1670, von ihm selbst erzählt. Zugleich ein Beitrag zur Geschichte des 30jährigen Kriegs in Franken* (Kitzingen, 1887).

17. The most recent print is Jochen Desel and Walter Mogk, eds., *Wege in eine neue Heimat: Fluchtberichte von Hugenotten aus Metz* (Sickte, 1987), 87–124.

18. On the Huguenots in the Landgraviate of Hesse–Kassel see Susanne Lachenicht, "Die Freiheitskonzession des Landgrafen von Hessen–Kassel, das Edikt von Potsdam

und die Ansiedlung von Hugenotten in Brandenburg–Preußen und Hessen–Kassel," in *Hugenotten und deutsche Territorialstaaten: Immigrationspolitik und Integrationsprozesse*, ed. Guido Braun and Susanne Lachenicht (Munich, 2007), 71–83.

19. On this aspect see Klaus Weber, "Zwischen Religion und Ökonomie: Sepharden und Hugenotten in Hamburg, 1580–1800," in *Religion und Mobilität: Zum Verhältnis von raumbezogener Mobilität und religiöser Identitätsbildung im frühneuzeitlichen Europa*, ed. Henning P. Jürgens and Thomas Weller (Göttingen, 2010), 137–68.

20. This seems to be a fruitful tendency in migration research of early modern Germany. See, among others, a number of contributions in Jürgens and Weller, eds., *Religion und Mobilität*; Alexander Schunka and Eckart Olshausen, eds., *Migrationserfahrungen—Migrationsstrukturen* (Stuttgart, 2010).

21. Alexander Schunka, "Migranten und kulturelle Transfers," in *Friedrich der Große in Europa: Geschichte einer wechselvollen Beziehung*, ed. Bernd Sösemann and Gregor Vogt-Spira, 2 vols. (Stuttgart, 2012), 2:80–96.

22. Christian Lehmann, *Historischer Schauplatz derer natürlichen Merckwürdigkeiten in dem Meißnischen Ober-Erzgebirge . . .* (Leipzig, 1699), 10–11.

23. Gustav Schmoller, "Die ländliche Kolonisation des 17. und 18. Jahrhunderts [1886]," in *Moderne Preußische Geschichte 1648–1947: Eine Anthologie*, ed. Otto Büsch and Wolfgang Neugebauer (Berlin and New York, 1981), 924.

24. Ratsschulbibliothek Zwickau, Diary of Wenzeslaus Altwasser, 11, 18.

25. Schunka, *Gäste*, 75, 151; Municipal Archives, Pirna C VI IV, 44–48 (Church Accounts, 1637) [old pagination].

26. See the subtitle of Georg Miller, *Ein Christliche Predig Zu Ehren vnd schuldiger Danckbarkeit der Kirchen Statt und Schulen in Straßburg gethon . . . Durch Georgen Miller der Heiligen Schrifft Doctorn a patria & Ecclesia Augustana exulantem* (Lauingen, 1584).

27. Fabianus Natus, *Vermahnungs-Predigt Zur Christlichen Beständigkeit. Gehalten in der Königlichen Haupt und alten Stadt Praga / bey der deutschen Evangelischen Kirchen zum Salvator genandt / den 11. Martii Anno 1622 . . .* (Leipzig, 1623); see also Schunka, "Constantia im Martyrium."

28. Critical toward the notion of a particular "theology of emigrants" is Henning P. Jürgens, "Die Vertreibung der reformierten Flüchtlingsgemeinden aus London: Jan Utenhoves Simplex et fidelis narratio," in *Religion und Mobilität*, ed. Jürgens and Weller, 13–40.

29. Johann Amos Comenius, *Trawren über Trawren / und Trost über trost / Sehr dienlich auf alle zeiten. Sonderlich bei ietziger noht der gantzen Christenheit* (Preßburg, 1626), 178: "Laß dich nicht verjagen / sondern gehe lieber gutwillig davon: vergönnen sie dir nicht da zu wohnen / gehe anders wohin. Da wirstu nicht wie ein vorjagter / sondern wie ein frembder bleiben oder wohnen können. Ein weiser und vernünftiger ist uberal daheim."

30. Sigismund Scherertz, *Zwey christliche Sendschreiben an die Evangelischen Präger; Sampt der Relation vom Abzug der vier Teutscher Prediger daselbst* (Wolfenbüttel, 1623); Fabianus Natus, *Des Ewigen viel frommen Gottes Hochthewrer Augapffel . . .* (Wittenberg, 1630).

31. See, among others, Andreas Kesler, *Patientia christiana: Außführlicher Tractat Von der Kirchen Christi Persecution* (Coburg, 1630).

32. The most recent monographical studies on the Bohemians in Saxony are Wäntig, *Grenzerfahrungen* and Schunka, *Gäste*. On Brandenburg-Prussia see Stefi Jersch-Wenzel, *Juden und "Franzosen" in der Wirtschaft des Raumes Berlin/Brandenburg*

zur Zeit des Merkantilismus (Berlin, 1978); Matthias Asche, *Neusiedler im verheerten Land: Kriegsfolgenbewältigung, Migrationssteuerung und Konfessionspolitik im Zeichen des Wiederaufbaus. Die Mark Brandenburg nach den Kriegen des 17. Jahrhunderts* (Münster, 2006).

33. See, for instance, the complaint of some municipal administrators in Dresden, 1638, Municipal Archives, Dresden, Ratsarchiv, H XXIX 4, Dresden 9 November, 1638 (no folio).

34. See the case of Pirna, Lenka Bobková, "Die Gemeinde der böhmischen Exulanten in der Stadt Pirna 1621–1639," in *Herbergen der Christenheit* 27 (2003): 37–56.

35. Ulrich Niggemann, *Immigrationspolitik zwischen Konflikt und Konsens: Die Hugenottenansiedlung in Deutschland und England 1681–1697* (Cologne, 2008), 93f.

36. See Schunka, *Gäste*, 108–16; Milan Svoboda, "Kryštof II. z Redernu, pobělohorský exulant," in *Víra nebo vlast? Exil v Českých dějinách raného novověku*, ed. Michaela Hrubá (Ústí nad Labem, 2001), 222–37; Wäntig, *Grenzerfahrungen*, 320–25.

37. Antonín Rezek, *Dějiny Saského vpádu do Čech (1631–1632) a návrat emigrace* (Prague, 1889).

38. See Étienne Bourdon, "La 'glorieuse rentrée' des Vaudois (1689), un voyage militaire et spirituel," in *Partir pour résister: S'expatrier pour sa foi ou ses idées (du XVIIe au XIXe siècle)* (Paris, 2009), 27–38.

39. Bedřich Šindelář, "Die böhmischen Exulanten in Sachsen und der Westfälische Friedenskongreß," in *Sborník Prací Filosofické Fakulty Brněnské University* 9 (1960), Řada Historická, C 7, 215–51; Barbara Dölemeyer, "Der Friede von Rijswijk und seine Bedeutung für das europäische Refuge," in *Hugenotten* 66 (2002): 51–73.

40. See Katy Gibbons, *English Catholic Exiles in Late Sixteenth-Century Paris* (Woodbridge and Rochester, 2011), 143–69; on Catholic print culture in exile around 1588 see Paul Arblaster, *Antwerp & The World: Richard Verstegan and the International Culture of Catholic Reformation* (Leuven, 2004), 61–63; Christoph von Ehrenstein, "Jakobiten in Europa 1688–1788," in *Enzyklopädie Migration in Europa*, eds. Klaus J. Bade et al., 3rd ed. (Paderborn et al., 2010), 707–10.

41. Dölemeyer, "Rijswijk", 63–65; Niggemann, *Immigrationspolitik*, 32f.

42. These aspects are treated, with varying emphasis on the obvious importance of generational changes among migrants, in Frank Metasch, *Exulanten in Dresden: Einwanderung und Integration von Glaubensflüchtlingen im 17. und 18. Jahrhundert* (Leipzig, 2011); Franziska Roosen, *Soutenir notre Église: Hugenottische Erziehungskonzepte und Bildungseinrichtungen im Berlin des 18. Jahrhunderts* (Bad Karlshafen, 2008); Manuela Böhm, *Sprachenwechsel: Akkulturation und Mehrsprachigkeit der Brandenburger Hugenotten vom 17. bis 19. Jahrhundert* (Berlin and New York, 2010).

43. See the edition of [Johann Amos Comenius et al.,] *Historia Persecutionum Ecclesiae Bohemicae* . . . , (n.p., 1648). On some practical outcomes in the making of immigrant traditions after 1648 see the case study of Alexander Schunka, "St. Johanngeorgenstadt zu kurfürstlicher Durchlaucht unsterblichem Nachruhm: Stadtgründung und städtische Traditionsbildung in der Frühen Neuzeit," *Neues Archiv für Sächsische Geschichte* 75/76 (2004): 175–205. An example of political pamphleteering for the Vaudois is *Kurtze Erzehlung Von dem letztern Außgang Der Armen Waldenser, So auff Ordre des Hertzogs von Savoyen, aus den Piemontesis. Thälern, ihr Hauß, Hof und Ländereyen verlassen, über Genff nach der Schweitz, dem Würtenbergischen und Darmstädtischen Land, wie auch Holland und Engeland, und anderswo hin sich begeben und daselbst niederlassen müssen* . . . , (Hamburg [?], 1699). Huguenot pamphleteering

started even before the peace treaty of Rijswijk was concluded, see *La Balance de la religion et de la politique, ou réfléxions par lesquelles on fait voir que les réformez de France on droit de prétendre d'être compris favorablement, par la médiation des puissances protestantes, dans le traité de paix, qui terminera la presente guerre* (Philadelphie, 1697).

44. See, for instance, the highly stylized report of Christian Gottlob Züge, *Der russische Colonist oder Christian Gottlob Züge's Leben in Rußland: Nebst einer Schilderung der Sitten und Gebräuche der Russen, vornehmlich in den asiatischen Provinzen* (Zeitz and Naumburg, 1802/1803).

45. See the correspondence of the Pietist German pastor in London, Friedrich Michael Ziegenhagen, in Archiv der Franckeschen Stiftungen, Halle/Mission Archives, 1 e 2, No. 48, London 7/18 November 1732; No. 58, London, 25 May 1733. On the larger context see Charlotte Haver, *Von Salzburg nach Amerika: Mobilität und Kultur einer Gruppe religiöser Emigranten im 18. Jahrhundert* (Paderborn, 2011).

46. I consider this a rather problematic embrace of older, often derogatory stereotypes against human mobility. Matthias Asche, "Migrationen im Europa der Frühen Neuzeit—Versuch einer Typologie," *Geschichte, Politik und ihre Didaktik: Beiträge und Nachrichten für die Unterrichtspraxis, Zeitschrift für historisch-politische Bildung* 32 (2004): 76.

47. Steve Hochstadt, "Migration in Preindustrial Germany," *Central European History* 3 (1983): 195–224.

Bibliography

Anonymous. *La Balance de la religion et de la politique, ou réfléxions par lesquelles on fait voir que les réformez de France on droit de prétendre d'être compris favorablement, par la médiation des puissances protestantes, dans le traité de paix, qui terminera la presente guerre.* Philadelphie, 1697.

———. *Kurtze Erzehlung Von dem letztern Außgang Der Armen Waldenser, So auff Ordre des Hertzogs von Savoyen, aus den Piemontesis. Thälern, ihr Hauß, Hof und Ländereyen verlassen, über Genff nach der Schweitz, dem Würtenbergischen und Darmstädtischen Land, wie auch Holland und Engeland, und anderswo hin sich begeben und daselbst niederlassen müssen . . . .* Hamburg [?], 1699.

Arblaster, Paul. *Antwerp & The World: Richard Verstegan and the International Culture of Catholic Reformation.* Leuven, 2004.

Asche, Matthias. "Glaubensflüchtlinge und Kulturtransfer—Perspektiven für die Forschung aus der Sicht der sozialhistorischen Migrations- und der vergleichenden Minderheitenforschung." In *Kultureller Austausch: Bilanz und Perspektiven der Frühneuzeitforschung,* ed. Michael North. Cologne, 2009.

———. "Migrationen im Europa der Frühen Neuzeit—Versuch einer Typologie." *Geschichte, Politik und ihre Didaktik: Beiträge und Nachrichten für die Unterrichtspraxis, Zeitschrift für historisch-politische Bildung* 32 (2004): 74–89.

———. *Neusiedler im verheerten Land. Kriegsfolgenbewältigung, Migrationssteuerung und Konfessionspolitik im Zeichen des Landeswiederaufbaus. Die Mark Brandenburg nach den Kriegen des 17. Jahrhunderts.* Münster, 2006.

Asche, Matthias. "Religionskriege und Glaubensflüchtlinge im Europa des 16. und 17. Jahrhunderts—Überlegungen zu einer Typendiskussion." In *Religionskriege im Alten Reich und in Alteuropa: Begriff, Wahrnehmung, Wirkmächtigkeit*, ed. Franz Brendle and Anton Schindling. Münster, 2006.

Bobková, Lenka. "Die Gemeinde der böhmischen Exulanten in der Stadt Pirna 1621–1639." *Herbergen der Christenheit* 27 (2003): 37–56.

Böhm, Manuela. *Sprachenwechsel: Akkulturation und Mehrsprachigkeit der Brandenburger Hugenotten vom 17. bis 19. Jahrhundert*. Berlin, 2010.

Bourdon, Étienne. "La 'glorieuse rentrée' des Vaudois (1689), un voyage militaire et spirituel." In *Partir pour résister: S'expatrier pour sa foi ou ses idées (du XVIIe au XIXe siècle)*. Paris, 2009.

Braun, Bettina. "Katholische Glaubensflüchtlinge: Eine Spurensuche im Europa der Frühen Neuzeit." *Historisches Jahrbuch der Görres-Gesellschaft* 130 (2010): 505–76.

Buchwald, Georg. "Wenzeslaus Altwasser: Evangelischer Pfarrer in Bergreichenstein, dann in Schüttenhofen, vertrieben im Jahre 1622." *Jahrbuch der Gesellschaft für die Geschichte des Protestantismus in Österreich* 12 (1891): 55–71.

Comenius, Johann Amos. *Trawren über Trawren / und Trost über trost / Sehr dienlich auf alle zeiten: Sonderlich bei ietziger noht der gantzen Christenheit*. Preßburg, 1626.

———, et al. *Historia Persecutionum Ecclesiae Bohemicae . . . .* n.p., 1648.

Corpis, Duane. *Crossing the Boundaries of Belief: Geographies of Religious Conversion in Southern Germany, 1648–1800*. Charlottesville, NC, 2014.

Desel, Jochen and Walter Mogk, eds. *Wege in eine neue Heimat: Fluchtberichte von Hugenotten aus Metz*. Sickte, 1987.

Deventer, Jörg. "Zu Rom übergehen: Konversion als Entscheidungshandlung und Handlungsstrategie." In *Staatsmacht und Seelenheil: Gegenreformation und Geheimprotestantismus in der Habsburgermonarchie*, ed. Rudolf Leeb, Susanne Claudine Pils, and Thomas Winkelbauer. Vienna, 2007.

Dölemeyer, Barbara. "Der Friede von Rijswijk und seine Bedeutung für das europäische Refuge." *Hugenotten* 66 (2002): 51–73.

von Ehrenstein, Christoph. "Jakobiten in Europa 1688–1788." In *Enzyklopädie Migration in Europa*, ed. Klaus J. Bade et al., 3rd ed. Paderborn, 2010.

Fejtová, Olga. *Rekatolizace na Novém Městě pražském v době pobělohorské: Já pevně věřím a vyznávám . . . .* Prague, 2012.

Francois, Etienne. "Vom preußischen Patrioten zum besten Deutschen." In *Die Hugenotten 1685–1985*, ed. Rudolf von Thadden and Michelle Magdelaine, 2nd ed. Munich, 1986.

Freist, Dagmar et al., eds. *Living with Religious Diversity in Early Modern Europe*. Farnham, 2009.

Gibbons, Katy. *English Catholic Exiles in Late Sixteenth-Century Paris*. Woodbridge, 2011.

Haver, Charlotte. *Von Salzburg nach Amerika: Mobilität und Kultur einer Gruppe religiöser Emigranten im 18. Jahrhundert*. Paderborn, 2011.

Hochstadt, Steve. "Migration in Preindustrial Germany." *Central European History* 16 (1983): 195–224.

Hoerder, Dirk. *Cultures in Contact: World Migrations in the Second Millennium.* Durham, 2002.

Janssen, Geert. "Quo Vadis? Catholic Perceptions of Flight and the Revolt of the Low Countries, 1566–1609." *Renaissance Quarterly* 64 (2011): 472–99.

Jersch-Wenzel, Stefi. *Juden und "Franzosen" in der Wirtschaft des Raumes Berlin/Brandenburg zur Zeit des Merkantilismus.* Berlin, 1978.

Jürgens, Henning P. "Die Vertreibung der reformierten Flüchtlingsgemeinden aus London: Jan Utenhoves Simplex et fidelis narratio." In *Religion und Mobilität,* ed. Jürgens and Weller.

Jürgens, Henning P., and Thomas Weller, eds. *Religion und Mobilität: Zum Verhältnis von raumbezogener Mobilität und religiöser Identitätsbildung im frühneuzeitlichen Europa* (Göttingen, 2010).

Kesler, Andreas. *Patentia Christiana: Außfürlicher Tractat von der Kirchen Christi Persecution oder Verfolgung bey diesen betrübten Zeiten.* Coburg, 1630.

Lachenicht, Susanne. "Die Freiheitskonzession des Landgrafen von Hessen-Kassel, das Edikt von Potsdam und die Ansiedlung von Hugenotten in Brandenburg-Preußen und Hessen-Kassel." In *Hugenotten und deutsche Territorialstaaten: Immigrationspolitik und Integrationsprozesse,* ed. Guido Braun and Susanne Lachenicht. Munich, 2007.

Leeb, Rudolf, Susanne Claudine Pils, and Thomas Winkelbauer, eds., *Staatsmacht und Seelenheil: Gegenreformation und Geheimprotestantismus in der Habsburgermonarchie.* Vienna, 2007.

Leeb, Rudolf, Martin Scheutz, and Dietmar Weikl, eds. *Geheimprotestantismus und evangelische Kirchen in der Habsburgermonarchie und im Erzstift Salzburg (17./18. Jahrhundert).* Vienna, 2009.

Lehmann, Christian. *Historischer Schauplatz derer natürlichen Merckwürdigkeiten in dem Meißnischen Ober-Erzgebirge* . . . . Leipzig, 1699.

Metasch, Frank. *Exulanten in Dresden: Einwanderung und Integration von Glaubensflüchtlingen im 17. und 18. Jahrhundert.* Leipzig, 2011.

Miller, Georg. *Ein Christliche Predig Zu Ehren vnd schuldiger Danckbarkeit der Kirchen Statt und Schulen in Straßburg gethon . . . Durch Georgen Miller der Heiligen Schrifft Doctorn a patria & Ecclesia Augustana exulantem.* Lauingen, 1584.

Moch, Leslie Page. *Moving Europeans: Migration in Western Europe since 1650.* 2nd edition. Bloomington, IN, 2003.

Natus, Fabianus. *Vermahnungs-Predigt Zur Christlichen Beständigkeit. Gehalten in der Königlichen Haupt und alten Stadt Praga / bey der deutschen Evangelischen Kirchen zum Salvator genannt / den 11. Martii Anno 1622* . . . . Leipzig, 1623.

———. *Des Ewigen viel frommen Gottes Hochthewrer Augapffel* . . . . Wittenberg, 1630.

Niggemann, Ulrich. *Immigrationspolitik zwischen Konflikt und Konsens: Die Hugenottenansiedlung in Deutschland und England (1681–1697).* Cologne, Weimar, Vienna, 2008.

Niggemann, Ulrich. *Hugenotten.* Cologne, 2011.

Rezek, Antonín. *Dějiny Saského vpádu do Čech (1631–1632) a návrat emigrace.* Prague, 1889.

Roosen, Franziska. *Soutenir notre Église: Hugenottische Erziehungskonzepte und Bildungseinrichtungen im Berlin des 18. Jahrhunderts.* Bad Karlshafen, 2008.

Scherertz, Sigismund. *Constantia Veritatis Evangelicae: Das ist / Christlich Bericht / Von Beständigkeit bey der Göttlichen Wahrheit des Heiligen Evangelii / Augspurgischer Confession: An die hinterlassenen Evangelischen Präger / (auff etlicher Begehren) einfeltig gefasset.* Lüneburg, 1623.

Schilling, Heinz. "Confessional Migration as a Distinct Type of Old European Long Distance Migration." In *Le migrazioni in Europa, Secc. XIII–XVIII,* ed. Simonetta Cavaciocchi. Prato, 1994.

Schmoller, Gustav. "Die ländliche Kolonisation des 17. und 18. Jahrhunderts [1886]." In *Moderne Preußische Geschichte 1648–1947: Eine Anthologie,* ed. Otto Büsch and Wolfgang Neugebauer. Berlin, 1981.

Schnabel, Werner W. *Österreichische Exulanten in oberdeutschen Reichsstädten: Zur Migration von Führungsschichten im 17. Jahrhundert.* Erlangen, 1990.

Schunka, Alexander. "Constantia im Martyrium: Zur Exilliteratur des 17. Jahrhunderts zwischen Humanismus und Barock." In *Frühneuzeitliche Konfessionskulturen,* ed. Thomas Kaufmann, Anselm Schubert, and Kaspar von Greyerz. Gütersloh, 2008.

———. "Exulanten, Konvertiten, Arme und Fremde: Zuwanderer aus der Habsburgermonarchie in Kursachsen im 17. Jahrhundert." In *Frühneuzeit-Info* 14 (2003): 66–78.

———. "Forgotten Memories—Contested Representations: Early Modern Bohemian Migrants in Saxony." In *Enlarging European Memory: Migration Movements in Historical Perspective,* ed. Mareike König and Rainer Ohliger. Ostfildern, 2006.

———. *Gäste, die bleiben: Zuwanderer in Kursachsen und der Oberlausitz im 17. und im frühen 18. Jahrhundert.* Hamburg, 2006.

———. "Immigrant Petition Letters in Early Modern Saxony." In *Letters across Borders: The Epistolary Practices of International Migrants,* ed. Bruce S. Elliott, David A. Gerber and Suzanne M. Sinke. New York, 2006.

———. "Konfession und Migrationsregime in der Frühen Neuzeit." In *Geschichte und Gesellschaft* 35 (January-March 2009): 28–63.

———. "Konfessionelle Liminalität: Kryptokatholiken im lutherischen Territorialstaat des 17. Jahrhunderts." In *Migration und kirchliche Praxis: Das religiöse Leben frühneuzeitlicher Glaubensflüchtlinge in alltagsgeschichtlicher Perspektive,* ed. Joachim Bahlcke and Rainer Bendel. Cologne, 2008.

———. "Lutheran Confessional Migration." In *European History Online (EGO),* ed. Leibniz Institute of European History (IEG). Mainz, 2012.

———. "Migranten und kulturelle Transfers." In *Friedrich der Große in Europa: Geschichte einer wechselvollen Beziehung,* ed. Bernd Sösemann and Gregor Vogt-Spira, 2 vols. Stuttgart, 2012.

————. "St. Johanngeorgenstadt zu kurfürstlicher Durchlaucht unsterblichem Nachruhm: Stadtgründung und städtische Traditionsbildung in der Frühen Neuzeit." *Neues Archiv für Sächsische Geschichte* 75, no. 76 (2004): 175–205.

Schunka, Alexander, and Eckart Olshausen, eds. *Migrationserfahrungen—Migrationsstrukturen*. Stuttgart, 2010.

Šindelář, Bedřich. "Die böhmischen Exulanten in Sachsen und der Westfälische Friedenskongreß." *Sborník Prací Filosofické Fakulty Brněnské University* 9 (1960).

Steiner, Stephan. *Reisen ohne Wiederkehr: Die Deportation von Protestanten aus Kärnten 1734–1736*. Vienna, 2007.

Svoboda, Milan. "Kryštof II. z Redernu, pobělohorský exulant." In *Víra nebo vlast? Exil v Českých dějinách raného novověku*, ed. Michaela Hrubá. Ústí nad Labem, 2001.

Walz, Rainer. "Die Ansiedlung der Salzburger Emigranten in Ostpreußen." In *Probleme der Migration und Integration im Preussenland vom Mittelalter bis zum Anfang des 20. Jahrhunderts*, ed. Klaus Militzer. Marburg, 2005.

Wäntig, Wulf. *Grenzerfahrungen: Böhmische Exulanten im 17. Jahrhundert*. Konstanz, 2007.

Wirth, Volkmar, ed. *Bartholomäus Dietwar: Leben eines evangelischen Pfarrers im früheren markgräflichen Amte Kitzingen von 1592–1670, von ihm selbst erzählt. Zugleich ein Beitrag zur Geschichte des 30jährigen Kriegs in Franken*. Kitzingen, 1887.

Weber, Klaus. "Zwischen Religion und Ökonomie: Sepharden und Hugenotten in Hamburg, 1580–1800." In *Religion und Mobilität*, ed. Jürgens and Weller.

Züge, Gottlob. *Der russische Colonist oder Christian Gottlob Züge's Leben in Rußland: Nebst einer Schilderung der Sitten und Gebräuche der Russen, vornehmlich in den asiatischen Provinzen*. Zeitz and Naumburg, 1802–03.

CHAPTER FOUR

~:~

Inventing Immigrant Traditions in Seventeenth- and Eighteenth-Century Germany
The Huguenots in Context

ULRICH NIGGEMANN

T housands of immigrants, often fleeing from persecution in other European countries, settled in German territories, principalities, and Imperial cities during and after the sixteenth century. Dutch and Walloon Protestants fled the confessional upheavals and the revolt in the Netherlands, founding Dutch- and French-speaking Reformed communities not only in Emden, Wesel, Aachen, and Cologne, but also in the Palatinate, Hanau, and Altona.[1] Catholics from the Low Countries escaped to German cities and towns during the Dutch war of independence from Spain, settling in Cologne.[2] In the seventeenth century, *Vaudois* from France and Savoy were driven out of their home countries, and many came to Württemberg or Hesse-Darmstadt.[3] Protestants from the Habsburg territories repeatedly emigrated from their home countries. For example, during and after the Thirty Years' War, Protestants from Bohemia crossed borders and settled in the electorate of Saxony.[4] As late as 1837, Protestants from the Austrian Zillertal were forced to leave their country and to settle in the Prussian parts of Silesia.[5] Most notably, Lutherans from the bishopric of Salzburg left their native soil in 1731–32 to look for new homes, not only in the southern Imperial cities and in the Protestant territories of Württemberg and Franconia, but also as far away as Prussia.[6]

The Huguenots—the migrant group that is the subject of this chapter— have a special significance in the history of German migration in the early modern period. After the Bartholomew's Day Massacre of 1572, French Huguenots left their homes and went to England, Germany, and the Netherlands. In the early years of exile, Huguenots preferred destinations near the French border, and many of them went home after the Edict of Nantes proclaimed a policy of toleration in 1598.[7] But during every period of renewed conflict and persecution, especially after 1680, new groups of Huguenot refugees (totaling about forty thousand) moved to German territories such as Brandenburg-Prussia, Hesse-Kassel, Brandenburg-Bayreuth, and Hanover.[8] The religious instabilities of the sixteenth and seventeenth centuries, in other words, prompted massive waves of migration throughout central Europe, and the Huguenot experience should be seen in this context.

Larger waves of immigration were often accompanied by broad publicity campaigns—pamphlets, broadsheets, and images were distributed in great quantities—aimed at gaining support for immigrants from the overall population as well as from state officials. Such campaigns can be observed in the case of the Salzburg Protestants as well as in the case of the Huguenots.[9] It would certainly be too easy to conclude that the substantial privileges that immigrant groups received were the result of these propaganda efforts, but one might ask what images and ideas about groups such as the Huguenots were constructed and communicated to a wider public that also included the princes and their counselors. It is known that reactions of the indigenous populations to these migrants were mixed; their attitudes varied from sympathy and charity to open hostility toward those people arriving in their communities.[10]

The evidence shows that these publicity campaigns sought to impact "public opinion," shifting the attitudes of the host population so that Huguenots would not face conflicts with their new neighbors while at the same time securing concessions from territorial lords. Pamphlets and other contemporary media did not offer just one homogenous message, but rather produced a broad range of possible meanings. Contemporaries did not understand the contents of these texts and images in just one way, but connected them to broader issues of public discussion. This chapter examines how and by which languages certain images and traditions were conveyed in the years following the mass immigration of Huguenots to Germany.

The Huguenot as Witness to Faith

Images of the Salzburg Protestants on their way through Germany are well-known even today. The exile of Protestants from the prince-bishopric of Salzburg was widely perceived as an act of intolerance, or a relic from another time, positions that reflected the influence of Enlightenment thought. Mass propaganda depicted their flight to Prussia, styling the Salzburgers as true exiles and martyrs for their faith.[11] However, this was by no means new or singular. There are earlier cases of broad publicity campaigns asking for solidarity with refugees and condemning the persecution and expulsion of religious minorities. Often, members of those minorities were actively involved in such campaigns.

The Huguenots are a very good example of the "self-fashioning"[12] of a group of migrants, attempting to shape their own present and past in very elaborate ways. Many of the exiled French Protestants as well as their progeny wrote and published narratives of their experience of persecution, thereby legitimizing and conceptualizing their own past. When persecution of the Huguenots increased after 1679, large quantities of pamphlets poured from the presses in the Netherlands, England, and other Protestant countries condemning the religious policy of the French Crown. Huguenot writers produced these texts while in exile, endeavoring to influence European public opinion to their advantage. One of the busiest among these writers was Pierre Jurieu, who lived in exile in Rotterdam. His *Lettres Pastorales* (Pastoral letters) were directed to those Huguenots who had decided to stay in France, either as *Nouveaux Convertis* (new converts) or as members of the secret *Église du désert* (Church of the desert).[13] Other tracts from his hand, as for example his *Les Soupirs de la France esclave qui aspire après la liberté* (The sighs of France in slavery, breathing after liberty), ran through several editions and were translated into Dutch, English, and German.[14] Pamphlets written by Jean Claude, Pierre Allix, Elie Benoît, along with many other anonymous publications, also enjoyed wide translation and distribution.[15]

Although adapted to very different contexts in the respective countries, the Huguenot pamphlets had some main lines of argument in common. One of them is the handling of history and historical narrative, defining their own place in history and interpreting persecution as a mark of divine election.[16] By identifying themselves with the early Christians under persecution by the emperors of Rome,[17] they construed themselves as the true Church of Christ, which was in distress in every age. They were the "innocent" and "poor" disciples of Christ, the "lambs" and "sheep" hunted by wolves.[18] Thus, they were persecuted because they formed the body of the true Church.[19] Suffering from the hands of evil, therefore, was a mark of election: when Christ himself had to endure persecution, how could his servants expect better treatment?[20] Furthermore, suffering in this world often came to be seen as a precondition for salvation in the next.[21]

Huguenot authors and intellectual leaders thus integrated their own history into the history of salvation and into a transhistorical tradition of the persecution of the Christian Church. They not only construed themselves as the elect few, but they also identified the Roman Catholic Church with this same old enemy of the true Church.[22] The Catholic Church was—in familiar Reformation language—depicted as the "cruel Babylon" and the "realm of Antichrist." In short, it was the home of evil, the Church of Satan.[23] The history of Christianity altogether was interpreted as a struggle between good and evil, between the true Church and the false Church. It was therefore an eschatological interpretation of history, using the powerful language of the apocalypse. Anti-Catholicism was rooted in this interpretation of history. This conception of history was especially powerful, because it included the Protestant movement in the history of salvation, and it gave sense to the sufferings of the Huguenots by providing them with certainty regarding good and evil, assuring them of their being on the side of goodness and righteousness, whereas Catholics were condemned as evil. This interpretation, moreover, coalesced with the expectation of the imminent end of the world. Pierre Jurieu even predicted in his *Accomplissement des propheties* (The accomplishment of the Scripture prophecies) published in 1686 that the overthrow of the Antichrist would come three years later, in 1689. Many other pamphlets give evidence of the pronounced millenarian expectations held by Huguenot communities both in France and in exile.[24]

This perception of the Huguenots as martyrs for their faith and as the elect persecuted by the enemies of Christ's Church drew upon longstanding traditions not only in late antiquity and the Middle Ages, but also in the narratives of the French Reformed Church. From the beginning of the civil wars of the sixteenth century, Huguenots developed narratives of persecution and martyrdom. The most influential undoubtedly was Jean Crespin's *Le livre des martyrs* (The book of martyrs), which was first published in Geneva in 1554 and extended after the shock of the St. Bartholomew's Day massacre in 1572.[25] In his preface, Crespin maintained: "Entre les marques de la vraye Eglise de Dieu, ceste-cy a esté l'une de principales, à sauoir, qu'elle a de tous temps soustenu les assauts des persecutions." (Among the marks of the true Church of God, its ability to endure persecution at all times has been one of its most characteristic features.)[26] The narratives by Crespin and the experience of civil war and massacre predetermined the view in which Huguenots conceived the renewed experience of persecution in the late seventeenth century, and this, in turn, influenced their image in foreign Protestant countries.

The Huguenots and their supporters made use of such images in the negotiations with those princes and rulers, who were prepared to allow the foundation of colonies in their territories. This becomes clear when we consider one of these petitions: the letter by Claude Brousson and Jean de la Porte,[27] originally written in Latin, which was printed under the title "Eines der Schreiben welches die Protestirende in Franckreich Bey Verlassung aller Haab An andre Protestirend- und Evangelische abgehen lassen" (One of the writings that the Protestants in France, upon leaving their possessions, had sent widely to all other Protestants and evangelicals), and again as part of Johann Friedrich Mayer's "Bewegliches Seufftzen Derer aus Franckreich geflüchteten Reformirten" (Affectionate sighs of those Calvinists who fled France). The first of these prints was, perhaps, ordered by the French Reformed consistory in Berlin.[28] However, not only in printed pamphlets, but also in a broad range of petition letters, Huguenots referred to themselves as "poor exiles" and "refugees for religion's sake."[29] In the same manner as other groups of persecuted Protestants petitioning for support or begging permission to settle in a foreign country, Huguenots styled themselves as pious victims of religious persecution.[30]

Even more remarkable is the response communicated through princely edicts and decrees. Often, the proclamations adopted the language used by refugees and pamphleteers. The edict of Potsdam, for example, mentioned the "hard persecutions and rigorous procedures" against the Protestants in France.[31] Because of his "just compassion," it claimed, Frederic William wanted to receive the refugees in his territories and grant them a number of privileges.[32] Allusions to the "cruel persecution" in France and appeals to the "compassion" of the host population were also usual in the orders of some German princes to carry out collections for the refugees.[33] Such edicts were widely distributed and usually read in churches during Sunday services. They had, therefore, an enormous impact on the images and ideas about the immigrants held by the native inhabitants. Thus, their image of being martyrs and exiles for their faith was enforced and widely distributed by a large variety of texts. In contrast to the case of the Salzburg Protestants, pictures, medals, and other pictorial sources are still largely neglected by historical research.

Huguenots as Victims of "French Tyranny"

Being martyrs and exiles for the true faith, however, was by no means the sole image used to depict Huguenots. The 1680s and the following decades were times of intense hostility toward France. Especially since the "Reunions", the seizure of territories of the Empire by using questionable legal claims, and the capture of the Imperial city of Strasbourg by Louis XIV and during the renewed war after 1689, anti-French sentiments ran high throughout Germany.[34] Thus, the persecution of the Huguenots could also serve as an example of "French tyranny."[35] A number of anti-French propaganda texts mentioned the fate of the refugees. The French king was depicted as the main actor of anti-Huguenot politics. According to the author of the 1686 publication *Franckreich: Die neuen Conjuncturen Werden dir den Compass gewaltig verrücken* (France: The new situation will mightily align your compass), Louis XIV was looking for glory and preeminence in Europe, and therefore he needed the money of the clergy of France. To get this money, he was prepared to extirpate heresy in his kingdom.[36] For another author under the pseudonym of Sincerus Catholicus, the persecution of Protestants was proof of the dishonesty and insidiousness of the French king, who dedicated all possible means to sow distrust and discord between Catholics and Protestants in order to avoid their concerted action against France.[37] The idea of France trying to create hostilities between German Protestants and Catholics was also prominent in pamphlets attempting to justify a broad, inter-confessional alliance.[38] Even the idea that France was preparing for a religious war, beginning with persecution at home, was a widely held belief among German Protestants.[39]

Some of the Huguenot pamphlets could also be read as anti-French sentiments. *Spiegel der Frantzösischen Tyranney* (Mirror of French tyranny), for example, characterized the French—without addressing the king or the clergy as main actors—as cruel and intolerant. It was the "French nation" that committed all the cruelties against the Huguenots,[40] who were victims of "French tyranny."[41] This was meant to be understood as a warning to German readers who should be aware of the French methods to convert his subjects to Catholicism. This was, as one pamphleteer stated, what the German Protestants had to expect, if parts of the Empire were seized by the French.[42] Concerns about French expansion were thus connected to religious fears. In a situation of renewed hostility against Catholic France and of intense efforts for Protestant unity, the Huguenots became an example of the threat to Germans posed by the French king.

Although both ideas were often intermingled, pamphlets focusing on France as a dangerous enemy could be quite different, both in language and in purpose, from those focusing on the threat of Catholicism. Whereas one group of pamphlets used the example of the Huguenots to strengthen pan-Protestant self-consciousness and certainty of salvation, another group of pamphlets used the Huguenots to enforce unity and accord within the Holy Roman Empire. Thus, one group had a potentially European Protestant focus, whereas the other group focused on Germany and included the Catholic parts of the Empire. It was perhaps significant for the political and religious climate in the late seventeenth century that confessional fears and enmities—at least in the pamphlet literature—were at the heart of the debates.[43]

Anti-French sentiments, however, were ambiguous with regard to the Huguenots. Although they could be seen as victims of the French and "French tyranny," Huguenots were nevertheless perceived as French. As such, they could suffer from the same anti-French attitudes that were enforced by their persecution. Ironically, Huguenots in London were even suspected of being crypto-Catholics,[44] and in Germany some state officials were worried about Huguenots spying on fortifications or poisoning wells.[45] Moreover, a pamphlet, *Der Teutsch-Französische Moden-Geist* (The German-French spirit of fashion), depicted the Huguenots by using common stereotypes of the French.[46]

In the long run, however, the image of the Huguenots as being "good" French as well as victims of the French prevailed. Especially in the Age of Enlightenment, the descendants of the late seventeenth-century refugees

styled themselves as bringers of civilization and education. The Enlightenment writers, Jean Pierre Erman and Pierre Chrétien Frédéric Reclam, in their
nine-volume work on the Huguenots in Prussia, expressed their pride in being
of French descent. The high standard of French culture was contrasted to the
backwardness of Brandenburg at the time of Huguenot immigration, and the
improvement of Brandenburg was depicted as mainly the result of Huguenot
settlement.[47] From this a tradition developed that separated the "Frenchness"
of the Huguenots from the French beyond the Rhine.[48]

Huguenots as Manufacturers and Entrepreneurs

One of the most enduring images of the Huguenots in Germany is that the
majority of them were successful entrepreneurs and transmitters of new tech-
nologies and manufactured goods. Whereas the perception of Huguenots as
martyrs of the true faith or as victims of "French tyranny" were aspects of
confessional or proto-national discourses, the expectations of their technological and economic know-how were connected to a mercantilist mode of thought.
Besides simple population politics[49]—*Peuplierung* as it was called in the post-
Thirty Years' War German principalities—many German princes hoped to
strengthen their economies and to gain economic independence by introduc-
ing French methods of manufacturing into their countries. The privileges and
concessions granted to Huguenot immigrants give clear evidence that their
settlement was highly desired by German princes.[50] Some of these edicts
also contained descriptions of the countries designed to attract immigrants.[51]
Moreover, Huguenots were purposefully recruited at Frankfurt, Rotterdam,
or in Switzerland, where they gathered after their flight from France.[52] Obviously, the agents of those princes, who wanted to receive Huguenot settlers,
preferred to recruit manufacturers, merchants or craftsmen with special skills.
Joseph Auguste du Cros, acting as an agent of Margrave Christian Ernest of
Brandenburg-Bayreuth, promised to recruit only such immigrants as were
useful for the country.[53] Similarly, Elector Frederic William of Brandenburg
demanded that only learned immigrants be recruited.[54]

The economic aims are also clear from the privileges themselves. Most of
them very directly addressed the manufacturers, and the wording of many
edicts also underscored this preference.[55] Margrave Christian Ernest even published a declaration explaining his motives of receiving the Huguenots. In this
declaration from 6 December 1686, he argued that as a result of the Thirty
Years' War his territories were largely depopulated and that all his measures to
repopulate them and to stimulate the economy of the country had been fruit-
less. The only hope was to admit strangers to settle and work there.[56] Although
we have to be careful about what to infer from the margrave's intentions from

such public documents, it seems likely that the mercantilist argumentation was thought to be plausible by the prince and his counselors. Only from such hopes and expectations of German rulers to take advantage of the economic and technological knowledge of French Huguenots—together with an idea of society in which different groups are defined by their rights and privileges—can we explain the numerous privileges of the Huguenots and their success in negotiating these concessions.[57]

The high expectations of German princes concerning the Huguenots had their parallel in—and were perhaps enforced by—the self-fashioning of the immigrants themselves. Some of the Huguenot manufacturers were not exactly moderate in praising their own abilities in order to get as far-reaching concessions as possible. Pierre André, Pierre Claparède, and Pierre Valentin, who wanted to build up textile manufacturing in Magdeburg, promoted their ability to operate no less than 110 looms and to employ a suitable number of workers.[58] Jean Poincheval, a dyer planning to settle in Königsberg/Prussia, boasted of his abilities to create colors never seen before in that country. His work, therefore, would be a great gain for the territory.[59] Huguenot manufacturers combined this self-fashioning with high demands: they negotiated credit, free houses and factory buildings, as well as the construction of mills and other facilities. Often, they got what they demanded, and the privileges and concessions not only reveal the hopes of the princes, but also the self-confidence of the Huguenots.[60] Reality, in many cases, did not suit the high expectations, and we have evidence for the frustration and disappointment on the part of the princes and their councils.[61] Surprisingly, the positive image of Huguenot manufacturers remained unstained, especially in historiography. Historians like Charles Ancillon or Jean Pierre Erman and Pierre Chrétien Frédéric Reclam hammered out the image of the Huguenots as skilled craftsmen and innovative manufacturers who contributed so much both to the ascendency of the German economy after the Thirty Years' War and to the rise of Brandenburg-Prussia.[62]

This image, however, was not without controversy. Whereas scholars argue that conflicts between Huguenot immigrants and indigenous craftsmen resulted from the envy of the latter and were therefore a clear indication of their acceptance of Huguenot technical superiority,[63] a closer examination of the sources reveals the ambiguity of attitudes. In fact, native craftsmen often doubted the qualification of their Huguenot colleagues. One reason for the suspicions was that Huguenot craftsmen were unable to produce evidence of their training, because they had lost their certificates during their flight from France.[64] But qualification, in the understanding of the craft guilds, was more than just training. Qualification was defined by a certain code of honor as well as by certain rites and customs, as for example to take the road as a journeyman. Having no evidence of apprenticeship according to the customs of the guilds, Huguenots were not accepted by German craftsmen as their equals. Often the natives complained about Huguenot craftsmen who established their own workshops as masters without entering the guild and without producing proof of qualification.[65] Perhaps it was the bad image of the craft guilds in the eighteenth and nineteenth centuries as backward and leaden institutions that helped to shape the contrasting ideas of the Huguenots as innovators.[66]

Huguenots as Loyal Subjects and "Best Germans"

When Elector Frederic William of Brandenburg-Prussia died in April 1688, the French Reformed community in Berlin held their own funeral service, and François Gaultier de Saint-Blancard, the preacher of the French Reformed Church, gave a funeral sermon that was printed afterwards.[67] The sermon was not only a panegyric on the deceased elector, but it was also an assurance of the loyalty and faithfulness of the Huguenots in Brandenburg to the house of Hohenzollern. Two years later, in 1690, Charles Ancillon, judge of the French colony in Berlin, published a small book on the history of the settlement of the Huguenots in the electoral territories.[68] Ancillon's work is, first, a plaudit for the elector who had rescued the refugees out of their distress and calamity, describing him as one who had displayed true Christian charity and tolera-tion.[69] However, Ancillon did more than this: he praised the Huguenot immi-grants for their industry and reassured the elector of Brandenburg of their loyalty.[70] After characterizing the happy situation of all sorts of refugees—from scholars and soldiers to artisans and merchants—Ancillon appealed to their thankfulness. Every refugee should be obliged to venerate the elector; the very name of "this hero" had to live on in the heart of every member of the Reformed communities.[71]

This idea of the loyalty of the Huguenots to their German hosts remained an important part of later stories. Erman and Reclam in the eighteenth as well as Henri Tollin in the nineteenth century depicted Huguenots not only as loyal subjects of the Hohenzollern dynasty and other princely houses, but also as some kind of élite within German society. Erman and Reclam wrote, it was the intention of their work "de conserver dans nos Colonies cet esprit, qui a toujours si bien secondé les vues du Gouvernement; en leur rappelant les bienfaits de leurs Souverains, nous cherchons à animer le sentiment du patriotisme par celui de la reconnaissance" (to preserve in our colonies that spirit, which has always well promoted the view of the government; by remind-ing them of the beneficence of their sovereigns, we seek to animate their spirit of patriotism with that of thankfulness)." And in his foundation manifest for a *Hugenottenbund* (Huguenot league), Henri Tollin stated that the Huguenots were "Deutsch durch und durch" (German to the core), and he went on, "königstreu aus innerster Seele, leben sie heute durch Deutschland zerstreut" (royalist from innermost soul, they live scattered through Germany).[72] They praised Huguenot patriotism, meaning a German patriotism, and Bismarck even called them "the best Germans," connecting the virtues of the Huguenots with those of the Germans.[73] Even during the Third Reich, the Huguenots were seen by some ideologists as descendants of the "Germanic" parts of the French people.[74] These are late phenomena, and as such they are part of another interesting story. However, they have their origin in the early histories of the Huguenot migration, for the most part written by the progeny of the immigrants themselves. It was the result of a process of defining and redefining identities within changing political situations and under differing circumstances.

The case of the Huguenots is a good example of the varieties of images created during times of persecution and migration. These images served several different interests: the interest of the Protestant churches in Germany and their efforts to define their own identities against the Catholic threat, the political interest of a broad alliance against France in the late seventeenth and early eighteenth centuries, as well as the interest of the Huguenots and their supporters to market themselves as attractive immigrants for German principalities. These strategies, however, were the cornerstone of a tradition of Huguenot history that had impact well into the twentieth century. In this tradition Huguenots, as well as the Salzburgers, were depicted as exemplarily pious, industrious, and loyal to authority. The works of eighteenth- and nineteenth-century historians enforced this image and transferred it into popular knowledge. Even today, the *Hugenottengesellschaft* (Huguenot society) and local societies are keen to preserve at least parts of the Huguenot image and defend it against any attempt to undermine it.

Ulrich Niggeman is director of the Institute of European Cultural History at the University of Augsburg. He received his doctorate at the University of Marburg in 2007. In 2015, he finished his habilitation at the University of Marburg. Niggemann is author of *Immigrationspolitik zwischen Konflikt und Konsens: Die Hugenottenansiedlung in Deutschland und England 1681–1697* (2008), *Hugenotten* (2011), *Revolutionserinnerung in der Frühen Neuzeit: Refigurationen der Glorious Revolution in Großbritannien (1688–1760)* (2017), and coeditor of *Antike als Modell in Nordamerika? Konstruktion und Verargumentierung 1763–1803* (2011) and *Sicherheit in der Frühen Neuzeit: Norm – Praxis – Repräsentation* (2013).

Notes

1. Heinz Schilling, *Niederländische Exulanten im 16. Jahrhundert: Ihre Stellung im Sozial-gefüge und im religiösen Leben deutscher und englischer Städte* (Schriften des Vereins für Reformationsgeschichte vol. 187. Gütersloh, 1972); Dagmar Freist, "Dutch Calvinist Refugees in Europe since the Early Modern Period," in *The Encyclopedia of Migration and Minorities in Europe: From the 17th Century to the Present*, ed. Klaus J. Bade et al. (Cambridge, 2011), 320f.

2. Geert Janssen, "Quo Vadis? Catholic Perceptions of Flight and the Revolt of the Low Countries, 1566–1609," *Renaissance Quarterly* 64 (2011): 472–99; Raingard Esser, "Rückkehr oder Unterwanderung? Niederländische Remigranten im Schatten des Achtzigjährigen Krieges," in *Sicherheit in der Frühen Neuzeit. Norm—Praxis—Repräsentation*, ed. Christoph Kampmann and Ulrich Niggemann (Frühneuzeit-Impuse vol. 2. Cologne, 2013).

3. Theo Kiefner, *Die Privilegien der nach Deutschland gekommenen Waldenser*, 2 vols. (Stuttgart, 1990); Matthias Asche, "Hugenotten und Waldenser im frühmodernen deutschen Territorialstaat zwischen korporativer Autonomie und obrigkeitlicher Aufsicht," in *Selbstverwaltung in der Geschichte Europas in Mittelalter und Neuzeit*, ed. Helmut Neuhaus, (Der Staat Beihefte, vol. 19; Berlin, 2010), 63–94.

4. Alexander Schunka, *Gäste, die bleiben: Zuwanderer in Kursachsen und der Oberlausitz im 17. und frühen 18. Jahrhundert* (Pluralisierung & Autorität, vol. 7; Hamburg, 2006). For the emigration from the Habsburg territories in general, for example, Arno Herzig, *Der Zwang zum wahren Glauben: Rekatholisierung vom 16. bis zum 18. Jahrhundert* (Göttingen, 2000); and the contributions to Rudolf Leeb, Martin Scheutz, Dietmar Weikl, eds., *Geheimprotestantismus und evangelische Kirchen in der Habsburgermonarchie und im Erzstift Salzburg (17./18. Jahrhundert)* (Veröffentlichungen des Instituts für Österreichische Geschichtsforschung vol. 51; Vienna and Munich, 2009).

5. Joachim Bahlcke, "'Die jüngste Glaubenscolonie in Preußen': Kirchliche Praxis und religiöse Alltagserfahrung der Zillertaler in Schlesien," in *Migration und kirchliche Praxis: Das religiöse Leben frühneuzeitlicher Glaubensflüchtlinge in alltagsgeschichtlicher Perspektive*, ed. Joachim Bahlcke and Rainer Bendel (Forschungen und Quellen zur Kirchen- und Kulturgeschichte Ostdeutschlands vol. 40; Cologne, Weimar, Vienna, 2008), 181–202.

6. Mack Walker, *The Salzburg Transaction: Expulsion and Redemption in Eighteenth-Century Germany* (Ithaca, NY, 1992); Gabriele Emrich, *Die Emigration der Salzburger Protestanten 1731–1732: Reichsrechtliche und konfessionspolitische Aspekte* (Historia profana et ecclesiastica vol. 7: Münster, 2002); Rudolf Leeb, "Die große Salzburger Emigration von 1731/32 und ihre Vorgeschichte (Ausweisung der Deferegger 1684)," in *Glaubensflüchtlinge: Ursachen, Formen und Auswirkungen frühneuzeitlicher Konfessionsmigration in Europa*, ed. Joachim Bahlcke (Religions- und Kulturgeschichte in Ostmittel- und Südosteuropa vol. 4; Berlin, 2008), 277–305.

7. For these early migrations, see Mack P. Holt, *The French Wars of Religion, 1562–1629*, 2nd ed. (Cambridge, 2005), 96; Myriam Yardeni, *Le Refuge protestant* (Paris, 1985), 15–17, 22–30; Matthias Asche, "Huguenots in Europe since the 16th Century," in *Encyclopedia of Migration*, ed. Bade et al., 476f.

8. There is an immense amount of research on the Huguenots in Germany; even smaller communities have found their historians. From the mass of studies compare Franz-

Anton Kadell, *Die Hugenotten in Hessen-Kassel* (Quellen und Forschungen zur hessischen Geschichte vol. 40; Darmstadt, 1980); Matthias Asche, *Neusiedler im verheerten Land: Kriegsfolgenbewältigung, Migrationssteuerung und Konfessionspolitik im Zeichen des Landeswiederaufbaus. Die Mark Brandenburg nach den Kriegen des 17. Jahrhunderts* (Münster, 2006); Ulrich Niggemann, *Immigrationspolitik zwischen Konflikt und Konsens: Die Hugenottenansiedlung in Deutschland und England (1681–1697)* (Norm und Struktur vol. 33; Cologne, Weimar, Vienna, 2008); Susanne Lachenicht, *Hugenotten in Europa und Nordamerika: Migration und Integration in der Frühen Neuzeit* (Frankfurt am Main, 2010); and generally Yardeni, *Refuge*; Barbara Dölemeyer, *Die Hugenotten* (Stuttgart, 2006); Ulrich Niggemann, *Hugenotten* (Cologne, Weimar, Vienna, 2011).

9. Compare, for example, Angelika Marsch, *Die Salzburger Emigration in Bildern* (Weissenhorn, 1977); Ulrich Niggemann, "Die Hugenottenverfolgung in der zeitgenössischen deutschen Publizistik (1681–1690)," *Francia* 32, no. 2 (2005): 59–108.

10. Niggemann, *Immigrationspolitik*, passim.

11. Marsch, *Salzburger Emigration*; Walker, *Salzburg Transaction*, 192–205.

12. For the concept of "self-fashioning," see Stephen Greenblatt, *Renaissance Self-Fashioning. From More to Shakespeare* (Chicago, 1984).

13. Frederik R.J. Knetsch, *Pierre Jurieu: Theoloog en politikus der Refuge* (Kampen, 1967); Pierre Jurieu, *Lettres pastorales adressées aux fidèles de France qui gémissent sous la captivité de Babylon*, ed. Robin Howells (Hildesheim, 1988).

14. [Pierre Jurieu] *Les Soupirs de la France esclave, Qui aspire après la Liberté* (Amsterdam, 1690); [Jurieu] *The Sighs of France in Slavery, Breathing after Liberty: By Way of Memorial. Done out of French* (London, 1689) [Wing / L1796]; [Jurieu] *De suchtingen van het slaefachtigh Vrankryk, wenschende naer desselfs vryheyt* (The Hague, 1689); [Jurieu] *Gründlicher Bericht / Von dem jetzigen jämmerlichen Zustand Der Cron Franckreich: Worauß umbständlich zu vernehmen / Wie der jetzige König Ludwig der XIV. . . . Das gantze Volck in eine solche Sclaverey und Dienstbarkeit gesetzt / daß das gantze Land darüber säuffzen und lamentiren muß* (s.l., 1689) [VD17 12:187865M].

15. For example, Jean Claude, *Les Plaintes des Protestants cruellement opprimez dans le royaume de France* (Cologne, 1686); Claude, *An Account of the Persecutions and Oppressions of the French Protestants to which is added, the Edict of the French King, Prohibiting all Publick Exercise of the pretended Reformed Religion in his Kingdom* (London, 1686) [Wing / C4589A]; compare Bernard Cottret, *The Huguenots in England: Immigration and Settlement c. 1550–1700* (Cambridge, 1991), 188f.

16. Heinz Schilling, "Peregrini und Schiffchen Gottes: Flüchtlingserfahrung und Exulantentheologie des frühneuzeitlichen Calvinismus," in *Calvinismus: Die Reformierten in Deutschland und Europa*, ed. Ansgar Reiss and Sabine Witt (Dresden, 2009), 160–68.

17. For example, *Außführliches doch Unvorgreifliches Bedencken über gegenwertige der Reformirten in Franckreich Glaubens- und Gewissens-Rüge* (Gera, 1686) [Wolfenbüttel, Herzog August Bibliothek Tq 90], 149–53.

18. *Spiegel der Frantzösischen Tyranney. Das ist: Ausführlich-Umständliche Erzehlung der unmenschlichen Grausamkeit / Welche die Französische Nation wider die so genannte Reformirte . . . verübet* (s.l., 1686) [Bonn, Universitäts- und Landesbibliothek Gg 245], 65, 71, 73, 83f., 86f., 91, 95, 99–102, 108f., 116, 135; *Hertzliche Bekummernus umb den Schaden Josephs: Bezeuget in etlichen Bedencken ueber die grausame bishero unerhoerte Verfolgung Der Evangelisch-Reformirten Kirche in Franckreich* (s.l., 1686)

[Bonn, Universitäts- und Landesbibliothek Gg 245], 79f.; Johann F. Mayer, *Beweglices Seufftzen Derer aus Franckreich geflüchteten Reformirten, Nach der Lutherischen Religions-Vereinigung* (Wittenberg, 1686) [Wolfenbüttel, Herzog August Bibliothek QuN 946 (19)], 77–79. Cf. Niggemann, "Hugenottenverfolgung," 79.

19. *Eines der Schreiben welches die Protestirende in Franckreich Bey Verlassung aller Haab An andre Protestirend- und Evangelische abgehen lassen* (s.l., 1686) [Halle, Universitäts- und Landesbibliothek AB 154365 (10)], unpag.; *Grosser Ludewig, Herr und Beherrscher der Frantzosen, siehe zu, daß von der Hugenotten Fall dein Franckreich nicht erzittere* (Frankfurt and Leipzig, 1686) [Wolfenbüttel, Herzog August Bibliothek Gv 1 Mischbd. (4)], 33, 68; *Spiegel der Frantzösischen Tyranney*, 97f., 101, 114, 121. Cf. Niggemann, "Hugenottenverfolgung," 79.

20. "Haben sie den HERRN verfolget / so werden ja die Knecht keine bessere Bequemlichkeit erwarten"; *Eines der Schreiben*, unpag. For this line of argument cf. Niggemann, "Hugenottenverfolgung," 78–80.

21. "Zumahlen wir durch viel Trübsal in das Reich Gottes eingehen müssen"; *Eines der Schreiben*, unpag.

22. Niggemann, "Hugenottenverfolgung," 78f.; Philippe Joutard, "1685—Ende und neue Chance für den französischen Protestantismus," in *Die Hugenotten, 1685–1985*, ed. Rudolf von Thadden and Michelle Magdalaine (Munich, 1985), 14.

23. *Eines der Schreiben*, unpag.; *Grosser Ludewig*, 46, 85; Mayer, *Bewegliches Seufftzen*, 80; *Hertzliche Bekummernus*, 0, 1f., 55, 63f., 75; *Unvorgreifliches Bedencken*, 54, 81. Cf. Niggemann, "Hugenottenverfolgung," 76f.

24. *Hertzliche Bekummernus*, 169f.; *Eines der Schreiben*, unpag.; *Unvorgreifliches Bedencken*, 139, 153.

25. Jean Crespin, *Le Livre des Martyrs, qui est vn Recveil de plusieurs Martyrs qui ont enduré la mort pour le Nom de nostre Seigneur Iesus Christ, depuis Iean Hus iusques à ceste année presente M.D.LIIII* ([Geneva] 1554). Cf. Jean-François Gilmont, *Jean Crespin: Un éditeur réformé du XVIe siècle* (Travaux d'humanisme et renaissance vol. 186; Geneva, 1981), 165–90.

26. Crespin, *Livre des Martyrs*, fo. *.ii.

27. Compare Niggemann, *Immigrationspolitik*, 82f.

28. Compare Henri Tollin and Richard Béringuier, *Die französische Colonie in Berlin* (Geschichtsblätter des Deutschen Hugenotten-Vereins vol. I.4. Magdeburg 1891), 16; Niggemann, "Hugenottenverfolgung," 71n65.

29. For example, Prudhomme to Elector Frederic William, Cologne on Spree, 14 October 1685, Geheimes Staatsarchiv Preußischer Kulturbesitz Rep. 9 Allg. Verwaltung D8 Fasz. 2, fo. 17–18; Spanheim to Danckelmann, Berlin, 29 June 1689, Geheimes Staatsarchiv Preußischer Kulturbesitz VI. HA Nl. Spanheim Nr. 4, fo. 2–3'; French settlers to Margrave Christian Ernest, Bayreuth, 21 January 1699, Staatsarchiv Bamberg C60 Nr. 5970, fo. 34–34a.

30. Compare Alexander Schunka, "Pragmatisierung konfessioneller Autorität. Zuwanderer im Kursachsen des 17. Jahrhunderts im Spiegel des Supplikenwesens," in *Glaubensflüchtlinge*, 235–56; Schunka, "Glaubensflucht als Migrationsoption. Konfessionell motivierte Migrationen in der Frühen Neuzeit," *Geschichte in Wissenschaft und Unterricht* 56 (2005): 552, 559f.

31. ". . . die harten Verfolgungen und rigoureusen procedure, womit man eine zeithero im dem Königreich Franckreich wider Unsere Evangelisch-Reformirten Religion zu gethane Glaubens-Genossen verfahren." Edict of Potsdam by Elector Frederic Wil-

liam, 29 October 1685, in *Das Recht der französisch-reformierten Kirche in Preußen: Urkundliche Denkschrift*, ed. Ernst Mengin (Berlin, 1929), 186.

32. Ibid.
33. Order by Landgrave Charles of Hessen-Kassel, 30 November 1685, Hessisches Staatsarchiv Marburg Best. 5 no. 9690, fo. 30–30'; order by Elector Frederic William of Brandenburg-Prussia, Cologne on Spree, 1 October 1685, Geheimes Staatsarchiv Preußischer Kulturbesitz, Berlin, I. HA Rep. 122 6a no. 1 vol. 1, fo. 8. Cf. for the issue of the collections, Niggemann, *Immigrationspolitik*, 118–46.
34. For the political situation compare Klaus Malettke, *Hegemonie, multipolares System, Gleichgewicht. Internationale Beziehungen 1648/1659—1713/1714* (Handbuch der Geschichte der internationalen Politik vol. 3. Paderborn, 2012), 343–407, 419–447; and for sentiments as expressed in pamphlets Jean Schillinger, *Les pamphlétaires allemandes et la France de Louis XIV* (Contacts, série 2: Gallo-Germanica vol. 27; Bern, 1999), 69–73; Franz Bosbach, "Der französische Erbfeind: Zu einem deutschen Feindbild im Zeitalter Ludwigs XIV," in *Feindbilder: Die Darstellung des Gegners in der politischen Publizistik des Mittelalters und der Neuzeit*, ed. Bosbach (Bayreuther Historische Kolloquien vol. 6; Cologne, 1992), 127f., 134–36.
35. *Spiegel der Frantzösischen Tyranney.*
36. *Franckreich / Die neuen Conjunkturen Werden dir den Compass gewaltig verrükken / Benebenst vielen remarqvablen Begebenheiten* (Leipzig, 1686) [Wolfenbüttel, Herzog August Bibliothek Gk 2142 (6)], 121. Similarly *Franckreich Uber Alles / wenn es nur könnte / Worinnen Die merckwürdigsten Französischen Staats- und Kriegs-Begebenheiten / . . . unpartheyisch beschrieben und angemercket werden* (Leipzig, 1686) [Wolfenbüttel, Herzog August Bibliothek Gk 2142 (7)], 226. Compare also Hubert Gillot, *Le règne de Louis XIV et l'opinion publique en Allemagne* (Nancy, 1914), 46f.
37. Sincerus Catholicus, *Entdeckungen Der listigen Kunst-Stücke Womit Die Frantzosen die Catholische und Protestirende Stände an einander zu hetzen gedencken* (s.l., 1689) [Stuttgart, Württembergische Landesbibliothek Franz G ql.k.196], unpag.
38. *Discours Von den Religions-Kriegen ins gemein / Und in specie, Ob auch der jetzige einer seye oder nicht? Occasione Verschiedener in solcher Materia im Truck außgegangener Schrifften . . .* (Freystadt (fake), 1689) [VD17 12:205189K].
39. A doctoral thesis on this topic by Christian Mühling (Marburg) is in preparation.
40. *Spiegel der Frantzösischen Tyranney*, 3f., 92, 96, 134.
41. Ibid., 94, 106 [that is, 126].
42. "Ihr könnet gar leicht aus dieser armen Leute Exempel euch gleichsam die Rechnung machen / was ihr künfftiger Zeit auch zu gewarten habet"; *Grosser Ludewig*, 92f. *Waagschale der Frantzosen / Oder Das auff die Schaubühne gestellte Franckreich* (s.l., 1689) [Wolfenbüttel, Herzog August Bibliothek 127 QuN (21)], 47 [that is, 59].
43. Compare Niggemann, "Hugenottenverfolgung," 101–3; David Onnekink and Gijs Rommelse, eds., *Ideology and Foreign Policy in Early Modern Europe (1650–1750)* (Politics and Culture in Europe, 1650–1750; Aldershot, 2011).
44. Daniel Statt, *Foreigners and Englishmen: The Controversy over Immigration and Population, 1660–1760* (Newark, 1995), 171; Cottret, *Huguenots*, 191–95; Niggemann, *Immigrationspolitik*, 467–69.
45. Kadell, *Hugenotten*, 668; Niggemann, *Immigrationspolitik*, 348.
46. *Der Teutsch-Französische Moden-Geist: Wer es lieset der verstehets* (Geyersbergk [fake], 1689) [Halle, Universitäts- und Landesbibliothek AB 155745(16)].

47. Jean P. Erman and Pierre C.F. Reclam, *Mémoires pour servir à l'histoire des Réfugiés françois dans les Etats du Roi*, 9 vols. (Berlin, 1782–99), e.g., 1:170–77, 302–4. Cf. Viviane Rosen-Prest, *L'historiographie des Huguenots en Prusse au temps des Lumières. Entre mémoire, histoire et légende: J.P. Erman et P.C.F. Reclam, Mémoires pour servir à l'histoire des Réfugiés françois dans les Etats du Roi (1782–1799)* (Vie des Huguenots vol. 23; Paris 2002), 266–68, 352f.

48. Compare Rudolf von Thadden, "Vom Glaubensflüchtling zum preußischen Patrioten," in von Thadden and Magdelaine, *Hugenotten*, 192f.

49. For the development of population politics, see Justus Nipperdey, *Die Erfindung der Bevölkerungspolitik: Staat, politische Theorie und Population in der Frühen Neuzeit* (Veröffentlichungen des Instituts für Europäische Geschichte Mainz. Abteilung für Universalgeschichte vol. 229; Göttingen, 2012).

50. Examples of such edicts granting privileges are printed by Dieter Mempel, ed., *Gewissensfreiheit und Wirtschaftspolitik: Hugenotten- und Waldenserprivilegien 1681–1699* (Wissenschaftlich-didaktische Arbeitshefte zur Geschichte des Mittelalters und der Neuzeit vol. 3; Trier, 1986). Compare also Dölemeyer, *Hugenotten*, 40–49; Ulrich Niggemann, "Hugenotten als wirtschaftliche Elite: Wahrnehmung und Selbstwahrnehmung in den immigrationspolitischen Auseinandersetzungen in Deutschland und England, 1680–1700," in *Religiöse und konfessionelle Minderheiten als wirtschaftliche und geistige Eliten (16. bis frühes 20. Jahrhundert). Büdinger Forschungen zur Sozialgeschichte 2006 und 2007*, ed. Markus A. Denzel, Matthias Asche, Matthias Stickler (Deutsche Führungsschichten in der Neuzeit vol. 28; St. Katharinen, 2009), 207f.

51. For example, "Concessions & privilèges" by Landgrave Charles of Hessen-Kassel, Kassel, 12 December 1685, printed by Mempel, *Gewissensfreiheit*, 55f.

52. Dölemeyer, *Hugenotten*, 37f.; and Michelle Magdelaine, "Frankfurt am Main: Drehscheibe des Refuge," in *Hugenotten*, ed. von Thadden and Magdelaine, 26–37.

53. Compare Andreas Jakob, *Die Neustadt Erlangen: Planung und Entstehung* (Erlanger Bausteine zur Fränkischen Heimatforschung, special vol. 33. Erlangen 1986), 237–40; Michael Peters, "Joseph Auguste du Cros als Agent des Markgrafen Christian Ernst von Brandenburg-Bayreuth: Ein Beitrag zur Vorgeschichte der Hugenotten-Kolonisation in Franken," *Erlanger Bausteine zur fränkischen Heimatforschung* 34 (1986): 168f.; Niggemann, "Hugenotten als wirtschaftliche Elite," 208f.

54. Compare Ingrid Mittenzwei, "Die Hugenotten in der gewerblichen Wirtschaft Brandenburg-Preußens," in *Hugenotten in Brandenburg-Preußen*, ed. Mittenzwei (Berlin, 1987), 115f.

55. For example, "Freyheits-Conceßion und Begnadigung für die fremden Manufacturiers," Kassel, 18 April 1685, printed by Mempel, *Gewissensfreiheit*, 47–51. Cf. also Walter Mogk, "Voraussetzungen für die Einwanderung von Hugenotten und Waldensern nach Hessen-Kassel," in *Die Hugenotten und Waldenser in Hessen-Kassel*, ed. Jochen Desel and Walter Mogk (Monographia Hassiae vol. 5; Kassel, 1978), 26; Peter Landgrebe, *Minoritätengruppe und wirtschaftliche Bedeutung: Zum Einfluß der Hugenotten auf die deutsche Wirtschaftsentwicklung* (Geschichtsblätter des Deutchen Hugenotten-Vereins e.V. vol. 17.7/10. Sickte 1977), 138–40; Barbara Dölemeyer, "Ökonomie und Toleranz: Wirtschaftliche Ziele, Mittel und Ergebnisse der Hugenottenaufnahme in europäischen Ländern," in *Wirtschaft und Wirtschaftstheorien in Rechtsgeschichte und Philosophie: Viertes deutsch-französisches Symposium vom 2–4. Mai in Wetzlar*, ed. Jean-François Kervégan and Heinz Mohnhaupt (Studien zur europäischen Rechtsgeschichte vol. 176; Frankfurt am Main, 2004), 79f.

56. Printed declaration by Margrave Christian Ernest, Bayreuth, 6 December 1686, Staatsarchiv Bamberg, Geheimes Archiv Bayreuth Nr. 5568, fo. 566–567'. Compare Niggemann, *Immigrationspolitik*, 78f.

57. For the negotiations between the Huguenots and the German princes compare Niggemann, *Immigrationspolitik*, 80–100; Barbara Dölemeyer, "'Tractat' oder 'Begnadigung'? Vertragselemente in Exulantenprivilegien," in *Gesellschaftliche Freiheit und vertragliche Bindung in Rechtsgeschichte und Philosophie: Zweites deutsch-französisches Symposium vom 12. bis 15. März 1997 in der Herzog August Bibliothek Wolfenbüttel*, ed. Jean-François Kervégan and Heinz Mohnhaupt (Ius Commune—Sonderhefte vol. 120. Frankfurt am Main 1999), 143–64.

58. Henri Tollin, *Geschichte der Französischen Colonie zu Magdeburg*, 6 vols. (Halle on Saale, 1886–1892), 2:416.

59. Jean Poincheval to Elector Frederic William, undated, but most certainly August or September 1686, Geheimes Staatsarchiv Preußischer Kulturbesitz, Berlin, I. HA Rep. 122 17b Nr. 1 vol. I, unpag. Compare Niggemann, "Hugenotten als wirtschaftliche Elite," 212.

60. Cf. Niggemann, "Hugenotten als wirtschaftliche Elite," 212f.

61. For examples, see Niggemann, "Hugenotten als wirtschaftliche Elite," 213–15; Niggemann, *Immigrationspolitik*, 304–6, 317–20.

62. Ancillon, *Geschichte*, 51–64; Erman and Reclam, *Mémoires*, vols. 5–6. Compare Rosen-Prest, *Historiographie*, 351–417.

63. Compare, for example, Yardeni, *Refuge*, 129.

64. See Tollin, *Geschichte*, vol. 3.1a, 27f.

65. Helga Schultz, *Das ehrbare Handwerk: Zunftleben im alten Berlin zur Zeit des Absolutismus* (Weimar, 1993), 44–50; Rudolf Wissell, *Des alten Handwerks Recht und Gewohnheit*, 6 vols. (Berlin 1971–88), 1:145–273; Niggemann, "Craft Guilds and Immigration: Huguenots in German and English Cities," in *Gated Communities? Regulating Migration in Early Modern Cities*, ed. Bert de Munck and Anne Winter (Farnham, 2012), 56.

66. Tollin, *Geschichte*, 1:408 and 425.

67. François Gaultier de Saint-Blancard, *Sermon sur la Mort de Tres-Haut & Tres-Puissant Prince, Monseigneur Frideric Guillaume, Marggrave de Brandebourg, Electeur, & Archichambellan du Saint Empire, &c. Arrivée le Dimanche 29. Avril 1688. Prononcé à Berlin, dans l'Eglise du Dôme, le Dimanche suivant 6. de Mai* (Berlin, 1688) [VD17 23:666212Y].

68. Charles Ancillon, *Histoire de l'établissement des François refugiez dans les Etats de S. Altesse Electorale de Brandebourg* (Berlin, 1690). For the present study, I only had access to the German translation: *Ancillon, Geschichte der Niederlassung der Réfugiés in den Staaten Seiner Kurfürstlichen Hoheit von Brandenburg* (Geschichtsblätter des Deutschen Hugenotten-Vereins e.V. vol. 15, 8. Berlin, 1939).

69. Ancillon, *Geschichte*, 9–11, 16–20 and *passim*. Compare Viviane Rosen-Prest, "Willkommene Fremde? Zwei Jahrhunderte Geschichtsschreibung über Hugenotten im deutschen Refuge (17–19. Jahrhundert)," in *Die Begegnung mit Fremden und das Geschichtsbewusstsein*, ed. Judith Becker and Bettina Braun (Veröffentlichungen des Instituts für Europäische Geschichte Main vol. 88. Göttingen, 2012), 139–41.

70. For example, he praised the loyalty and courage of the Huguenot soldiers; Ancillon, *Geschichte*, 42–50.

71. "Alle aber sind gleicherweise verpflichtet, dem Kurfürsten zu danken und ihn zu verehren. Der Name dieses Helden muß ewig in den Herzen aller Reformierten fortleben;" Ancillon, *Geschichte*, 74.
72. Erman and Reclam, *Mémoires*, vol. 5, unpag. preface.; Tollin quoted from Friedrich Centurier, "Die Hugenotten-Nachkommen und der Deutsche Hugenotten-Verein," in von Thadden and Magdelaine, *Hugenotten*, 215f. Cf. Ursula Fuhrich-Grubert, "Zwischen Patriotismus und Internationalismus. Hugenotten im 19. und 20. Jahrhundert," in *Zuwanderungsland Deutschland: Die Hugenotten*, ed. Sabine Beneke and Hans Ottomeyer (Berlin, 2005), 163–72.
73. Etienne François, "Vom preußischen Patrioten zum besten Deutschen," in *Hugenotten*, ed. von Thadden and Magdelaine, 205; François, "Die Traditions- und Legendenbildung des deutschen Refuge," in *Der Exodus der Hugenotten: Die Aufhebung des Edikts von Nantes 1685 als europäisches Ereignis* (Archiv für Kulturgeschichte, Beihefte vol. 24; Cologne and Vienna 1985), 188; Rudolf von Thadden, "Hugenotten und Hugenottengedenken 1685–1985," in *Wege und Grenzen der Toleranz. Edikt von Potsdam 1685–1985* ed. Manfred Stolpe and Friedrich Winter (Berlin, 1987), 17.
74. Compare Ursula Fuhrich-Grubert, *Hugenotten unterm Hakenkreuz: Studien zur Geschichte der Französischen Kirche zu Berlin 1933–1945* (Veröffentlichungen der Historischen Kommission zu Berlin vol. 85. Berlin and New York, 1994), 420–70.

Bibliography

Ancillon, Charles. *Histoire de l'établissement des François refugiez dans les Etats de S. Altesse Electorale de Brandebourg.* Berlin, 1690.

———. *Geschichte der Niederlassung der Réfugiés in den Staaten Seiner Kurfürstlichen Hoheit von Brandenburg.* Berlin, 1939.

Anonymous. *Außführliches doch Unvorgreifliches Bedencken über gegenwertige der Reformirten in Franckreich Glaubens- und Gewissens-Rüge.* Gera, 1686.

———. *Discours Von den Religions-Kriegen ins gemein / Und in specie, Ob auch der jetzige einer seye oder nicht? Occasione Verschiedener in solcher Materia im Truck außgegangener Schrifften (. . .). . . . Freystadt* (fake), 1689.

———. *Eines der Schreiben welches die Protestirende in Franckreich Bey Verlassung aller Haab An andre Protestirend- und Evangelische abgehen lassen.* s.l., 1686.

———. *Franckreich / Die neuen Conjunkturen Werden dir den Compass gewaltig verrücken / Benebenst vielen remarqvablen Begebenheiten.* Leipzig, 1686.

———. *Franckreich Uber Alles / wenn es nur könnte / Worinnen Die merckwürdigsten Frantzösischen Staats- und Kriegs-Begebenheiten / . . . unpartheyisch beschrieben und angemercket warden.* Leipzig, 1686.

———. *Grosser Ludewig, Herr und Beherrscher der Frantzosen, siehe zu, daß von der Hugenotten Fall dein Franckreich nicht erzittere.* Frankfurt and Leipzig, 1686.

———. *Hertzliche Bekummernus umb den Schaden Josephs: Bezeuget in etlichen Bedencken ueber die grausame bishero unerhoerte Verfolgung Der Evangelisch-Reformirten Kirche in Franckreich.* s.l., 1686.

———. *Spiegel der Frantzösischen Tyranney. Das ist: Ausführlich-Umständliche Erzehlung der unmenschlichen Grausamkeit / Welche die Französische Nation wider die so genannte Reformirte . . . verübet.* Bonn, 1686.

———. *Der Teutsch-Französische Moden-Geist: Wer es lieset der verstehets.* Geyersbergk [fake], 1689.

———. *Waagschale der Frantzosen / Oder Das auff die Schaubühne gestellte Franckreich.* s.l., 1689.

Asche, Mattias. "Huguenotten und Waldenser im frühmodernen deutschen Territorialstaat zwischen korporativer Autonomie und obrigkeitlicher Aufsicht." In *Selbstverwaltung in der Geschichte Europas in Mittelalter und Neuzeit*, ed. Helmut Neuhaus. Der Staat. Beihefte, vol. 19. Berlin, 2010.

———. "Huguenots in Europe since the 16th Century." In *The Encyclopedia of Migration and Minorities in Europe: From the 17th Century to the Present*, ed. Klaus Bade et al. Cambridge, 2011.

———. *Neusiedler im verheerten Land. Kriegsfolgenbewältigung, Migrationssteuerung und Konfessionspolitik im Zeichen des Landeswiederaufbaus. Die Mark Brandenburg nach den Kriegen des 17. Jahrhunderts.* Münster, 2006.

Bahlcke, Joachim. "'Die jüngste Glaubenscolonie in Preußen': Kirchliche Praxis und religiöse Alltagserfahrung der Zillertaler in Schlesien." In *Migration und kirchliche Praxis: Das religiöse Leben frühneuzeitlicher Glaubensflüchtlinge in alltagsgeschichtlicher Perspektive*, ed. Joachim Bahlcke and Rainer Bendel. Cologne, Weimar, Vienna, 2008.

Bahlcke, Joachim, ed. *Glaubensflüchtlinge: Ursachen, Formen und Auswirkungen frühneuzeitlicher Konfessionsmigration in Europa.* Berlin, 2008.

Bosbach, Franz. "Der französische Erbfeind. Zu einem deutschen Feindbild im Zeitalter Ludwigs XIV." In *Feindbilder: Die Darstellung des Gegners in der politischen Publizistik des Mittelalters und der Neuzeit*, ed. Franz Bosbach. Cologne, 1992.

Claude, Jean. *An Account of the Persecutions and Oppressions of the French Protestants to which is added, the Edict of the French King, Prohibiting all Publick Exercise of the pretended Reformed Religion in his Kingdom.* London, 1686.

———. *Les Plaintes des Protestants cruellement opprimez dans le royaume de France.* Cologne, 1686.

Centurier, Friedrich. "Die Hugenotten-Nachkommen und der Deutsche Hugenotten-Verein." In *Die Hugenotten, 1685–1985*, ed. Rudolf von Thadden and Michelle Magdelaine. Munich, 1985.

Crespin, Jean. *Le Livre des Martyrs, qui est vn Recveil de plusieurs Martyrs qui ont enduré la mort pour le Nom de nostre Seigneur Iesus Christ, depuis Iean Hus iusques à ceste année presente M.D.LIIII.* Geneva, 1554.

Dölemeyer, Barbara. *Die Hugenotten.* Stuttgart, 2006.

———. "Ökonomie und Toleranz: Wirtschaftliche Ziele, Mittel und Ergebnisse der Hugenottenaufnahme in europäischen Ländern." In *Wirtschaft und Wirtschaftstheorien in Rechtsgeschichte und Philosophie. Viertes deutsch-französisches Symposium vom 2–4. Mai in Wetzlar*, ed. Jean-François Kervégan and Heinz Mohnhaupt. Main, 2004.

Dölemeyer, Barbara. "'Tractat' oder 'Begnadigung'? Vertragselemente in Exulanten-privilegien." In *Gesellschaftliche Freiheit und vertragliche Bindung in Rechtsgeschichte und Philosophie. Zweites deutsch-französisches Symposium vom 12. bis 15. März 1997 in der Herzog August Bibliothek Wolfenbüttel*, ed. Jean-François Kervégan and Heinz Mohnhaupt. Frankfurt am Main, 1999.

Elector Frederic William, Edict of Potsdam, 29 October 1685, in *Das Recht der französisch-reformierten Kirche in Preußen: Urkundliche Denkschrift*, ed. Ernst Mengin. Berlin, 1929.

Erman, Jean P. and Pierre C.F. Reclam. *Mémoires pour servir à l'histoire des Réfugiés françois dans les Etats du Roi*, 9 vols. Berlin, 1782–99.

Esser, Raingard. "Rückkehr oder Unterwanderung? Niederländische Remigranten im Schatten des Achtzigjährigen Krieges." In *Sicherheit in der Frühen Neuzeit. Norm—Praxis—Repräsentation*, ed. Christoph Kampmann and Ulrich Nigge-mann. Cologne, 2013.

François, Etienne. "Die Traditions- und Legendenbildung des deutschen Refuge." In *Der Exodus der Hugenotten: Die Aufhebung des Edikts von Nantes 1685 als europäisches Ereignis*. Cologne, 1985.

Freist, Dagmar. "Dutch Calvinist Refugees in Europe since the Early Modern Period." In *The Encyclopedia of Migration and Minorities in Europe: From the 17th Century to the Present*, ed. Klaus J. Bade et al. Cambridge, 2011.

Fuhrich-Grubert, Ursula. *Hugenotten unterm Hakenkreuz: Studien zur Geschichte der Französischen Kirche zu Berlin 1933–1945*. Berlin and New York, 1994.

———. "Zwischen Patriotismus und Internationalismus: Hugenotten im 19. und 20. Jahrhundert." In *Zuwanderungsland Deutschland: Die Hugenotten*, ed. Sabine Beneke and Hans Ottomeyer. Berlin, 2005.

Gillot, Hubert. *Le règne de Louis XIV et l'opinion publique en Allemagne*. Nancy, 1914.

Gilmont, Jean-François. *Jean Crespin: Un éditeur réformé du XVIe siècle*. Geneva, 1981.

Greenblatt, Stephen. *Renaissance Self-Fashioning: From More to Shakespeare*. Chicago, 1984.

Herzig, Arno. *Der Zwang zum wahren Glauben: Rekatholisierung vom 16. bis zum 18. Jahrundert*. Göttingen, 2000.

Holt, Mack P. *The French Wars of Religion, 1562–1629*. 2nd ed. Cambridge, 2005.

Jakob, Andreas. *Die Neustadt Erlangen: Planung und Entstehung*. Erlangen, 1986.

Janssen, Geert. "Quo Vadis? Catholic Perceptions of Flight and the Revolt of the Low Countries, 1566–1609." In *Renaissance Quarterly* 64 (2011): 472–99.

Joutard, Philippe. "1685—Ende und neue Chance für den französischen Protestant-ismus." In *Die Hugenotten, 1685–1985*, ed. Rudolf von Thadden and Michelle Magdalaine. Munich, 1985.

Jurieu, Pierre. *Gründlicher Bericht / Von dem jetzigen jämmerlichen Zustand Der Cron Franckreich: Worauß umbständlich zu vernehmen / Wie der jetzige König Ludwig der XIV. . . . Das gantze Volck in eine solche Sclaverey und Dienstbarkeit gesetzt / daß das gantze Land darüber säuffzen und lamentiren muß*. s.l., 1689.

———. *Lettres pastorales adressées aux fidèles de France qui gémissent sous la captivité de Babylon*, ed. Robin Howells. Hildesheim, 1988.

———. *The Sighs of France in Slavery, Breathing after Liberty: By Way of Memorial; Done out of French*. London, 1689.

———. *Les Soupirs de la France esclave, Qui aspire après la Liberté*. Amsterdam, 1690.

———. *De suchtingen van het slaefachtigh Vrankryk, wenschende naer desselfs vryheyt*. The Hague, 1689.

Kadell, Franz-Anton. *Die Hugenotten in Hessen-Kassel*. Darmstadt, 1980.

Kiefner, Theo. *Die Privilegien der nach Deutschland gekommenen Waldenser*, 2 vols. Stuttgart, 1990.

Knetsch, Frederik R.J. *Pierre Jurieu: Theoloog en politikus der Refuge*. Kampen, 1967.

Lachenicht, Susanne. *Hugenotten in Europa und Nordamerika: Migration und Integration in der Frühen Neuzeit*. Frankfurt am Main, 2010.

Landgrebe, Peter. *Minoritätengruppe und wirtschaftliche Bedeutung: Zum Einfluß der Hugenotten auf die deutsche Wirtschaftsentwicklung*. Sickte, 1977.

Leeb, Rudolf. "Die große Salzburger Emigration von 1731/32 und ihre Vorgeschichte (Ausweisung der Deferegger 1684)." In *Glaubensflüchtlinge: Ursachen, Formen und Auswirkungen frühneuzeitlicher Konfessionsmigration in Europa*, ed. Joachim Bahlcke. Berlin, 2008.

Leeb, Rudolf, Martin Scheutz, Dietmar Weikl, eds. *Geheimprotestantismus und evangelische Kirchen in der Habsburgermonarchie und im Erzstift Salzburg (17./18. Jahrhundert)*. Vienna and Munich, 2009.

Malettke, Klaus. *Hegemonie, multipolares System, Gleichgewicht. Internationale Beziehungen 1648/1659–1713/1714*. Paderborn, 2012.

Marsch, Angelika. *Die Salzburger Emigration in Bildern*. Weissenhorn, 1977.

Mayer, Johann F. *Bewegliches Seufftzen Derer aus Franckreich geflüchteten Reformirten, Nach der Lutherischen Religions-Vereinigung*. Wittenberg, 1686.

Mempel, Dieter, ed. *Gewissensfreiheit und Wirtschaftspolitik: Hugenotten- und Waldenserprivilegien 1681–1699*. Trier, 1986.

Mittenzwei, Ingrid. "Die Hugenotten in der gewerblichen Wirtschaft Brandenburg-Preußens." In *Hugenotten in Brandenburg-Preußen*, ed. Ingrid Mittenzwei. Berlin, 1987.

Mogk, Walter. "Voraussetzungen für die Einwanderung von Hugenotten und Waldensern nach Hessen-Kassel." In *Die Hugenotten und Waldenser in Hessen-Kassel*, ed. Jochen Desel and Walter Mogk. Kassel, 1978.

Niggemann, Ulrich. "Craft Guilds and Immigration: Huguenots in German and English Cities." In *Gated Communities? Regulating Migration in Early Modern Cities*, ed. Bert de Munck and Anne Winter. Farnham, 2012.

———. *Hugenotten*. Cologne, Weimar, Vienna, 2011.

———. "Hugenotten als wirtschaftliche Elite: Wahrnehmung und Selbstwahrnehmung in den immigrationspolitischen Auseinandersetzungen in Deutschland und England, 1680–1700." In *Religiöse und konfessionelle Minderheiten als wirtschaftliche und geistige Eliten (16. bis frühes 20. Jahrhundert): Büdinger Forschungen zur Sozialgeschichte 2006 und 2007*, ed. Markus A. Denzel, Matthias Asche, Matthias Stickler. St. Katharinen, 2009.

Niggemann, Ulrich. "Die Hugenottenverfolgung in der zeitgenössischen deutschen Publizistik (1681–1690)." *Francia* 32, no. 2 (2005): 59–108.

———. *Immigrationspolitik zwischen Konflikt und Konsens: Die Hugenottenansiedlung in Deutschland und England (1681–1697)*. Cologne, Weimar, Vienna, 2008.

Nipperdey, Justus. *Die Erfindung der Bevölkerungspolitik: Staat, politische Theorie und Population in der Frühen Neuzeit*. Göttingen, 2012.

Onnekink, David and Gijs Rommelse, eds. *Ideology and Foreign Policy in Early Modern Europe (1650–1750)*. Aldershot, 2011.

Peters, Michael. "Joseph Auguste du Cros als Agent des Markgrafen Christian Ernst von Brandenburg-Bayreuth: Ein Beitrag zur Vorgeschichte der Hugenotten-Kolonisation in Franken." *Erlanger Bausteine zur fränkischen Heimatforschung* 34 (1986): 163–74.

Rosen-Prest, Viviane. *L'historiographie des Huguenots en Prusse au temps des Lumières. Entre mémoire, histoire et légende: J.P. Erman et P.C.F. Reclam, Mémoires pour servir à l'histoire des Réfugiés françois dans les Etats du Roi (1782–1799)*. Paris, 2002.

———. "Willkommene Fremde? Zwei Jahrhunderte Geschichtsschreibung über Hugenotten im deutschen Refuge (17–19. Jahrhundert)." In *Die Begegnung mit Fremden und das Geschichtsbewusstsein*, ed. Judith Becker and Bettina Braun. Göttingen, 2012.

de Saint-Blancard, François Gaultier. *Sermon sur la Mort de Tres-Haut & Tres-Puissant Prince, Monseigneur Frideric Guillaume, Marggrave de Brandebourg, Electeur, & Archichambellan du Saint Empire, &c. Arrivée le Dimanche 29. Avril 1688. Prononcé à Berlin, dans l'Eglise du Dôme, le Dimanche suivant 6. de Mai*. Berlin, 1688.

Schilling, Heinz. *Niederländische Exulanten im 16. Jahrhundert*. Gütersloh, 1972.

———. "Peregrini und Schiffchen Gottes: Flüchtlingserfahrung und Exulantentheologie des frühneuzeitlichen Calvinismus." In *Calvinismus: Die Reformierten in Deutschland und Europa*, ed. Ansgar Reiss and Sabine Witt. Dresden, 2009.

Schillinger, Jean. *Les pamphlétaires allemandes et la France de Louis XIV*. Bern, 1999.

Schultz, Helga. *Das ehrbare Handwerk: Zunftleben im alten Berlin zur Zeit des Absolutismus*. Weimar, 1993.

Schunka, Alexander. *Gäste, die bleiben: Zuwanderer in Kursachsen und der Oberlausitz im 17. und im frühen 18. Jahrhundert*. Hamburg, 2006.

———. "Glaubensflucht als Migrationsoption." In *Geschichte in Wissenschaft und Unterricht* 10 (2005): 547–564.

———. "Pragmatisierung konfessioneller Autorität. Zuwanderer im Kursachsen des 17. Jahrhunderts im Spiegel des Supplikenwesens." In *Glaubensflüchtlinge*, ed. Joachim Bahlcke. Berlin, 2008.

Sincerus Catholicus. *Entdeckungen Der listigen Kunst-Stücke Womit Die Frantzosen die Catholische und Protestirende Stände an einander zu hetzen gedencken*. s.l., 1689.

Statt, Daniel. *Foreigners and Englishmen: The Controversy over Immigration and Population, 1660–1760*. Newark, 1995.

von Thadden, Rudolf. "Hugenotten und Hugenottengedenken 1685–1985." In *Wege und Grenzen der Toleranz. Edikt von Potsdam 1685–1985*, ed. Manfred Stolpe and Friedrich Winter. Berlin, 1987.

―――. "Vom Glaubensflüchtling zum preußischen Patrioten," in von Thadden and Magdelaine, *Hugenotten* (Munich, 1985).

von Thadden, Rudolf, and Michelle Magdelaine, eds. *Die Hugenotten, 1685–1985.* Munich, 1985.

Tollin, Henri. *Geschichte der Französischen Colonie zu Magdeburg,* 6 vols. Halle on Saale, 1886–1892.

Tollin, Henri, and Richard Béringuier. *Die französische Colonie in Berlin.* Magdeburg, 1891.

Walker, Mack. Gabriele Emrich, *Die Emigration der Salzburger Protestanten 1731– 1732: Reichsrechtliche und konfessionspolitische Aspekte. Historia profana et ecclesiastica* vol. 7. Münster, 2002.

―――. *The Salzburg Transaction: Expulsion and Redemption in Eighteenth-Century Germany.* Ithaca, NY, 1992.

Wissell, Rudolf. *Des alten Handwerks Recht und Gewohnheit.* 6 vols. Berlin 1971–88.

Yardeni, Myriam. *Le Refuge protestant.* Paris, 1985.

CHAPTER FIVE

❧

Between Economic Interest and Nationalism

The Policy Regarding Polish Seasonal Rural Workers in the German Empire before 1914

ROLAND GEHRKE

Polish Migration to Germany in the Long Nineteenth Century: Reasons and Preconditions

Scholars of the prominent movements of migrants in central Europe from the second half of the eighteenth century onward need to keep track of the way borders have repeatedly shifted across this geographical space. People have not only moved across borders, but borders have also moved across people,[1] thus bestowing upon the issue an additional layer of complexity as newly drawn borders always define and redefine the spaces in which migration takes place.[2]

Following the three partitions of Poland in 1772, 1793, and 1795, Russia appropriated 60 percent, and thus the lion's share, of the territory of the Polish-Lithuanian *Rzeczpospolita*, while Prussia and Austria integrated more or less equal shares of what remained into their respective territories. After Napoleon created the Duchy of Warsaw as a satellite state in the years 1807–1815 from the territory acquired by Prussia and Austria with the partitions of 1793 and 1795, the borders were once more redrawn at the Congress of Vienna. While the western part of its territorial acquisitions—the "Grand Duchy of Posen" as it was known from then on—was returned to Prussia, the remaining territory of the earlier Duchy of Warsaw was turned into the Kingdom of Poland (or, as it was derisively called, "Congress Poland" [*Kongresspolen*]). At its head, ruling on the basis of a personal union with Russia, stood the Russian Tsar. A weighty 80 percent of the area of the old Polish state therefore from 1815 onward fell into the area where Russia wielded power. As the demise of Polish sovereignty also extinguished the Polish rights of citizenship, the rubric of "Polish migrants," as it will be used in what follows and as it applied to Prussian Germany, comprehended all those persons who spoke Polish whether they originated from the Austrian area (Galicia) or from the Russian area (and in this case especially from the "Kingdom of Poland"). The equally important phenomenon of Polish internal migration—meaning the movements from the partly Polish-speaking areas of the Prussian Hohenzollern monarchy (Posen, West Prussia, Upper Silesia, Southern East Prussia) into other regions of Prussian-Germany and particularly into the Ruhr[3]—fall beyond the scope of this essay.

The presence of Poles in foreign countries both in Europe and further abroad was closely connected to the wish for a restoration of national independence and therefore must usually be understood within a military context. Units of Polish volunteers formed in Strasbourg and Milan, who fought on the side of Napoleon and allegedly patronized the Polish struggle for liberty, ended up as far afield as Haiti in the Caribbean—an undertaking that ended in disaster.[4]

Despite the long distances that some Poles traveled in their migrations, German territory remained unaffected. The German public first came face-to-face with the ramifications of the Polish question following the failure of the Polish November Uprising of 1830–31 against Russia. The widespread solidarity felt within the bourgeois public for the Polish struggle for liberty led, under the forbearance of the authorities, to the creation of "Poland Associations" (*Polenvereine*).[5] This was particularly the case in the constitutional states of Germany's southwest where comparatively moderate rule was the norm. These associations devoted themselves to forms of charitable support by collecting donations, providing medical supplies, and sending doctors to tend to the wounded. From the autumn of 1831—after the uprising had been suppressed by military force—Polish officers and soldiers, who had rejected Russian amnesty and opted for exile, found public sympathy in several German states. In the course of their procession through Germany's southwest these Polish exiles were given board and succor and were mostly enthusiastically celebrated. It is important to note that the path followed by most migrants took them through rather than to Germany; thus, their stay was of limited duration. The actual destination of the refugees lay in western Europe. Paris in particular became the center of the Great Emigration (*Wielka Emigracja*), and these circles of emigrants created the forum in which debates took place about the future territory and the desirable political and social constitution of the Polish nation for the next three decades.[6]

The Polish charity movement in Germany—a movement already described at the time as "Poland enthusiasm" (*Polenbegeisterung*)[7]—reveals on closer inspection a crypto-political character, since the Polish struggle for liberty served as a movement onto which German liberals living through the Restoration period could project their own political aspirations. In this respect it is revealing that the attitude of society toward the Polish struggle for independence shifted as the Polish question lost its functional meaning within German political discourse.[8] A Polish conspiracy, which was brought to light in 1846 in the Grand Duchy of Posen, and a failed military uprising in the territory two years later caused feelings of solidarity within German liberals to wane. Instead these events were linked to threats to Germany's national interests. It was a liberal representative, Wilhelm Jordan, who recommended in a plenary debate of the Frankfurt National Assembly in July 1848 that Germans should counter Polish demands in the future on the basis of a "healthy ethnic pride" (*gesunder Volksegoismus*).[9] In this manner he indicated the course that the majority of German society would follow for many subsequent decades.

In any case, Polish migrants to Germany were perceived in a political context until well after the middle of the nineteenth century. As long as the German states remained countries of net emigration, then a more economically motivated attitude to Polish labor migration did not emerge. The immigration from Russian Poland or from Galicia to Germany was in numerical terms too negligible to give rise to any need for administrative regulation.[10] At the end of the 1860s there were still only a few hundred Poles coming from Galicia annually, and almost 90 percent of these opted for Prussia as their destination—without this leading to any noteworthy problems.[11]

The increase in population that followed the unification of the Reich in 1870–71 was accompanied by a discernible migration into cities, fuelling the growth of the industrial centers. Meanwhile, the number of Germans emigrating overseas peaked in the 1880s.[12] The structural transformation wrought in agriculture by the final dissolution of the feudal order as well as the internal migration of rural workers leaving their homes east of the Elbe and heading to the more industrialized regions of Prussia and initially into the province of Saxony[13] bled the rural labor market dry in East Prussia. Owing to these developments, it increasingly suffered from a "dearth of people" (*Leutenot*) and was therefore increasingly dependent upon foreign workers.[14] At the same time, social pressure intensified in both Galicia and the Kingdom of Poland due to the lack of economic perspectives for the peasant population. In contrast to Prussia the comprehensive agrarian reforms in Russia and Austria were not only implemented considerably later (in 1848 and 1861, respectively), but they also left the class of land-owning peasants with their miniscule forms of ownership largely untouched. This situation increased the numbers of those who possessed no land or, as was especially the case in Galicia, those who owned parcels so small that sustaining a family was no longer possible. This promoted the willingness on the part of Poles to move on and to seek better prospects elsewhere, and in offering such prospects a number of options competed with each other: either permanent emigration overseas or different forms of seasonal migration.[15]

In order to explain the phenomenon of migratory movements that continually occur from certain lands of origin to certain lands as destinations, the research into historical migration has recently discovered the concept of the "migration system." This phrase captures the planning of long-term or even permanent residency in a destination land as well as forms of temporary migration, termed "shuttle migration" (*Pendelmigration*) in the case of regular repetition.[16] The deployment of Polish seasonal laborers, which as a practice spread throughout Germany's agriculture in the east from the end of the nineteenth century and which is the focus of this chapter, did not reflect the free volition of the migrants but rather resulted from state planning and policy. This strategy took on the form of a finely tuned mechanism that was progressively refined up until the outbreak of World War I. The recruitment scheme targeted Polish laborers, but at the same time, these same laborers became victims of discrimination, and numerous administrative measures aimed to nip in the bud any chance these laborers might have had to permanently settle in the German Reich. In the words of Dirk Hoerder, Polish seasonal migration amounted to "the extreme case of recruiting foreign labor under a policy of nonimmigration."[17]

To understand this seeming contradiction, it is imperative not to lose sight of the political context. Discrimination against Polish migrants on the basis of ideological concerns can be explained by noting how the Prussian-German government encouraged a view (which was subsequently amplified by its supporters) of eastern Prussia as the location of an existential struggle between the Polish and German nations. The fear that this area of the Hohenzollern monarchy, which was already partly Polish-speaking, might be irrevocably lost for the German Volk (*Deutschtum*) as a result of yet more Polish immigration stood in stark contrast to the economic interest in a supply of cheap labor from the east, an interest pursued in particular by Prussian estate owners. The German policy toward the Poles, which, when questions of migration are for the moment pushed to the side, focused on attempts at linguistic assimilation, especially in the education system, and then later on the suppression and expulsion of the Polish element through legislatively authorized resettlement and dispossession,[18] had to confront a form of Polish nationalism, which from the end of the nineteenth century onward became increasingly aggressive.[19] This nationalism latched onto the cross-border mobility of a divided Poland as a lever for pursuing a form of national "expansion," even in the absence of a sovereign nation-state.[20] As a result, adherents of this Polish nationalism devoted special attention to questions of Polish migration. In Lviv (also known as Lemberg, Lwów, or Lvov depending on the linguistic context) in Galicia, for example, the Polish Society for Emigration (*Polskie Towarzystwo Emigracyjne*) was founded, an organization equipped with its own newspaper to spread its message.[21]

The "Dearth of People" vs. Fears of Being Swamped by Foreigners: Changing Premises of the Prussian Policy toward Foreigners after 1880

In a climate riven by nationalist hostilities the conviction grew that Prussia had to defend its eastern territories (*Ostmarken*, as they were frequently termed at the time) against the Polish struggle for independence. From a German nationalist perspective, areas that had only recently been won by Germans and integrated into Germany were at risk first of being swamped by Poles and ultimately "polonized." Polish-speaking immigrants from beyond the eastern border were seen as invaders who not only quantitatively strengthened the Polish element but who could also contaminate it with Polish nationalist creeds.[22] The Prussian estate owners belonged to a social elite whose political-ideological beliefs induced them to join the chorus of those espousing a policy of anti-Polish pushback. At the same time, they felt the direct repercussions of the structural transformations in the economy, and the challenges created by these transformations could only be surmounted if there was a steady supply of foreign labor. This situation reflected a volatile mix of political and economic interests; interests that, as subsequent history demonstrated, could obviously no longer be reconciled with each other.

Chancellor Otto von Bismarck chose to continue a course of minimizing the number of foreign Poles in the German Reich. This policy reached its highpoint in 1885–86 with the expulsion of close to forty thousand non-naturalized Poles—a third of them being Jewish—who until then lived in the eastern provinces of Prussia. On the grounds of their brutal implementation alone, these measures provoked widespread criticism among the German public.[23] The government linked the expulsion with a categorical proscription against any further migration from Galicia or Russian Poland. As an unintended result, this policy exacerbated the already noticeable "dearth of people," particularly in Prussian agriculture. In addition, the cultivation of sugar beets, which had been promoted since the late 1870s and was more labor-intensive than other crops, demanded a highly variable input of labor through the seasons and thus required the seasonal employment of rural workers.[24] In this respect there were repeated attempts to bring about a reconciliation between economic interests and the salient guidelines of Prussian-German policy toward the Poles. Continuing up until the first decade of the twentieth century, German agricultural leaders discussed how to engage other groups of migrants as seasonal labor instead of Poles. Among the candidates were Estonians, Latvians, Belarusians, and Ukrainians, but also Flemings and Italians and even ethnicities from further afield, including Brazilians and Chinese "coolies." With the exception of recruiting Ukrainians, such plans revealed themselves again and again to be premised on ideas largely divorced from reality.[25]

With the complete closure of the eastern border in 1885–86 the problem took on such existential weight that in the following years the wish was articulated ever more forcefully for at least a seasonally restricted readmission of labor migrants. By 1889–90 this had consolidated itself into a campaign organized by large Prussian estate owners. The new Reich chancellor Leo von Caprivi was petitioned by over seventy branch associations to approve a measure to "allow Russian laborers [i.e., laborers from Russian Poland] temporary abode in Prussia so that they might be employed by the agricultural enterprises for the requisite time."[26]

Against the backdrop of a more conciliatory tone in the Prussian-German policy toward Poles ushered in with the change of chancellor, the government relented. In three ordinances from November and December 1890, the chief president of the four eastern provinces of Prussia was authorized to readmit laborers from Russian Poland and Galicia in agricultural enterprises for a "test phase" of at first three years. As a strict precondition for this, the laborers had to come unaccompanied (which meant for the most part that they were not married), and, furthermore, their residency was limited to only part of the year. In correspondence with the cycle of crop production and harvesting, the duration of the stay was at first fixed for the period from 1 April to 15 November, but in response to pressure exerted by the owners of large estates this was extended. From 1907 onward those seasonal laborers in question only had to leave Prussia from 20 December to 1 February.[27] Their employment stretched over forty-six of the fifty-two weeks of a calendar year so that the term used by those at the time, summer contracts (*Sommerverträge*),[28] had little to do with the reality of the situation.

The enforced "leave of absence" (known as *Karenzzeit*) might have seemed absurdly short, but in the minds of those working at the Prussian Ministry of the Interior it was "the only means of reminding the foreign laborers that they were only tolerated as alien subjects and that their permanent settlement was out of the question."[29] The degree to which this *Karenzzeit* rule served as an instrument of Prussian-German policy toward Poles became clear by 1905, at the latest, when ethnic Ukrainians—the second largest group of seasonal laborers—were exempted from the forced rotation. Since their national-political claims, as far as they found articulation at all before 1914, primarily touched upon Austrian state interests, they were perceived in the eyes of German policy-makers as far less threatening.[30]

In any case, the phase of a moderately tolerant policy toward Poland ended with the downfall of Chancellor Caprivi in the autumn of 1894. Two nationalist pressure groups were founded almost simultaneously in the form of the German Association for the Eastern Marks (*Deutscher Ostmarkenverein*)[31] and the All-German Union (*Alldeutscher Verband*).[32] These organizations assiduously cultivated the image of the Pole as enemy and thus left their imprint upon the social mood in the German Reich, even if their actual influence upon government decisions should not be exaggerated. Despite the increasing tensions within the atmosphere of national politics, the Prussian Minister for the Interior pointed to the vital interests of agriculture when instructing the chief president of the four eastern provinces to continue to permit the employment of foreign Polish workers. At the same time he demanded a more vigorous use of those instruments designed to prevent a permanent settlement of foreigners.[33]

The practice of employing Polish seasonal laborers on the basis of an enforced rotation system could thus continue. If in 1890 at least 17,000 seasonal laborers from Russian Poland were working in Prussian agriculture, in 1895 it had risen to 56,000, and by 1900 the figure was 119,000.[34] This enormous increase gave rise to numerous organizational problems that posed a challenge to Prussian policy-makers dealing with the employment of foreigners at the turn of the century.

The Procurement of Labor and the Imposition of Identification Procedures (Legitimationszwang): Polish Seasonal Labor in the Prussian East after 1900

Recruiting from the multitude of those who were headed to the border and who were willing to work had, at first, hardly been a direct activity engaged in by the estate owners. For the most part they left the actual work of negotiating contracts and tending to the seasonal laborers to foremen (*Vorschnitter*) who could usually also speak Polish.[35] The rapidly increasing need for a mechanism to bring employer and employee together could admittedly not be managed for long on this basis. While in Russian Poland every form of mediating the procurement of trade labor remained officially forbidden, private agencies in the Prussian-Austrian border areas pursued a lively and lucrative trade in laborers and contract work from the second half of the 1890s onward.[36] The complaints about unethical agents and the "slave trade" overseen by their profession became more vociferous due to some of the disreputable figures who numbered among the seven thousand agents operating in 1905 in the border area.[37] Just as attempts were made by the Galician administration after 1900 to curtail the excesses of the unregulated procurement of labor, the German authorities and the agrarian associations undertook initiatives to bring the agents under their own control.[38]

In order to offer an alternative to what had until then been the standard practice, the Central Office for the Procurement of German Settlers and Field Workers (*Centralstelle zur Beschaffung deutscher Ansiedler und Feldarbeiter*) was established in 1903 under the protection of the Prussian Ministry for Agriculture. The initiative had its origins in the German Association for the Eastern Marks. Even the name of the organization reveals how it represented a renewed effort to substitute other workers for the foreign Poles who allegedly represented a "danger to the nation." As the idea to persuade Hungarian and Galician Germans to relocate to Prussia quickly proved illusory, the Central Office entered into close cooperation with the Ukrainian nationalist Ruthenian National Committee (*Ruthenisches Nationalkomitee*) in the hope that this body would facilitate the procurement and conveyance of large numbers of Ukrainian seasonal laborers from Galicia to Prussia.[39] This strategy achieved moderate success, but it could not change the fact that between 1907 and 1910 up to two-thirds of the Galician seasonal laborers were ethnic Poles.[40] In the face of such realities, there was no course of action left to the Central Office for German Rural Labor (*Deutsche Feldarbeiter-Centralstelle*, as it was officially known after 1905) to pursue, except to promote and organize the deployment of Polish seasonal laborers, although this was exactly what it had set out to combat.

Admittedly the Central Office increasingly encountered resistance in its attempts to move beyond its character as an unofficial body based on private initiative and to secure a monopoly in the business of procuring labor. On the one hand, it aroused the ire of the Chambers for Agriculture in the eastern provinces, which espied in the Central Office unwelcome competition in the provision of seasonal laborers. On the other hand, rural councils or individual estate owners who found themselves bereft of seasonal laborers complained repeatedly about the incompetence of the Central Office.[41] The government finally heeded the protests by turning the Central Office into a de facto state organization. On the basis of a charter approved on 23 August 1907,[42] the German Head Office for Rural Labor (*Deutsche Feldarbeiterzentrale*) was transformed into a legal association affiliated formally to the Prussian Chambers of Agriculture and based in Berlin. It had thereby become an official institution, even if it coexisted with the regular provincial authorities.[43] At the same time, the sober calculation of economic interests by the Prussian estate owners had won the upper hand over a political ideology that initially had counted the rural elites among its potential supporters. Measured against the original goals pursued four years earlier by the German Association for the Eastern Provinces, practically nothing of this program remained.[44]

Economic utility had won the day, but it came at the cost of a drastically more intrusive regime of police control imposed upon seasonal workers. Already at the beginning of 1896 the Prussian Ministry for the Interior had instructed the rural councils to register all foreigners in lists containing their personal details,[45] but it was now the individual who at any time had to prove their "legitimate" presence to the authorities. Prussia reacted in this manner to breaches of contract, which had been increasing in number for a long time. These broken contracts normally took the form of unauthorized leave from the farm of the contractual employer and were usually motivated by the hope of being hired at better conditions somewhere else. After 1900, on average every tenth foreign migrant worker breached their contract, but in some regions the rate exceeded this considerably.[46]

Instead of investigating the causes for this refusal to honor the original contracts—a refusal that represented for the seasonal laborers the only form of resistance with any prospect of success against intolerable working conditions—a system of identification cards (*Legitimationskarten*) was introduced. Those to whom this regulation applied were to carry their card at all times, which supplied their names as well as their country or place of origin, the name of their employer, the duration of the agreed period of work, along with a description of personal features (including "stature," "face," "eyes," and "hair"). The color of the cards revealed the ethnicity without any consideration of the official nationality: ethnic Poles received red cards, Ukrainians yellow cards.[47] For the card to be issued, those seeking work had to pay a charge of two Marks out of their own pocket. The pendant to the identification card was the work card (*Arbeitskarte*), which contained the same information and was to be given to the estate-owner upon the commencement of work.[48]

In order to prevent future breaches of contract, an amendment to the card on the basis of a new employer was only possible with a notation recognizing the regular dissolution of the previous work relationship; if this notation was missing, then the cardholder faced immediate expulsion.[49] In addition to the wish of agricultural operators to secure as binding an employment relationship to their seasonal workers as possible, one should not overlook the other political circumstances that made the introduction of such a regime seem advisable. The Russian Revolution of 1905 aroused once more the concern that migrant workers might also import dangerous political ideas to Prussia.[50] Nevertheless, the goals of this policy were not fully achieved. The directors of the head office for field workers estimated that as much as 20 percent of the seasonal laborers in Prussia in 1907 were illegal, meaning that they were without an officially recognized right to be there.[51]

After 1907, the monopoly on enforcing legitimate residency formed the essential reason for the Head Office for Rural Labor to exist, but when it came to the actual procurement of labor the claim to monopoly and the reality never matched up. In the report year of 1913–14, the organization "legitimized" approximately 433,000 seasonal workers in Prussian agriculture—the highest number reached before the outbreak of war. However, it had acted as the procuring agent for only 78,000 of these laborers, which was less than a fifth of the total number of seasonal migrants. Just as before, commercial agents hired most Polish workers, and the Prussian government remained grudgingly dependent on their cooperation.[52]

If the Prussian policy toward foreigners rested on the duty imposed on workers to provide legitimate identification and to return home each year, then it needs to be remembered that all questions relating to immigration fell within the jurisdiction of the individual states of the German Empire. In order to achieve a greater degree of homogeneity in these policies, Prussia exerted pressure upon the other states to adopt identical regulations but encountered only middling success. Only the Kingdom of Saxony, Saxony-Meiningen, and Brunswick introduced the Prussian model in its entirety. Other states adopted only the regulation of enforced annual return (*Karenzzeit-Regel*) or the principle of providing legitimate identification, while Bavaria and Württemberg in particular went their own way in formulating a policy toward foreigners.[53] Admittedly, Polish migrant workers hardly featured in the thoughts of southern German authorities.

Social Reality and Criticism of the Prussian Foreign Policy before 1914

The fact that Polish seasonal laborers were recruited mostly from a rural, relatively uneducated milieu complemented the interest of the employers in the smooth and unobstructed management of their enterprises. A simple preliminary school education was the rule, but illiteracy remained widespread.[54] The laborers were generally between 16 and 25 years old and were therefore at the peak of their stamina and resilience. Noteworthy is the high proportion of women, which according to different estimates was between 50 and 60 percent; most of these women were unmarried girls.[55]

As a "segregated, sub-proletarian class,"[56] the Polish seasonal laborers were completely excluded from the German society within which they lived, and personal contacts extending beyond the immediate working environment represented the absolute exception. The efforts undertaken in the name of Polish nationalism—a nationalism that feared few things more than long-term "Germanization"—found, ironically enough, a source of support in the Prussian model of seasonal work.[57] At the same time, it was neither possible nor sensible for the Polish seasonal laborers to build a parallel cultural world like the "Ruhr Poles" with their network of associations and clubs.[58] The conditions imposed by the duty to legitimately identify oneself and by the enforced annual "leave of absence" meant that the workplace could hardly become a center of social life.

The concrete working and living conditions of Polish seasonal laborers as well as their treatment at the hands of their employers or their supervisors generated on repeated occasions harsh criticism from certain corners in German politics; here the labor movement as well as the Catholic Church, to which the overwhelming majority of the Polish migrant workers belonged, played prominent roles.[59] The problems began as early as the recruitment phase. In the effort to achieve a high rate of procurement and to provide agricultural enterprises with a larger field to choose from, the Head Office for Rural Labor often lured far more candidates to the border than were actually needed. This frequently created chaotic conditions and gave rise on occasion to mass brawls between the agents and those whom they had rejected. Those who managed to find prospective employment were brought to their place of work in overcrowded trains, which, as noted bitterly by a speaker at the SPD party conference in Essen in 1907, gave the impression of being a form of "transport for convicts."[60]

In most cases, the living quarters provided for the workers could hardly have been more primitive. The sleeping quarters were often an empty barn or empty stables, in which some hay had been strewn but which otherwise contained no furniture.[61] However, what unsettled the German public was less the living conditions themselves, but rather the fact that little heed was given to separating the sexes. It was thought that this might encourage moral degeneration (*Entsittlichung*) among the workers. As one example, the Social Democrat Karl Kautsky polemicized against this "rabbit-hutch form of employment (*Karnickelwirtschaft*), which had been created by those very same defenders of marriage and the family."[62] At least in this regard, the new police regulations at the turn of the century enforced the implementation of basic standards of hygiene and separate living quarters for the sexes.[63]

With regard to discipline, the seasonal laborers were, for the most part, at the mercy of their masters. The "certificate of duty" (*Verpflichtungsschein*) specified not only arbitrary and malleable concepts like the "local standards of working time," but it also listed numerous rules and prohibitions where transgression would incur wage deductions (for example, for missing work or for inebriation) or even expulsion (for example, as a result of disobedience and "rabble-rousing," but also as a result of pregnancies).[64] Numerous cases document the excessive harshness and maltreatment meted out by the employers.[65] In such circumstances, recourse to litigation was hardly an option for the laborers. Nevertheless, sweeping statements should be avoided; the fact that some former seasonal laborers later left behind reminiscences that emphasized the benefits and advantages of this form of labor migration allows one to conclude that in many cases the treatment was fair, as hard as the everyday work on a farming estate might have been.[66]

The rate of remuneration was fixed in the "Conditions for Contracting Rural Migrant Workers" (*Bedingungen für den Bezug landwirtschaftlicher Wanderarbeiter*) as formulated in 1907 by the Head Office for Rural Labor. Differentiating between "men and strong lads, who can swing the scythe" and "weaker lads, women and girls," the daily wage was set between one Mark and one Mark fifty.[67] This was less than what was normally paid to German rural laborers, but more than what one could earn working the fields in Russian Poland (on average 22 Marks a month) or in Galicia (14 Marks a month),[68] and for this reason it represented an attractive option. From the point of view of the employers, the model of seasonal labor had the additional advantage of saving on the costs that otherwise had to be paid as social security in the case of local workers.[69] To prevent breaches of contract, the masters adopted the practice of holding on to a retainer (*Kaution*), which was set at a month's wage deducted at the beginning of the working relationship.[70]

In the political discourse carried out internally within the German Reich the payment of seasonal laborers always remained a contested issue. It is hardly surprising that arguments submitted by those on the right of the political spectrum took the employment practices in Prussian agriculture to task for the possible displacement of local German workers by foreigners—foreigners, who were furthermore seen as a danger to the German nation.[71] Meanwhile, the widespread conviction that cheap seasonal laborers forced wages down (in other words, that they were *Lohndrücker*) stirred resentments in the German labor movement. There were demands to put an end to the import of cheap labor and to prohibit the entry of foreigners who were restricted by seasonal contracts in the use of their labor.[72] Such demands reveal the limits to the solidarity that German Social Democrats were willing to invoke when this was trumped by their interest in looking after their own constituents.

Conclusion

In summary, it once more becomes apparent "that in the question of employing foreigners, economic and ideological options of interest to the social elites in the *Kaiserreich* stood opposed to each other and that this generated far-reaching conflicts over matters of principle."[73] The outcome of these conflicts was a strenuously negotiated compromise that made Prussia into a land importing labor rather than a destination for migrants. This illusion of exploiting foreign labor for the benefit of the German economy, while at the same time preventing genuine immigration with all its social and cultural consequences, continues to inform attitudes about the recent past. It is reflected in a right of citizenship based upon the principle of ethnic descent rather than the principle of territory. In this manner all those living inside Germany's border but who were not of German descent were deprived of any right of naturalization, regardless of where they were born or how long they had been living in Germany.[74]

August 1914 put an end to the system of seasonal labor developed since the 1890s. For all foreign laborers from "enemy states" (meaning from Russia) who were in German territory at the outbreak of hostilities, the previous enforced leave suddenly turned into the denial of any right to leave: their internment in barracks ensued.[75] The two-way movement represented by seasonal "shuttle migration" suddenly became an enforced one-way emigration.

Roland Gehrke is Professor of Modern History and History of East Central Europe at the University of Stuttgart. He received his doctorate in History at the University of Hamburg in 1999. He has specialized in the history of Prussia, Poland, and Silesia focusing notably on the history of political ideas, the constitutional history, and the history of the nobility. Publications include *Der polnische Westgedanke bis zur Wiedererrichtung des polnischen Staates nach Ende des Ersten Weltkrieges* (2001), *Landtag und Öffentlichkeit: Provinzialständischer Parlamentarismus in Schlesien* (2009), some edited volumes and a number of articles and book chapters.

Notes

Translated by Andrew McKenzie-McHarg.

1. Thus the title of a volume edited by Klaus J. Bade, ed., *Die multikulturelle Herausforderung: Menschen über Grenzen—Grenzen über Menschen* (Munich, 1996); see Jochen Oltmer, "Wanderungsraum Deutschland im 19. und 20. Jahrhundert," in *Polnische Einwanderung: Zur Geschichte und Gegenwart der Polen in Deutschland*, ed. Basil Kerski and Krzysztof Ruchniewicz (Osnabrück, 2011), 13.
2. Peter Kriedte, "Wirtschaftliche Not, massiver Druck und physische Gewalt: Wanderungen in der deutsch-polnischen Beziehungsgeschichte des 19. und 20. Jahrhunderts," in *Społeczeństwo w dobie modernizacji: Polacy i Niemcy w XIX i XX wieku. Studia ofiarowane profesorowi Kazimierzowi Wajdzie w siedemdziesiątą rocznicę urodzin* [Society in the age of its modernization: Poles and Germans in the 19th and 20th centuries. Festschrift for Kazimierz Wajda on the occasion of his 70th birthday], ed. Roman Bäcker (Toruń, 2000), 26.
3. Oltmer, "Wanderungsraum Deutschland," 13; Andrzej Brożek, "Ruchy migracyjne z ziem polskich pod panowaniem pruskim w latach 1850–1918" [Migratory movements from Polish areas under Prussian rule 1850–1918], in *Emigracja z ziem polskich w czasach nowożytnych i najnowszych (XVIII–XX w.)* [Emigration from the Polish areas in recent and more recent periods (18th–20th C.)], ed. Andrzej Pilch (Warsaw, 1984), 161–64; for the comparatively well-researched phenomenon of the "Ruhr Poles" compare the exemplary contribution from Christoph Kleßmann, "Einwande-

rungsprobleme im Auswanderungsland: Das Beispiel der 'Ruhrpolen','' in *Deutsche im Ausland—Fremde in Deutschland: Migration in Geschichte und Gegenwart*, ed. Klaus J. Bade (Munich, 1992), 303–10.

4. See Jan Pachoński, Reuel K. Wilson, *Poland's Caribbean Tragedy: A Study of Polish Legions in the Haitian War of Independence 1802–1803* (Boulder, CO, 1986).

5. Gabriela Brudzyńska-Němec, *Polenvereine in Baden: Hilfeleistung süddeutscher Liberaler für die polnischen Freiheitskämpfer 1831–1832* (Heidelberg, 2006); Roland Gehrke, "Praktische Solidarität als Ausdruck politischer Gesinnung: Die Aktivität der südwestdeutschen 'Polenvereine' von 1831/32," in *Migration als soziale Herausforderung: Historische Formen solidarischen Handelns von der Antike bis zum 20. Jahrhundert*, ed. Joachim Bahlcke et al. (Stuttgart, 2011), 273–91.

6. Sławomir Kalembka, *Wielka Emigracja 1831–1863* [The great emigration 1831–1863] (Toruń, 2003).

7. Compare Dieter Langewiesche, "Humanitäre Massenbewegung und politisches Bekenntnis: Polenbegeisterung in Südwestdeutschland," in *Blick zurück ohne Zorn: Polen und Deutsche in Geschichte und Gegenwart*, ed. Dietrich Beyrau (Tübingen, 1999), 11–37.

8. Eberhard Kolb, "Polenbild und Polenfreundschaft der deutschen Frühliberalen: Zur Motivation und Funktion außenpolitischer Parteinahme im Vormärz," *Saeculum* 26 (1975): 126.

9. Martin Broszat, *Zweihundert Jahre deutsche Polenpolitik* (Munich, 1963), 85.

10. Andrzej Brożek, "Polityka imigracyjna w państwach docelowych emigracji polskiej (1850–1939)" [The immigration policy in the countries of destination for emigrants from the Polish areas (1850–1939)], in *Emigracja z ziem polskich*, ed. Pilch, 121.

11. Andrzej Pilch, "Emigracja z ziem zaboru austriackiego (od połowy XIX w. do 1918 r.)" [Emigration from the Austrian areas (from the middle of the nineteenth century to 1918)], in *Emigracja z ziem polskich*, ed. Pilch, 257.

12. Ulrich Herbert, *Geschichte der Ausländerpolitik in Deutschland: Saisonarbeiter, Zwangsarbeiter, Gastarbeiter, Flüchtlinge* (Munich, 2001), 14.

13. To this phenomenon of the Saxony pilgrimage (*Sachsengängerei*), which was intensified by the addition of seasonal workers from Austria and Russian Poland, see Johannes Frackowiak, "Arbeitsmigranten und/oder Einwanderer? Polen in Mitteldeutschland 1880–1945," *IMIS-Beiträge* 29 (2006): 71–98; Kriedte, "Wirtschaftliche Not," 34; Edward Pietraszek, "Zwischen Geldverdienen und Aufstieg: Polnische Arbeitsmigranten in Deutschland von 1870 bis 1939," in *Vom Wandergesellen zum "Green Card"-Spezialisten. Interkulturelle Aspekte der Arbeitsmigration im östlichen Mitteleuropa*, ed. Klaus Roth (Münster et al., 2003), 110.

14. Klaus J. Bade, "Labour, Migration, and the State: Germany from the Late 19th Century to the Onset of the Great Depression," in *Population, Labour and Migration in 19th- and 20th-Century Germany*, ed. Klaus J. Bade (Leamington Spa et al., 1987), 59, 63; Bade, "'Billig und willig'—die 'ausländischen Wanderarbeiter' im kaiserlichen Deutschland," in *Deutsche im Ausland*, ed. Bade, 314.

15. Kriedte, "Wirtschaftliche Not," 36f.; cf. Leslie Page Moch, *Moving Europeans: Migration in Western Europe since 1650*, 2nd ed. (Bloomington, IN, 2003), 104; Pilch, "Emigracja z ziem zaboru austriackiego," 254–56; a detailed overview for the motives behind the decision to migrate along with a compendium of contemporary opinions with regard to migration from the Polish territories is offered by Piotr Kraszewski, *Polska emigracja zarobkowa w latach 1870–1939. Praktyka i refleksja* [Polish economic migration in the years 1870–1939: The practice and reflections upon it] (Poznań, 1995), 26–42, 209–78.

16. Christoph Pallaske, "Die Migration von Polen nach Deutschland: Ein europäisches Migrationssystem," in *Die Migration von Polen nach Deutschland: Zu Geschichte und Gegenwart eines europäischen Migrationssystems*, ed. Christoph Pallaske (Baden-Baden, 2001), 13; compare the classification of different forms of migrations provided by Andrzej Pilch, "Wstęp" [Introduction], in *Emigracja z ziem polskich*, ed. Pilch, 15; an overview of Polish research on this topic is offered by Ewa Kępińska, *Migracje sezonowe z Polski do Niemiec: Mechanizmy rekrutacji, rola rodziny i zróżnicowanie według płci* [Seasonal migration from Poland to Germany: The mechanisms of recruitment, the role of the family and the differences with regard to the sexes] (Warsaw, 2008), 68–72.

17. Dirk Hoerder, *Cultures in Contact: World Migrations in the Second Millennium* (Durham, NC, 2002), 351.

18. For the preconditions of the Prussian-German policy towards the Poles after 1871, the instruments applied in this matter and the national stereotypes that framed the issue, see, among others, Broszat, *Zweihundert Jahre*; Hans-Ulrich Wehler, "Die Polenpolitik im Deutschen Kaiserreich," in *Krisenherde des Kaiserreichs 1871–1918: Studien zur deutschen Sozial- und Verfassungsgeschichte*, ed. Hans-Ulrich Wehler (Göttingen, 1970), 181–200; Richard Blanke, *Prussian Poland in the German Empire: 1871–1900* (Boulder, CO, 1981); Christoph Kleßmann, Johannes Frackowiak, "Die Polenpolitik des Deutschen Kaiserreichs 1871–1918," in *Nationalistische Politik und Ressentiments: Deutsche und Polen von 1871 bis zur Gegenwart*, ed. Johannes Frackowiak (Göttingen, 2013), 24–38; Uwe Müller, "Wirtschaftliche Maßnahmen der Polenpolitik in der Zeit des Deutschen Kaiserreichs," *Nationalistische Politik und Ressentiments*, ed. Frackowiak , 39–62.

19. Compare for a thorough treatment of this Roland Gehrke, *Der polnische Westgedanke bis zur Wiederrichtung des polnischen Staates nach Ende des Ersten Weltkrieges: Genese und Begründung polnischer Gebietsansprüche gegenüber Deutschland im Zeitalter des europäischen Nationalismus* (Marburg, 2001); Brian Porter, *When Nationalism Began to Hate: Imagining Modern Politics in Nineteenth-Century Poland* (New York et al., 2000).

20. See Gehrke, *Der polnische Westgedanke*, 119f.

21. For more details see Kraszewski, *Polska emigracja zarobkowa*, 78–100.

22. Herbert, *Ausländerpolitik*, 15f.

23. Helmut Neubach, *Die Ausweisungen von Polen und Juden aus Preußen 1885/86: Ein Beitrag zu Bismarcks Polenpolitik und zur Geschichte des deutsch-polnischen Verhältnisses* (Wiesbaden, 1967); Czesław Łuczak, *Od Bismarcka do Hitlera: Polsko-niemieckie stosunki gospodarcze* [From Bismarck to Hitler: Polish-German economic relations] (Poznań, 1988), 41f.; Jack Wertheimer, *Unwelcome Strangers: East European Jews in Imperial Germany*, 2nd ed. (New York et al., 1991), 60–63.

24. Herbert, *Ausländerpolitik*, 18; Kępińska, *Migracje sezonowe*, 113.

25. For more details see Johannes Nichtweiss, *Die ausländischen Saisonarbeiter in der Landwirtschaft der östlichen und mittleren Gebiete des Deutschen Reiches: Ein Beitrag zur Geschichte der preußisch-deutschen Politik von 1890 bis 1914* ([East-]Berlin, 1959), 58–66, 81–86, 103–6. Despite its ideological slant this study remains until today the most detailed, source-based, comprehensive treatment of this topic.

26. Cited in ibid., 35; cf. Herbert, *Ausländerpolitik*, 19–21; Gerhard Brunn, "Ausländische Arbeiter und die Debatte um die, Überfremdungsgefahr' im Deutschen Kaiserreich," in *Migracja i integracja jako doświadczenie europejskie na przykładzie*

niemieckich metropolii w XIX i XX w. Polacy w Zagłębiu Ruhry i Berlinie—Migration und Integration als europäische Erfahrung am Beispiel deutscher Metropolen im 19. und 20. Jahrhundert. Die Polen im Ruhrgebiet und Berlin, ed. Detlef Briesen et al. (Wrocław, 1996), 15.

27. Nichtweiss, *Saisonarbeiter*, 43; Brożek, "Polityka imigracyjna," 122; Łuczak, *Od Bismarcka do Hitlera*, 108.

28. Panikos Panayi, "Irish, Poles and Other Migrants: A Comparative Study of Migration to Britain and Germany, 1820–1918," in *Irish and Polish Migration in Comparative Perspective*, ed. John Belchem and Klaus Tenfelde (Essen, 2003), 41.

29. Cited in Brunn, "Ausländische Arbeiter," 15.

30. Kriedte, "Wirtschaftliche Not," 36; cf. Bade, "Labour," 71, according to whom in 1913 of approximately 270,000 Polish foreign workers in actual fact only around 3,200 (corresponding to 1.2 percent) remained in Prussia throughout the *Karenzzeit*.

31. Sabine Grabowski, *Deutscher und polnischer Nationalismus: Der Deutsche Ostmarkenverein und die polnische Straż 1894–1914* (Marburg, 1998); Adam Galos et al., *Dzieje Hakaty* [The History of the Hakata] (Poznań, 1966). The Polish insult "Hakata" (for the *Ostmarkenverein*) is an acronym formed from the first letters of the surnames of the association's founders—the estate-owners Hansemann, Kennemann, and Tiedemann from the province of Posen.

32. Rainer Hering, *Konstruierte Nation: Der Alldeutsche Verband 1890 bis 1939* (Hamburg, 2003).

33. Nichtweiss, *Saisonarbeiter*, 49.

34. At this time only an insignificant number of seasonal laborers came from Galicia (in 1902 approx. 42,000). Shortly after the outbreak of the war, a move in the direction of equal numbers can be observed in the contingents from Russian and Austrian Poland. The numbers are found in Kraszewski, *Polska emigracja zarobkowa*, 51, 56.

35. Nichtweiss, *Saisonarbeiter*, 77f.

36. Klaus J. Bade, "Ausländerbeschäftigung, Staatsräson und Sicherheitspolitik: Der Sonderfall Preußen," in *Europa in Bewegung: Migration vom späten 18. Jahrhundert bis zur Gegenwart*, ed. Klaus J. Bade (Munich, 2000), 227f.

37. Bade, "Billig und willig," 316–18; Panayi, "Irish, Poles and Other Migrants," 35; Herbert, *Ausländerpolitik*, 33f, 38f.; Sebastian Conrad, *Globalisierung und Nation im Deutschen Kaiserreich*, 2nd ed. (Munich, 2010), 129f.

38. Nichtweiss, *Saisonarbeiter*, 79.

39. Ibid. 79–92; Conrad, *Globalisierung*, 164f.; see Panayi, "Irish, Poles and Other Migrants," 41.

40. Pilch, "Emigracja," 284.

41. Nichtweiss, *Saisonarbeiter*, 92, 102f.

42. The essential points are summarized by Otto Becker, *Die Regelung des ausländischen Arbeiterwesens in Deutschland: Unter besonderer Berücksichtigung der Anwerbung und Vermittlung* (Berlin, 1918), 6f.

43. Nichtweiss, *Saisonarbeiter*, 111–13.

44. Ibid., 109.

45. Ibid., 49.

46. Herbert, *Ausländerpolitik*, 32f.

47. A facsimile of such an identification card may be found in the appendix in Nichtweiss, *Saisonarbeiter*, 255f.; see Jochen Oltmer, "'Rückkehr historischer Migrationsmuster?' Migration und Integration in Deutschland im frühen und im späten 20. Jahrhun-

dert," in *Die Russlanddeutschen in den Migrationsprozessen zwischen den GUS-Staaten und Deutschland,* ed. Otto Luchterhandt and Alfred Eisfeld (Göttingen, 2008), 49f.; Brożek, "Polityka imigracyjna," 122.

48. Herbert, *Ausländerpolitik,* 36.
49. Nichtweiss, *Saisonarbeiter,* 139.
50. Ibid., 134; see Łuczak, *Od Bismarcka do Hitlera,* 109.
51. Herbert, *Ausländerpolitik,* 37.
52. The numbers in Nichtweiss, *Saisonarbeiter,* 142f.; see Bade, "Labour," 75f.
53. An enumeration of the different regulations for each state can be found in Nichtweiss, *Saisonarbeiter,* 142f.; see Brożek, "Polityka imigracyjna," 122f.; Krzysztof Groniowski, "Emigracja z ziem zaboru rosyjskiego (1864–1918)" [Emigration from Russian Poland (1864–1918)], in *Emigracja z ziem polskich,* ed. Pilch, 218f.
54. Pietraszek, "Zwischen Geldverdienen und Aufstieg," 112.
55. Kępińska, *Migracje sezonowe,* 112f.; Pilch, "Emigracja z ziem zaboru austriackiego," 283; Oltmer, "Wanderungsraum Deutschland," 18.
56. Brunn, "Ausländische Arbeiter," 21.
57. Łuczak, *Od Bismarcka do Hitlera,* 115f.
58. Pietraszek, "Zwischen Geldverdienen und Aufstieg," 112.
59. A compact overview on this topic can be found in Nichtweiss, *Saisonarbeiter,* 154–86.
60. Ibid., 218n13.
61. Łuczak, *Od Bismarcka do Hitlera,* 114; Herbert, *Ausländerpolitik,* 40.
62. Karl Kautsky, *Die Agrarfrage: Eine Übersicht über die Tendenzen der modernen Landwirthschaft und die Agrarpolitik der Sozialdemokratie* (Stuttgart, 1899), 370.
63. Nichtweiss, *Saisonarbeiter,* 229.
64. Ibid., 220f.
65. In 1913 an enumeration of concrete cases was conveyed by the Prince-Bishop in Wrocław, Georg Kardinal Kopp, to the Prussian Ministry of Education. See Herbert, *Ausländerpolitik,* 40f.
66. See Pietraszek, "Zwischen Geldverdienen und Aufstieg," 122–127, 129f., where he examines the recorded memories of seven former Polish migrant laborers.
67. Printed in the appendix in Nichtweiss, *Saisonarbeiter,* 251.
68. Panayi, "Irish, Poles and Other Migrants," 40.
69. Herbert, *Ausländerpolitik,* 29.
70. Nichtweiss, *Saisonarbeiter,* 221.
71. See Brunn, "Ausländische Arbeiter, " 16f.
72. Herbert, *Ausländerpolitik,* 65; see for more details Bade, "Billig und willig," 320–24.
73. Herbert, *Ausländerpolitik,* 43.
74. Dieter Gosewinkel, "Wer ist Deutscher? Deutsche Staatsangehörigkeit im 19. und 20. Jahrhundert, " in *Zuwanderungsland Deutschland. Migrationen 1500–2005,* ed. Rosemarie Beier-de Haan (Wolfratshausen, 2005), 90–105; Dieter Gosewinkel, *Einbürgern und Ausschließen: Die Nationalisierung der Staatsangehörigkeit vom Deutschen Bund bis zur Bundesrepublik Deutschland* (Göttingen, 2001), 310–27; Rogers Brubaker, *Staats-Bürger: Deutschland und Frankreich im historischen Vergleich* (Hamburg, 1994), 156–83.
75. Kriedte, "Wirtschaftliche Not," 37f.; Herbert, *Ausländerpolitik,* 91–98.

Bibliography

Bade, Klaus J. "Ausländerbeschäftigung, Staatsräson und Sicherheitspolitik: Der Sonderfall Preußen." In *Europa in Bewegung: Migration vom späten 18. Jahrhundert bis zur Gegenwart*, ed. Klaus J. Bade. Munich, 2000.

———. "'Billig und willig'—die 'ausländischen Wanderarbeiter' im kaiserlichen Deutschland." In *Deutsche im Ausland, Fremde in Deutschland: Migration in Geschichte und Gegenwart*, ed. Klaus J. Bade. Munich, 1992.

———. "Labour, Migration, and the State: Germany from the Late 19th Century to the Onset of the Great Depression." In *Population, Labour and Migration in 19th- and 20th-Century Germany*, ed. Klaus J. Bade. Leamington Spa et al., 1987.

Bade, Klaus J. ed. *Die multikulturelle Herausforderung: Menschen über Grenzen—Grenzen über Menschen.* Munich, 1996.

Becker, Otto. *Die Regelung des ausländischen Arbeiterwesens in Deutschland: Unter besonderer Berücksichtigung der Anwerbung und Vermittlung.* Berlin, 1918.

Blanke, Richard. *Prussian Poland in the German Empire: 1871–1900.* Boulder, CO, 1981.

Broszat, Martin. *Zweihundert Jahre deutsche Polenpolitik.* Munich, 1963.

Brożek, Andrzej. "Polityka imigracyjna w państwach docelowych emigracji polskiej (1850–1939)" [The immigration policy in the countries of destination for emigrants from the Polish areas (1850–1939)]. In *Emigracja z ziem polskich w czasach nowożytnych i najnowszych (XVIII–XX w.)* [Emigration from the Polish areas in recent and more recent periods (18th–20th C.)], ed. Andrzej Pilch. Warsaw, 1984.

———. "Ruchy migracyjne z ziem polskich pod panowaniem pruskim w latach 1850–1918" [Migratory movements from Polish areas under Prussian rule 1850–1918]. In *Emigracja z ziem polskich w czasach nowożytnych i najnowszych (XVIII–XX w.)* [Emigration from the Polish areas in recent and more recent periods (18th–20th C.)], ed. Andrzej Pilch. Warsaw, 1984.

Brubaker, Rogers, *Staats-Bürger: Deutschland und Frankreich im historischen Vergleich.* Hamburg, 1994.

Brudzyńska-Němec, Gabriela. *Polenvereine in Baden: Hilfeleistung süddeutscher Liberaler für die polnischen Freiheitskämpfer 1831–1832.* Heidelberg, 2006.

Brunn, Gerhard. "Ausländische Arbeiter und die Debatte um die ‚Überfremdungsgefahr' im Deutschen Kaiserreich." In *Migracja i integracja jako doświadczenie europejskie na przykładzie niemieckich metropolii w XIX i XX w. Polacy w Zagłębiu Ruhry i Berlinie—Migration und Integration als europäische Erfahrung am Beispiel deutscher Metropolen im 19. und 20. Jahrhundert. Die Polen im Ruhrgebiet und Berlin*, ed. Detlef Briesen et al. Wrocław, 1996.

Conrad, Sebastian. *Globalisierung und Nation im Deutschen Kaiserreich.* 2nd ed. Munich, 2010.

Frackowiak, Johannes. "Arbeitsmigranten und/oder Einwanderer? Polen in Mitteldeutschland 1880–1945." *IMIS-Beiträge* 29 (2006): 71–98.

Galos, Adam, et al. *Dzieje Hakaty* [The History of the Hakata]. Poznań, 1966.

Gehrke, Roland. *Der polnische Westgedanke bis zur Wiederrichtung des polnischen Staates nach Ende des Ersten Weltkrieges: Genese und Begründung polnischer Gebietsansprüche gegenüber Deutschland im Zeitalter des europäischen Nationalismus.* Marburg, 2001.

———. "Praktische Solidarität als Ausdruck politischer Gesinnung: Die Aktivität der südwestdeutschen 'Polenvereine' von 1831/32." In *Migration als soziale Herausforderung: Historische Formen solidarischen Handelns von der Antike bis zum 20. Jahrhundert,* ed. Joachim Bahlcke et al. Stuttgart, 2011.

Gosewinkel, Dieter. *Einbürgern und Ausschließen: Die Nationalisierung der Staatsangehörigkeit vom Deutschen Bund bis zur Bundesrepublik Deutschland* (Göttingen, 2001).

———. "Wer ist Deutscher? Deutsche Staatsangehörigkeit im 19. und 20. Jahrhundert." In *Zuwanderungsland Deutschland: Migrationen 1500–2005,* ed. Rosemarie Beier-de Haan. Wolfratshausen, 2005.

Grabowski, Sabine. *Deutscher und polnischer Nationalismus: Der Deutsche Ostmarkenverein und die polnische Straż 1894–1914.* Marburg, 1998.

Groniowski, Krzysztof. "Emigracja z ziem zaboru rosyjskiego (1864–1918)" [Emigration from Russian Poland (1864–1918)]. In *Emigracja z ziem polskich w czasach nowożytnych i najnowszych (XVIII–XX w.)* [Emigration from the Polish Areas in recent and more recent periods (18th–20th C.)], ed. Andrzej Pilch. Warsaw, 1984.

Herbert, Ulrich. *Geschichte der Ausländerpolitik in Deutschland: Saisonarbeiter, Zwangsarbeiter, Gastarbeiter, Flüchtlinge.* Munich, 2001.

Hering, Rainer. *Konstruierte Nation: Der Alldeutsche Verband 1890 bis 1939.* Hamburg, 2003.

Hoerder, Dirk. *Cultures in Contact: World Migrations in the Second Millennium.* Durham, NC, 2002.

Kalembka, Sławomir. *Wielka Emigracja 1831–1863* [The great emigration 1831–1863]. Toruń, 2003.

Kautsky, Karl. *Die Agrarfrage: Eine Übersicht über die Tendenzen der modernen Landwirthschaft und die Agrarpolitik der Sozialdemokratie.* Stuttgart, 1899.

Kępińska, Ewa. *Migracje sezonowe z Polski do Niemiec: Mechanizmy rekrutacji, rola rodziny i zróżnicowanie według płci* [Seasonal migration from Poland to Germany: The mechanisms of recruitment, the role of the family and the differences with regard to the sexes]. Warsaw, 2008.

Kleßmann, Christoph. "Einwanderungsprobleme im Auswanderungsland: Das Beispiel der 'Ruhrpolen'." In *Deutsche im Ausland—Fremde in Deutschland: Migration in Geschichte und Gegenwart,* ed. Klaus J. Bade. Munich, 1992.

Kleßmann, Christoph, and Johannes Frackowiak. "Die Polenpolitik des Deutschen Kaiserreichs 1871–1918." In *Nationalistische Politik und Ressentiments: Deutsche und Polen von 1871 bis zur Gegenwart,* ed. Johannes Frackowiak. Göttingen, 2013.

Kolb, Eberhard. "Polenbild und Polenfreundschaft der deutschen Frühliberalen: Zur Motivation und Funktion außenpolitischer Parteinahme im Vormärz." *Saeculum* 26 (1975): 111–27.

Kraszewski, Piotr. *Polska emigracja zarobkowa w latach 1870–1939: Praktyka i refleksja* [Polish economic migration in the years 1870–1939: The practice and reflections upon it]. Poznań, 1995.

Kriedte, Peter. "Wirtschaftliche Not, massiver Druck und physische Gewalt: Wanderungen in der deutsch-polnischen Beziehungsgeschichte des 19. und 20. Jahrhunderts." In *Społeczeństwo w dobie modernizacji: Polacy i Niemcy w XIX i XX wieku: Studia ofiarowane profesorowi Kazimierzowi Wajdzie w siedemdziesiątą rocznicę urodzin* [Society in the age of its modernization: Poles and Germans in the 19th and 20th centuries: Festschrift for Kazimierz Wajda on the occasion of his 70th birthday], ed. Roman Bäcker. Toruń, 2000.

Langewiesche, Dieter. "Humanitäre Massenbewegung und politisches Bekenntnis: Polenbegeisterung in Südwestdeutschland." In *Blick zurück ohne Zorn: Polen und Deutsche in Geschichte und Gegenwart*, ed. Dietrich Beyrau. Tübingen, 1999.

Łuczak, Czesław. *Od Bismarcka do Hitlera: Polsko-niemieckie stosunki gospodarcze* [From Bismarck to Hitler: Polish-German economic relations]. Poznań, 1988.

Moch, Leslie Page. *Moving Europeans: Migration in Western Europe since 1650.* 2nd edition. Bloomington, IN, 2003.

Müller, Uwe. "Wirtschaftliche Maßnahmen der Polenpolitik in der Zeit des Deutschen Kaiserreichs." In *Nationalistische Politik und Ressentiments: Deutsche und Polen von 1871 bis zur Gegenwart*, ed. Johannes Frackowiak. Göttingen, 2013.

Neubach, Helmut. *Die Ausweisungen von Polen und Juden aus Preußen 1885/86: Ein Beitrag zu Bismarcks Polenpolitik und zur Geschichte des deutsch-polnischen Verhältnisses.* Wiesbaden, 1967.

Nichtweiss, Johannes. *Die ausländischen Saisonarbeiter in der Landwirtschaft der östlichen und mittleren Gebiete des Deutschen Reiches: Ein Beitrag zur Geschichte der preußisch-deutschen Politik von 1890 bis 1914.* [East-]Berlin, 1959.

Oltmer, Jochen. "'Rückkehr historischer Migrationsmuster?' Migration und Integration in Deutschland im frühen und im späten 20. Jahrhundert." In *Die Russlanddeutschen in den Migrationsprozessen zwischen den GUS-Staaten und Deutschland*, ed. Otto Luchterhandt and Alfred Eisfeld. Göttingen, 2008.

———. "Wanderungsraum Deutschland im 19. und 20. Jahrhundert." In *Polnische Einwanderung: Zur Geschichte und Gegenwart der Polen in Deutschland*, ed. Basil Kerski and Krzysztof Ruchniewicz. Osnabrück, 2011.

Pachoński, Jan, and Reuel K. Wilson. *Poland's Caribbean Tragedy: A Study of Polish Legions in the Haitian War of Independence 1802–1803.* Boulder, CO, 1986.

Pallaske, Christoph. "Die Migration von Polen nach Deutschland: Ein europäisches Migrationssystem." In *Die Migration von Polen nach Deutschland: Zu Geschichte und Gegenwart eines europäischen Migrationssystems*, ed. Christoph Pallaske. Baden-Baden, 2001.

Panayi, Panikos. "Irish, Poles and Other Migrants: A Comparative Study of Migration to Britain and Germany, 1820–1918." In *Irish and Polish Migration in Comparative Perspective*, ed. John Belchem and Klaus Tenfelde. Essen, 2003.

Pietraszek, Edward. "Zwischen Geldverdienen und Aufstieg: Polnische Arbeitsmigranten in Deutschland von 1870 bis 1939." In *Vom Wandergesellen zum "Green Card" Spezialisten: Interkulturelle Aspekte der Arbeitsmigration im östlichen Mitteleuropa*, ed. Klaus Roth. Münster et al., 2003.

Pilch, Andrzej. "Emigracja z ziem zaboru austriackiego (od połowy XIX w. do 1918 r.)" [Emigration from the Austrian areas (from the middle of the nineteenth century to 1918)]. In *Emigracja z ziem polskich w czasach nowożytnych i najnowszych (XVIII–XX w.)* [Emigration from the Polish Areas in recent and more recent periods (18th–20th C.)], ed. Andrzej Pilch. Warsaw, 1984.

———. "Wstęp" [Introduction]. In *Emigracja z ziem polskich w czasach nowożytnych i najnowszych (XVIII–XX w.)* [Emigration from the Polish Areas in recent and more recent periods (18th–20th C.)], ed. Andrzej Pilch. Warsaw, 1984.

Porter, Brian. *When Nationalism Began to Hate: Imagining Modern Politics in Nineteenth-Century Poland*. New York et al., 2000.

Wehler, Hans-Ulrich. "Die Polenpolitik im Deutschen Kaiserreich." In *Krisenherde des Kaiserreichs 1871–1918. Studien zur deutschen Sozial- und Verfassungsgeschichte*, ed. Hans-Ulrich Wehler. Göttingen, 1970.

Wertheimer, Jack. *Unwelcome Strangers: East European Jews in Imperial Germany*. 2nd ed. New York, 1991.

CHAPTER SIX

⁓:⁓

Elite Migration to Germany
The Anglo-American Colony in Dresden before World War I

NADINE ZIMMERLI

In 1908, an American resident of Dresden reported on the existence of a shop sign found on the Saxon capital's most exclusive retail avenue, Prager Strasse, that read "English spoken, American understood." This American resident could not say whether the shop and its sign were apocryphal but concluded that the sign ought to be invented if it did not exist.[1] He was right, because this alleged sign displayed by a high-end retailer both reflects the large and affluent Anglo-American presence in Dresden before World War I and nicely illustrates that Dresdeners specifically courted an elite Anglo-American clientele and tried to make them feel welcome.

A brochure titled "Dresden—The Jewel of Northern Europe," published in 1910 by Dresden's tourist association, the self-titled Strangers' Protection Society [founded in 1875 as *Verein Einheimischer und Fremder zur Wahrung gegenseitiger Interessen*, since 1895 *Verein zur Förderung Dresdens und des Fremdenverkehrs*] further highlights that a large British and American community existed in Dresden and confirms the city's active recruitment of Anglo-American visitors and residents. This English-language publication—the association's only foreign-language guide—stated that "the foreigner, indeed, is very much a privileged person in Dresden."[2] After the brochure detailed Dresden's Anglo-American facilities, from sports venues such as golf links and tennis courts to shops stocking the latest English and American goods, the Society revealed its mission: "the English or American visitor *and intending resident* literally finds in Dresden a 'home away from home.'"[3]

Not only did the local tourist association appeal to Anglo-American visitors, but it also hoped to attract ever more British and American permanent residents. In fact, most of the brochure highlighted Dresden's amenities for a prolonged, rather than a short, stay. As this makes clear, Dresden's tourist association actively encouraged Anglo-American migration to Dresden and invited English-speaking foreigners to settle permanently in the city. To do so, the Society highlighted Dresden's already existing, extensive British and American infrastructure.

Anglo-American migration to Dresden, and the resulting infrastructure, was but one aspect of the mobility brought about by the increasingly globalized world around 1900. As scholars, most notably Sebastian Conrad, have recently come to recognize, the "late nineteenth century was an era of worldwide inter-action and exchange," but "this fact is returning to historical consciousness only now, in the context of the current wave of globalization."[4] Conrad focuses his attention on migratory laborers in imperial Germany, which leads him to argue that globalization conditioned nationalist responses. He dismisses the movements of economic elites, diplomats, or artists—people such as the Anglo-Americans Dresdeners encouraged to migrate to their city—as less significant than the mass mobility of the peasant and proletarian masses in the minds of contemporaries.[5]

Yet in Dresden, at least, elite foreign migration was very much on the minds of municipal, social, and cultural leaders, as exemplified by the members of the Strangers' Protection Society, whose encouragement of Anglo-American foreigners to settle in their city highlights a different German response to the globalized world of the late nineteenth century. While Conrad convinc-ingly argues that migratory laborers contributed to increasing national fervor in imperial Germany, another type of migration, socially elite in nature, led Germans to embrace foreign residents at the same time. It is important to point this out in order to emphasize that Germans responded with nuance, rather than uniformity, to the opportunities and challenges presented by the globalizing world around 1900.

Indeed, at the turn of the last century, Dresden's Anglo-American commu-nity was a major and welcome feature of the city's social, cultural, and physical landscape. It supported English, American, and Scottish churches, which were all located in the so-called English and American quarters of the city northeast and southeast of Dresden's main train station.[6] The community had also estab-lished a number of private preparatory schools for boys and girls. Foremost among these schools was Franklin College, one of only four European centers at which American University Board examinations were held.[7] Originally founded in 1890 to "provide for English-speaking boys a thorough English, Classical and Mathematical Education, and at the same time to give such advantages in Modern Languages, as could not possibly be obtained under Home conditions," Franklin College started admitting girls as well in 1901 and had enrolled over five hundred pupils by 1904.[8] Upon its founding, the College admitted only students aged nine and older, but in 1907, "as the result of several applications," the College formed a class for English and American children between the ages of six and ten.[9] Over the years, the College thus expanded into a comprehensive school for Anglo-American children of both sexes and all ages. Overall, it strove to "combine all that is best in American with all that is best in German life," making it a prominent Anglo-American institution mediating between foreign and local society in Dresden.[10]

In general, Anglo-Americans often migrated to Dresden for educational purposes, to learn German or to take instruction in the fine and musical arts. The foyer of the opera house at times even "resounded with nothing save the English tongue" due to the "countless young ladies from England and America who are acquiring a 'finishing education' in Dresden."[11] To support this burgeoning community, three English-language newspapers appeared at varying intervals—the weekly *Stranger's Guide to Dresden*, founded in 1871; the *Daily Record*, Germany's only English-language daily newspaper, published between 1906 and 1910; and the *Continental Express*, the weekly publication of the Anglo-American Club.

All these elements combined to make the city indeed an ideal "home away from home" for British and American sojourners abroad. One temporary American resident stated in 1909 that "Dresden had impressed her as quite the finest city for foreign residents she knew in Europe, being infinitely superior to Paris or Berlin as far as climate, pretty surroundings, opportunities for artistic and musical education, and homelike conditions were concerned."[12] Broadly speaking, by the early twentieth century Dresden proved attractive to British and American residents on account of its artistic and educational facilities, especially its art galleries, the opera house, its various theaters, and its schools, coupled with a beautiful location and a relatively low cost of living.

Over a century earlier, some of these very same reasons had led to the establishment of an English-speaking community in Dresden in the first place, when the city had featured as a destination of the Grand Tour on account of its royal art gallery, its reputation as a center of music, and the natural beauty of the Elbe valley.[13] English travelers increasingly visited Dresden, as it was "less forbidding than Berlin and more cosmopolitan than both Berlin and Hanover," and as early as 1792, a traveling party of English aristocrats noted that they had found "a numerous society of English" in the city.[14] After the Napoleonic wars, American travelers also began taking up temporary residence in the city, and one prominent American resident in the early nineteenth century, the academic George Ticknor, resided in Dresden for a year in 1835–36. During his stay the future president of Harvard University struck up a friendship with Prince Johann, the future king of Saxony, and upon his return to the United States popularized Dresden as a travel destination for Americans.[15]

By mid-century, Dresden's permanently residing Anglo-Americans had formed a community, putting down roots by instituting their own religious and civic associations. In 1841, English residents founded an Anglican Church congregation, which met at a temporary chapel, and about two hundred English residents lived in the city in 1845.[16] In 1858, eighteen British and American men founded the Anglo-American Club, the first such institution on the European continent, which existed continuously until World War I.[17] When an American dentist, who would reside in Dresden until 1916, moved to the city in 1866, he already mentioned the presence of a "considerable English and American colony."[18] About 340 Anglicans and Episcopalians lived in Dresden in the late 1860s, and the year 1869 saw the founding of an American Episcopalian church congregation as well as the consecration of the newly-built Anglican Church of All Saints', which literally cemented the presence of English-speakers in Dresden in stone.[19]

Not accidentally, the permanent formation of the Anglo-American community coincided with the advent of leisure-based mass tourism and mass migration fueled by the invention of the steam engine and subsequent rise of mass transportation made possible by steamships and ever-expanding rail networks in the middle decades of the nineteenth century.[20] Not just British and American travelers visited Dresden in greater numbers; the number of all registered visitors to the city jumped from 13,900 in 1831 to 71,010 by 1846.[21] After the revolutionary upheavals of 1848, Dresden registered a renewed influx of travelers and recorded a total of 103,792 visitors in 1868.[22]

As Dresden transformed into a popular travel destination, the local population began to associate the category of *Fremde* [strangers] with resident, not transitory, foreigners. An 1859 travel guide stated that Dresden

> has been elevated, as if through quiet accord, to a rendezvous of strangers of all nations . . . Yet where else do art and nature come together in such glorious unity as they do here! . . . This is why so many foreigners choose it as their place of residence, especially those who have retired from business and want to lead a comfortable life in every respect.[23]

Just as it had during the Grand Tour, Dresden continued to appeal to affluent foreigners on account of its extraordinary combinations of artistic and natural treasures, and many of them took up permanent residence.

Regarding non-local visitors as potential residents rather than transient tourists became engrained in Dresdeners' thinking about foreigners in subsequent years. In 1864, an economist wrote that tourists in cities such as Munich and Breslau outnumbered those registered in Dresden, but "[i]t is less travelers of whom the Dresdner thinks when he speaks of strangers. He thinks of those thousands who reside here permanently or for long periods of time, [and] who benefit not only the inns, but almost all classes of society and trade."[24] Thus, permanently residing migrants, not transient travelers, constituted the most important and economically beneficial category of visitors. In the 1860s, then,

Dresdeners began to value foreign migrants over tourists; affluent foreign permanent residents and Dresden's prosperity had become inextricably linked.

After German unification in 1871, and Dresden's loss of political importance to Berlin, this link took on even more salience. In the 1870s, Dresden's municipal elites made a conscious decision to actively recruit affluent foreigners to take up permanent residence. Fueled by fears that Dresden had lost its appeal as an international travel destination, the municipal government commissioned the city's first and only *Fremdenstudie*, a detailed statistical account of resident foreigners and their economic contributions as based on the 1875 census.[25] This report was the first effort by city authorities to systematically document the city's foreign residents and also the first time that officials commented on the importance of foreigners to municipal affairs.

The report assuaged local fears about Dresden losing its international pull, since the number of resident foreigners stood at 8,026 in 1875, which represented a substantial increase over the numbers in 1871 (6,250) and 1867 (4,658).[26] In terms of economic stratification, of the four largest foreign groups in the city the vast majority of Austrians had come to Dresden for work and earned wages or salaries as craftsmen, factory workers, or servants. In contrast, the majority of Russian, British, and American residents had come to Dresden for purposes of entertainment and leisure, to retire in the city, or to attain an education. Thus, the majority of Austrians belonged to the poorer, dependent stratum of society, whereas the Russians, British, and Americans enjoyed relative affluence and economic independence.[27]

The Statistical Bureau for the most part did not elaborate on economic categories predominated by Austrians. Rather, the statisticians deemed self-employed foreign artists and teachers "highly significant," emphasized that the contributions of the independent entrepreneurs had a "profound influence" on Dresden, and acknowledged that "an affluent, consumption-oriented population of foreigners" was extremely important for the "economic prosperity of the city's inhabitants."[28] In other words, the statisticians emphasized the importance of the 2,396 Russian, British, and American residents who predominantly belonged to the leisure class over the 4,407 Austrians who belonged to the working class.[29] Although the focus on affluent Russians and Anglo-Americans might have been due to an implicit prejudice against Catholic Austrians, the report did not track religious affiliation and offered no commentary on the religious views of foreign migrants living in Dresden. The report focused solely on the economic contributions foreigners made to the city, especially the fine arts, and the Bureau's discussion strongly endorsed the presence and continued recruitment of affluent American, British, and Russian migrants, while remaining silent on labor migrants from Austria-Hungary.

Whereas the *Fremdenstudie* simply collected economic information on foreigners in Dresden and recommended continued recruitment of affluent migrants, Dresden's tourist association actively recruited them. Founded in 1875, the Strangers' Protection Society represented Dresden's bourgeois, intellectual elite; its founding executive committee included two academics, one lawyer, one bookseller and publisher, a consul, and an art purveyor to the royal court. Much like the *Fremdenstudie*, these men claimed to have founded the association due to the "economic importance of the foreigners' question." It catered to members of the leisure class from the start, stating outright that its definition of "stranger" did not include "menial laborers, servants, and so forth" but instead focused on "affluent strangers with disposable incomes, namely Americans and Englishmen."[30] Just like the Statistical Bureau had done, the Society consciously excluded the majority of foreigners in Dresden, laboring Austrians, from consideration and privileged the affluent, predominantly English-speaking elites.

Civic authorities thus merely acknowledged one type of migration, the laboring masses, but they actively encouraged another type, elite migration. On the national level, debates on immigration mainly focused on migratory laborers, especially Russian and Galician Poles, which resulted in calls for restrictions, better border controls, and the Germanization of Polish migrants.[31] Yet this was not the only German response to the increased foreign presence in their midst. Rather, in Dresden, municipal leaders carefully distinguished between types of migrants and openly embraced and recruited socially elite foreigners, especially from Great Britain and the United States.

Indeed, the Strangers' Protection Society's annual reports document an increasing shift toward an exclusive focus on Dresden's British and American temporary and permanent residents. In 1875, Russians outnumbered the British and American members of Dresden's foreign leisure class, but just five years later their numbers had diminished to the point of relative parity—679 British, 654 Russian, and 580 American permanent residents.[32] Yet despite the continued presence of over 600 Russians in 1880, the Society merely narrated the decline of that colony in its annual reports and focused most of its discussion and efforts on the ever-increasing number of English-speaking migrants. In 1882 it announced that "[a]s usual, this year once again the British and American nation was in the vast majority" of foreigners seeking information from the Society.[33] Over the first few years of its existence, then, the Strangers' Protection Society came to see the Americans and British—collapsed into members of one English-speaking nation—as its most numerous, visible, and important clientele, and directed its efforts toward attracting English-speakers and catering to their needs.

To this end, in 1880, the Society published a small brochure in German and English that featured Dresden's most important sights and contained the addresses of businesses whose owners were members of the Strangers' Protection Society and who would therefore submit to mediation by the Society should differences with foreigners arise.[34] That same year, a member of the Anglo-American community, Dr. Charles Eales, was elected to the Society's executive committee.[35] In 1881, the committee commented on the heightened visibility of English-speakers in Dresden's public life—"[w]hoever associates a lot in the English and American quarter, or often visits our institutes of art will be able to confirm this on account of his own perceptions"—and pointed out that local business owners who depended on foreign clients "had been able to notice a pleasing increase in their sales on account of the stronger influx of non-locals."[36] Thus, the Society could report a noteworthy increase of English and American temporary and permanent residents just six years after its founding and once again reiterated and established the significance of these English-speakers to art institutions and local businesses more generally. Increasingly, the Society catered to the needs of permanent migrants, not transient tourists, and in 1886 happily reported that "as is known, representatives of the British and American Nation . . . have constituted the strongest contingent of our foreign colony for many years and have become devoted friends of our association."[37]

Whether due to the activities of the Strangers' Protection Society or simply as a result of the ever-increasing volume of British and American visitors to the European continent, by the 1880s, the Anglo-American colony had become entrenched in Dresden and remained an important feature of municipal life for the next three decades.[38] A Scottish Presbyterian Church was built in 1884 and the American Episcopal Church of St. John's was consecrated in 1886.[39] The community also continued to grow in size. By 1895, 2,279 Anglo-Americans were permanent residents of Dresden, 1,184 of whom were British subjects and 1,095 of whom were Americans. In 1910, the numbers still held strong at 1,868, with 931 British and 937 American residents.[40]

Although Dresden's population quadrupled between the 1870s and the 1910s, the number of British and American residents remained relatively stable. Yet observers consistently perceived Dresden's Anglo-American population as a sizeable one. For example, in 1907 a local observer stated that "[i]n Dresden, the contingent of foreigners is more noticeable than in other major cities, and none more so than the English and the Americans."[41] This quotation is also informative when it comes to Dresdener's usage of the term *Fremde*. As the original German makes clear—"Bedeutend mehr, als in einer anderen großen Stadt fällt in Dresden das Kontigent seiner Fremden auf, und von diesen bei weitem am meisten die Engländer und Amerikaner"—this observer specifically applied a term to English-speaking foreigners that in German usually encompasses all non-locals, Germans and non-Germans alike. Indeed, Dresdeners translated the term *Fremdenstadt* as "city of foreigners" and proclaimed their city to be "Germany's preferred *Fremdenstadt*" in 1911.[42] Dresden was not just any tourist destination. It was a city patronized by English-speakers.

Foreign residents, especially Anglo-Americans, clearly mattered to the city's self-perception and domestic standing vis-à-vis perceived rivals.

These rival cities included the national and regional German capitals of Berlin, Munich, Hamburg, Stuttgart, and Wiesbaden, and spa towns such as Baden-Baden, which all had Anglo-American colonies.[43] In terms of size and their status as fellow royal residence cities, Stuttgart and Munich were Dresden's closest competitors. By 1908, though, Stuttgart was reported to have "lost its once flourishing English-speaking colony."[44] Munich, however, much like Dresden, attracted American students to its art academy in great numbers.[45] In addition, Americans studied in old university towns such as Göttingen and Leipzig. Yet the numbers of Americans in Dresden far outweighed numbers of Americans in these university towns. In 1877, twenty-five to thirty Americans studied in Göttingen, whereas the 1875 census had counted 584 permanent American residents in Dresden. In 1895, 556 Americans resided in Leipzig, whereas Dresden was home to over one thousand Americans that same year. In general, a little more than twice as many British subjects and Americans resided in Dresden than in Leipzig.[46]

Overall, perception of size and importance mattered most, and Dresden ranked high among German centers of Anglo-American life in the eyes of contemporary observers. The English-language editions of the Baedeker guidebooks consistently stated that in Dresden "a considerable English community resides here," a phrase not used to describe any other German city.[47] In 1909, a British journal asserted that "Dresden is emphatically a comfortable and pleasant place of residence. Without the grandeur of Berlin or the commercial bustle of Frankfort-on-Main [sic], it has attracted a larger English colony than any other town in Germany."[48] Even as late as 1917, the New York Times stated that Dresden "still harbors the largest American colony" in Germany.[49]

The presence of this large colony and the thousands of Anglo-American visitors every year suffused Dresden with English sounds. German observers noted that Dresden felt like an English or American city during certain times of day when more English than German could be heard on the city's promenades and in its museums.[50] Dresden's illustrated journal, the Salonblatt, tried to capture some of this atmosphere in 1906 when printing a seemingly random conversation with an American woman about giving a public talk. The American's speech is a mixture of German and English, such as "No, ich will lieber nicht vortragen. My mother sagt, ich sei überanstrengt und soll sonnenbaden."[51] The paper did not draw attention to the conversation as a special occurrence, but rather conveyed it as if it was one of many happening on the prominent Brühl Terrace every day.

A number of decades earlier, a young Theodore Roosevelt, who studied German for six months as a guest of the elite von Minckwitz family, had also captured the mixture of English and German that even long-term residents employed. In one letter, Roosevelt related a conversation between his aunt, a permanent resident of Dresden, and a German servant girl on how to pre-serve a goose. The American's instructions were "[e]s muss gechopped-up in little pieces sein," much to the consternation of the servant.[52] Roosevelt's recollections show that Americans and Germans interacted on a variety of levels—upper-class families such as the von Minckwitzes and the Roosevelts intermingled as social equals whereas members of the German lower-class interacted with Americans as servants. Collectively, this established Anglo-Americans as members of the elite in Germans' minds.

While English-speakers might have expected their German friends or employees to speak a modicum of English, Germans might also not have made it easy for Anglo-Americans to learn the native language. A letter writer to the *Daily Record* in 1907 complained that foreign students of German were "materially hindered by shop and boarding-house keepers who insist on speak-ing English" in this endeavor. Although this was "often well-meant," many for-eign residents "refuse to live in or recommend certain pensions because of the English-speaking proclivities of proprietors and others."[53] Germans who were keen on attracting an affluent British and American clientele hoped to appear welcoming by speaking English. Yet whereas this might have been expected by some Anglo-Americans, it drove away others hoping for more immersion in local culture. It most likely also prevented some English-speakers such as Roosevelt's aunt from ever becoming truly fluent in German.

Aside from making an effort to speak English, Dresdeners tried to make the British and American residents in their midst feel welcome in general. For example, Dresden restaurants catered to American patriotism but suppressed overtly German national behavior. A letter to the Dresden Pan-Germans in 1911 revealed that a café owner had refused to allow the nationalistic song "Wacht am Rhein" to be played in his establishment, but that a few months earlier a band performing at the popular Belvedere restaurant on the Fourth of July had played nothing but American patriotic songs for the Americans present. This had led to loud toasts and a sing-along of the American national anthem by all involved.[54]

Relations between local Germans and members of the Anglo-American community were on the whole very friendly. Reports on fundraisers at the community's three churches routinely included language about the "numerous German friends of the parishioners" in attendance, from the 1890s through August 1914.[55] Yet it was predominantly the arts, especially music, that linked the Anglo-American and German communities. It was one of the main fac-tors for the presence of English-speaking foreigners in Dresden in the first place. When the *Daily Record* characterized life in Dresden as "the reverse of unpleasant" in 1908, it linked this sentiment to the fact that the "best of music is to be had everywhere for a most modest outlay."[56]

Anglo-American students flocked to Dresden to study music in some form. Samuel Clemens (Mark Twain), for example, came to spend "a portion of the winter at Dresden, where his daughters [were] studying music" in the early 1890s.[57] Young Anglo-Americans studied music alongside fellow German students at the famous Royal Conservatory, founded in 1856; the privately owned Rollfuss Academy of Music for Ladies, founded in 1875; and Ehrlich's Music Academy, founded in 1878. These private institutions printed informational brochures in German and English, a testament to the clientele these academies wished to attract.[58] Both also advertised in Dresden's English-language papers, which in turn printed myriad reports on pupils' recitals and always carefully noted the contributions by young British or American musicians.[59]

Aside from Anglo-American students, these academies also featured Anglo-American instructors. English composer Percy Sherwood gave lessons at the Rollfuss Academy, while American piano teacher Emmeline Potter-Frissell worked at Ehrlich's Music Academy.[60] Both moved seamlessly in German circles. As the *Stranger's Guide* noted in 1911, Sherwood had "a host of friends in Dresden among German residents as well as in the English-speaking colony."[61] When King Friedrich August III of Saxony conferred upon Sherwood the title of Professor of Music, Sherwood appeared just like any other of the German honorees in the *Salonblatt* and was simply identified as *Tonkünstler*.[62] Emmeline Potter-Frissell also appeared in the *Salonblatt* as simply another local figure, being identified as "the famous Dresden piano teacher" in one announcement.[63] She had moved to Dresden in 1898 and her musical "At Homes" and student soirees, which saw up to 150 guests, brought together prominent members of the American colony as well as notable German musicians.[64]

Like Sherwood and Potter-Frissell, most members of the colony moved fluidly between foreign and native society and understood their lives in Dresden as engaged in "cosmopolitan residence."[65] Since the 1850s English-speakers in Dresden had built an extensive infrastructure of diplomatic, social, cultural, religious, educational, and even medical amenities that facilitated this cosmopolitan residence and in turn proved an incentive for more Anglo-Americans to spend at least one season in the city or to settle there permanently. Several social nodes, such as the three churches, the Anglo-American Club, sports clubs, and a myriad of schools, added to the pleasantness of life by facilitating social interaction among English-speakers and with local German society and as such constituted the backbone of the Anglo-American community.

However, the international tensions of the time, especially the great-power rivalry between Great Britain and Germany, did reverberate locally. For example, Anglo-German relations in Dresden became quite strained as a consequence of German pro-Boer sentiments during the South African

War. In March of 1900, Dresden made headlines in British and American papers as the foremost Anglophobic German city.[66] Children pelted English women with snowballs in the streets and vandals defaced the walls of the Anglo-American Club and the English Church with insulting epithets and red paint.[67]

Although the Dresden papers, German and English alike, downplayed the attacks as the acts of a few ruffians and called upon Dresdeners to move past the incidents and restore cordial relations between British subjects and the Saxons with whom they interacted every day, relations between the locals and English-speaking residents remained strained, which translated into decreasing numbers of Anglo-Americans in the city.[68] Aware of this decline, Dresden's municipal elites started a number of initiatives in 1905 that sought to repair Dresden's international reputation, improve Anglo-German relations, and attract English-speaking tourists and residents once more.

For example, Dresden participated in several private and municipal initiatives aimed at improving Anglo-German international relations after the first Morocco Crisis, such as a visit of British mayors to Germany in the summer of 1905 and a large British-German friendship demonstration in January 1906.[69] The city's daily English-language newspaper was established in the wake of this January meeting to "foster the entente cordiale, a true union of hearts, between the Anglo-American colony and their German hosts in Dresden."[70] Communication and exchange between the English-speaking and German communities lay at the heart of the young paper's mission. In its second issue, the editor outright stated that "[o]ur aim is to be useful to the community, whether English-speaking or German; to either or to both, as a link of good metal between the two."[71]

Although municipal Anglo-German friendship demonstrations also took place in other German localities, such as Munich, Cologne, and Stuttgart, only the event in Dresden led to a tangible outcome—the founding of a newspaper dedicated to forging an Anglo-German (and American) *entente cordiale*. As this example shows, international tensions did not just reverberate on the local level; local efforts also alleviated these tensions. After the second Morocco Crisis, Dresden's Society for the Promotion of International Friendship—founded in 1911 to promote mutual understanding between members of the various nationalities present in Dresden, and led by two Germans, two Englishmen, and a Scotsman—served much the same purpose. In fact, the Strangers' Protection Society's 1910 brochure "Dresden—The Jewel of Northern Europe" should be seen in the same light: it sought to bolster Dresden's international reputation by portraying the city as a friendly Anglo-German-American meeting space and in so doing hoped to attract more English-speaking migrants.

Perhaps the most interesting aspect of this brochure and the 1911 Friendship Society is their use of the term "cosmopolitan." Not only did British and Americans themselves perceive their residence as a cosmopolitan endeavor, the Anglo-American presence in Dresden also transformed the Saxon capital into "literally a cosmopolitan hub" in the view of the Strangers' Protection Society.[72] The founding of the Friendship Society, likewise, was regarded as "a great addition to the social and intellectual attractions of Dresden, further emphasizing the delightful cosmopolitan spirit already existing."[73] These two assertions explain why Dresdeners actively recruited English-speaking migrants, aside from their economic importance to the city—in the estimation of contemporaries, the resident Anglo-American community conferred a cosmopolitan distinction upon Dresden. It is important to emphasize once more that Dresden commentators only referenced cosmopolitan life with regard to the British and American migrants, ignoring the more than 24,000 Austro-Hungarians living in the city by 1910.[74]

Generally speaking, then, Dresdeners seized on elite migration as something positive and saw cosmopolitan encounters with permanent Anglo-American residents as a sign of Dresden's continued importance after the city had lost political power to Berlin following German unification. Dresden teetered on the brink of provincialism after 1871, and officials constantly worried about the city losing its international stature. Therefore, Dresden's embrace of elite Anglo-American migrants represented one municipal strategy to avoid descent into perceived mediocrity. As a principal for a boarding school catering to English-speaking girls succinctly put it in 1896, "without the foreigners, Dresden would be a village."[75]

Kathleen Courtney, one of the many young English ladies in Dresden and a pupil at this principal's school, painted a metaphorical picture of the intersection of German and Anglo-American life in the city before World War I. Sitting in her room at school in the American quarter in 1896, she observed in a letter that she was "being enlivened by strains from the band which is playing in the Bergkeller," a local restaurant. Courtney called the music—which she implied featured patriotic German songs—"really very good," and then added that "a short time ago the organ in the American Church was also going, and may be doing so still, but it is drowned by the band." A while later, the band stopped for a minute and Courtney noted that the organ in the American Church was still playing. She then heard the singing of "Eternal Father" emanating from the church even though there was hardly any wind carrying the music.[76]

This story makes for a lovely musical metaphor of the Anglo-American community in Dresden. In the city, German and foreign cultural spheres inhabited the same space, crossed, intersected, and overlapped. Although the American voice was quieter and less dominant, it nonetheless existed and persisted, contributing a clear and recognizable foreign voice to Dresden's public sphere. In turn, these English sounds conferred upon and confirmed for Dresden a much vaunted and prized cosmopolitan distinction. As such, the strains of the American Church choir added a welcome English voice to Dresden's urban soundscape, as did the thousands of Anglo-American residents in general.

Nadine Zimmerli is Associate Editor of Books at the Omohundro Institute of Early American History and Culture in Williamsburg, Virginia. She also offers courses on modern Europe as an adjunct assistant professor of history at the College of William & Mary. She earned her Ph.D. in modern European history from the University of Wisconsin-Madison and is completing a book on "American Dresden."

Notes

1. Quotation taken from A. Meff, "Dr. Grimshaw on Americanisms," *Stranger's Guide to Dresden*, 18 January 1908, 5.
2. Verein zur Förderung Dresdens und des Fremdenverkehrs, "Dresden—The Jewel of Northern Europe" (Dresden: 1910), 23. The inside flap of the brochure states: "Presented with the compliments of the Verein zur Förderung Dresdens und des Fremdenverkehrs (Strangers' Protection Society)." The association translated its name as Strangers' Protection Society, although this was not a literal translation.
3. Ibid., 20. Emphasis added.
4. Sebastian Conrad, *Globalization and the Nation in Imperial Germany*, trans. Sorcha O'Hagan (Cambridge, 2010), 1.
5. Ibid., 11.
6. For the exact location, see *Dresden und das Elbgelände*, ed. Friedrich Kummer, 5th ed. (Dresden, 1910), 122, 123.
7. "Franklin College," *Stranger's Guide to Dresden*, 9 September 1899, 1.
8. For the founding mission statement, see Franklin College, Dresden, Saxony, *Prospectus* 18, no. 7 (1893–94): 9. For the change in admission policy, see "Franklin College," *Stranger's Guide to Dresden*, 2 November 1901, 1. An article in 1903 specifically praised Franklin College for admitting girls and preparing them for university courses as well. See "Education for American Boys and Girls," *Stranger's Guide to Dresden*, 22 August 1903, 3. For the number of pupils enrolled, see "Franklin College Closing Festival," *Stranger's Guide to Dresden*, 16 July 1904, 1.
9. "Franklin College," *Stranger's Guide to Dresden*, 2 November 1907, 1.
10. "Franklin College," *Stranger's Guide to Dresden*, 10 September 1904, 1. The school functioned as a community center of sorts; it held annual closing festivals, its instructors gave lectures open to all members of the Anglo-American Colony free of charge, and its students formed the nucleus of community-wide sporting clubs.
11. "Wagner's 'Ring'," *Dresden Daily*, 5 April 1906, 2.

12. "Mrs. Elizabeth A. Bolton," *Daily Record*, 17 December 1909, 3.

13. Andrea Dietrich, "Die Entwicklung der Stadt Dresden zu einer Tourismusmetropole von den Anfängen bis zum Vorabend des ersten Weltkrieges," vol. 1 (PhD diss., Leipzig University, 1992); Jeremy Black, *The British and the Grand Tour* (London, 1985), 12; 218–19; Brian Dolan, *Ladies of the Grand Tour: British Women in Pursuit of Enlightenment and Adventure in Eighteenth-Century Europe* (New York, 2001), 105.

14. Black, 12; Dolan, 105.

15. Thomas Adam and Gisela Mettele, eds., *Two Boston Brahmins in Goethe's Germany: The Travel Journals of Anna and George Ticknor* (Lanham, MD, 2009). For overviews of American travelers in Dresden in the early nineteenth century, see Eberhard Brüning, "'Elb-Florenz' versus 'Spree-Athen': Die amerikanische Bildungselite des 19. Jahrhunderts und ihr Bild von Dresden," *Amerikastudien/American Studies* 36, no. 2 (1991): 195-208; Eberhard Brüning, "Sachsen mit amerikanischen Augen gesehen – Das Sachsenbild amerikanischer Globetrotter im 19. Jahrhundert," *Neues Archiv for Sächsische Geschichte* 67 (1996): 109–131; and Eberhard Brüning, "Saxony Is a Prosperous and Happy Country: American Views of the Kingdom of Saxony in the Nineteenth Century," in *Traveling between Worlds: German-American Encounters*, eds. Thomas Adam and Ruth Gross (Arlington, TX, 2006), 20–50. See also Ashley Sides, "'That Humane and Advanced Civilization': Interpreting Americans' Values from Their Praise of Saxony, 1800–1850" in *Crossing the Atlantic: Travel and Travel Writing in Modern Times*, eds. Thomas Adam and Nils H. Roemer (Arlington, TX, 2011), 11–49.

16. Paul W. Schniewind, *Anglicans in Germany: A History of Anglican Chaplaincies in Germany until 1945* (Darmstadt, 1988), 89.

17. "Anglo-American Club," *Stranger's Guide to Dresden*, 5 November 1898, 1–3; Victor von Hüben, *Mein Dresden lob ich mir*, 2nd ed. (Dresden, no date [1908]), 59.

18. Newell Sill Jenkins, *Reminiscences of Newell Sill Jenkins* (Princeton, NJ, 1924), 90.

19. Numbers based on the 1867 census, as reported in *Mittheilungen des Statistischen Amtes der Stadt Dresden*, vol. 1, nos. 3 and 4 (1891): 11. Also Schniewind, 92.

20. Shelley Baranowski and Ellen Furlough, eds., *Tourism, Consumer Culture, and Identity in Modern Europe and North America* (Ann Arbor, MI, 2001).

21. Dietrich, 1:114.

22. R. Jannasch, ed., *Zeitschrift des Statistischen Bureaus der Stadt Dresden*, no. 1 (Dresden, 1875), 7.

23. Friedrich Gottschalck, *Dresden, seine Umgebungen und die sächsische Schweiz: Ein Führer für Reisende* (Dresden, 1859), 10.

24. Cited in Dietrich, 1:146.

25. "Statistik der in Dresden sich aufhaltenden Fremden," in *Mittheilungen des Statistischen Bureaus der Stadt Dresden*, no. 4A, Part II, ed. R. Jannasch (Dresden, 1877), 73–100.

26. Ibid., 73.

27. Ibid., 92–93.

28. Ibid., 86–88.

29. Numbers taken from R. Jannasch, ed., *Mittheilungen des Statistischen Bureaus der Stadt Dresden*, no. 4A, Part I (Dresden, 1877), 37. The following nine countries counted one hundred or more permanent residents in Dresden in the 1875 census: Austria—4,407 / Russia—1,033 / Great Britain—779 / United States—584 / Switzerland—218 / Hungary—166 / France—148 / Italy—147 / Netherlands—100.

30. *Dritter Rechenschafts-Bericht des Vereins Einheimischer und Fremder zur Wahrung gegenseitiger Interessen* (Dresden, 1878), 6–7.

31. Conrad, *Globalization and the Nation in Imperial Germany*; also Klaus J. Bade, *Deutsche im Ausland, Fremde in Deutschland: Migration in Geschichte und Gegenwart* (Munich, 1992); Klaus J. Bade, ed., *Population, Labour, and Migration in 19th- and 20th-century Germany* (New York, 1987).

32. *Sechster Rechenschafts-Bericht des Vereins Einheimischer und Fremder zur Wahrung gegenseitiger Interessen* (Dresden, 1881), 8.

33. *Siebenter Rechenschafts-Bericht des Vereins Einheimischer und Fremder zur Wahrung gegenseitiger Interessen* (Dresden, 1882), 6.

34. *Fünfter Rechenschafts-Bericht des Vereins Einheimischer und Fremder zur Wahrung gegenseitiger Interessen* (Dresden, 1880), 5.

35. Ibid., 7.

36. *Sechster Rechenschafts-Bericht*, 3.

37. *Elfter Rechenschafts-Bericht des Vereins zur Förderung des Fremdenverkehrs in Dresden* (Dresden, 1886), 5–6.

38. For the ever-increasing numbers of Americans in Europe, see Christopher Endy, "Travel and World Power: Americans in Europe, 1890–1917," *Diplomatic History* 22, no. 4 (Fall 1998): 565–94.

39. For the Scottish Church, see Jürgen Helfricht, *Dresden und seine Kirchen* (Leipzig, 2005), 126. For the American Church, see the report from Consul Jos. F. Mason to Department of State on "The Consecration of the American Church of St. John in Dresden," 26 January 1887, no. 187, in *Despatches from United States Consuls in Dresden, 1837–1906* (Washington, DC, 1961).

40. Statistics for 1895 and 1905 are taken from a table comparing resident British subjects and American citizens in Dresden for 1895, 1900, and 1905 as printed in "Die Volkszählung vom 1. Dezember 1905," *Zeitschrift des K. Sächsischen Statistischen Landesamtes* 1 (1908): 10. The numbers for 1910 are from Ralf Richter, "Reichsausländer in Dresden zwischen 1871 und 1914" (Diplomarbeit, 1996), 54.

41. Eva Gräfin von Baudissin, "Die Amerikanische und Englische Kolonie," in *Dresden und die Dresdener—Ein lustiges Vademecum*, ed. Freiherr von Schlicht (Wolf Graf von Baudissin) (Dresden, 1907), 62.

42. The quotation is part of an advertisement found in Zeitungsausschnittsammlung, Z/ Bd. 1, "I. Internationale Hygiene-Ausstellung Dresden 1911" (I. IHA). Sächsisches Hauptstaatsarchiv Dresden. The organizers of the International Hygiene Exhibition printed promotional materials in German and English, and they translated *Fremdenstadt* as "international city of foreigners" in these materials. For the German original, see "Internationale Hygiene–Ausstellung Dresden 1911, Mai bis Oktober," [1911], 7, Signatur H. Sax. G 126 SC, Sächsische Landesbibliothek—Staats- und Universitätsbibliothek Dresden (SLUB). For the English equivalent, see "International Hygiene Exhibition Dresden 1911," 7, Ebling Library for the Health Sciences, University of Wisconsin–Madison.

43. Studies only exist for Baden-Baden and Hamburg. See Ursula Perkow, *Residents and Visitors: Die englisch-amerikanische Gemeinde in Baden-Baden* (Baden-Baden, 1990) and Anne D. Petersen, *Die Engländer in Hamburg, 1814–1914* (Hamburg, 1993).

44. "The Complaint is Made . . .," *Daily Record*, 12 September 1908, 3.

45. See Susanne Böller, "American Artists at the Academy of Fine Arts in Munich, 1850–1920," in *American Artists in Munich: Artistic Migration and Cultural Exchange*

Processes, ed. Christian Fuhrmeister, Hubertus Kohle, and Veerle Thielemans (Berlin, 2009), 43–56.

46. For Göttingen, see Paul G. Buchloh and Walter T. Rix, eds., *American Colony of Göttingen: Historical and Other Data Collected Between the Years 1855 and 1888* (Göttingen, 1976), 79. For Americans at German universities in general, but especially at Leipzig, see Anja Werner, *The Transatlantic World of Higher Education: Americans at German Universities, 1776–1914* (New York, 2013). For statistics, see "Die Volkszählung vom 1. Dezember 1905," *Zeitschrift des K. Sächsischen Statistischen Landesamtes* 1 (1908): 10.

47. Karl Baedeker, *Northern Germany as far as the Bavarian and Austrian Frontiers— Handbook for Travellers*, 13th rev. ed. (Leipzig, 1900), 272; and Baedeker, *Northern Germany*, 15th rev. ed. (Leipzig, 1910), 181.

48. "The Dresden Exhibition," *British Journal of Photography* (4 June 1909): 436.

49. "Many Americans to Stay in Germany," *New York Times*, 9 February 1917, 2.

50. von Baudissin, 63; von Hüben, 65.

51. Mephisto, "Hochfluten und kritische Tage in Elbflorenz," *Salonblatt* vol. 1, no. 4 (1906): not paginated.

52. Theodore Roosevelt to his mother, Dresden, 5 October 1873, in *The Letters of Theodore Roosevelt*, ed. Elting E. Morrison (Cambridge, MA, 1951), 12.

53. Letter to the editor from "Amerigo," *Daily Record*, 11 December 1907, 2.

54. E.R. to Hopf, containing a clipping from *Dresdner Anzeiger* of 7 September 1911, Bestand: Alldeutscher Verband, Signatur 13.1, Akte 38, Blatt 103, Stadtarchiv Dresden. It is important to note that membership numbers of the nationalistic Pan-German League paled in comparison to those of the Strangers' Protection Society, which encouraged (elite) foreign migration. In 1903, the Dresden Pan-Germans peaked at five hundred members, but the Strangers' Protection Society counted 861 supporters. By 1912, the Strangers' Protection Society had 1,426 members, whereas support for the Pan-Germans had diminished to 342 members.

55. "Sale of Work," *Stranger's Guide to Dresden*, 25 November 1899, 1; and "The All Saints' Ladies Work Society Sale of Work," *Stranger's Guide to Dresden*, 24 November 1906, 1; "Annual Bazaar at American Church," *Stranger's Guide to Dresden*, 4 July 1914, 1, 3.

56. "Anglo-American Colonists," *Daily Record*, 5 September 1908, 1. For Anglo-American estimations of German music before World War I, see Sven Oliver Müller, "'A Musical Clash of Civilizations?' Musical transfers and Rivalries around 1900," in *Wilhelmine Germany and Edwardian Britain: Essays on Cultural Affinity*, ed. Dominik Geppert and Robert Gerwarth (Oxford, 2008): 305–30.

57. As reported in the *New York Times*, 20 December 1891, 5.

58. See *Adreßbuch für Dresden und seine Vororte 1904*, part 3, subsection 4, page 118.

59. For one example, see *Stranger's Guide to Dresden*, 17 April 1897, 4.

60. See notices in the *Stranger's Guide to Dresden*, 17 September 1904, 1; *Stranger's Guide to Dresden*, 5 November 1904, 1.

61. "A Well-deserved Honour," *Stranger's Guide to Dresden*, 3 June 1911, 1.

62. See *Salonblatt*, 24 June 1911, 716.

63. "Frau Potter-Frissell," *Salonblatt*, 17 June 1911, 697.

64. As reported in the *Stranger's Guide to Dresden*, 26 May 1906, 1.

65. "A Merry Christmas," *Daily Record*, 25 December 1907, 1.

66. The *New York Times* reported for Germany that "[i]n Dresden and other places, English residents have been insulted." See "Anglophobia in Germany: Hatred of All Things British is Manifested by the People," *New York Times*, 8 April 1900, 21; E.J. Walker, "German Animosity in Dresden—To the Editor of the Times," *Times* (London), 12 March 1900, 10.
67. E.J. Walker, "German Animosity in Dresden—To the Editor of the Times," *Times* (London), 12 March 1900, 10.
68. "Örtliches: Wie bekannt," *Dresdner Journal*, 6 March 1900; "Verschiedene Mittheilungen: Wie bekannt," *Dresdner Anzeiger*, 7 March 1900, 32; "Das 'Dresdn. Journ.' theilt mit," *Dresdner Nachrichten*, 7 March 1900, 9; "Verschiedene Mittheilungen," *Dresdner Anzeiger*, 17 March 1900, 21; "The Greatest Babble and Bluster," *Stranger's Guide to Dresden*, 31 March 1900, 1.
69. Gerald Deckart, "Deutsch-Englische Verständigung: eine Darstellung der nichtoffiziellen Bemühungen um eine Wiederannäherung der beiden Länder zwischen 1905 und 1914" (PhD diss., Ludwig-Maximilians University Munich, 1967).
70. "Merry Christmas," *Dresden Daily*, 25 December 1906, 1.
71. "A Second Word," *Dresden Daily*, 4 February 1906, 1.
72. "Dresden—The Jewel of Northern Europe," 5.
73. "Society for International Friendship," *Stranger's Guide to Dresden*, 6 May 1911, 13.
74. For the figures on Austrians, see Richter, 54. In contemporary overviews of Dresden, the Anglo-American community consistently served as the one and only example of international life in the city; this is especially evident in von Hüben's 1908 account *Mein Dresden lob ich mir.*
75. As reported by Kathleen D'Olier to Mamma, 2 February 1896, Papers of Kathleen D'Olier Courtney, 7KDC/A/2, The Women's Library, London Metropolitan University.
76. Kathleen D'Olier to Mamma, 17 May 1896, Papers of Kathleen D'Olier Courtney, 7KDC/A/2, The Women's Library, London Metropolitan University.

Bibliography

"A Merry Christmas." *Daily Record*, 25 December 1907.
"A Second Word." *Dresden Daily*, 4 February 1906.
"A Well-deserved Honour." *Stranger's Guide to Dresden*, 3 June 1911.
Adam, Thomas, and Gisela Mettele, eds. *Two Boston Brahmins in Goethe's Germany: The Travel Journals of Anna and George Ticknor.* Lanham, MD, 2009.
Adreßbuch für Dresden und seine Vororte 1904.
"The All Saints' Ladies Work Society Sale of Work." *Stranger's Guide to Dresden*, 24 November 1906.
"Anglo-American Colonists." *Daily Record*, 5 September 1908.
"Anglophobia in Germany: Hatred of All Things British is Manifested by the People." *New York Times*, 8 April 1900.
"Annual Bazaar at American Church." *Stranger's Guide to Dresden*, 4 July 1914.
"Anglo-American Club." *Stranger's Guide to Dresden*, 5 November 1898.

Anonymous. "The Dresden Exhibition." *British Journal of Photography*, 4 June 1909.

———. *Dritter Rechenschafts-Bericht des Vereins Einheimischer und Fremder zur Wahrung gegenseitiger Interessen*. Dresden, 1878.

———. *Elfter Rechenschafts-Bericht des Vereins zur Förderung des Fremdenverkehrs in Dresden*. Dresden, 1886.

———. *Fünfter Rechenschafts-Bericht des Vereins Einheimischer und Fremder zur Wahrung gegenseitiger Interessen*. Dresden, 1880.

———. *Mittheilungen des Statistischen Amtes der Stadt Dresden*, vol. 1, nos. 3 and 4 (1891).

———. *Sechster Rechenschafts-Bericht des Vereins Einheimischer und Fremder zur Wahrung gegenseitiger Interessen*. Dresden, 1881.

———. *Siebenter Rechenschafts-Bericht des Vereins Einheimischer und Fremder zur Wahrung gegenseitiger Interessen*. Dresden, 1882.

———. "Die Volkszählung vom 1. Dezember 1905." *Zeitschrift des K. Sächsischen Statistischen Landesamtes* 1 (1908).

Bade, Klaus J. *Deutsche im Ausland, Fremde in Deutschland: Migration in Geschichte und Gegenwart*. Munich, 1992.

Bade, Klaus J., ed. *Population, Labour, and Migration in 19th- and 20th-century Germany*. New York, 1987.

Baedeker, Karl. *Northern Germany as far as the Bavarian and Austrian Frontiers—Handbook for Travelers*. 13th revised ed. Leipzig, 1900.

———. *Northern Germany as far as the Bavarian and Austrian Frontiers—Handbook for Travelers*. 15th revised ed. Leipzig, 1910.

Baranowski, Shelley, and Ellen Furlough, eds. *Tourism, Consumer Culture, and Identity in Modern Europe and North America*. Ann Arbor, MI, 2001.

Baudissin, Eva Gräfin von. "Die Amerikanische und Englische Kolonie." In *Dresden und die Dresdener—Ein lustiges Vademecum*, ed. Freiherr von Schlicht. Dresden, 1907.

Black, Jeremy. *The British and the Grand Tour*. London, 1985.

Böller, Susanne. "American Artists at the Academy of Fine Arts in Munich, 1850–1920." In *American Artists in Munich: Artistic Migration and Cultural Exchange Processes*, ed. Christian Fuhrmeister, Hubertus Kohle, and Veerle Thielemans. Berlin, 2009.

Buchloh, Paul G., and Walter T. Rix, eds. *American Colony of Göttingen: Historical and Other Data Collected Between the Years 1855 and 1888*. Göttingen, 1976.

"The Complaint is Made . . . ." *Daily Record*, 12 September 1908.

Conrad, Sebastian. *Globalization and the Nation in Imperial Germany*. Trans. Sorcha O'Hagan. Cambridge, 2010.

Deckart, Gerald. "Deutsch-Englische Verständigung: eine Darstellung der nichtoffiziellen Bemühungen um eine Wiederannäherung der beiden Länder zwischen 1905 und 1914." PhD diss., Ludwig-Maximilians University Munich, 1967.

Dietrich, Andrea. "Die Entwicklung der Stadt Dresden zu einer Tourismusmetropole von den Anfängen bis zum Vorabend des ersten Weltkrieges" vol. 1. PhD diss., Leipzig University, 1992.

Dolan, Brian. *Ladies of the Grand Tour: British Women in Pursuit of Enlightenment and Adventure in Eighteenth-Century Europe.* New York, 2001.

"Das 'Dresdn. Journ.' theilt mit." *Dresdner Nachrichten,* 7 March 1900.

"Education for American Boys and Girls." *Stranger's Guide to Dresden,* 22 August 1903.

Endy, Christopher. "Travel and World Power: Americans in Europe, 1890–1917." *Diplomatic History* 22, no. 4 (Fall 1998): 565–94.

"Franklin College." *Stranger's Guide to Dresden,* 9 September 1899.

"Franklin College, Dresden, Saxony." *Prospectus* vol. 18, no. 7 (1893–94).

"Franklin College." *Stranger's Guide to Dresden,* 2 November 1901.

"Franklin College." *Stranger's Guide to Dresden,* 10 September 1904.

"Franklin College." *Stranger's Guide to Dresden,* 2 November 1907.

"Franklin College Closing Festival." *Stranger's Guide to Dresden,* 16 July 1904.

"Frau Potter-Frissell." *Salonblatt,* 17 June 1911.

Gottschalck, Friedrich. *Dresden, seine Umgebungen und die sächsische Schweiz: Ein Führer für Reisende.* Dresden, 1859.

"The Greatest Babble and Bluster." *Stranger's Guide to Dresden,* 31 March 1900.

Helfricht, Jürgen. *Dresden und seine Kirchen.* Leipzig, 2005.

Hüben, Victor von. *Mein Dresden lob ich mir.* 2nd ed. Dresden, no date [1908].

Kummer, Friedrich, ed. *Dresden und das Elbgelände.* 5th ed. Dresden, 1910.

Jannasch, R., ed. *Zeitschrift des Statistischen Bureaus der Stadt Dresden,* no. 1. Dresden, 1875.

———. *Mittheilungen des Statistischen Bureaus der Stadt Dresden,* no. 4A, Part I. Dresden, 1877.

Jenkins, Newell Sill. *Reminiscences of Newell Sill Jenkins.* Princeton, NJ, 1924.

Letter to the editor from "Amerigo." *Daily Record,* 11 December 1907.

"Many Americans to Stay in Germany." *New York Times,* 9 February 1917.

Mason, Consul Jos. F. to Department of State on "The Consecration of the American Church of St. John in Dresden," 26 January 1887, no. 187. In *Despatches from United States Consuls in Dresden, 1837–1906.* Washington, DC,1961.

Meff, A. "Dr. Grimshaw on Americanisms." *Stranger's Guide to Dresden,* 18 January 1908.

Mephisto. "Hochfluten und kritische Tage in Elbflorenz." *Salonblatt* 1, no. 4 (1906).

"Merry Christmas." *Dresden Daily,* 25 December 1906.

"Mrs. Elizabeth A. Bolton." *Daily Record,* 17 December 1909.

Müller, Sven Oliver. "'A Musical Clash of Civilizations?' Musical transfers and Rivalries around 1900." In *Wilhelmine Germany and Edwardian Britain: Essays on Cultural Affinity,* ed. Dominik Geppert and Robert Gerwarth. Oxford, 2008.

"Örtliches: Wie bekannt." *Dresdner Journal,* 6 March 1900.

Perkow, Ursula. *Residents and Visitors: Die englisch-amerikanische Gemeinde in Baden-Baden.* Baden-Baden, 1990.

Petersen, Anne D. *Die Engländer in Hamburg, 1814–1914.* Hamburg, 1993.

Richter, Ralf. "Reichsausländer in Dresden zwischen 1871 und 1914." Diplomarbeit, Humboldt University Berlin, 1996.

Roosevelt, Theodore. *The Letters of Theodore Roosevelt,* ed. Elting E. Morrison. Cambridge, MA, 1951.

"Sale of Work." *Stranger's Guide to Dresden*, 25 November 1899.

Salonblatt, 24 June 1911.

"Statistik der in Dresden sich aufhaltenden Fremden." In *Mittheilungen des Statistischen Bureaus der Stadt Dresden*, no. 4A, Part II, ed. R. Jannasch. Dresden, 1877.

Schniewind, Paul W. *Anglicans in Germany: A History of Anglican Chaplaincies in Germany until 1945*. Darmstadt, 1988.

"Society for International Friendship." *Stranger's Guide to Dresden*, 6 May 1911.

Verein zur Förderung Dresdens und des Fremdenverkehrs. "Dresden—The Jewel of Northern Europe." Dresden, 1910.

"Verschiedene Mittheilungen." *Dresdner Anzeiger*, 17 March 1900.

"Verschiedene Mittheilungen: Wie bekannt." *Dresdner Anzeiger*, 7 March 1900.

"Wagner's 'Ring'." *Dresden Daily*, 5 April 1906.

Walker, E.J. "German Animosity in Dresden—To the Editor of the Times." *Times* (London), 12 March 1900.

Werner, Anja. *The Transatlantic World of Higher Education: Americans at German Universities, 1776–1914*. New York, 2013.

CHAPTER SEVEN

~:~

Foreign Policy and Migration in Central Europe
Functions of the German-Polish Recruitment Treaty of 1927

JOCHEN OLTMER

After World War I, German-Polish relations were long marked by a diplomatic "cold war." In the 1920s, German foreign policy developed the concept of a policy of mutual agreement with the West (*Verständigungspolitik*) with the goal of suspending the limitations to sovereignty set by the Treaty of Versailles. This policy of mutual agreement with the West found no corresponding foreign policy concept toward the East in a similarly crafted collective security system. A widely agreed upon and fundamental goal of the German political parties and of the public sought to revise the eastern border of Germany, specifically the boundary shared with Poland. The loss of German territory to Poland after World War I was generally referred to in Germany as the "Polish robbery."

At the cost of frictions in the policy of reconciliation toward the West, for example in the context of the question of Germany's accession into the League of Nations, the goal of eastern border revision was maintained. The result was a conflict-ridden relationship with Poland. Armed conflicts in Posen and Upper Silesia, as well as fierce voting controversies in the south of East Prussia and in Upper Silesia, defined the formative phase of the German-Polish relationship in the early postwar years. These conflicts found their equivalent policy on the level of international contractual arrangements in the anti-Polish alignment of the German-Soviet Treaty of Rapallo in 1922. The German point of view in the Locarno Treaty of 1925 also had an anti-Polish perspective. At the same time the German-initiated breakdown of the German-Polish economic negotiations led to a "tariff war," or rather an "economic war," lasting several years. After Germany was admitted into the League of Nations in the autumn of 1926, the conflicts shifted increasingly to that scene. The most important disputes involved minority policies. Anti-Polish revisionist policies remained an important component of German foreign policy until the end of the Weimar Republic. The German policies, which were principally prepared for conflict with Poland, were to a great degree ideologically loaded and characterized by an ethno-nationally motivated line of confrontation.

Despite the diplomatic "cold war" between Germany and Poland, which had existed since the end of World War I in 1918, and despite the "tariff war" or "economic war," which influenced German-Polish relations in the second half of the 1920s, the two nations still worked together to regulate migration. Accordingly, the German-Polish Treaty on Polish Farm Workers was passed on 24 November 1927. This treaty, which regulated the recruitment of Polish workers for the German economy, demonstrates why bilateral control of the migration relationship was so important for both states in a period of sharpened foreign political conflicts.

A mesh of socio-political interests, labor market policy, economic policy matters, nationality policies, security issues, and foreign policy interests influenced German migration politics after World War I as well as the contemporary discussion about their content and form.[1] Against the background of the recently arisen scientific historical interests in the interrelationship[2] between foreign policy and migration, a look at the German-Polish migratory relationship focusing on the foreign relations of Germany and Poland offers a concentrated approach to the constellation of conflicts and to the conditions, objectives, and results of discussions about the control and regulation of migratory movements across borders. The emphasis here will be on the examination of German interests and their place in the migration policies of the Weimar Republic. Unequally distributed interests formed as a result because unlike the Poles, the German side expected distinctly greater advantages of a stipulation to the migratory relationship.

The first section introduces foreign employment in the Reich after World War I as well as German foreign employment policies. The second section discusses the central goal of preventing the permanent migration of Polish workers into the Reich. The result of this policy was the German effort to conclude a migration treaty; the constellation of interests and the lengthy debates about its realization is laid out in the third section. The concluding remarks summarize the results and offer a short overview on the promotion of the increased employment of labor migrants of German descent from the German minorities in east-central and southeastern Europe in the sense of an ethno-nationally oriented anti-Polish "defense policy."

Foreign Employment in the Reich and German Foreign Employment Policy

Before World War I, Germany had developed into the second most important "labor import country" after the United States.[3] In the boom period since the 1890s, the number of foreigners employed in the German economy had significantly increased and reached a height of around 1.2 million just before World War I. Up to a third of these migrant workers were Russian or Austria-Hungarian citizens of Polish nationality. A differentiated system of control of the foreign workers aimed at a strict observation and regulation of Polish immigration out of Russia and Austria-Hungary. This Prussian anti-Polish "defense policy" did not strive to curtail or to completely block the migration itself, and it functioned wholly independently from the development of the labor market. Its main goal was, for reasons of nationality politics, not to let the migration of the Polish from abroad turn out to be permanent immigration into Prussian Germany. The *Rückkehrzwang* (forced return) policy in particular served this end and compelled the Polish workforce to leave Prussian Germany in the winter every year. The guiding basis for its introduction had been the dread of rebuilding the Polish state through a reinforcement of the Polish minority in the Prussian east through permanent immigration.[4]

After 1918, the feared reemergence of Poland at the cost of German territory became reality. Furthermore, economic considerations of the German migration policies in the Weimar Republic were placed in the foreground for the admission of a Polish workforce, and the prevention of their long-term settling still stood at the forefront of immigration policy measures. Despite the considerable decline of the Polish minority in the Reich after World War I due to the surrender under the terms of the Treaty of Versailles, the ethnonationalist fear of a Polish infiltration resulting in a "Polonization" of the Prussian east remained the basis of the anti-Polish "defense policy." It understood the immigration of Poles into the Reich as a threat to Germany's internal security, economy, labor market, society, and culture, a threat that was thought to be especially acute in the East Elbian region of Prussia.

The employment of foreigners in the Weimar Republic was considerably less than it had been during the German Empire. The number of legitimate foreign workers decreased overall from around 715,000 during the last year of the war in 1918 to approximately 279,000 in the first year of peace in 1919. This meant a decrease to about forty percent of the initial value, which affected the agricultural and non-agricultural areas of employment equally. The period of inflation was characterized by a high rate of employment of foreigners in comparison to the years of the Weimar Republic, which ended with the hyperinflation of 1923 and stabilization of 1924. A short interphase in 1925 then let the number of foreigners rise again before the crisis of 1926 again marked a break. The years 1927–30 represented another peak in the employment of foreigners, and the following years of world economic crisis represented the absolute low point. Among the foreign workforce, those of Polish citizenship made up a substantial share. In the 1920s, 50 to 60 percent of all foreign workers were from Poland, while the share of foreign farm hands stood even higher at 80 to 90 percent (Table 7.1).

In light of the tense job market situation in the Weimar Republic, where a clear *Inländervorrang* (priority for nationals) was considered to be the guideline for the foreign national policies in the labor market, the foreign workforce only had a replacement or complementary function. For the implementation of foreign employment dependent on the development of the job market, a permit was required beginning in April 1920. According to this requirement foreign farm workers were only permitted to be employed if a farmer or a large estate owner had successfully applied for a work permit at the labor administration office. Along with requiring work permits for foreign national agricultural laborers, the immigration of foreign industrial workers who did not possess an entry visa was forbidden. The German diplomatic and consular representatives abroad were henceforth not allowed to issue visas if there were unemployed nationals of the same qualifications registered in the area where

Table 7.1. Authorization of Foreign Workers 1918–1932

Year	Total	Agriculture	Non-Agriculture
1918	715,770	372,274	343,496
1919	278,896	145,194	133,702
1920	274,552	136,274	138,278
1921	293,903	147,413	146,490
1922	287,584	148,086	139,498
1923	225,217	118,526	106,691
1924	210,677	110,892	99,781
1925	263,417	142,694	120,723
1926	218,636	134,869	83,767
1927	227,090	137,411	89,679
1928	236,870	145,871	90,999
1929	232,030	140,857	91,173
1930	219,992	132,810	87,182
1931	155,689	79,777	75,912
1932	108,662	43,391	65,271

Source: Oltmer, *Migration und Politik*, 404.

requests were made and there was no available accommodation. With this, the immigration of industrial workers was also in fact made dependent upon the job market situation in Germany.[5]

Standardization of a comprehensive regulation of all foreign workers occurred in 1922–23. The "Ordinance on the Employment and Occupation of Foreign Workers,"[6] published on 2 January 1923, brought together a multitude of already existing provisions that kept its orientation on the employers. Employers were obliged to apply for an employment permit for their foreign workers, and these foreign workers were only allowed to be employed in companies that had successfully obtained such a work permit. Beyond that, foreigners could only be legally employed if they possessed a proper identification card from the German Worker's Agency (*Deutsche Arbeiterzentrale*), which, as a semi-public organization in the Weimar Republic, was responsible for the recruitment and authorization of foreign workers.[7]

The authorization requirement did not apply to foreign workers who had stayed in Germany uninterrupted for several years (effective 1 January 1913 for agricultural workers, 1 January 1919 for industrial). These foreign workers could obtain a certificate that exempted them from working exclusively for companies that possessed the required permits. However, this freedom of movement did not apply to more recent arrivals who were subject to the requirement of proper authorization. Apart from only being permitted to change employment between companies that possessed a work permit, they were also only allowed to leave a regular work position if the employer had given written confirmation that he agreed to the dissolution of the contract. The change of a foreign worker from an agriculturally bound position to a nonagricultural sector had to be permitted by the responsible regional employment office.

In 1923, these regulations were tied to the system of foreigner admission and employment, which was labor market development-oriented. This system remained valid with no serious changes for a decade. By linking foreign employment to the general labor market through the residency and work permit requirements for foreigners, broad control became possible so that foreign employment could be kept at a considerably lower level during the Weimar Republic in comparison to the prewar period.

Re-Seasonalization of the Polish Labor Migration: The Factual Reintroduction of the Rückkehrzwang Policy in 1925–26

In the years 1925–26, the cornerstone of the Weimar Republic's system of recruitment, placement, and control of foreign workers in the permit process began in earnest with the actual enforcement of the *Rückkehrzwang* policy, which had been interrupted since the beginning of the war in 1914. The reintroduction of the *Rückkehrzwang* policy was not governed primarily by economic intentions with the goal of making foreign employment in agricultural labor markets flexible. Rather, it was driven by anti-Polish policies that sought to hinder "seasonal" Polish labor migrants from permanently staying by requiring them to return to their regions of origin for the winter. This process was known as "re-seasonalizing."

At the beginning of World War I, foreign Polish agricultural workers were no longer obligated to return and instead a prohibition against returning was put in place, which remained in effect over the following four years of war. Until the war the obligation for this group had been to return to their region of origin without exception during the winter period from 20 December to 1 February (the *Karenzzeit*, or waiting period). However, after the end of World War I the unconditional obligation to return was not eliminated but was repeatedly suspended.

The reasons for the alleged necessity of the obligatory return had not changed dramatically in comparison to the prewar period. The Reich's Minister of Labor argued that Polish labor migration would develop as follows: "If they remain in Germany over the winter, they will gradually become permanent workers instead of seasonal workers and with this transformation will come a danger for native German farm hands and for the German character of the rural population of large districts."[8] After 1918 the argument was used that foreign agricultural workers remaining in the winter prevented efforts toward "the protection of the national labor market" owing to decreased control and reduced flexibility in the recruitment process.

In addition to labor market policies and ethnically motivated opinions, the question of security also lent support to the strict enforcement of the *Rückkehrzwang* policy. Only the *Rückkehrzwang* policy would improve "the general security during the winter months" because "a large portion of capital crime in rural areas" would have to be "attributed to the roving reapers," so—among others—the district president (*Regierungspräsident*) in Stralsund in 1922 was given to understand.[9] Not least was the perception of the remaining foreign labor migrants as a social-political problem, as the number of homeless and urban asylum seekers would rise in the wintertime because many of the foreign labor migrants were unable to find employment in the winter.[10]

A renewed enforcement of the *Rückkehrzwang* policy with the goal of re-seasonalization could not be realized immediately after the war. Many were concerned that it would not be possible to enforce the *Rückkehrzwang* policy because Germany would then be unable to recruit a sufficient number of Polish agricultural workers in light the Polish measures seeking to impede border crossings into Germany.[11] But foreign policy considerations also played a role: at the beginning of the 1920s the Foreign Office feared that the enforcement of the *Rückkehrzwang* policy could be interpreted by the Polish as a repression measure that could lead to the expulsion of former citizens of the German Reich from the regions that had been ceded to Poland.[12]

Not until 1924–25 did the enforcement of the *Rückkehrzwang* policy seem to become more realistic for the Reich and Prussian departments responsible for its enforcement. Foreign policy considerations of the Polish state were continually given less priority. Important in this context was Germany's improving foreign policy position, which found expression primarily in the signing of the Treaties of Locarno in October 1925. These treaties strengthened the German position in Europe considerably, while at the same time considerably weakening that of Poland.[13] Moreover, according to the assessment of the Federal Foreign Office, the "systematic de-Germanization of the former Prussian provinces ceded to Poland . . . had made such progress that in the next year [1925] the reintroduction of the *Rückkehrzwang* policy for foreign farm hands could be arranged without having to fear drastic reprisals from the Polish side."[14] In the summer of 1925 the conflict escalated—for one, the German-Polish "tariff war," or "economic war," led to severe conflicts. In this context the Poles unilaterally terminated the Treaty on Border Crossing of December 1920, which had intended to lift the passport and visa requirement for the Polish labor migrants and to recognize the identification card issued by the German Workers' Agency as a fully valid document for the attainment of a border crossing certificate.

The responsible Prussian and Reich authorities had already begun the planning of the implementation of the *Rückkehrzwang* policy at the end of 1924, which is how the German Workers' Agency could already report in March of 1925 that they had

> made practical arrangements . . . to enable and to facilitate the return migration of seasonal workers despite the difficulties created by the [Polish] consulate. For these purposes the German Workers' Agency created facilities in their border organizations to offer the possibility to transport the Polish workers back to their homeland who had either not obtained the border crossing certificate in sufficient time or at all.

The police authorities had been informed about the possibilities of crossing the border "in the interest of a smooth execution of the return migration."[15] Because the Treaty on Border Crossing was revoked, the winter return of Polish labor migrants to Poland in 1925–26 still appeared to be possible (albeit illegal) from the standpoint of the Prussian and Reich authorities.[16]

At the end of September 1925, the German Workers' Agency had confirmed the ability to transport around 50,000 recruited Polish agricultural workers across the German-Polish border through illegal means over the course of the year. Thereupon, it was decided on 7 October 1925 to induce as many Poles as possible to return home. Notably, the Foreign Office and the Prussian Interior Ministry spoke out against the formal reintroduction of the *Rückkehrzwang* policy without a treaty with the Polish government. They asserted that initially the agricultural employers were only requested to refrain from signing contracts with their Polish workers for the winter.[17] At the same time a confidential decree was issued to the governor and district presidents in Prussia with measures for the encouragement of the winter emigration of the Polish labor migrants. The decree served, superficially and in title, to regulate the return migration of all foreign farm hands. In the relevant specifications of the decree, however, it becomes clear that it only dealt with Polish agricultural workers. The goal was "to do its utmost to encourage their voluntary emigration" preferably before the beginning of the winter waiting period on 15 December that had been valid in the prewar period. The concrete implementation and degree of "voluntariness," however, remained unclear: "But such employees, who are not willing to return home, can also be influenced by their employers in appropriate ways to leave the country." Transport to the border should be ensured for all dismissed Polish farm hands, as in the prewar period, to prevent their "accumulat[ion] inside or on the border of the country and that new sources of danger do not emerge for the public health, public security or for the labor market." An employer who did not take care of this "would jeopardize the interests of the fatherland."[18]

The decree to the district presidents of the border provinces called for the enforcement to begin on 28 October 1925. They were instructed to support the measures put in place by the German Workers' Agency for the illegal transport of Polish workers over the border. The border officials should be given tasks, in the strictest of confidence and exclusively verbally, of inaction: to not prevent the movement of Polish labor migrants in the direction of the border, to not conduct controls, and to not hinder the (again, illegal) border crossing of the confidants of the German Workers' Agency who would cross the border from the Polish side. The customs and railroad administration were likewise instructed not to interfere with the return migration and to take measures to support the German Workers' Agency.[19]

Already on 6 November 1925, immediately after the beginning of the return migration, border officials reported to the German Workers' Agency about the success of the measures they had taken. For example, the Upper Silesian frontier services in Zawisna stated outright: "Although none of the laborers were in possession of a border crossing certificate, we have succeeded, with the help of our confidants, to illegally lead all the workers over the border to Poland without difficulty."[20] The frontier services in Pomeranian Lauenburg likewise knew to report about the successful duty that was eased by the minimal activity of the Polish border police: "The crossing took place without incident during settled weather. The return became difficult in the last few days because the footprints in the fresh snow along the smugglers' routes were easy to follow. In spite of this, however, unpleasant incidents have not yet occurred."[21]

According to the German Workers' Agency, the transport to the border went smoothly based on arrangements with the Reich railroad administration and customs:

> The border officials are notified mostly already twenty-four hours before the arrival of large transports to the border and therefore are able to make their preparations. Notification is passed from our regional authorities to the next junction of the route of stationed D.A.Z. [German Workers' Agency] officials, and from this on to the next and so forth up to the border, so that the whole stretch is made aware of the transport and the officials can intervene in a timely manner if need be.

Large amounts of luggage made the illegal transport of Polish workers more difficult, but: "We saw to it that there were enough wagons available on this side as well as the Polish side—the farmers gladly take their earnings along in this quiet time—so that the transfer of the baggage has also been successful."[22]

Over the course of the months October and November of 1925, as the German Workers' Agency phrased it in the face of the large number of illegal border crossings from Germany to Poland, "the Polish border authorities have adapted to the state of affairs and do not ask at all for any kind of papers."[23] Here the local initiatives by the Polish border police, which led to a loosening of the restrictive Polish entry provisions due to protests by the regional *Sejm* (the Polish parliament) representatives, appear to have been essential. While in the beginning almost all return migrants registered with the German Workers' Agency crossed the border illegally, the share decreased considerably by December, above all due to the contribution of the installation of a Polish passport station at the central station in Breslau for the return trip of the Polish labor migrants.[24]

Information given by the German Workers' Agency from the last week of November 1925 demonstrates the change that had already taken place by that point in time—of the 6,771 registered border crossers in that week, 4,329 went over the border legally and only 2,442 illegally.[25] The number of return migrants who had a proper border-crossing certificate from the Polish consulate was even higher than the number of legal border crossers, standing at 5,355. But still, if more than a thousand Polish return migrants with correct papers sought to cross the border by illegal means, then this resulted primarily from direct instructions from the German Workers' Agency to bypass the Polish customs provision: the DAZ saw to it that "convoys with particularly a lot of valuable baggage on which a high Polish import tariff was to be paid [was] secretly brought over the border, in spite of having available passports."[26] On 8

December 1925, the Polish government showed itself ready to issue passports free of charge to the Polish workers to be recruited as well as to permit their departure to Germany at the beginning of the following year. This is how the German side was able to secure the recruitment for the next year. Noteworthy services in return were not put into writing.[27] In an outright fight with Poland for the return migration, the aggressive German policies prevailed at every step.

For the German side, the success in the conflict over the factual reintroduction of the *Rückkehrzwang* policy meant an important stride toward the understanding of re-seasonalization of Polish labor migrants as an essential element of the immigration policy. An important stage was missing, however, so long as Polish agricultural workers, already settled in Germany for several years, had not yet been included under the re-seasonalization measures. The resistance of the Polish government stood in the way of a regulation; it was not ready to tolerate a return migration in the case of Poles who had already been residents in Germany for many years, many of whom had unresolved citizenship issues. A German-Polish migration treaty appeared to offer a solution.

Bilaterally Defining the Rückkehrzwang Policy through the German-Polish Recruitment Treaty of 1927

After the German and Austro-Hungarian initiatives to establish a new Polish state in 1916, Germany had considered signing a recruitment treaty with the newly founded Polish state, one dictated unilaterally by German interests. This treaty was supposed to help secure the unlimited recruitment of agricultural workers for the Reich in the long term. With the end of the war and the establishment of the Polish state, the question of recruitment of Polish workers for German farming was unregulated and urgent. Despite the signing of a French-Polish recruitment treaty in September 1919,[28] there were no promising approaches to a German-Polish migration agreement in the face of foreign policy tensions.

In January 1921, the Polish government suggested signing a German-Polish treaty on migration issues in order to remove what they perceived as the many abuses of labor migration from Poland to Germany. The Polish Consulate General in Berlin asserted that the issued guidelines about the recruitment of Polish workers by the Germans carried, without exception, "the characteristics of one-sided arrangements" and "did not take into consideration either the interests of the seasonal emigrants nor did they comply with the customary principles and customs in international relations." Proceedings of dealing with Polish labor migrants would, moreover, not meet the Polish legal provisions, which is why "in the Polish areas or along the border, seasonal workers who were hired illegally and had illegally crossed over into Germany" came "into . . . conflict with the Polish border regulations" or were led to do it by German agents. However, the most important problem for the Polish Consulate General was the recruitment of Polish labor migrants at the German border without the participation of the Polish administration. Such a measure would be "completely unthinkable in normal, loyal international relations." Establishing this measure could only be done, according to the Polish opinion, by a German-Polish recruitment treaty that corresponded at its core to the French-Polish Treaty of September 1919. Should the German side not be ready to find a contractual solution, the Polish Consulate General threatened, Poland would use the means of a general immigration freeze for those going to Germany.[29]

The Polish initiative of January 1921 led to negotiations, which were broken off after a short time, however, due to the German-Polish conflicts over Upper Silesia in the spring/summer of 1921. Discussions taken up again at the beginning of 1922 likewise ran without a result. Not until three years later, in March 1925, were the negotiations resumed once more. They stayed tense in light of difficult German-Polish relations and of the simultaneously occurring conflicts over the closing of a trade treaty.[30] The main points of negotiations were, for one, questions of the determination of citizenship of the labor migrants situated in Germany, characterized by the Germans as Poles; and for another, questions of recruitment and employment agencies. The basis of negotiations regarding the statement of citizenship was the German demand for the reintroduction of the *Rückkehrzwang* policy in the winter waiting period. This policy should extend to labor migrants who had been employed for many years in Germany and had been able to settle there because of the failed implementation of the obligation to return. From the Polish point of view, the border crossing of labor migrants required checking citizenship because a considerable share had been living in Germany before the reestablishment of the Polish state and who therefore did not possess official proof of their citizenship.

From the start the Polish delegation stressed that they only wanted to deal with those Poles who had been settled for years in Germany during the winter waiting period if a decision of yearly fixed quotas were made and if, over the course of a transitional period of several years, the *Rückkehrzwang* policy was first extended to all Polish labor migrants in agriculture.[31]

Regarding the question of recruitment and employment, the Polish side demanded a complete renunciation by the German Workers' Agency of what they considered to be the illegal recruitment practices on Polish territory and at the German-Polish border. According to the Polish authorities, the recruitment itself should only be permitted to be undertaken by their own employment agencies. Moreover, the German authorities would have to guarantee protection of the Polish labor migrants and, regarding the wage and working conditions and labor law positions, make the possibilities of perception of freedom of association as well as of social security in the region equal to that of the German workers. The Polish embassy and consulates would also be entitled to the right of control in the job positions.[32] The German delegation stressed in return that there were no objections to the inclusion of the Polish employment agencies for the recruitment of Polish labor migrants, but the recruitment and placement of the workers would have to be carried out by the German offices. Equalization in all areas of social security was not desired; moreover, the Polish diplomatic and consular representatives could not be entitled to the right of control in the job positions.[33]

As of the end of May 1925, negotiations were interrupted in light of the German-Polish "tariff war," or more accurately, "economic war," that had broken out in connection with the failure of the German-Polish economic negotiations that had been going on since the end of 1924. The "tariff war" could not be brought to an end until 1934. Accompanied by heavy national-istic positioning on both sides, the economic actions intensified in June and July of 1925, culminating in an open tariff war through the imposition of higher import tariffs. Only when the German side forced the return of Polish labor migrants in the winter waiting period, as illustrated, and successfully implemented it by means of large quantities of illegal border crossings over the German-Polish border in December 1925, did the Polish side finally relent.[34]

The head of the Polish delegation, Director Dr. Stanislaw Gawroński of the Polish immigration department, in his rationale for the Polish conces-sion, spoke of the "extremely alarming" conditions that would have developed because of the German policies on the illegal repatriation of Polish labor migrants. The conditions "meant a severe injury to the authority of the Polish state." That is why the Poles were forced "for their part to support the illegal actions of the German Workers' Agency" and to facilitate the issuance of pass-ports against Polish legal provisions. Delegation leader Gawroński therefore suggested a provisional agreement for the regulation of the return of Polish labor migrants to Germany in spring, which the German side accepted, stipu-lating that passports should be given free of charge and labor migrants would no longer be required to have a visa. The Polish delegation also conceded on the question disputed before the breaking off of negations: the return migra-tion of settled Poles already living in Germany for many years. The person-nel in the Polish consulate were strengthened in order to be able to perform citizenship tests more quickly. However, the requirement for the acceptance of the *Rückkehrzwang* policy remained, according to Director Gawroński, the return migration directed by the German side so that it would extend over several years.[35]

As the German authorities reported in the spring of 1926, the Polish authorities complied with the provisional agreement. Passports for the journey to Germany were issued to those wishing to migrate. However, the German border police did not follow the established obligation in the provisional agreement to prosecute all illegal border crossings, but on the contrary, those Polish border crossers who could not be placed in a job in Germany were "deported over the green border."[36]

In June 1926, the German delegation developed a proposal for the specific arrangement of the process for the return migration of Polish labor migrants in the waiting period, in which the Polish demand for an extension of the period of transition over several years was accepted, however, the Polish influence on the structure of the return migration was limited. Neither involvement of the Polish commission in the selection of the return migrants, nor an examination of citizenship in individual cases was acceptable. According to investigations by the German Workers' Agency, around 80,000 Polish agricultural workers were situated in Germany during the winter waiting period in 1925–26. It was assumed that for 10 percent of these workers, a feeling of guilt on the Polish side about Polish citizenship could be discerned. Another 10 percent were cases of hardship that should not be forced to return. To this 10 percent in particular belonged those Poles that had lived in the territory of the Reich since 1913, those who had built up a secure economic existence in Germany, or those who had married German spouses. Apart from these roughly 16,000 Poles that should have been sanctioned, there were about 64,000 long-term settled Polish labor migrants in Germany under the 80,000 that came into question, and, according to the German proposal of June 1926, should have been deported back to Poland in five "yearly installments" until the winter of 1930–31.[37]

The German-Polish negotiations were taken up again in September 1926. The Polish delegation declared the readiness of its government to assume a total of 36,000 returning Polish citizens in a time frame of ten years, which was only 60 percent of the quoted number in the German proposal and a time period twice as long. This proposal was unacceptable from the German governmental representative's point of view because only if "the settled Poles are utterly done away with as quickly as possible" was there interest in a recruitment treaty with the Polish. In light of the Polish proposals, the German delegation recommended a revision of the initiative for the acceleration of the return migration, which had been evaluated as successful the year prior.[38]

Although the Ministry of Foreign Affairs, the Prussian Ministries of the Interior and of Agriculture, as well as the German Workers' Agency signaled their disinterest in signing a treaty in light of the Polish demands, a breakthrough was achieved in the negotiations in November 1926 because of the German preparedness to make concessions. First, at the initiative of the Reich's Ministry of Labor, the number of Poles who had already been settled for years and were to be forced under the signum "Reclassification in Migration" to return home had been reduced to 45,000. It should be concluded within six instead of five years, according to the new initiative.[39] In the middle of November 1926, a proposal by the German ambassador in Warsaw, Ulrich Rauscher, proceeded and was immediately accepted by the Polish delegation evidently without the knowledge of the German delegation: 42,000 Poles were to be "reclassified" in the "migration."[40] In accord with the Ministry of Foreign Affairs, Rauscher's interests lay in accelerating the negotiations on the recruitment agreement and hindering a threatening severance of those negotiations for reasons of improvement of German-Polish relations.

At the beginning of December 1926, another provisional agreement on return migration for the winter of 1926–27 was finalized,[41] based on the agreement of the year prior, but at the same time including important elements of the general recruitment treaty signed in November 1927. According to the agreed upon scaling of the return migration, the Polish agricultural workers who had long been settled in Germany were appointed as the first year's quota of eight thousand "to be queued" in the "migration" in the winter of 1926–27. Thereby the German side committed itself to "not exercise any influence on the dismissal and emigration of those people," though it wanted to influence the employers not to dismiss certain categories of Polish farm workers but to continue to employ them in the winter of 1926–27.

Social and legal considerations especially played a role in this: those farm hands should continue to be employed who did not originate in the former Congress Poland or former Galicia, who were married to German citizens, who had many children, and/or could show proof of continuous residency in Germany since 1 January 1919. Also included were recipients of accident or disability annuities. All dismissed workers who returned in the winter waiting period were furthermore to be hired again if possible in the spring of the following year.[42]

The Prussian Ministry of the Interior reported "strictly confidentially" in March 1927 on the impact of the initial measures coordinated with the Polish government for the re-seasonalization of the Polish labor migration. According to the police examinations of the farms in August 1926, of the total 81,647 Polish labor migrants employed in Prussia, 31,211 could still be found after the revision of the examination in January 1927. Hence, over fifty thousand Polish labor migrants had set off on their return. This number, based on the police examinations on the farms, corresponded almost exactly to the return migration number gathered by the German Workers' Agency with a slight difference of around three hundred between 1 October 1926 and 31 January 1927. The police examinations allowed an overview of the question of the entry date of the returning Poles in the winter of 1926–27. Of all the farm hands who immigrated in 1926, 91 percent could not be found in Prussia during the winter waiting period. Furthermore, 47 percent of all the Polish labor migrants who immigrated in the years 1919 to 1925 and 19 percent before 1918 also returned to Poland during the winter. The set quota of eight thousand in the German-Polish negotiations for the winter waiting period of 1926–27 was far exceeded in December 1926 with a number of almost 15,000 Poles who immigrated to Prussia before 1925.[43]

After the protracted negotiations in which the German side was able to exercise considerable pressure on the Polish side due to its preparedness for conflict and successful re-seasonalization policies, the German-Polish treaty on Polish agricultural workers was signed on 24 November 1927 in Warsaw.[44] At the same time both sides signed two execution agreements for the two most important items. First, the accords dealt with an "agreement over the recruitment, employment, obligation as well as the transport of the Polish agricultural migrant workers." Second, they enjoined an "agreement on the Polish agricultural workers that came to Germany before 31 December 1925 and stayed there." In the treaty it was decided that those Polish agricultural workers who had already gone to Germany before 1 January 1919 were allowed to continue to remain there and were to be granted exemption certificates. All other Polish labor migrants were under the *Rückkehrzwang* policy during the winter waiting period. Under this policy, the Polish farm workers who had come between 1 January 1919 and 31 December 1925 and remained in the Reich were supposed to "again join the migration." It was in this context that yearly quotas were based on 4,500 people. After six years the re-seasonalization was to be completed and, with the help of the German Workers' Agency, citizenship was checked through questionnaires in each individual case.

The German-Polish recruitment treaty moreover regulated the process of recruitment, employment, and the duties of the Polish farm hands. On the Polish side, only state employment agencies were allowed to take action in this field, while on the German side organizations exclusively requested by the Reich government (the German Workers' Agency and its regional bureaus) were allowed; agencies, foremen, and other private people were not permitted to recruit at all. Through the cooperation between the Polish and German recruitment authorities the center of recruitment, employment, and duties of the Polish agricultural workers was shifted from the border to Poland's interior. The Polish employment agencies took over the task of recruiting appropriate farm hands from whom employees of the German Workers' Agency made their selection. Work contracts based on a model contract agreed upon by the German and Polish were signed in the presence of the government officials from the Polish Labor Administration.[45]

According to the opinion of the Reich Labor Ministry, the set of agreements as a whole was "of meaning not to be underestimated for the general relations of both states to each other." According to the words of the *Ministerialrat* (head of section), Philipp Beisiegel, who had participated in the negotiations on the side of the Reich labor ministry, it removed "a dangerous matter for conflict" and in the future could promote "another pleasant approach of both states." But the set of agreements was important "also for the migratory being," because "for the first time it regulated the technical and legal questions that were connected with such a large migration in a thorough way."[46]

With the signing of the German-Polish recruitment treaty in November 1927, the *Rückkehrzwang* policy for Polish agricultural labor was reintroduced after a fourteen-year interruption. This was counted as a success on the German side for two reasons: first, it appeared to become possible on the road to the consistent implementation of the *Rückkehrzwang* policy to decrease the unemployment of native farm hands in the winter months. Second, the German government believed itself able to prevent permanent settlement of Poles in the Reich in light of continuing employment of Polish workers, which was seen as necessary, with only these instruments.

Moreover, the treaty also facilitated the recruiting activities of the German Workers' Agency. According to the agreement recruitment and duties of the Polish farm hands lay formally as a priority for the Polish labor administration. The German Workers' Agency reported, however, that after a short period of transition the Polish authorities proceeded to "leave the selection and recruitment of the workers" to them. The job of the German Workers' Agency was supported and facilitated by the Polish labor administration "in every respect": "We may recognize with thanks that the Polish authorities have fulfilled their duties set out in the agreement in a loyal manner and have also given efforts to take the German interests into account in every direction, which are certainly here also their own interests."[47] As a result, the situation in the border departments of the German Workers' Agency fundamentally changed in comparison to the previous years, as an evaluation of the Reich Labor Ministry showed in the spring of 1928. "Masses of non-obliged people seeking work" would now "no longer" convene there "like they used to." Now there would only be Polish farm hands who had proper Polish emigration passes and had been recruited by employees of the German Workers' Agency in their places of origin. It thus became possible to make "many better selected people" available to German agricultural businesses and to include "particularly troops with an almost unlimited percentage of female workers." In this manner the gender distribution shifted even further in favor of high demand, low wage female farm hands, which made up 80 percent of all members of the work hands, according to the Reich labor administration.[48] The study of the agronomist Walther Vohland, conducted in the three Saxon districts of Torgau, Delitzsch, and Saalkreis, shows that this tendency found its correspondence in the jobs in the Reich. In 1925, the share of women had stood at around 56 percent, there being minimal differences between the three districts, but by 1930 it reached around 80 percent.[49]

Conclusion and Perspective:
Anti-Polish Recruitment Policies in the Weimar Republic

In the middle of the 1920s, German immigration policies succeeded in again enforcing the *Rückkehrzwang* policy for Polish farm hands, which had been required since the immediate postwar era. One of the requirements for this was the establishment of a closed system of surveillance of foreigners in the beginning of the 1920s, which was directed at labor market development, and second the increase of the offers to Polish workers in agriculture, which occurred in Germany after first overcoming postwar inflation.

The aggressive German return migration policies in place since 1924–25 operating by means of massive illegal Polish labor migrant border crossings at the beginning of the waiting period forced the Polish authorities to make concessions in this area. The German-Polish recruitment treaty then formally confirmed the *Rückkehrzwang* policy and included the Polish labor migrants who had been settled in Germany for years. Moreover, the treaty facilitated the recruitment of Polish farm workers through the German Workers' Agency.

In addition to securing a potential source of foreign agricultural workers, the recruitment treaty signed with Poland in 1927 served mainly to prevent a permanent settlement of Polish labor migrants in the winter waiting period that stemmed from the Prussian anti-Polish defense policies. Clear settlement tendencies had already developed over the decade after the suspension of the *Rückkehrzwang* policy. The implementation of the anti-Polish *Rückkehrzwang* policy built the crucial motive for the Prussian and Reich departments responsible for the signing of a treaty with Poland.

Although foreign employment in the Weimar Republic had become a problem area of the labor market policies, anti-Polish defense policies, ethnonational notions, and the corresponding political semantics in no way completely lost their meaning. The overarching goal of preventing the permanent settlement of Poles that came seamlessly from the anti-Polish defense policies of the *Kaiserreich* associated itself in the late 1920s with an ethno-national component that aimed to encourage the recruitment of people of "German descent" as labor migrants.

At the end of the 1920s, Germany signed other recruitment agreements with Czechoslovakia, Hungary, Yugoslavia, and Austria. They did not arise primarily from the impetus of securing sufficient numbers of potential foreign farm workers. Behind them, rather, were foreign political considerations that, for one, aimed at breaking up the continued existence of Germany's foreign policy isolation via legal agreements in questions of migration. Also behind these agreements, and more importantly, was the attempt to reduce the number of Polish farm hands in the German agricultural sector through the strengthened recruiting of seasonal workers from the German minorities in east-central and southeastern Europe or of Germans from Austria.

The encouragement of farm hands of German descent abroad appeared to the Foreign Office as the sole essential possibility to preserve, or rather to promote, German minorities. In all Prussian and Reich departments in the late 1920s, an "agreement [prevailed that] all permanent emigration of ethnic Germans from all the German settlements in eastern and southeastern Europe, as well as such a movement toward Germany, was undesired and in no way to be encouraged." A strengthened recruitment of ethnic German seasonal workers for the German agriculture sector did not contribute to replacing "the Polish element by an element [that was] economically equal and nationally more welcome." Apart from an economic function, according to which the earning potential in Germany could support the economic development of the settlement regions, from the point of view of the Foreign Office, the labor migration to Germany had moreover a cultural function of equal value: the opportunity "to remain in cultural contact with the motherland" must be offered to German minorities in east-central, eastern, and southeastern Europe "in whose preservation we are strongly interested."[50]

The responsible policies carried out by the Reich's Ministry of Labor on the forced recruitment of ethnic Germans, in particular through the signing of migration treaties with those states of east-central and southeastern Europe that possessed strong German minorities, were able to increase the share of ethnic Germans in relation to the Polish farm hands in the late 1920s. However, it was not so successful in recruiting so many non-Polish workers that the employment of Poles came to an end. Workers of Polish citizenship remained, with a considerable decrease of the total numbers, the strongest group among the foreign workers in the Reich, even in the global economic crisis.

Jochen Oltmer is associate professor of history and board member of the Institute for Migration Research and Intercultural Studies (IMIS) at Osnabrück University. Author and editor of books on the history of migration, including *The Encyclopedia of Migration and Minorities in Europe: From the Seventeenth Century to the Present* (with Klaus J. Bade, Pieter C. Emmer, and Leo Lucassen, eds, Cambridge, 2013); *Handbuch Staat und Migration in Deutschland vom 17. Jahrhundert bis zur Gegenwart* (ed, Berlin/Boston, 2016); *Globale Migration: Geschichte und Gegenwart* (2nd edition Munich, 2016); *Migration im 19. und 20. Jahrhundert*, 3nd edition (Berlin/Boston, 2016).

Notes

1. For a comprehensive look, see Jochen Oltmer, *Migration und Politik in der Weimarer Republik* (Göttingen, 2005).
2. For more information, see, e.g., Donna Gabaccia, *Foreign Relations: American Immigration in Global Perspective* (Princeton, NJ, 2012).
3. Imre Ferenczi, *Kontinentale Wanderungen und die Annäherung der Völker: Ein geschichtlicher Überblick* (Jena, 1930), 21.
4. Klaus J. Bade, "Politik und Ökonomie der Ausländerbeschäftigung im preußischen Osten 1885–1914: die Internationalisierung des Arbeitsmarkts im 'Rahmen der preußischen Abwehrpolitik,'" in *Preußen im Rückblick*, ed. Hans-Jürgen Puhle and Hans-Ulrich Wehler (Göttingen, 1980), 273–99.
5. "Verfügung betr. Einwanderung ausländischer Arbeiter, March 15, 1920," *Der Arbeitsnachweis in Deutschland* 7 (1919–20): 213.
6. Walter Kaskel and Friedrich Syrup, Annotation. *Arbeitsnachweisgesetz* (Berlin, 1923), 22–30.
7. Stephan, "Die Verordnungen der Reichsarbeitsverwaltung zur Regelung der Beschäftigung ausländischer Arbeitnehmer," *Neue Zeitschrift für Ausländerrecht* 3 (1923): col. 345–58.
8. *Memorandum in the Reich Department of Labor (RAM), October 22, 1922*. Bundesarchiv Berlin (BArch B), R 3901, no. 782.
9. *District president in Stralsund to the Prussian Ministry of the Interior, May 2, 1922*, BArch B, R 3901, no. 782.
10. Arthur B. Krause, "Landwirtschaftliche Wanderarbeiter im Asyl für Obdachlose," *Arbeit und Beruf* 4 (1925), no. 8: 154–57; no. 9: 178–94.
11. For more information, see, e.g., *Referendum RAM, September 21, 1921; Referendum on the result of the discussions affecting the reintroduction of the Rückkehrzwang policy for foreign farm hands in the Prussian Ministry of the Interior, December 7, 1922, RAM, December 16, 1922*, both in BArch B, R 3901, no. 782.
12. *Referendum RAM, October 22, 1921; Transcript of the discussions on December 10, 1924 in the Prussian Ministry of the Interior about the reintroduction of the Rückkehrzwang policy for foreign farm hands*, both in BArch B, R 3901, no. 782.
13. Helmut Lippelt, "'Politische Sanierung': Zur deutschen Politik gegenüber Polen 1925/26" *Vierteljahrshefte für Zeitgeschichte* 19, no. 4 (1971): 334–36.
14. *Transcript of the discussions on December 10, 1924 in the Prussian Ministry of the Interior about the reintroduction of the Rückkehrzwang policy for foreign farm hands*, BArch B, R 3901, no. 782. On the emigration of Germans from the new Polish western regions, see as a whole: Oltmer, *Migration und Politik in der Weimarer Republik*, 89–138.
15. *Deutsche Arbeiterzentrale (DAZ) to the governor of the Brandenburg province, March 31, 1925*, BArch B, R 3901, no. 782.
16. Horst Kahrs, "Die Verstaatlichung der polnischen Arbeitsmigration nach Deutschland in der Zwischenkriegszeit," in *Arbeitsmigration und Flucht: Vertreibung und Arbeitskräfteregulierung im Zwischenkriegseuropa*, ed. Eberhard Jungfer et al. (Berlin/Göttingen, 1993), 152.
17. *Memorandum on department meeting on September 24, 1925, RAM, September 30, 1925*, BArch B, R 901, no. 35226.

18. *Prussian Ministry of the Interior to the governors and district presidents, November 3, 1925,* BArch B, R 901, no. 35228.

19. *Prussian Ministry of the Interior to the governors and district presidents in the border districts in the East, October 28, 1925; central office of the Reich's railroad company to the railway administration in the districts near the border, October 31, 1925,* both in BArch B, R 901, no. 35228; Kahrs, *Verstaatlichung der polnischen Arbeitsmigration,* 153f.

20. *DAZ frontier services in Zawisna (Upper Silesia) to the DAZ, November 6, 1925,* BArch B, R 3901, no. 782.

21. *DAZ frontier services in Lauenburg (Pomerania) to the DAZ, November 30, 1925,* BArch B, R 3901, no. 782.

22. *DAZ to the RAM, November 20, 1925,* BArch B, R 3901, no. 782.

23. *DAZ to the RAM, December 16, 1925,* BArch B, R 3901, no. 782.

24. *DAZ to the RAM, November 20,1925, November 26, 1925,* both in BArch B, R 3901, no. 782; *DAZ to the Foreign Office (AA), December 2, 1925; Reich's Ministry of Food and Agriculture to the RAM, December 15, 1925,* both in: BArch B, R 901, no. 35228.

25. *DAZ to the RAM, December 2, 1925,* BArch B, R 3901, no. 782.

26. *DAZ to the RAM, December 15, 1925,* BArch B, R 3901, no. 782.

27. *RAM circular letter, December 11, 1925; Minutes about the German-Polish Negotiations on a recruitment treaty, January 12, 1926,* both in: BArch B, R 901, no. 35228.

28. Janine Ponty, *Polonais méconnus: Histoire des travailleurs immigrés en France dans l'entre-deux-guerres* (Paris, 1990): 35–50. From a macrohistorical perspective, see Christoph Rass, *Institutionalisierungsprozesse auf einem internationalen Arbeitsmarkt: Bilaterale Wanderungsverträge in Europa zwischen 1919 und 1974* (Paderborn, 2010).

29. *Polish Consulate General in Berlin to the AA, February 15, 1921,* BArch B, R 901, no. 35226.

30. Peter Krüger, *Die Außenpolitik der Republik von Weimar,* 2nd ed. (Darmstadt, 1993), 280f., 290f., 304f.

31. *Memorandum on the meeting with President Gawroński on 9.4.1925, RAM,* BArch B, R 901, no. 35226.

32. *Principles of the German-Polish emigration and immigration agreement of the Polish delegation, March 11, 1925,* BArch B, R 901, no. 35226.

33. *Ministerial draft bill for the counterstatement of the German delegation to the principles of the German-Polish emigration and immigration agreement presented to the Polish delegation, AA, March 23, 1925,* BArch B, R 901, no. 35226.

34. *RAM to the German delegation members in the German-Polish negotiations on a recruitment treaty, December 11, 1925,* BArch B, R 901, no. 35227; see also Wolfram Hennies, "Zu den deutsch-polnischen Verhandlungen vor dem Vertrag über Wanderarbeiter 1927," *Fremdarbeiterpolitik des Imperialismus* 16 (1985): 68; Janusz Sobczak, "Die polnischen Wanderarbeiter in Deutschland in den Jahren 1919 bis 1939 und ihre Behandlung," in *Fremdarbeiterpolitik des Imperialismus* 2 (1977): 53f.

35. *RAM to the German delegation members in the German-Polish negotiations on a recruitment treaty, December 11, 1925;* this provisional regulation was established in a *general report from both delegation leaders on January 6, 1926,* both in: BArch B, R 901, no. 35227.

36. *District president in Marienwerder to the Prussian Ministry of the Interior, March 30, 1926,* BArch B, R 901, no. 35227.

37. *Draft of the German delegation about the return of Polish labor migrants, RAM, June 1925,* BArch B, R 901, no. 35227.

38. *Transcript of the German delegation session for the German-Polish negotiations on the labor migrants on September 26, 1926, RAM, October 28, 1926,* BArch B, R 901, no. 35227.
39. *Head of the German delegation for the negotiations on Polish labor migrants in Berlin to the head of the Polish delegation in Warsaw, November 2, 1926,* BArch B, R 901, no. 35227.
40. *Transcript of the meeting between Geheimrat Dr. Weigert, Regierungsrat Lämmle and Emigrationsrat Dr. Dalbor on November 19, 1926 in the RAM,* BArch B, R 901, no. 35227; *The ambassador in Warsaw, Rauscher, to the AA, November 11, 1926,* in *Akten zur deutschen Auswärtigen Politik 1918–1945,* Series B: 1925–1933 (Göttingen, 1967), vol. II: 2 June to December 1926, 328–30; *The ambassador in Warsaw, Rauscher, to the AA, Telegram, December 5, 1926,* in *Akten zur deutschen Auswärtigen Politik 1918–1945,* Series B: 1925–1933, 389f.
41. "Negotiations with Regard to Polish Seasonal Immigration to Germany during 1927," *The Monthly Record of Migration* 2, no. 3 (1927): 87–89.
42. *German-Polish agreement affecting return migration of Polish farm hands in the winter half year 1926/27, December 8, 1926,* BArch B, R 901, no. 35228.
43. *Prussian Ministry of the Interior to the AA, March 2, 1927,* BArch B, R 901, no. 35228.
44. "German-Polish Agreement Concerning Agricultural Migrants," *The Monthly Record of Migration* 2, no. 12 (1927): 453f.
45. Philipp Beisiegel, "Der deutsch-polnische Vertrag über polnische landwirtschaftliche Arbeiter," in *Reichsarbeitsblatt N.F.* 8, no. 1 (1928): 1–4.
46. Ibid., 4. The ratification of the treaty in the *Reichstag* remained undisputed. There was only a statement by the KPD who spoke out against the treaty; Session 407, March 22, 1928, Negotiations of the German Reichstag. Stenographic report 3, voting period 1925, vol. 395, 13161–13619.
47. *DAZ to the Prussian Ministry of Agriculture, Domains and Forests, March 8, 1927; Report by the Director of the DAZ, Minutes of the DAZ supervisory board meeting on April 24, 1926,* both in the Geheimes Staatsarchiv Preußischer Kulturbesitz, Berlin-Dahlem, Rep. 87 B, no. 122.
48. *Memorandum on an official trip from March 27–30, 1928 to the border offices of the DAZ, RAM, April 7, 1928,* BArch B, R 3901, no. 775.
49. Walther Vohland, "Die ausländischen Wanderarbeiter und ihr Ersatz in den Kreisen Torgau, Delitzsch und Saalkreis," *Kühn Archiv: Arbeiten aus den Landwirtschaftlichen Instituten der Universität Halle* 32 (1932): 34.
50. *AA to RAM, July 27, 1929,* BArch B, R 901, no. 35198. On the policies of the Weimar Republic towards the "ethnic German" population in eastern-central, southeast and eastern Europe, see Oltmer, *Migration und Politik in der Weimarer Republik,* 139–217.

Bibliography

Akten zur deutschen Auswärtigen Politik 1918–1945, Series B: 1925–1933. Göttingen, 1967.

Anonymous. "German-Polish Agreement Concerning Agricultural Migrants." In *The Monthly Record of Migration* 2, no. 12 (1927): 453f.

Anonymous. "Negotiations with Regard to Polish Seasonal Immigration to Germany during 1927." In *The Monthly Record of Migration* 2, no. 3 (1927): 87–89.

———. "Verfügung betr. Einwanderung ausländischer Arbeiter, March 15, 1920." In *Der Arbeitsnachweis in Deutschland* 7 (1919–20).

Bade, Klaus J. "Politik und Ökonomie der Ausländerbeschäftigung im preußischen Osten 1885–1914: die Internationalisierung des Arbeitsmarkts im 'Rahmen der preußischen Abwehrpolitik.'" In *Preußen im Rückblick*, ed. Hans-Jürgen Puhle and Hans-Ulrich Wehler. Göttingen, 1980.

Beisiegel, Philipp. "Der deutsch-polnische Vertrag über polnische landwirtschaftliche Arbeiter." In *Reichsarbeitsblatt N.F.* 8, no. 1 (1928): 1–4.

Ferenczi, Imre. *Kontinentale Wanderungen und die Annäherung der Völker: Ein geschichtlicher Überblick.* Jena, 1930.

Gabaccia, Donna. *Foreign Relations: American Immigration in Global Perspective.* Princeton, NJ, 2012.

Hennies, Wolfram. "Zu den deutsch-polnischen Verhandlungen vor dem Vertrag über Wanderarbeiter 1927." In *Fremdarbeiterpolitik des Imperialismus* 16 (1985): 66–71.

Kahrs, Horst. "Die Verstaatlichung der polnischen Arbeitsmigration nach Deutschland in der Zwischenkriegszeit." In *Arbeitsmigration und Flucht: Vertreibung und Arbeitskräfteregulierung im Zwischenkriegseuropa*, ed. Eberhard Jungfer et al. Berlin/Göttingen, 1993.

Kaskel, Walter, and Friedrich Syrup. Annotation. *Arbeitsnachweisgesetz.* Berlin, 1923.

Krause, Arthur B. "Landwirtschaftliche Wanderarbeiter im Asyl für Obdachlose." In *Arbeit und Beruf* 4 (1925), no. 8: 154–57; no. 9: 178–94.

Krüger, Peter. *Die Außenpolitik der Republik von Weimar.* 2nd edition. Darmstadt, 1993.

Lippelt, Helmut. "'Politische Sanierung': Zur deutschen Politik gegenüber Polen 1925/26." *Vierteljahrshefte für Zeitgeschichte* 19, no. 4 (1971): 323–73.

Oltmer, Jochen. *Migration und Politik in der Weimarer Republik.* Göttingen, 2005.

Ponty, Janine. *Polonais méconnus: Histoire des travailleurs immigrés en France dans l'entre-deux-guerres.* Paris, 1990.

Rass, Christoph. *Institutionalisierungsprozesse auf einem internationalen Arbeitsmarkt. Bilaterale Wanderungsverträge in Europa zwischen 1919 und 1974.* Paderborn, 2010.

Reichsarbeitsministerium archives. Bundesarchiv Berlin-Lichtefelde (BArch B), R 3901.

Sobczak, Janusz. "Die polnischen Wanderarbeiter in Deutschland in den Jahren 1919 bis 1939 und ihre Behandlung." In *Fremdarbeiterpolitik des Imperialismus* 2 (1977): 47–66.

Stephan. "Die Verordnungen der Reichsarbeitsverwaltung zur Regelung der Beschäftigung ausländischer Arbeitnehmer." In *Neue Zeitschrift für Ausländerrecht* 3 (1923): col. 345–58.

Vohland, Walther. "Die ausländischen Wanderarbeiter und ihr Ersatz in den Kreisen Torgau, Delitzsch und Saalkreis." In *Kühn Archiv: Arbeiten aus den Landwirtschaftlichen Instituten der Universität Halle* 32 (1932): 1–84.

CHAPTER EIGHT

~:~

Returning Home?
Italian and German Jews' Remigration to Their Countries of Origin after the Holocaust

ANNA KOCH

In December 1940 Giorgina Levi, an Italian Jewish schoolteacher and author from Turin, who had left Italy for Bolivia after the issuing of the racial laws in 1938, wrote to a friend, "we [Levi and her husband] tried to imagine our excitement at the moment of return, when you can see Genoa looming from afar: it seemed too much to both of us. Homesickness truly is a disease."[1] Levi never felt at home in her Bolivian exile, and like many other Italian Jews who had left Italy because of anti-Semitic persecution, she planned to go back as soon as possible.[2] She returned in 1946. Like Giorgina Levi, Alfred Kantoro-wicz, a German Jewish author, had to leave his home country. He emigrated in 1933, first to Paris and later to the United States. Like Levi, Kantorowicz decided to return after the war. Born only ten years apart, they shared not only the experience of persecution, exile, and return, but also a strong belief in communism. The ways in which they imagined their return, however, could hardly have been more different. In his diary Kantorowicz wrote of his "black fears" and doubts about a future in Germany.[3] Many friends tried to discourage him from returning to the country of his birth, and he expected to "find there hunger and hatred, open and hidden Nazism, material and moral destruc-tion."[4] But, he explained, he felt too old to adjust to life in the United States, and growing anti-communism made living there increasingly difficult. Like Levi, he returned in 1946.

The distinct ways that Levi and Kantorowicz imagined their return from exile mirror broader differences in the stories of German and Italian Jewish remigration. While Italian Jews generally maintained a strong sense that Italy was still where they belonged; German Jews were uncertain they could still call Germany home. The different roles fascist Italy and Nazi Germany played in the murder of European Jews,[5] as well as the distinct postwar discourses and narratives in East Germany, West Germany, and Italy, shaped the ways in which they related to their home countries after 1945. The extent to which German and Italian Jews felt at home depended largely on how and what they remembered from their pre-emigration lives and on their ability to reconstruct a positive image of their country, be it by romanticizing its past or by envisioning a better future.[6]

In the immediate aftermath of the war most German Jews unsurprisingly found the idea of returning to Germany inconceivable.[7] The *Interessenvertretung Jüdischer Gemeinden*, the postwar organization that represented the German Jewish communities, debated whether Jews could and should remain in Germany at length. At a June 1947 meeting, one person maintained, "German Jewry had ceased to exist."[8] International Jewish organizations also vigorously opposed the reconstruction of Jewish life in Germany. In 1948 the World Jewish Congress stated that Jews should never again live on "blood-soaked German soil,"[9] and Rabbi Leo Baeck declared during a visit there that the history of Jews in Germany had ended.[10]

Friends and family confronted those German Jews who chose to return, accusing them of stupidity, naiveté, or even betrayal.[11] Articles in Jewish newspapers, statements of Jewish organizations and public figures impacted the ways in which surviving Jews could explain their decision to return. A Jewish discourse that strongly condemned their choice left little room for emphasizing homesickness or attachment. Rather, the repeated condemnations caused some to feel defensive and others outright guilty about living in the wrong place.[12] In 1946 Grete Weil, who wished to return from the Netherlands, wrote about the difficulty of standing by her unpopular choice: "I live against the world's opinion, which understandably finds it nonsensical that I want to go to Germany, and sometimes I lose breath swimming against the current."[13]

German Jews resettled in their home country with ambivalent feelings, and they pondered at length whether to stay or to go. Whether or not to return was an individual choice and numerous factors, some voiced, some kept private, played a role. Some returnees provided multiple reasons, such as health concerns, familial obligations, or professional opportunities.[14] Others maintained that their postwar return had not been a choice at all, but rather a matter of contingencies or simply the absence of other options.[15]

In contrast, most Italian Jews did not feel they needed to explain their return to Italy. Arrigo Levi and his family escaped fascist persecution and moved to Argentina in 1942. They returned four years later, without seriously considering the option of staying in Buenos Aires. As he put it, returning was just the "natural choice."[16] In a letter to a friend, an Italian Jewish refugee in Switzerland writing of her difficulties in finding work concluded, "we hope to return home soon, that would be the only and the best solution."[17] For her, Italy remained home, and most Italian Jews felt the same. A questionnaire composed by Swiss authorities asked Italian Jewish refugees where they wanted to go after the war had ended. Almost every respondent replied "back to Italy."[18] Italian Jewish returnees did not need to defend their choice, as neither Italian Jewish newspapers, nor Jewish communities, nor international Jewish organizations ever questioned Jews living on the Italian peninsula.[19]

While memoirs and diaries of Italian Jews mention the enactment of the racial laws as a radical turning point in their lives, in most cases their suffering under the anti-Semitic legislation had little impact on how they perceived Italy after 1945. Rather most Italian Jews subscribed and contributed to the myth of the "good Italian" who had protected Jews during the war. They promoted the view that anti-Semitism did not exist among Italians and emphasized the benevolent and humane behavior of their fellow citizens. Like Italian non-Jews, most Jews shared the widespread belief that Mussolini had issued the racial laws due to German pressure, and they saw Germany as solely responsible for the deportations, having forgotten or suppressed Italy's role.[20] Adriana Luzatti, a Jew from Asti who had survived the war in exile in Switzerland, declared for instance, "the Germans had influenced Mussolini; making him enact the racial laws and making him do whatever Hitler wanted."[21]

Italian postwar discourses promoted a sharp contrast between the "good Italian" and the "bad German," emphasizing the difference in the nature of the two people as well as in the character of the two regimes. Long-held stereotypes of "the Italians" as undisciplined but humane and "the Germans" as cold and obedient helped in constructing a view of the past that underestimated Italian violence and relieved Italian historical actors from any agency.[22] Most Italian Jews shared this view. Leone Maestro, a Jewish doctor from Florence, wrote in his diary, "I do not think that Hitler holds onto power longer than Capone [Mussolini] because he is more intelligent, but because he followed for better or for worse the historical line of imperial and bellicose Germany while Mussolini in all regards went against the nature, the character of Italy (from the black uniforms to the total militarization, from the goose-stepping to the racism)."[23]

Many Italian Jews viewed fascist anti-Semitism and collaboration as disconnected from what they understood as the "true Italy." Vittorio Foa, a Jewish antifascist from Turin, explained for instance that the racial laws were "a shameful stain on Italy that we were trying to wipe out in order to return the country to its tradition of democracy and tolerance."[24] The postwar image of Italy as a nation united in resistance against the Germans further strengthened the notion of fascism as a mere detour in Italian history. The *Resistenza* represented the "true Italy," the Italy, as an article in the Italian Jewish journal *Israel* stated, "that we love and expect to rise again."[25] The belief in this "true

Italy" allowed Italian Jews to connect the place to which they returned with something beyond memories of persecution.

Most German Jews experienced the period under the Nazi regime as a total rupture. With many of their friends, relatives, and colleagues expelled or murdered and their cities destroyed, the country they returned to had little in common with the place they had left behind.[26] "I had to return to understand how foreign it all had become to me, in Germany," wrote the author Hermann Kesten to a friend in 1949. Likewise, the literary scholar Hans Mayer, who returned from Switzerland to the Soviet Occupied Zone, exclaimed "And what is Germany? None of this exists anymore."[27]

While Italian Jews connected postwar Italy with a positive past, German Jews remembered above all their suffering under Nazism. An article in *Der Weg* referred to the "emotional burden" of being in Germany, "because every house and every stone reminds them [Jewish survivors] of the sufferings of the past and of the dear ones they have lost."[28] Karl Marx, who returned from London in 1946, emphasized that: "the majority of us do not feel at home in Germany and we do not know if we can ever feel at home again. All too often we are reminded of the horrific years by a house that we connect with past times, or by the sight of a square on which a synagogue used to stand, or by a cemetery."[29]

Traumatic memories also shaped how German Jews expressed longing for their home country. If they referred to *Heimweh* (homesickness) at all, they often alluded to the years of persecution at the same time.[30] Grete Weil wrote in a letter in 1946, "I would much rather be in Germany [than in Amsterdam] . . . And take walks with you. Not in the rubble of the cities, but in the countryside, after all it is still my country."[31] In her letters Weil repeatedly expressed her wish to be back in a place where she belonged. At the same time she seemed hesitant to leave Amsterdam: Germany remained her country, but it could be her country only "still" and "after all." Her past experiences of persecution and the murder of her first husband in Mauthausen continued to shape her relationship with postwar Germany.

Italian Jews rarely connected their return to their hometowns with memories of their suffering under fascism. While German Jews often seemed to feel the need to explain their attachment to Germany despite what happened, Italian Jews referred to their homesickness without mentioning their experiences of persecution. "I felt such homesickness for Italy," wrote Bruno di Cori remembering his time in Palestine, "that when I heard a record with Neapolitan songs that we had at home, I was moved to tears."[32] Lea Ottolenghi, a young Jewish girl from Livorno who had found refuge in Switzerland filled her diary in the weeks following Italy's liberation with her impatience to finally return. At one point, she decided to take a boat to the middle of a nearby lake and swim, so she could "bathe . . . in Italy!"[33]

Italian and German Jews also described their arrival in distinct ways. Most Italian Jews conveyed strong emotions about their homecoming. One described her return from Switzerland: "And . . . over the border we went! It was a really emotional moment, my heart leapt and the tears streamed down my cheeks";[34] another wrote "the Simplon tunnel was interminable, especially when one's heart was beating anxiously in the hope of finding some remnants of a home . . . We left the tunnel in a cloud of acrid black smoke: the trees that I saw along the railroad were Italian trees, Italian grass and stones, which moved me deeply."[35] Clara Levi Coen, who returned from Switzerland with her husband and young son, remembered the "wonderful feeling, when the train . . . arrived at the border to Italy. We returned to our homeland, so painfully loved and remembered during the time of exile."[36]

These writings form a stark contrast to two German Jewish recollections of arrival. "What does a man feel, who returns after fifteen years to his country of birth?" wrote Hans Sahl, "he has no mood. He does not feel anything. He does not know what he feels."[37] Fellow writer Ludwig Marcuse, who likewise returned in the late 1940s used similar words in a letter written in 1949: "What I felt? That I had slept only four hours at night, that I had a cold, that I wished the border was behind us . . . That, after sixteen years of anticipation of this hour, I felt nothing."[38] By emphasizing their lack of emotions these German Jewish returnees underlined the distance they felt towards their former home country.

Italian Jews' outpouring of emotions, on the other hand, marked the connection they still felt. Fulva di Segni Jesi, who returned from Brazil shortly after the end of the war, filled her memoir with images that encapsulated a strong sense of familiarity. About the night of her arrival she wrote, "the small polar star once again greeted me from the skies."[39] Another Italian Jewish returnee from South America, Alma Morpurgo, addressed her hometown, Trieste, directly: "every stone is familiar to me. There is a real bond of affection, of belonging between you and me."[40] Bruno di Cori recalled this enthusiasm in the letters he received from his parents after their return to Italy in 1946. His father, who had great difficulty adjusting to life in Palestine, "re-entered his world."[41] Di Cori's father did not merely move back to Italy, he returned home—to the food, the language, and the family and friends he knew and loved. Italian Jewish returnees frequently wrote about drinking Italian coffee, eating Italian food, smelling pine trees, and hearing the familiar language.[42]

The different ways in which Italian and German Jews constructed the first days after their return are also apparent in their divergent descriptions of the weather. Adriana Luzzati recalled that the day she returned to Turin was a beautiful, warm day in July,[43] and Max Donati, who like the young woman returned from Switzerland, wrote "Italy waited for us with its blue sky."[44] Fulvia di Segni Jesi remembered that it was snowing when her ship arrived in Italy but claimed she did not feel the cold.[45] Livio Steindler wrote about his first winter in Italy, after years in Israel, "the snow covered the city like a blanket," evoking an image of warmth and safety.[46] In contrast German Jews wrote of suffering under the cold temperatures, and Marcuse, who arrived in the summer, described the climate as oppressive.[47]

Italian and German Jews also depicted the destruction of their hometowns differently. Italian Jews emphasized their pain at seeing their hometowns in ruins. "My God, what have they done to my beautiful Milan?" one Italian Jew wrote upon her arrival in April 1946, and another exclaimed four months later, "How many ruins, in what state was my poor fatherland!"[48] A third spoke of the martyrdom of her father's poor city.[49] All three women personified their city or country in their writings and, by so doing, expressed their emotional attachment.

In contrast German Jews often linked the devastation with a sense of distance. The ruined streets, churches, and housing blocks rendered the city they had known so well unfamiliar and added to the already widespread feelings of estrangement. Kantorowicz described his loss of orientation: "even the victory column, which as if mocking itself still towered among rubble and ruins, was, so it seemed to me, no longer standing at the same place; I had not known that it had been moved during Hitler's time."[50]

Lotte Winter unveiled a different way in which encounters with the destroyed country reinforced feelings of estrangement. In her memoir she described her shock about the destruction she encountered after her return from Sweden in 1946: "Yet, as it would soon become clear, a city of ruins was horrifying, but much, much more horrifying were the morally ruined and demoralized people."[51] Other German Jews likewise drew a connection between the devastated cities and the moral decay of the non-Jewish population.[52] For them the destruction symbolized the damage that Nazi propaganda had caused in the people's minds.

How surviving Jews perceived the role their fellow citizens had played in their persecution affected the extent to which they felt at home.[53] Many Jewish returnees in postwar Germany underscored that they could not help but feel suspicious towards other Germans, most of whom had turned against them or had watched silently. Hans Mayer had no "inkling of liking for his former compatriots," and Ludwig Marcuse wrote that he felt "nowhere as lonely as in [his] hometown."[54] In a letter written in 1946 a German Jewish returnee from Portugal framed his return as "going back to these people who tortured his [sic] own family and killed six million Jews!"[55] German Jews' wartime experiences separated them from the majority population, and non-Jewish Germans' self-perception as victims worsened the situation. Moreover, most Germans reacted with indifference or even hostility to the return of emigrants, making them feel unwelcome.[56]

Whereas German Jews by and large understood their wartime experiences in stark contrast to those of non-Jewish Germans, Italian Jews often asserted that all Italians had suffered during the war and emphasized the similarity between their own fate and the majority population's experiences. "Their shoulders were also burdened with stories of poverty, separations and grief," remembered one Italian Jew about her non-Jewish coworkers, and another described the "common pain and common hope" of Italians after the war.[57] Rather than pointing to the particularity of their fate, many Italian Jews wished to integrate their individual experiences into the collective memory. The literary critic Giacomo Debenedetti rejected any notion that the Jewish fate was unique. In his work *Eight Jews*, written in 1944, he maintained that "what Jews would prefer is that the suffering of those of them presently liberated and of those still being persecuted, be poured into, mixed, mingled with the long collective, the common levy of tears and pleas that all humans worthy of the name have sacrificed, and are still sacrificing."[58]

The notion that they had all suffered during the war, and that Jewish and non-Jewish Italians had been united in their antifascist resistance, allowed Italian Jews to regain a sense of belonging. Dan Segre, who had immigrated to Israel but whose family had stayed behind, portrayed Jewish and non-Jewish Italians as united against the Germans and the "Fascist Republicans." He wrote, "this grotesque situation . . . combined a deep sense of human solidarity with an equally deep hate for the Germans and the Fascist Republicans. It also gave an idea of the links between my family and the seven hundred or so villagers."[59] Like Segre, other Italian Jews understood Italian perpetrators as the exceptions among a benign people, as a treacherous minority that did not represent the "true Italy."[60]

While many Italian Jews supported the myth of the "good Italian," others challenged this concept; they adopted a more critical stance vis-à-vis their fellow citizens and emphasized the differences between the Jewish and the non-Jewish fate.[61] In a letter written in 1944 Fernanda Di Segni Sermoneta explained why she decided to leave Italy after the war: "We feel that this is not our homeland . . . We feel different, we see among these people, these Italians, many of those spies who have contributed to our downfall in that fateful period."[62] For Di Segni Sermoneta the fascist period constituted a rupture, as for so many German Jews. She could no longer connect with her life before the racial laws and thus chose to leave. Others like Umberto Beer, who had immigrated to Brazil after the 1938 racial laws, decided to remain in their place of exile. "The punch I had received," Beer explained, "still hurt and continues to hurt."[63] Beer could not forget the persecution, and these memories made it impossible for him to consider Italy home.

These examples show that while the majority of Italian Jews described their return as unproblematic, some felt, like most German Jews, estranged from the place they had once considered home. At the same time a few German Jews expressed feelings of closeness rather than distance. Hans Rothfels for instance, a German Jewish historian who had left his home country in 1938 and returned shortly after the war, remained strongly attached to Germany. Rothfels continued to perceive Germany as distinct from Nazism, and claimed the existence of a "true" or "other" Germany that had resisted Hitler. Like many Italian Jews, he connected the time before 1933 with the postwar years, bridging over the Nazi period.[64] Other German Jews likewise maintained a positive outlook on their home country. Replying to the many articles published in *Der Weg* that questioned the future for Jews in Germany, one author argued that Jews should feel no shame because in their hearts Germany remained their "fatherland." He continued to perceive Germany as *Heimat* and insisted on the continuous existence of a "true Germany," the home of Goethe and Schiller.[65]

While few German Jews expressed such strong emotional bonds, others likewise pointed to Germany's cultural achievements in their effort to rescue at least some remnants of home from the stench of Nazism. Jewish publications from the immediate postwar were filled with articles that sought to free the German "Greats," such as Goethe or Nietzsche, from suspicions of anti-Semitism. Other articles focused on the Jewish contribution to German culture, pointing to the rootedness of German Jews in Germany.[66] Both ultimately aimed to separate German culture from Nazism and thus to reclaim it.[67]

Others expressed their love for a particular region. Grete Weil wrote in 1946 that Bavaria remained the place "to which she belonged in the deepest way."[68] Many shared this loyalty to a specific region or city, while asserting that they no longer had a strong connection to the country as a whole.[69] German Jews found themselves caught between their love for certain parts of their home country—its culture, its language, its landscapes—and the knowledge of Germany's horrific crimes. By emphasizing their attachment to a specific aspect, some found a niche in which they could feel at home.

The hope of building a different and better Germany in the Soviet-occupied part of the country, the first "socialist state on German soil," enabled those German Jews who strongly identified as Communists to regain a sense of home.[70] "I still believe in the moral strength of the better Germany," explained Kantorowicz in August 1946,[71] and another German Jew maintained in 1947 that antifascist emigrants in their various countries of exile prepared to "return home to be present when the foundation for a new and better Germany was laid."[72] The dream of a better future allowed them to envision a place to which they would belong. This idea of actively building a new home is apparent in Lotte Winter's writing. She declared that she had "through persistent fighting against the reactionary heritage, professionally, politically and personally conquered for herself a new home."[73]

While most of these German Jewish communists shared other German Jews' feelings of distance and suspicion, their vision of a radically different country, a future home that they would build together with the like-minded, separated them from others. Their belief in the communist collective allowed them, in some ways similarly to Italian Jews, to feel they belonged to a community that had shared some of the same experiences. Like Jews, communists had been victims of Nazi persecution; therefore Jewish communists could find similarities between their own fate and the experiences of non-Jewish communists. For them the East German state offered not only the prospect of idealizing their dream of a socialist society but also a place of belonging.[74] Yet while Italian Jews tended to look at the entire population as having stood on their side during the war, these German Jews usually were well aware that the communist resistance had constituted a small minority in Nazi Germany. Thus while the party provided them with a social network, they appeared hardly less mistrustful of the general population than German Jews in the West. One German Jewish communist, for example, recounted that she felt at home among her comrades, but was afraid of other Germans.[75]

While an idealistic outlook was more dominant among German communists of Jewish origin who had opted for the East German zone, or later the GDR, some Jews in the West likewise dreamed of building a better, more democratic Germany.[76] Their sense of mission, and hope for a better future, made them more positive about finding a home again in Germany. The jurist Fritz Bauer, who returned from Sweden hoping to impact the development of the postwar justice system, wrote in a letter a few days after his arrival, that "for the time being" he "felt—much more than expected—at home again."[77]

Some Italian Jews likewise expressed the wish to contribute to the postwar reconstruction. Tullia Calabi Zevi, a journalist who returned to Italy from New York in 1946, came back to "participate in the reconstruction of the traumatized, unsettled communities and also to participate, after the defeat of Fascism, in the rebirth of democracy in Italy."[78] Yet in contrast to Jews in East or West Germany who hoped to build a new and different country, Zevi aimed for the "rebirth" of the "true Italy" that had existed before the rise of fascism.

Hope for a better future played a crucial role in deciding to return and in regaining a sense of home.[79] A feeling of belonging, however, depended also on how returning Jews remembered their past in their former home country. The constant reminders of Germany's crimes made it difficult for German Jews to feel or express attachment, and the general discourse of disapproval colored the way German returnees could perceive and narrate their return. Among surviving German Jews loving their homeland remained outside the "norms of emotional expression and value."[80] People like Fritz Bauer, who primarily identified as a Social Democrat and jurist, and who mainly associated with other political emigrants, proved less affected by the condemnations of a return to Germany. The same holds true for communists like Anna Seghers or Alfred Kantorowicz, who settled in the Soviet Occupied Zone.

Italian Jews on the other hand were never confronted with a similar negative discourse, as neither the Italian nor the international Jewish community disapproved of their choice to live in Italy. They could more easily focus on positive recollections of their pre-emigration lives in Italy, and most Italian Jews continued to express strong nationalism even after the issuing of the racial laws. They perceived fascist anti-Semitism as separate from their home country and constructed a memory, in which the Italian people, as antifascists, had stood on the side of their Jewish fellow citizens. Perhaps it was their wish to reintegrate, their longing to belong and their need for a home that rendered Italian Jews so forgetful or forgiving. After all, as Jean Améry observed, "it is not good to have no home."[81]

Whether or not German and Italian Jews could feel at home depended to a large extent on their ability to find something they could connect with, be it the familiarity of the culture, the romanticization of the past, or the vision of building a better place. The conviction that the "true Italy" had only been temporarily overshadowed, or the notion that there was an "other," better Germany, made returning home conceivable. In that sense Italian and German Jews' relation to their home was similar. Yet while the "true Italy" was rather easy to find, fewer succeeded in locating the "better Germany."[82]

Anna Koch is currently a Teaching Fellow in Jewish History and Culture at the University of Southampton.. She has received her PhD from the Departments of Hebrew and Judaic Studies and History at New York University in May 2015. Her manuscript titled "Home after Fascism? Italian and German Jews after the Holocaust, 1944-1952" compares the experiences of Jews who resettled in West Germany, East Germany and Italy after 1945. Anna's work has been supported by the Social Science Research Council, the Studienstiftung des Deutschen Volkes, and the Memorial Foundation for Jewish Culture, among others. Anna Koch has previously held fellowships at the Center for Jewish History, the German Historical Institute in Rome, and the NYU Tikvah Center for Law & Jewish Civilization.

Notes

I would like to thank Leora Auslander, Laura Honsberger, Marion Kaplan, Larissa Kopytoff, Silvano Longhi, Shaul Mitelpunkt, Mary Nolan, and the editors of this volume for their careful reading and helpful comments.

1. Giorgina Levi to Francesco Lemmi, 12/25/1940, Lemmi Francesco and Giorgina Levi, . . . *Caro Professore, eccomi di nuovo viva (1940–1948), Epistolario.* Archivio Diaristico Nazionale (hereinafter ADN), E/Adn. Unless otherwise noted, all translations are my own.

2. The number of Italian Jewish returnees from the United States and South America has not been determined. About 12 percent of Italian Jews who had immigrated to Israel returned after the war. See Arturo Marzano, *Una terra per rinascere: gli ebrei italiani in Palestina prima della guerra (1920–1940)* (Genoa, 2003), 361–71. Almost all Italians Jews who had fled to Switzerland returned. See Renata Broggini, *Frontier of Hope: Jews from Italy Seek Refuge in Switzerland 1943–1945* (Milan, 2003); Reuben Resnik to Communità Israelita, Milan and Turin, 06/28/1945, American Jewish Joint Distribution Committee Archives, New York, AR 45/54 # 629.

3. Alfred Kantorowicz, *Deutsches Tagebuch* (Munich, 1964), 102.

4. Ibid., 63.

5. Without trying to equate the roles played by fascist Italy and Nazi Germany in the Holocaust, the persecution both Italian and German Jews experienced in their home countries because of policies issued by their own governments, and their shared experiences of emigration, loss, and return, render the two cases similar enough to allow for a comparison. It is through this comparative analysis that the impact of the postwar narratives on surviving Jews' relationships to their homelands becomes apparent. Between 1938 and 1943 Fascist Italy introduced a set of anti-Jewish laws, primarily before World War II and without German interference. Like Jews in Nazi Germany, Italian Jews increasingly lost their economic security and were excluded from society. While the Nazis planned and executed the murder of Italy's Jews, the Salò Fascists provided necessary assistance in the deportations. Moreover, it was not the Nazis but the Repubblica Sociale Italiana that looted Jewish property and disenfranchised Italian Jews. Michele Sarfatti, *The Jews in Mussolini's Italy: From Equality to Persecution* (Madison, WI, 2006); Ilaria Pavan, *Tra Indifferenza E Oblio: Le Conseguenze Economiche Delle Leggi Razziali in Italia 1938–1970* (Florence, 2004).

6. When writing about "home" I refer to the local community, the home country, as well as to an environment that had offered Italian and German Jews a sense of belonging and security.

7. About 4–5 percent of German Jews who had emigrated decided to return after World War II. Marita Krauss, "Jewish Remigration: An Overview of an Emerging Discipline," *Leo Baeck Institute Year Book* 49 (2004). This chapter focuses on those who remigrated during the first postwar decade. The numbers of German Jewish returnees increased slightly over the next decades when Germany provided financial assistance to returnees, but most emigrants continued to reject the idea of a return.

8. Sitzungsprotokoll der Interessenvertretung der jüdischen Gemeinden, 06/08/1947, United States Holocaust Memorial Museum Archives (hereinafter USHMM), RG 14.053 M. See also "Die problematische Stellung der Juden in Deutschland," *Der Weg* 1 (1946).

9. Resolutions adopted by the Second Plenary assembly of the World Jewish Congress, Montreux June 27th–July 6th, 1948, cited as in Michael Brenner, *After the Holocaust: Rebuilding Jewish Lives in Postwar Germany* (Princeton, NJ, 1997), 66.

10. Rede Leo Baeck, 10/14/1948, Zentralarchiv zur Erforschung der Geschichte der Juden in Deutschland, Frankfurt—B.1/13, Serie A 722, Blatt 39.

11. See Ron Chernow, *Die Warburgs: Odyssee einer Familie* (Berlin, 1994), 707; Lotte Winter, *Unsere Vergangenheit, Unsere Zukunft 1933–1955*, Leo Baeck Institute (hereinafter LBI), ME 961, 244; Kantorowicz, *Deutsches Tagebuch*, 63; Inge Deutschkron, *Mein Leben nach dem Überleben* (Munich, 2001), 91; Ursula Bernhardt and Peter Lange, *Der Riss durch mein Leben: die Erinnerungen von Ursula Bernhardt* (Berlin, 2000), 284.

12. Anthony Kauders, *Unmögliche Heimat: eine deutsch-jüdische Geschichte der Bundesrepublik* (Munich, 2007).

13. Grete Weil to Walter Jokisch, 02/24/1946, Literaturarchiv der Monacensia (hereinafter Monacensia), GW B 96. Grete Weil survived in hiding in Amsterdam and returned to Germany in 1947.

14. Regarding motivations for return, see Ronald Webster, "Jüdische Rückkehrer in der BRD nach 1945: Ihre Motive, ihre Erfahrungen," *Aschkenas* 5 (1995).

15. See for example Rolf Hertz, *Macht und Ohnmacht*, LBI, ME 387, 10; Interview with Kurt Cohen in Franz Jürgens, *Wir waren ja eigentlich Deutsche: Juden berichten von Emigration und Rückkehr* (Berlin, 1997), 201; Interview with Boris Schachtel [name changed by the author] in Douglas Morris, *The Lives of Some Jewish Germans Who Lived in Nazi Germany and Live in Germany Today: An Oral History* (BA thesis, Wesleyan University, 1976), LBI, 79.

16. Account of Arrigo Levi in Eleanora Maria Smolensky, Vera Vigevani Jarach, *Tante voci, una storia: Italiani ebrei in Argentina 1938–1948* (Bologna, 1998), 374.

17. Letter from Giulia [last name unknown] to Franco Levi, 10/21/1944, AA.VV, . . . *Mio caro Franco* (1944–1947), *Epistolario*, ADN, E/Adn.

18. Broggini, *Frontier of Hope*, 361.

19. International onlookers perceived Italians likewise as harmless. See Ruth Ben-Ghiat, "A Lesser Evil? Italian Fascism in/and the Totalitarian Equation," in *The Lesser Evil: Moral Approaches to Genocide Practices*, ed. Helmut Dubiel and Gabriel Motzkin (London; New York, 2004), 140.

20. See, for example, Adriana Luzzati, *La mia vita*, ADN, MP/02; Emilio Levi, *Ricordo di Maria*, ADN, MG/90; Leona Maestro, *Tempo di guerra / Tempo di pace*, ADN, DG/88; Giuseppe Luft, *La mia guerra da civile*, ADN, MG/91. See also Carla Forti, *Il Caso Pardo Roques: Un eccidio del 1994 tra memoria e oblio* (Torino, 1998), 225–26; Guri Schwarz, *Ritrovare se stessi: Gli ebrei nell'Italia postfascista* (Rome, 2004), 167–68.

21. Luzzati, *La mia vita*, ADN, MP/02.

22. Filippo Focardi, "La memoria del fascismo e il "demone del' analogia"" *Faschismen im Gedächtnis*, ed. Andrea Di Michele and Gerald Steinacher (Innsbruck, 2004), 61–65; Ben-Ghiat, "A Lesser Evil?" 140.

23. Leone Maestro, *Tempo di guerra / Tempo di pace*, ADN, DG/88.

24. Cited as in Alexander Stille, *Benevolence and Betrayal: Five Italian Jewish Families Under Fascism* (New York, 1991), 321.

25. "Liberazione," *Israel* XXX-1 (1944).

26. See Rainer Nicolaysen, *Siegfried Landshut: die Wiederentdeckung der Politik: eine Biographie* (Frankfurt am Main, 1997), 344; Hermann Kesten, "Die vergebliche Heimkehr," in *"Ich hatte Glück mit den Menschen": Zum 100. Geburtstag des Dichters Hermann Kesten. Texte von ihm und über ihn*, eds. Wolfgang Buhl, Ulf von Dewitz (Nuremberg, 2000), 17.

27. Hermann Kesten to Manès Sperber, 08/21/1949, Monacensia, HKB 2353; Interview with Hans Mayer in Herlinde Koelbl, *Jüdische Porträts: Photographien und Interviews von Herlinde Koelbl* (Frankfurt, 2010), 183.

28. Hans-Erich Fabian, "Liquidationsgemeinden?" *Der Weg* 18 (1947).
29. Cited as in Wolfgang Blaschke, Karola Fings, and Cordula Lissner, *Unter Vorbehalt: Rückkehr aus der Emigration nach 1945* (Köln, 1997), 155. See similarly also the interview with Stefan Heym in Koelbl, *Jüdische Porträts*, 116 and Hermann Kesten to Joseph Wittlin, 02/05/1950, Monacensia, HKB 2510.
30. See for example Wilhelm Meier, "Auswanderer—Rückwanderer" *Der Weg*, 6 (1947).
31. Weil to Jokisch, 08/05/1946, Monacensia, GW B 96.
32. Bruno di Cori, *Memorie di un italiano in Medio Oriente*, ADN MP/94. See similarly also Fulva di Segni Jesi, *La lunga strada azzurra*, Centro bibliografico dell'Unione delle Comunità ebraiche italiane (hereinafter UCEI); Adriana Luzzati, *La mia vita*, ADN, MP/02.
33. Lea Ottolenghi, *Ricordi e impressioni di un'internata*, ADN, DG/92.
34. Cited in Broggini, *Frontier of Hope*, 373.
35. Cited in Ibid., 373. See similarly also Gualtiero Morpurgo, *Diario di un rifugiato in svizzera 1943–1945*, ADN, DG 99 and Max Donati, *Diario d'Esilio*, Archivio della Fondazione Centro di Documentazione Ebraica Contemporanea (hereinafter ACDEC), Vicissitudini Max Donati.
36. Clara Levi Coen, *Ebrei nell'occhio del ciclone*, ACDEC, Vicissitudini. Giu 9889.
37. Hans Sahl, *Memoiren eines Moralisten* (Frankfurt am Main, 1990), 217.
38. Marcuse to von Hofe and Townsend, 06/17/1949, in von Hofe, ed., *Briefe von und an Ludwig Marcuse*, 64. Interestingly, Marcuse described the same moment differently in his memoir: "When we reached the German border I felt overwhelmed." Ludwig Marcuse, *Mein zwanzigstes Jahrhundert; auf dem Weg zu einer Autobiographie* (Munich, 1960), 361.
39. Di Segni Jesi, *La lunga strada azzurra*, 149.
40. Alma Morpurgo, *Queste mie figlie*, ADN, MP/86, 72.
41. Di Cori, *Memorie di un italiano in Medio Oriente*.
42. Di Cori, *Memorie di un italiano in Medio Oriente*; Di Segni Jesi, *La lunga strada azzurra*; Anonymous, "Una Italiana Reduce da Auschwitz Racconta," ACDEC, Vicissitudini dei singoli, Saralvo Corrado, 1.2. N. 700, Roberta di Camerino, *R come Roberta* (Milano, 1981), 62.
43. Luzzati, *La mia vita*. Similarly Donati, *Diario d'Esilio*.
44. ACDEC Vicissitudini Max Donati: Diario d'Esilio. Similar also Camerino, *R come Roberta*, 65.
45. Di Segni Jesi, *La lunga strada azzurra*.
46. Steindler, *Viandante del XX secolo*, ADN MP/88.
47. See Interview with Ms. C. in Kliner-Fruck, *Es ging ja ums Überleben*, 297; Kantorowicz, *Deutsches Tagebuch*, 121; Marcuse to von Hofe and Townsend, 07/17/1949, in Hofe, ed., *Briefe von und an Ludwig Marcuse*, 80.
48. Becky Behar, *Diary 1943–1947*, ACDEC, Vicissitudini dei singoli, 1.2., N. 57; Ottolenghi, *Ricordi e impressioni di un'internata*.
49. Di Segni Jesi, *La lunga strada azzurra*.
50. Kantorowicz, *Deutsches Tagebuch*, 144. See also the letter from Peter Reiche to relatives 01/01/1946, Archiv des Jüdischen Museums Berlin, Sammlung Peter H Reiche, 2005/51/01–14. Similar also Marcuse, *Mein zwanzigstes Jahrhundert*, 361, 363.
51. Winter, *Unsere Vergangenheit*, 275.
52. Kesten, "Die vergebliche Heimkehr," 24.

53. Regarding the connection between the feeling of belonging to a collective and a sense of home, see Marc Fried, "Grieving for a Lost Home: Psychological Costs of Relocation," in *Urban Renewal: The Record and the Controversy*, ed. James Q. Wilson (New York, 1966), 363; Christina Twomey, "Double Displacement: Western Women's Return Home from Japanese Internment in the Second World War," in *Homes and Homecomings*, ed. Adler, Hamilton, 671.

54. Interview with Mayer in Koelbl, *Jüdische Porträts*, 183; Marcuse to von Hofe and Townsend, Berlin 07/17/1949, in Harold von Hofe, ed., *Briefe von und an Ludwig Marcuse*, 80.

55. Letter of a German Jewish returnee to the German Jewish representative Committee affiliated with the World Jewish Congress, 09/18/1946, Central Zionist Archives, C3/349.

56. See Krauss, "Jewish Remigration," 113.

57. Sonia Oberdorfer, *A Marco*, ADN MP/06; Jenny Ravenna, *Relazione, Testimonianze sui campi di concentramento*, UCEI, Busta 44A, Fascicolo 3.

58. Giacomo Debenedetti, *Eight Jews*, trans. Estelle Gilson (Notre Dame, IN, 2001), 84.

59. Dan Vittorio Segre, *Memoirs of a Fortunate Jew: An Italian Story* (Bethesda, MD, 1987), 75.

60. See, for example, Liliana Briefel, *My Story of Life in Italy during the Holocaust* (USHMM, 2005), 387; Raffaele Cantoni, "Il saluto dell'unione delle comunità israelitiche italiane a Riccardo Bachi," *Rassegna mensile d'Israel* 34 (1950): 22.

61. See "Privati 1944–1945," Busta 65A, Fascicolo 8, UCEI.

62. Cited as in Frederica Barozzi, "L' uscita degli ebrei di Roma dalla clandestinità," in *Il ritorno alla vita: Vicende e diritti degli ebrei in Italia dopo la seconda guerre mondiale*, ed. Michele Sarfatti (Florence, 1998), 41.

63. Umberto Beer, *Va' Fuori d'Italia*, UCEI.

64. Nicolas Berg, "Hidden Memory and Unspoken History: Hans Rothfels and the Postwar Restoration of Contemporary German History," *Leo Baeck Institute Yearbook* (2004), 49. The concept of the "other Germany" related to those Germans who had remained uncorrupted, either by emigrating or by resisting. It was widely used and debated among emigrants. Marita Krauss, *Heimkehr in ein fremdes Land: Geschichte der Remigration nach 1945* (Munich, 2001), 19.

65. "Juden in Deutschland oder Deutsche Juden," *Der Weg* 6 (1946).

66. See for example August Kruhm, "Goethe und Felix Mendelsohn-Bartholdy," *Zwischen den Zeiten* 2 (1947); Ludwig Misch, "Juedischer Anteil an der Deutschen Kultur, Felix Mendelssohn-Bartholdy," *Jüdisches Gemeindeblatt für die britische Zone*, 17 (1946); Richard May, "Juedischer Anteil an der Deutschen Kultur, Heinrich Heine," *Jüdisches Gemeindeblatt für die britische Zone* 19 (1947); Carl Heinz, "Der Anti-Antisemit Friedrich Nietzsche" *Zwischen den Zeiten* 2 (1947).

67. Regarding returnees' attachment to German culture and language, see also the interviews with Helmut Stern and Edith Reifenberg in Jürgens, "Wir waren ja eigentlich Deutsche;" Hermann Kesten, *Das ewige Exil* (Munich, 1963), 28; Marcuse, *Mein zwanzigstes Jahrhundert*, 296.

68. Weil to Jokisch, 07/06/1946, also 11/28/1946, Monacensia, GW B 96.

69. Inge Deutschkron, Leon Spierer, Erich Cohn, Ursula Bernhardt and Helmut Stern expressed a strong connection with Berlin. Deutschkron, *Mein Leben*, 270, 271; Interviews with Leon Spierer and Helmut Stern in Jürgens, *"Wir waren ja eigentlich Deutsche,"*18, 27; Michael Czollek, "Cohn sagt"—Interview Michael Czollek mit

Erich Cohn in *"Sind allet Berlina"—Geschichten und Gedichte,* ed. Petra Grande (Berlin, 1986); Bernhardt "Der Riß durch mein Leben," 297; Ralph Giordano described similar feelings for Hamburg, Ralph Giordano, "Ich bin geblieben—warum?" in *Ich bin geblieben—warum?: Juden in Deutschland, heute,* ed. Katja Behrens (Gerlingen, 2002), 124; Walter Grünwald explained that he identified as Swabian. Interview with Walter und Lotte Grünwald, in Jürgens, *"Wir waren ja eigentlich Deutsche,"* 224.

70. Interview with Ruth Benario in John Borneman and Jeffrey M. Peck, *Sojourners: The Return of German Jews and the Question of Identity* (Lincoln, NE, 1995); Recha Rothschild, *Memoirs,*173, LBI, ME 243; Interview with Sophie Marum in Vincent von Wroblewsky, *Zwischen Thora und Trabant: Juden in der DDR* (Berlin, 1993), 27.

71. Kantorowicz, *Deutsches Tagebuch,* 103.

72. Rothschild, *Memoirs,* 171.

73. Winter, *Unsere Vergangenheit,* 290.

74. See, for example, Stephan Hermlin, "Ballade von der Überwindung der Einsamkeit in den großen Städten," in *Gedichte und Nachdichtungen* (Berlin, 1990), 53; Hans Mayer, *Ein Deutscher auf Widerruf, Erinnerungen,* Vol. I (Frankfurt am Main, 1982), 305. See also Barbara Einhorn, "Nation und Identität: Erzählungen von Exil und Rückkehr," in *Zwischen Politik und Kultur—Juden in der DDR,* ed. Moshe Zuckermann (Göttingen, 2002), 113; Frank Stern, "The Return to the Disowned Home: German Jews and the Other Germany," *New German Critique* 67 (1996), 60.

75. Interview with Maria Einhorn in Einhorn, "Nation und Identität: Erzählungen von Exil und Rückkehr," 109.

76. See Andrea Sinn, "'Aber ich blieb trotzdem hier' Karl Marx und die Anfänge jüdischen Lebens im Nachkriegsdeutschland," in *Schwerpunktthema Leben danach— Jüdischer Neubeginn im Land der Täter* (Nuremberg, 2010); Deutschkron, *Mein Leben nach dem Überleben,* 21–22; Meier, "Auswanderer—Rückwanderer"; Ute Benz, "'Für den Vater war es sehr schwer' Lucy Geigers Auswanderung und Rückkehr," in *Das Exil der kleinen Leute,* ed. Wolfgang Benz (Munich, 1991), 330.

77. Fritz Bauer to Kurt Schuhmacher, 04/24/1948, cited in Wojak, *Fritz Bauer 1903– 1968,* 228.

78. Tullia Calabi Zevi, "La mia autobiografia politica." Una testimonianza letta al 'Convegno del Circolo Rosselli di Firenze del 15 novembre 1999 dedicato al Centenario della nascita di Carlo Rosselli, in 'Quaderni del Circolo Rosselli, 1/2000, Alinea editrice, Firenze, 83–89.

79. Krauss, "Jewish Remigration," 11.

80. Barbara Rosenwein, *Emotional Communities in the Early Middle Ages.* (Ithaca, NY, 2006), 2.

81. Jean Améry, "How Much Home Does a Person Need?" in *At the Mind's Limits: Contemplations by a Survivor on Auschwitz and Its Realities,* trans. Sidney Rosenfeld and Stella P. Rosenfeld (Bloomington, IN, 1980.)

82. In an interview in 1992 Hermann Kesten expressed his disappointment with Germany's postwar development: "We had not been emigrants ... We all had hoped to return to a better Germany, but for many it had, after all, been difficult to discover this better Germany." Norbert Schmidt, *Hermann Kesten-eine späte Annäherung.* Medienwerkstatt Franken Film, 1992.

Bibliography

Améry, Jean. "How Much Home Does a Person Need?" In *At the Mind's Limits: Contemplations by a Survivor on Auschwitz and Its Realities*, trans. Sidney Rosenfeld and Stella P. Rosenfeld. Bloomington, IN, 1980.

Anonymous. "Juden in Deutschland oder Deutsche Juden." *Der Weg* 6 (1946).

——. "Liberazione." In *Israel* XXX-1. 1944.

——. "Die problematische Stellung der Juden in Deutschland." *Der Weg* 1 (1946).

Barozzi, Frederica. "L'uscita degli ebrei di Roma dalla clandestinità." In *Il ritorno alla vita: Vicende e diritti degli ebrei in Italia dopo la seconda guerre mondiale*, ed. Michele Sarfatti. Florence, 1998.

Behrens, Katja, ed. *Ich bin geblieben—warum?: Juden in Deutschland, heute.* Gerlingen, 2002.

Ben-Ghiat, Ruth. "A Lesser Evil? Italian Fascism in/and the Totalitarian Equation." In *The Lesser Evil: Moral Approaches to Genocide Practices*, ed. Helmut Dubiel and Gabriel Motzkin. London; New York, 2004.

Benz, Ute. "'Für den Vater war es sehr schwer' Lucy Geigers Auswanderung und Rückkehr." In *Das Exil der kleinen Leute*, ed. Wolfgang Benz. Munich, 1991.

Berg, Nicolas. "Hidden Memory and Unspoken History: Hans Rothfels and the Postwar Restoration of Contemporary German History." *Leo Baeck Institute Yearbook*. 2004.

Bernhardt, Ursula, and Peter Lange. *Der Riss durch mein Leben: die Erinnerungen von Ursula Bernhardt*. Berlin, 2000.

Blaschke, Wolfgang, Karola Fings, and Cordula Lissner. *Unter Vorbehalt: Rückkehr aus der Emigration nach 1945.* Cologne, 1997.

Borneman, John, and Jeffrey M. Peck. *Sojourners: The Return of German Jews and the Question of Identity.* Lincoln, NE, 1995.

Brenner, Michael. *After the Holocaust: Rebuilding Jewish Lives in Postwar Germany.* Princeton, NJ, 1997.

Broggini, Renata. *Frontier of Hope: Jews from Italy Seek Refuge in Switzerland 1943–1945.* Milan, 2003.

di Camerino, Roberta. *R come Roberta.* Milan, 1981.

Chernow, Ron. *Die Warburgs: Odyssee einer Familie.* Berlin, 1994.

Debenedetti, Giacomo. *Eight Jews*, trans. Estelle Gilson. Notre Dame, IN, 2001.

Deutschkron, Inge. *Mein Leben nach dem Überleben.* Munich, 2001.

Einhorn, Barbara. "Nation und Identität: Erzählungen von Exil und Rückkehr." In *Zwischen Politik und Kultur—Juden in der DDR*, ed. Moshe Zuckermann. Göttingen, 2002.

Fabian, Hans-Erich. "Liquidationsgemeinden?" *Der Weg* 18 (1947).

Focardi, Filippo. "La memoria del fascismo e il 'demone del' analogia'." In *Faschismen im Gedächtnis*, ed. Andrea Di Michele and Gerald Steinacher. Innsbruck, 2004.

Forti, Carla. *Il Caso Pardo Roques: Un eccidio del 1994 tra memoria e oblio.* Torino, 1998.

Fried, Marc. "Grieving for a Lost Home: Psychological Costs of Relocation." In *Urban Renewal: the Record and the Controversy*, ed. James Q. Wilson. New York, 1966.

Grande, Petra, ed. *"Sind allet Berlina"—Geschichten und Gedichte*. Berlin, 1986.

Heinz, Carl. "Der Anti-Antisemit Friedrich Nietzsche." *Zwischen den Zeiten* 2 (1947).

Hermlin, Stephan. "Ballade von der Überwindung der Einsamkeit in den großen Städten." In *Gedichte und Nachdichtungen*. Berlin, 1990.

Jürgens, Franz. *Wir waren ja eigentlich Deutsche: Juden berichten von Emigration und Rückkehr*. Berlin, 1997.

Kantorowicz, Alfred. *Deutsches Tagebuch*. Munich, 1964.

Kauders, Anthony. *Unmögliche Heimat: eine deutsch-jüdische Geschichte der Bundesrepublik*. Munich, 2007.

Kesten, Hermann. *Das ewige Exil*. Munich, 1963.

———. "Die vergebliche Heimkehr." In *"Ich hatte Glück mit den Menschen": Zum 100. Geburtstag des Dichters Hermann Kesten. Texte von ihm und über ihn*, ed. Wolfgang Buhl and Ulf von Dewitz. Nuremberg, 2000.

Koelbl, Herlinde. *Jüdische Porträts: Photographien und Interviews von Herlinde Koelbl*. Frankfurt, 2010.

Krauss, Marita. *Heimkehr in ein fremdes Land: Geschichte der Remigration nach 1945*. Munich, 2001.

———. "Jewish Remigration: An Overview of an Emerging Discipline." *Leo Baeck Institute Year Book* 49 (2004).

Kruhm, August. "Goethe und Felix Mendelsohn-Bartholdy." In *Zwischen den Zeiten* 2. 1947.

Marcuse, Ludwig. *Mein zwanzigstes Jahrhundert; auf dem Weg zu einer Autobiographie*. Munich, 1960.

Marzano, Arturo. *Una terra per rinascere: gli ebrei italiani in Palestina prima della guerra (1920–1940)*. Genoa, 2003.

May, Richard. "Juedischer Anteil an der Deutschen Kultur, Heinrich Heine." *Jüdisches Gemeindeblatt für die britische Zone* 19 (1947).

Mayer, Hans. *Ein Deutscher auf Widerruf, Erinnerungen*, Vol. I. Frankfurt am Main, 1982.

Meier, Wilhelm. "Auswanderer—Rückwanderer." *Der Weg* 6 (1947).

Misch, Ludwig. "Juedischer Anteil an der Deutschen Kultur, Felix Mendelssohn-Bartholdy." *Jüdisches Gemeindeblatt für die britische Zone* 17 (1946).

Morris, Douglas. *The Lives of Some Jewish Germans Who Lived in Nazi Germany and Live in Germany Today: An Oral History*. BA thesis, Wesleyan University, 1976.

Nicolaysen, Rainer. *Siegfried Landshut: die Wiederentdeckung der Politik: eine Biographie*. Frankfurt am Main, 1997.

Pavan, Ilaria. *Tra Indifferenza E Oblio: Le Conseguenze Economiche Delle Leggi Razziali in Italia 1938–1970*. Florence, 2004.

Rosenwein, Barbara. *Emotional Communities in the Early Middle Ages*. Ithaca, NY, 2006.

Sahl, Hans. *Memoiren eines Moralisten*. Frankfurt am Main, 1990.

Sarfatti, Michele. *The Jews in Mussolini's Italy: From Equality to Persecution.* Madison, WI, 2006.

Schmidt, Norbert. *Hermann Kesten-eine späte Annäherung.* Medienwerkstatt Franken Film, 1992.

Schwarz, Guri. *Ritrovare se stessi. Gli ebrei nell'Italia postfascista.* Rome, 2004.

Segre, Dan Vittorio. *Memoirs of a Fortunate Jew: An Italian Story.* Bethesda, MD, 1987.

Sinn, Andrea. "'Aber ich blieb trotzdem hier' Karl Marx und die Anfänge jüdischen Lebens im Nachkriegsdeutschland." In *Schwerpunktthema Leben danach— Jüdischer Neubeginn im Land der Täter,* ed. Jim Tobias and Peter Zinke. Nuremberg, 2010.

Smolensky, Eleanora, and Maria Vera Vigevani Jarach. *Tante voci, una storia: Italiani ebrei in Argentina 1938–1948.* Bologna, 1998.

Stern, Frank. "The Return to the Disowned Home: German Jews and the Other Germany." *New German Critique* 67 (1996).

Stille, Alexander. *Benevolence and Betrayal: Five Italian Jewish Families Under Fascism.* New York, 1991.

Twomey, Christina. "Double Displacement: Western Women's Return Home from Japanese Internment in the Second World War." In *Homes and Homecomings: Gendered Histories of Domesticity and Return,* ed. K.H. Adler and Carrie Hamilton. Chichester, 2010.

Webster, Ronald "Jüdische Rückkehrer in der BRD nach 1945: Ihre Motive, ihre Erfahrungen." *Aschkenas* 5 (1995).

von Wroblewsky, Vincent. *Zwischen Thora und Trabant: Juden in der DDR.* Berlin, 1993.

CHAPTER NINE

❦

On the Move and Putting Down Roots

Transnationalism and Integration among Yugoslav Guest Workers in West Germany

CHRISTOPHER A. MOLNAR

In a recent essay, the Croatian writer Dubravka Ugrešić portrays Yugoslav guest workers, who began arriving in the Federal Republic of Germany (FRG) in large numbers in the late 1960s, as maintaining powerful emotional and economic ties to their homeland during their time abroad:

> Many of them never learned the language of the countries where they worked for years. There was never time. They spent every free moment "going back down" (from north to south!), bringing presents for everyone, arranging with masons and tile layers to lay a bathroom, a new floor, install a window, or put on a roof... Most of them did not invest their money "wisely," because they had no idea how. That is why they built houses in their villages, bought television sets, refrigerators, cars and—built lavish family tombs. See who has the fanciest gravestone! Most of them were guided by one thought alone, to come back one day and leave their bones in their homeland.[1]

This description of the Yugoslav guest workers has much to recommend it. Many guest workers did make frequent return trips home, their cars loaded with prized consumer goods to be given as gifts to family and friends. The majority did use their earnings to renovate an existing house or build a new family home. And most of them did remain committed to making a permanent return to Yugoslavia, even when the stay abroad stretched from the intended two or three years to a decade or more.[2] But Ugrešić's description of Yugoslav guest workers also conveys the impression that their intensive homeland-directed activity hindered their integration into the host society. Indeed, she suggests that all the time Yugoslavs spent "going back down" to their homeland prevented many of them from learning the language of their host country, a strong indication that they had not integrated into the host society. Ugrešić's brief essay is a nostalgic recollection of the guest worker era, not a scholarly intervention in the field of migration studies. Nonetheless, by subtly but clearly linking immigrants' homeland-directed activity to their degree of integration into the host society, she put her finger on a question that has occupied migration scholars for the last twenty years: what effect does intensive engagement in transnational networks have on immigrants' integration?[3]

Transnational theories of immigration burst onto the academic scene in the early 1990s when the American anthropologist Nina Glick Schiller and her colleagues developed a theory of transnational migration that, within a decade, fundamentally transformed the interdisciplinary field of migration studies.[4] In this field, transnationalism refers to immigrants' long-term attachment to their country of origin, as shown by participation in homeland politics, frequent returns home, consumption of cultural products from the homeland, the maintenance of transnational family structures, and significant economic connections to the homeland, whether in the form of remittances or border-crossing entrepreneurial activity. These activities often lead to the creation of dense transnational networks linking immigrants' country of origin and their adopted homeland. Since the advent of the transnational turn in migration studies, scholars have grappled with the question of how participation in transnational networks affects immigrants' integration into the host society. Some contend that immigrants' transnational practices hinder their integration into the host society, while others claim that transnational engagement does not necessarily forestall integration, and in some cases actually promotes it.[5]

Yugoslav migration to the FRG has some distinctive features that can shed light on the historically conditioned relationship between transnationalism and integration. Although scholars from around the world have studied immigrant transnationalism, many of the most influential theories of transnational migration have been based on case studies of recent immigration to the United States, a traditional country of immigration in which immigrants have historically been encouraged to integrate and where legal immigrants have a clear path to citizenship.[6] The FRG, in contrast, premised its postwar labor recruitment program on the notion that it was not a country of immigration and that guest workers would return to their homelands as soon as their labor was no longer required.[7] The Yugoslav government also conceived of its citizens in the FRG as temporary migrants who would soon return home, and it went to great lengths to maintain Yugoslavs' attachment to the homeland during their time abroad.[8] Thus, both the sending and receiving state encouraged Yugoslavs to maintain a connection to the homeland and to plan for an eventual return.

I contend that, through at least the mid-1970s, immigration policies in the FRG and Yugoslavia encouraged Yugoslavs' transnational practices and discouraged integration. This promotion of transnational engagement proved extremely effective, as most Yugoslavs remained oriented toward their homeland even after years in the FRG, but their attempts to forestall Yugoslavs' integration failed miserably. While other scholars have argued that Yugoslavs' transnational practices facilitated their relatively successful integration into West German society, I argue that the abilities and work qualifications that Yugoslavs brought with them to West Germany made a decisive contribution to their integration.[9]

The Development of Yugoslav Migration to West Germany

The Yugoslav lands had a long history of labor migration, with immigrants heading to destinations in the Americas and Europe in large numbers during the nineteenth and early twentieth century.[10] In the years immediately preceding World War I even the young Josip Broz Tito left his homeland to find work in Germany and Austria.[11] In Marxism-Leninism, however, labor migration was viewed as a form of capitalist oppression that had no place in socialist societies that promised full employment.[12] As the leader of socialist Yugoslavia after World War II, Tito therefore made emigration illegal; those who emigrated were seen as enemies of the state. But beginning in the 1950s, the combination of rising unemployment in Yugoslavia and booming economies in Western Europe led tens of thousands of Yugoslavs to leave Yugoslavia illegally.[13] Facing difficult economic conditions and the reality that Yugoslavs were already migrating, the Yugoslav regime began quietly tolerating migration at some point between the late 1950s and early 1960s, and it legalized labor migration in a series of steps between 1962 and 1965.[14] Yugoslavia's legalization of labor migration to the west was unique among the communist states of Eastern Europe. It was a response to economic problems, but it also flowed from Yugoslavia's position as a nonaligned communist state that had developed friendly relations with the Western world. In practice, this meant that Yugoslavs, unlike the citizens of the Warsaw Pact states, were able to leave their country for a stint working abroad and then return home. Following the legalization, migration from Yugoslavia took off in the mid-1960s, and the FRG was by far the favorite destination.[15]

Beginning in the early 1960s the FRG had an almost insatiable demand for foreign labor, and Yugoslavs, in particular, were in great demand.[16] German labor officials allowed Yugoslavs to take up employment in the FRG, but the severely strained relationship between the two states after Yugoslavia extended diplomatic recognition to East Germany in 1957, together with the fear that

Yugoslav migration would allow a communist infiltration of the FRG, led German officials to refuse to sign a labor recruitment agreement with Yugoslavia. These obstacles were overcome by Willy Brandt, who, as foreign minister in the Grand Coalition (1966–69), pushed for the signing of a labor recruitment agreement as a means of improving the FRG's relations with Yugoslavia. Brandt's efforts resulted in the conclusion of a labor recruitment treaty with Yugoslavia in October 1968.[17] With the treaty in place, Yugoslav migration to the FRG accelerated at a rapid pace; in 1968 there were 119,100 Yugoslav guest workers in the FRG, five years later the number had climbed to 535,000, and when dependents are included their number reached 673,300. In 1970 Yugoslavs constituted the largest immigrant group in the FRG and since 1972 have been, after Turks, the second largest group in Germany.[18] Munich had by far the largest Yugoslav population of any German city, and so this essay, while primarily based on federal immigration policy and statistics, will at times focus on the experiences of Yugoslavs in Bavaria and the Bavarian state government's immigration policies.[19]

State-Supported Transnationalism

Yugoslav officials actively encouraged their citizens abroad to build transnational networks and to maintain economic and emotional bonds with Yugoslavia. They did so for two primary reasons. First, remittances from Yugoslavs laboring abroad constituted an important source of foreign currency for Yugoslavia. They spurred consumption within Yugoslavia and improved the state's balance of payments.[20] The more connected an immigrant felt to his or her homeland in Yugoslavia, the more likely it was that remittances would keep flowing back home. Second, Yugoslav authorities feared that their citizens abroad would fall prey to Serbian and Croatian nationalist organizations that political émigrés had established in West Germany in the aftermath of World War II.[21] Guest workers' support for émigrés and their nationalist and anti-Yugoslavia agenda would represent a direct threat to the Yugoslav state, which was founded upon the ideal of "brotherhood and unity" among the various national groups.[22]

For the economic and political wellbeing of the state, Yugoslav authorities developed and implemented policies that sought to bind their citizens abroad to the homeland. They developed and broadcast radio and television shows for Yugoslavs living abroad, incentivized the sending of remittances, supported the establishment of separate Yugoslav classes for the children, and established and supported social clubs that aimed to link Yugoslavs to their homeland in order to encourage a spirit of brotherhood and unity among Yugoslavia's national groups and discourage integration into German society.[23] Yugoslav officials increasingly conceived of Yugoslavs abroad as collectively constituting a "seventh republic" that needed to be governed and whose loyalty to the state had to be maintained.[24]

The Federal Republic also encouraged guest workers to maintain transnational bonds with their countries of origin. German authorities supported immigrant transnationalism, or at a minimum the continuing identification with the homeland, not out of any liberal multicultural impulse, but rather in order to support the fiction that *Deutschland ist kein Einwanderungsland*. West Germany's labor recruitment program, begun in 1955 and brought to a halt in late 1973, was premised on the notion that foreign workers were temporary residents who would return to their homelands once their labor was no longer required. The German labor bureaucracy called for guest workers to work on short-term contracts, with the expectation that they would return home and be replaced by new immigrants, thereby significantly reducing the likelihood that immigrants would permanently settle in the Federal Republic.[25]

Although this rotation model was never enforced, the logic behind it continued to shape West Germany's policy toward immigrants.[26] Short-term contracts long remained the norm, restrictive citizenship policies made most immigrants and their offspring legal outsiders, and restrictive family reunification laws contributed to the frequent separation of immigrants from their families. Echoing federal policy, in 1973 the Bavarian Labor Ministry stated that all labor migration had to be temporary so that "foreign workers are able to maintain the necessary connection to *Heimat* and family."[27] Without this connection to the homeland, permanent settlement in Germany became more likely, a highly undesirable development for Bavarian officials. Many immigrants, and the vast majority of Yugoslavs, planned to return to their country of origin even after a decade or more of living in West Germany, in part because that had been their original intention, but also because German policy toward immigrants created a sort of permanent insecurity that made it difficult to make plans for permanent settlement in the Federal Republic.[28] At least through the 1970s, German immigration policy encouraged immigrants to integrate just enough to be effective workers and to prevent them from being socially disruptive, but not enough to break their connection to their countries of origin.[29]

Yugoslav authorities who sought to maintain the loyalty and patriotism of their citizens abroad therefore found willing helpers in the Federal Republic. Indeed, the two states had a clear convergence of interests on this point. Officials in the FRG allowed Yugoslav authorities to select and send hundreds of their citizens to staff separate Yugoslav sections within German labor unions and welfare institutions and to send hundreds of teachers to teach Yugoslav children a curriculum that differed little from that used in schools in Yugoslavia.[30]

In 1971 West Germany's federal minister for education and science reported that "the Federal Republic regards its foreign workers as guest workers and not immigrants. The concern for the reintegration of foreign workers in their homeland economy and the children's return to the school system in their land of origin has therefore from the outset also co-determined social and school policies in the Federal Republic."[31] Following this logic, in the early 1970s Bavaria introduced separate "model classes" for foreigners.[32] Parents were given the option of enrolling their children in classes taught in their native tongue by Yugoslav teachers selected by the Yugoslav government and sent to Bavaria. Naturally, Yugoslav officials were quite pleased with Bavaria's model classes because they allowed them to gain significant cultural and political influence over immigrants' children. Textbooks used in Yugoslav model classes, for instance, lionized Tito, completely ignored religion, asked children to join the Pioneers—Yugoslavia's communist youth organization—and, in general, conformed to Yugoslavia's communist ideology.[33] The Bavarian Ministry of Culture vigorously defended the model classes even when German critics argued that they would result in the ghettoization of the immigrant population and allow authoritarian foreign governments to broadcast antidemocratic ideals at odds with the Federal Republic's liberal, democratic order.[34] In 1975 the Bavarian Ministry of Culture responded to its critics by asserting that West Germany's economic crisis would lead to many guest workers returning home and that Bavaria's system for educating foreign students was therefore "far more suitable than an inflexible system aimed at integration, because the Bavarian model . . . made it possible for guest workers' children to maintain a connection to the *Heimat*, to not tear down the bridges leading there."[35]

A similar situation existed with regard to the hundreds of "Yugo clubs" that popped up throughout West Germany in the 1970s. These social clubs, which Yugoslav consuls in Germany and ultimately government authorities in Yugoslavia sought to control, were a key institution in Yugoslavia's plan to ensure the loyalty and patriotism of its citizens abroad and to hinder integration into West German society.[36] Among other purposes, the clubs were a means of keeping Yugoslavs oriented toward the homeland, and they did this in a number of ways, including organizing bus trips back to Yugoslavia and sending Yugoslav folklore groups, sports teams, and even children to take part in activities in the Yugo clubs abroad. Despite frequently voiced—and entirely justified—concerns that Yugoslav authorities used the clubs to exert undue political influence over Yugoslav guest workers, German officials took a hands-off approach to the clubs and sometimes even offered support.[37] In 1973 the Federal Republic's ambassador to Yugoslavia wrote approvingly of Yugoslavia's plans to construct two information-cum-propaganda centers for Yugoslav guest workers in West Germany, noting that "it has never been our goal to alienate guest workers from their native regime."[38] Less than a decade earlier the thought of communist cultural and social centers linked to a foreign authoritarian government operating freely in West Germany would have set off alarm bells, but now the Federal Republic supported these institutions because they encouraged immigrants to maintain intense bonds with their homeland, which Germans hoped would facilitate their eventual return.

Transnational Practices among Yugoslav Guest Workers

Most Yugoslav guest workers in the FRG came from northern and western Yugoslavia, particularly from the republics of Croatia and Bosnia-Herzegovina, and they settled heavily in southern Germany, most notably in Baden-Württemberg and southern Bavaria.[39] Most of them were therefore close enough to Yugoslavia to make frequent return trips home.[40] Planning only a short stay abroad and living relatively near their homeland, many Yugoslavs elected to live in transnational families in which one or more members of the nuclear family migrated to West Germany while a spouse or children or both stayed behind in Yugoslavia.[41] In 1968, 76 percent of male Yugoslav guest workers were married, but of those only 34 percent had their spouses with them in the FRG, making them and Turks the two immigrant group most likely to have a spouse still living in the country of origin.[42] By 1972 many Yugoslavs had had their spouses join them in the FRG, but in surveys conducted semi-regularly from 1980 onward, they have consistently been the immigrant group most likely to have a spouse living in the homeland.[43] In 1985, when over 80 percent of Yugoslav immigrants had resided in the FRG for a decade or more, 25 percent of married Yugoslav men still had spouses in Yugoslavia, a far higher percentage than other immigrant groups.[44] Yugoslavs also left their children behind in the country of origin, usually with a spouse or grandparents, more often than did guest workers from other states, and they did so at a very high rate: throughout the 1980s more than 40 percent of the children of Yugoslav guest workers still lived in Yugoslavia.[45]

Yugoslavs did not, however, break ties with their families in Yugoslavia. Prior to West Germany's decision to end its labor recruitment program in November 1973, tens of thousands of Yugoslavs who worked in construction and other seasonal jobs spent the winter months with their families in Yugoslavia and then returned to the FRG in the spring as soon as their employers needed them. The end of the recruitment program made this voluntary rotation impossible, as Yugoslavs who left the FRG for an extended period of time were no longer readmitted.[46] But many still visited Yugoslavia with great regularity. Indeed, they returned to Yugoslavia so frequently that some observers referred to them as *Pendlergastarbeiter* (commuting guest workers). It was not uncommon for Munich's central train station to fill up with Yugoslavs by early

Friday afternoon, where they caught buses back to Yugoslavia to spend the weekend with their families.[47] Already in 1969 a Yugo club in Munich organized bus trips back to Yugoslavia for thousands of guest workers, and by the mid-1970s private for-profit clubs headed by Yugoslav businessmen provided the same service for Yugoslavs throughout Bavaria.[48] By the mid-1980s, more than a decade after the end of large-scale migration from Yugoslavia, Yugoslavs still averaged four trips back home per year, but in southern Germany the number of return trips was much higher, with some returning nearly every weekend.[49] Even the wars in Yugoslavia in the early 1990s could not deter Yugoslavs from returning to their homeland. Busloads of Croats and Serbs still poured into Yugoslavia, into the war zone, to visit friends and families just as they had always done, and some guest workers, particularly Croats in southern Germany, became weekend warriors in the most literal sense: they fought as volunteers for the Croatian army during long weekends at home.[50]

Yugoslavs used a significant portion of their earnings in the FRG to support their families in Yugoslavia and to improve their own economic and social standing in preparation for their eventual return. They sent remittances back to their families, but also used their earnings to renovate their homes or build new houses in Yugoslavia.[51] Surveys of thousands of Croatian immigrants throughout Europe during the winter of 1970–71 showed that nearly half of them emigrated in order to save enough money to improve their housing situation in Yugoslavia.[52] In the FRG Yugoslavs were both the most prolific savers among all of the immigrant groups and the most likely to state that they were saving to build a house in their homeland.[53] And they carried through with their plans; in a 1985 survey, two-thirds of Yugoslavs in the FRG reported that they had already invested in the construction, renovation, or expansion of a house in Yugoslavia.[54] The construction of family homes in Yugoslavia attests, in the most concrete way, to Yugoslavs' commitment to return and their homeland-directed orientation more generally. A 1985 survey confirmed just how strong that orientation remained: an amazing 86 percent of Yugoslavs in Germany still planned to return permanently to Yugoslavia.[55]

Putting Down Roots: The Integration of Yugoslav Guest Workers

Many Yugoslavs in Germany clearly lived intensely transnational lives, and their transnational activity was encouraged explicitly by the Yugoslav state and implicitly by the Federal Republic. And yet, contrary to what might be expected, Yugoslavs' participation in transnational networks in no way precluded their relatively successful integration into West German society. In 1985 two German migration scholars concluded that there was "an internal hierarchy among the foreigners themselves, with the Yugoslavs at the top and the Turks at the bottom. This stratification," they continued, "affects nearly all areas of social life: jobs, education, qualifications, unemployment, housing, social prestige, and so on."[56] A more recent study shows that from the mid-1980s onward first and second generation Yugoslavs identified with Germany more often than did other immigrant groups, were the most likely to have close personal relationships with Germans, and had better command of the German language.[57] By the mid-1980s Yugoslavs had by and large moved out of the communal housing offered by employers and into private apartments. Perhaps most importantly, the vast majority felt accepted at the workplace and by the wider German society.[58] In 1987 a major study coauthored by Yugoslavia's leading migration expert concluded that Yugoslavs' "professional and social integration into West German society has to a great extent succeeded."[59]

How do we account for Yugoslavs' relatively successful integration? Kaja Shonick claims that Germans came to see Yugoslavs as a more desirable immigrant group in the 1970s when the German media began to fixate on the rapid growth of the Turkish immigrant community and the threat posed by Turks' purportedly alien culture.[60] This development surely eased Yugoslavs' integration, but presumably all immigrants from European areas would have benefited from the near-exclusive focus on Turkish immigrants, so it cannot explain why Yugoslavs integrated more successfully than, for example, Italian immigrants. Some migration scholars argue that transnational practices allow immigrants to tap into economic resources and social capital accumulated in the homeland, which then fosters their integration into the host society.[61] Without denying this possibility, I offer a different explanation: Yugoslavs' integration into West German society is due, in large measure, to the skills and abilities that they brought with them from Yugoslavia.

The overwhelming majority of guest workers in the FRG had been peasants or workers in their homelands, but the qualifications and skills that they brought to the FRG often differed considerably as a result of economic conditions and government policies in their countries of origin. Yugoslav guest workers benefited from an education system in Yugoslavia that required eight years of school. A significant percentage of Yugoslavs did not fulfill this requirement, but the policy nonetheless made the first generation of Yugoslavs the best-educated immigrants in the FRG by a sizeable margin. In 1972 a major survey commissioned by the German government showed that 52 percent of male and 58 percent of female Yugoslav guest workers had completed eight or more years of schooling in Yugoslavia. Spanish immigrants had the next highest level of education, with 39 percent of both men and women having completed eight or more years of education in Spain.[62] The difference in education between Yugoslavs and Turks and Italians is even more striking. Only 17 percent of Italian and 10 percent of Turkish men had more than eight years of schooling in their homelands. Immigrants from Portugal had by far the lowest educational attainment, a fact that can be attributed to Portugal's government only requiring four years of school.[63] By 1980 Yugoslavs' edge over other immigrant groups in terms of years of education in the homeland had grown even more pronounced.[64]

The content of the education they received also gave Yugoslavs an advantage over other immigrants. Despite not having arrived in the FRG in large numbers until the late 1960s, years later than the other main guest worker groups, by 1972 Yugoslavs already had the best German-language ability among the guest workers.[65] Although the vast majority of all guest workers reported that they learned German at the workplace, Yugoslavs had a leg up, as they learned German in school in the homeland almost twice as frequently (13 percent) as any other immigrant group.[66] Yugoslavs, and particularly men, also attended vocational schools in the homeland more than twice as frequently as any other immigrant group and they thus obtained qualifications as semi-skilled or skilled workers in school far more often than any other immigrant groups.[67] This likely explains why Yugoslavs were for the most part the only immigrants who had qualifications earned in the homeland recognized by German employers.[68]

A historical accident over which Yugoslav guest workers had no control may have been even more decisive than their advantage in education for their relatively successful integration. Worried that migration from Yugoslavia represented a potential security threat, in June 1962 German officials decided that henceforth only skilled workers from Yugoslavia would be allowed to enter the FRG.[69] This policy remained in place until West Germany and Yugoslavia signed a labor recruitment agreement in late 1968.[70] German officials assumed that the restrictive measure would reduce the number of Yugoslavs migrating to the FRG, but it quickly proved to be a mistaken assumption. In 1962, the year the year the restrictive policy took effect, there were only 23,600 Yugoslav guest workers in the FRG, but their number nearly doubled (44,000) in 1963 and more than qudrupled (96,700) by 1966.[71]

The restrictive policy was not uniformly enforced, but it was effective enough that by 1968 Yugoslav men were employed as skilled workers more than four times as frequently as any other immigrant group. In that year, 55 percent of Yugoslav men were employed as skilled workers, compared to 16 percent of Turkish, 13 percent of Italian, and 7 percent of Greek men. Moreover, only 14 percent of Yugoslav men were employed as unskilled workers, far less than any other immigrant group. In 1980 Yugoslavs were still employed as skilled workers far more often than were immigrants from any of the major immigrant-sending countries.[72] This concentration in skilled work not only earned Yugoslavs the largest paychecks, it also helped them improve their German, as many worked in craft enterprises that required more contact and communication with German coworkers than did, for example, working on an assembly line.[73] Taken together, Yugoslavs' advantages in education, German-language ability, and work qualifications, combined with West Germany's policy of only accepting skilled workers from Yugoslavia (from 1962 through 1968) meant that a significant proportion of Yugoslavs began their lives in the FRG a rung or two higher on the social ladder than did most guest workers. These advantages facilitated Yugoslavs' successful labor market integration and likely aided their more general integration into West German society.

Conclusion

In a sense, it is surprising that Yugoslavs integrated at all. They left a state that conceived of migration as temporary and actively sought to bind its citizens to the homeland while they were abroad and settled in a state that likewise viewed immigration as a temporary phenomenon, encouraged immigrants to orient themselves toward their countries of origin, and, until recently, refused even to acknowledge that it was a country of immigration. The states' interests and policies shaped Yugoslavs' expectations and planning for their stay in West Germany. The overwhelming majority of them planned only a brief stay of a few years or so in the Federal Republic, and even when those few years turned into a decade or more, most Yugoslavs still envisioned themselves returning to Yugoslavia. Many did return, but hundreds of thousands settled permanently in the FRG.[74] For them, the expectation that they would return, nurtured for many years, led them to construct and maintain dense transnational networks binding them to their families and friends in the homeland and, more generally, to the Yugoslav state. And still, Yugoslavs became one of the best-integrated guest worker populations in the Federal Republic.

The history of Yugoslav migration to West Germany suggests quite forcefully that transnationalism should not be viewed as standing in opposition to integration. It also highlights the significance of locality. For all their engagement in transnational networks, most immigrants spend the vast majority of their time in the host country and build meaningful networks and communities there. This essay thus bears out Ewa Morawska's contention that "transnational involvements of immigrants and their children and their assimilation into the host society typically are concurrent."[75] The experiences of Yugoslav guest workers in the Federal Republic suggest that scholars who focus exclusively on immigrant transnationalism run the risk of obscuring the significant steps toward integration that most immigrants and their offspring take.[76] While the study of immigrant transnationalism has undoubtedly yielded important insights and provided new perspectives on the history of immigration, my research supports calls by Rogers Brubaker and other scholars for students of migration to pay more attention to the process of immigrant assimilation, a concept too long shunned because of its negative connotations.[77]

Christopher A. Molnar is Assistant Professor of German and European history at the University of Michigan-Flint. He has published a number of articles on the history of migration from Yugoslavia to West Germany, and his book, *Memory, Politics, and Yugoslav Migrations to Postwar Germany*, will be published by Indiana University Press in 2018. He is currently working on a history of anti-foreigner sentiment in the years immediately after German reunification as well as an edited volume (with Mirna Zakić), entitled *From Berlin to the Bosphorus: German-Balkan Entangled Histories in the Twentieth Century.*

Notes

1. Dubravka Ugrešić, "A Requiem for the Yugoslav Guest Worker," in *Nobody's Home: Essays*, trans. Ellen Elias-Bursać (Rochester, NY, 2008), 230; for statistics on labor migration from Yugoslavia to Western Europe, see Othmar Nikola Haberl, *Die Abwanderung von Arbeitskräften aus Jugoslawien: Zur Problematik ihrer Auslandsbeschäftigung und Rückführung* (Munich, 1978), 276.
2. Ivo Baučić et al., *Rückkehr und Reintegration jugoslawischer Arbeitnehmer aus der Bundesrepublik Deutschland: Deutsch-Jugoslawische Untersuchung der Zukunftspläne jugoslawischer Arbeitsmigranten und ihrer Realisierung nach der Rückkehr: Endbericht einer empirischen Untersuchung im Auftrag des Bundesministers für Arbeit und Sozialordnung,* (Saarbrücken, 1987), 46, 62, 75.
3. Steven Vertovec, *Transnationalism* (London, 2009), 77–84.
4. For their initial formulation of a theory of transnational migration, see Nina Glick Schiller, Linda G. Basch, and Cristina Szanton-Blanc, "Transnationalism: A New Analytic Framework for Understanding Migration," in *Towards a Transnational Perspective on Migration: Race, Class, Ethnicity, and Nationalism Reconsidered,* ed. Nina Glick Schiller, Linda G. Basch, and Cristina Szanton-Blanc (New York, 1992), 1–24. The best introduction to the voluminous literature on transnational migration is Vertovec, *Transnationalism.*
5. For a brief summary of this debate, see Vertovec, *Transnationalism,* 77–84.
6. For an important exception, see Thomas Faist, *The Volume and Dynamics of International Migration and Transnational Social Spaces* (Oxford, 2000).
7. Douglas B. Klusmeyer and Demetrios G. Papademetriou, *Immigration Policy in the Federal Republic of Germany: Negotiating Membership and Remaking the Nation* (New York, 2009), 97–99.
8. William Zimmerman, *Open Borders, Nonalignment, and the Political Evolution of Yugoslavia* (Princeton, NJ, 1987), chapter five.
9. Pascal Goeke, *Transnationale Migrationen : Post-Jugoslawische Biografien in Der Weltgesellschaft* (Bielefeld, 2007).
10. Ulf Brunnbauer, "Labour Emigration from the Yugoslav Region from the late 19th Century until the End of Socialism: Continuities and Changes," in *Transnational Societies, Transterritorial Politics: Migrations in the (Post-) Yugoslav Region, 19th–21st Century,* ed. Ulf Brunnbauer (Munich, 2009), 19–22.
11. Geoffrey Swain, *Tito: A Biography* (London, 2011), 6.

12. Haberl, *Die Abwanderung von Arbeitskräften*, 22–27, and Karolina Novinšćak, "Der jugoslawische 'Gastarbeiter-Export' auf dem Sonderweg zwischen Sozialismus und Kapitalismus," in *Wahl und Wagnis Migration: Beiträge des Promotionskollegs Ost-West*, ed. Silke Flegel, Anne Hartmann, and Frank Hoffmann (Berlin, 2007), 143–44.

13. Karolina Novinšćak, "The Recruiting and Sending of Yugoslav 'Gastarbeiter' to Germany: Between Socialist Demands and Economic Needs," in *Transnational Societies*, ed. Ulf Brunnbauer (Munich, 2009), 125.

14. Ivo Baučić, "Die Auswirkung der Arbeitskräftewanderung in Jugoslawien," in *Ausländerbeschäftigung und international Politik: Zur Analyse transnationaler Sozialprozesse*, ed. Reinhard Lohrmann and Klaus Manfrass (Munich, 1974), 195–96; Haberl, *Die Abwanderung von Arbeitskräften*, 62–69.

15. Haberl, *Die Abwanderung von Arbeitskräften*, 276.

16. See, for example, Bundesvereinigung der Deutschen Arbeitgeberverbände to BMI, Betr.: Zusicherung der Aufenthaltserlaubnis für jugoslawische Arbeitnehmer, August 20, 1963, BAK, B 149 / 6420, 1–2.

17. On the labor recruitment agreement and the development of West German-Yugoslav relations, see Novinšćak, "The Recruiting and Sending of Yugoslav 'Gastarbeiter,'" 121–43; and Kaja Shonick, "Politics, Culture, and Economics: Reassessing the West German Guest Worker Agreement with Yugoslavia," *Journal of Contemporary History* 44, no. 4 (2009): 719–36.

18. Ulrich Herbert, *A History of Foreign Labor in Germany, 1880–1980: Seasonal Workers, Forced Laborers, and Guest Workers*, trans. William Templer (Ann Arbor, MI, 1990), 203. For statistics from the late 1970s to 2006, see Christian Babka von Gostomski, *Türkische, griechische, italienische und polnische Personen, sowie Personen aus den Nachfolgestaaten des ehemaligen Jugoslawien in Deutschland: Erste Ergebnisse der Repräsentativbefragung "Ausgewählte Migrantengruppen in Deutschland 2006/2007"* (Nuremberg, 2008), 8.

19. Baučić et al., *Rückkehr und Reintegration*, 19–21.

20. Baučić, "Die Auswirkung der Arbeitskräftewanderung," 188–93.

21. On political emigration from Yugoslavia, see Mate Nikola Tokić, "Landscapes of Conflict: Unity and Disunity in post-Second World War Croatian Émigré Separatism," *European Review of History* 16, no. 5 (October 2009): 739–53; and Kaja Shonick, "Émigrés, Guest Workers, and Refugees: Yugoslav Migrants in the Federal Republic of Germany, 1945–1995" (PhD diss., University of Washington, 2008), chapter one.

22. On "brotherhood and unity," see Vjekoslav Perica, *Balkan Idols: Religion and Nationalism in Yugoslav States* (Oxford, 2002), chapter six.

23. Zimmerman, *Open Borders*, 118–24; Botschaft der BRD to AA, Betr.: Jug. Wanderarbeiterpolitik; hier: Resolution der Sozialistischen Allianz der Werktätigen (SAW) vom 14.10.76 zur "Förderung der sozialen Selbstorganization," October 28, 1976, PA AA, B 85 / 1266, 1.

24. Zimmerman, *Open Borders*, chapter five.

25. Herbert, *A History of Foreign Labor*, 214–15.

26. Karen Schönwälder, "Assigning the State its Rightful Place? Migration, Integration and the State in Germany," in *Paths of Integration: Migrants in Western Europe (1880–2004)*, ed. Leo Lucassen, David Feldman, and Jochen Oltmer (Amsterdam, 2006), 85.

27. *Ausländische Arbeitnehmer in Bayern: Sonderdruck eines Berichts an den Bayerischen Landtag über Probleme der Arbeits- und Wohverhältnisse, der Familienzusammen-*

führung und der gesellschaftlichen Integration ausländischer Arbeitnehmer in Bayern (Munich, 1973), 37.

28. The overwhelming majority of Yugoslavs planned to return to their homelands, even after years of living in the FRG, see Baučić et al., *Rückkehr und Reintegration*, 59–60.

29. On the debate over immigrant integration during the 1970s and 1980s, see Rita Chin, *The Guest Worker Question in Postwar Germany* (Cambridge, 2007), 89–105; and Klusmeyer and Papademetriou, *Immigration Policy*, 97–107.

30. Zimmerman, *Open Borders*, 109–10, 118–19, 121–23.

31. Dohnanyi, Deutsche Bundestag, 6. Wahlperiode, Drucksache VI/2071, Der Bundesminister für Bildung und Wissenschaft an den Herrn Präsidenten des Deutschen Bundestages, Betr.: Schul- und Berufsausbildung der Kinder ausländischer Arbeitnehmer in der Bundesrepublik Deutschland, March 30, 1971, BHStA, StK / 17606, 2.

32. Gerhart Mahler, "Ausländische Schüler: Das bayerische Modell—Vorbild einer ländereinheitlichen Regelung," *Schulreport* no. 4 (1976): 16–19.

33. Sabel an das Staatsministerium für Unterricht und Kultus, Zulassung von Schulbüchern für Kinder ausländischer Arbeitnehmer; hier: Prüfung der Eignung zum Gebrauch im muttersprachlichen Klassen, October 22, 1974, BHStA, MK / 64580.

34. Peter Dyckhoff, "Schulen Ausländerkinder," *Deutsche Presse-Agentur*, 23 July 1974, BHStA, StK / 17606.

35. Das Kultusministerium weist Angriffe auf das bayerische Modell zur schulischen Betreuung der Kinder ausländischer Arbeitnehmer zurück, November 4, 1975, StaM, Schulamt / 7857, 1.

36. Botschaft der BRD to AA, Betr.: Jug. Wanderarbeiterpolitik; hier: Resolution der Sozialistischen Allianz der Werktätigen (SAW) vom 14.10.76 zur "Förderung der sozialen Selbstorganisation," October 28, 1976, PA AA, B 85 / 1266.

37. On these concerns see, for example, Heinz Richter an Dieter Bricke, in Botschaft der BRD [in Belgrade], April 13, 1976, DGBA im AdsD, BuVo AAN / 5/DGAZ566, 1.

38. Jaenicke to AA, Betr.: Jugoslawische Informationszentren in westlichen Ausland und in der Bundesrepublik, February 12, 1973, PA AA, B 85 / 1147, 3.

39. Baučić et al., *Rückkehr und Reintegration*, 17, 19, 45–49.

40. Ibid., 46.

41. On transnational family structures among Yugoslavs in Germany, see Jasna Čapo Žmegač, "Family Dispersal Across National Borders: A Strategy for Betterment," in *Transnational Societies*, ed. Ulf Brunnbauer (Munich, 2009), 267–82; and Christopher A. Molnar, "The Transnational Family: Yugoslav Guest-Workers and War Refugees in Munich," in *Update! Perspektiven der Zeitgeschichte: Zeitgeschichtetage 2010*, eds. Linda Erker et al. (Innsbruck, 2012), 529–35.

42. *Repräsentativuntersuchung '72 über die Beschäftigung ausländischer Arbeitnehmer im Bundesgebiet und ihre Familien- und Wohnverhältnisse* (Nuremberg, 1973), 19.

43. Ibid.; Mathias Venema and Claus Grimm, *Situation der ausländischen Arbeitnehmer und ihrer Familienangehörigen in der Bundesrepublik Deutschland: Repräsentativuntersuchung 2001: Teil A, Tabellenband* (Bonn, 1981), 61.

44. Venema and Grimm, *Situation der ausländischen Arbeitnehmer*, 61, 145.

45. Ibid., 68; in *Rückkehr und Reintegration*, Baučić et al. come up with an even higher percentage of children of guest workers living in Yugoslavia, 28.

46. Untitled report from DGB Bundesvorstand, Jugoslawisches Zentralbüro, December 1973, DGBA im AdsD / BuVo AAN / 5/DGAZ498, 3–4. On the decision to end

the labor recruitment program, see Karen Schönwälder, "The Difficult Task of Managing Migration: The 1973 Recruitment Stop," in *German History from the Margins*, ed. Neil Gregor, Nils Roemer, and Mark Roseman (Bloomington, IN, 2006), 252–67.

47. Marian Mihelić, *Jugoslawische Jugendliche : Intraethnische Beziehungen und ethnisches Selbstbewusstsein : Ergebnisse einer empirischen Untersuchung* (Munich, 1984), 20.
48. Protokoll über die Mitgliederversammlung des Klub Jugoslavena e.V., München, March 21, 1970, StAM / AGMüRG, 16505, 2; Georg Hrska, DGB Landesbezirk Bayern an Hans Maier; Betreff: Jugoslawische Klubs und Vereine in Bayern, January 29, 1975, IG-Metall Archiv im Archiv der sozialen Demokratie / Bundesvorstand Abteilung Ausländische Arbeitnehmer / 5/DGAZ566, 2.
49. Baučić et al., *Rückkehr und Reintegration*, 46.
50. Heike Faller, "Heimaturlaub an der Front," *Süddeutsche Zeitung Magazin*, 31 January 1992, 18, 20; "Urlaub an der Front," *Der Spiegel*, 18 November 1991, 16.
51. On the scale of remittances, see Baučić et al., *Rückkehr und Reintegration*, 73.
52. Ivo Baučić, *The Effects of Emigration from Yugoslavia and the Problems of Returning Emigrant Workers* (The Hague, 1972), 26.
53. Ursula Mehrländer, *Situation der ausländischen Arbeitnehmer und ihrer Familienangehörigen in der Bundesrepublik Deutschland: Repräsentativuntersuchung '80* (Bonn, 1981), 257, 261, 278.
54. Baučić et al., *Rückkehr und Reintegration*, 75.
55. Ibid., 62.
56. Hartmut Esser and Hermann Korte, in Tomas Hammar, *European Immigration Policy: A Comparative Study* (Cambridge, 1985), 196.
57. Claudia Diehl and Rainer Schnell, "'Reactive Ethnicity' or 'Assimilation'? Statements, Arguments, and First Empirical Evidence for Labor Migrants in Germany," *International Migration Review* 40 no. 4 (2006): 800, 801, 803.
58. Baučić et al., *Rückkehr und Reintegration*, 52, 54–55.
59. Ibid., 57.
60. Shonick, "Émigrés, Guest Workers, and Refugees," 167–68, 184–90.
61. Faist, *The Volume and Dynamics*; and Alejandro Portes, William Haller, and Luis E. Guarnizo, "Transnational Entrepreneurs: The Emergence and Determinants of an Alternative Form of Immigrant Economic Adaptation," *American Sociological Review* 67, no. 2 (2002): 278–98; Goeke, *Transnationale Migrationen*.
62. *Repräsentativuntersuchung '72*, 28.
63. Ibid., 27, 28.
64. Mehrländer, *Situation der ausländischen Arbeitnehmer*, 26.
65. *Repräsentativuntersuchung '72*, 29.
66. Ibid., 31.
67. Mehrländer, *Situation der ausländischen Arbeitnehmer*, 28–32.
68. Ibid., 33.
69. Weicken, Arbeitskreis für Fragen der Beschäftigung ausländischer Arbeitnehmer beim Bundesministerium für Arbeit und Sozialordnung, Bonn; hier: Besprechung am 8. Juni 1962, June 8, 1962, BAK, B 119 / 3027, 1–2; and Blank, Deutsche Bundestag, 4. Wahlperiode; Der Bundesminister für Arbeit und Sozialordnung an den Herren Präsidenten des Deutschen Bundestages, Betr.: Arbeitserlaubnis für jugoslawische Hilfsarbeiter; Bezug: Kleine Anfrage der Fraktion der SPD—Drucksache IV/629, September 21, 1962.

70. Müller-Dethard, Aufzeichnung,; betr.: Verhandlungen mit Jugoslawien über eine Anwerbevereinbarung, eine Abkommen über Soziale Sicherheit und ein Arbeitslosenversicherungsabkommen, July 1968, PA AA, B 85 / 898, 2.
71. Herbert, *A History of Foreign Labor*, 203.
72. Mehrländer, *Situation der ausländischen Arbeitnehmer*, 121.
73. Ibid., 234, 492, 494.
74. For statistics on return to Yugoslavia, see Baučić et al., *Rückkehr und Reintegration*, 9.
75. Ewa Morawska, "Immigrant Transnationalism and Assimilation: A Variety of Combinations and the Analytic Strategy it Suggests," in *Towards Assimilation and Citizenship: Immigrants in Liberal Nation-States*, ed. Christian Joppke and Ewa Morawska (New York, 2003), 133.
76. For recent works emphasizing the integration of postwar immigrants in Europe and the United States, see Leo Lucassen, *The Immigrant Threat: The Integration of Old and New Migrants in Western Europe since 1850* (Urbana, 2005); and Richard D. Alba and Victor Nee, *Remaking the American Mainstream: Assimilation and Contemporary Immigration* (Cambridge, MA, 2003).
77. Rogers Brubaker, "The Return of Assimilation? Changing Perspectives on Immigration and its Sequels in France, Germany, and the United States," *Ethnic and Racial Studies* 24 no. 4 (2001): 531–48.

Bibliography

Alba, Richard D. and Victor Nee. *Remaking the American Mainstream: Assimilation and Contemporary Immigration*. Cambridge, MA, 2003.
Ausländische Arbeitnehmer in Bayern: Sonderdruck eines Berichts an den Bayerischen Landtag über Probleme der Arbeits- und Wohverhältnisse, der Familienzusammenführung und der gesellschaftlichen Integration ausländischer Arbeitnehmer in Bayern. Munich, 1973.
Baučić, Ivo. "Die Auswirkung der Arbeitskräftewanderung in Jugoslawien." In *Ausländerbeschäftigung und international Politik: Zur Analyse transnationaler Sozialprozesse*, ed. Reinhard Lohrmann und Klaus Manfrass. Munich, 1974.
———. *The Effects of Emigration from Yugoslavia and the Problems of Returning Emigrant Workers*. The Hague, 1972.
Baučić, Ivo, et al. *Rückkehr und Reintegration jugoslawischer Arbeitnehmer aus der Bundesrepublik Deutschland: Deutsch-Jugoslawische Untersuchung der Zukunftspläne jugoslawischer Arbeitsmigranten und ihrer Realisierung nach der Rückkehr: Endbericht einer empirischen Untersuchung im Auftrag des Bundesministers für Arbeit und Sozialordnung*. Saarbrücken, 1987.
Brubaker, Rogers. "The Return of Assimilation? Changing Perspectives on Immigration and its Sequels in France, Germany, and the United States." *Ethnic and Racial Studies* 24, no. 4 (2001): 531–48.
Brunnbauer, Ulf. "Labour Emigration from the Yugoslav Region from the late 19th Century until the End of Socialism: Continuities and Changes." In *Transnational Societies, Transterritorial Politics: Migrations in the (Post-) Yugoslav Region, 19th–21st Century*, ed. Ulf Brunnbauer. Munich, 2009.

Chin, Rita. *The Guest Worker Question in Postwar Germany.* Cambridge, 2007.

Diehl, Claudia, and Rainer Schnell. "'Reactive Ethnicity' or 'Assimilation'? Statements, Arguments, and First Empirical Evidence for Labor Migrants in Germany." *International Migration Review* 40, no. 4 (2006): 786–816.

Dyckhoff, Peter. "Schulen Ausländerkinder." *Deutsche Presse-Agentur*, 23 July 1974.

Esser, Hartmut, and Hermann Korte. "Federal Republic of Germany." In *European Immigration Policy: A Comparative Study*, ed. Tomas Hammar. Cambridge, 1985.

Faist, Thomas. *The Volume and Dynamics of International Migration and Transnational Social Spaces.* Oxford, 2000.

Faller, Haike. "Heimaturlaub an der Front." *Süddeutsche Zeitung Magazin*, 31 January 1992.

Goeke, Pascal. *Transnationale Migrationen: Post-Jugoslawische Biografien in Der Weltgesellschaft.* Bielefeld, 2007.

Gostomski, Christian Babka von. *Türkische, griechische, italienische und polnische Personen, sowie Personen aus den Nachfolgestaaten des ehemaligen Jugoslawien in Deutschland: Erste Ergebnisse der Repräsentativbefragung "Ausgewählte Migrantengruppen in Deutschland 2006/2007."* Nuremberg, 2008.

Haberl, Othmor Nikola. *Die Abwanderung von Arbeitskräften aus Jugoslawien: Zur Problematik ihrer Auslandsbeschäftigung und Rückführung.* Munich, 1978.

Herbert, Ulrich. *A History of Foreign Labor in Germany, 1880–1980: Seasonal Workers, Forced Laborers, and Guest Workers*, trans. William Templer. Ann Arbor, MI, 1990.

Klusmeyer, Douglas B., and Demetrios G. Papademetriou. *Immigration Policy in the Federal Republic of Germany: Negotiating Membership and Remaking the Nation.* New York, 2009.

Lucassen, Leo. *The Immigrant Threat: The Integration of Old and New Migrants in Western Europe since 1850.* Urbana, IL, 2005.

Mahler, Gerhart. "Ausländische Schüler: Das bayerische Modell—Vorbild einer ländereinheitlichen Regelung." *Schulreport* no. 4 (1976): 16–19.

Mehrländer, Ursula. *Situation der ausländischen Arbeitnehmer und ihrer Familienangehörigen in der Bundesrepublik Deutschland: Repräsentativuntersuchung '80.* Bonn, 1981.

Mihelić, Marian. *Jugoslawische Jugendliche : Intraethnische Beziehungen und ethnisches Selbstbewusstsein : Ergebnisse einer empirischen Untersuchung.* Munich, 1984.

Molnar, Christopher A. "The Transnational Family: Yugoslav Guest-Workers and War Refugees in Munich." In *Update! Perspektiven der Zeitgeschichte: Zeitgeschichtetage 2010*, ed. Linda Erker et al. Innsbruck, 2012.

Morawska, Ewa. "Immigrant Transnationalism and Assimilation: A Variety of Combinations and the Analytic Strategy it Suggests." In *Towards Assimilation and Citizenship: Immigrants in Liberal Nation-States*, ed. Christian Joppke and Ewa Morawska. New York, 2003.

Novinšćak, Karolina. "Der jugoslawische 'Gastarbeiter-Export' auf dem Sonderweg zwischen Sozialismus und Kapitalismus." In *Wahl und Wagnis Migration: Beiträge des Promotionskollegs Ost-West*, ed. Silke Flegel, Anne Hartmann, and Frank Hoffmann. Berlin, 2007.

Novinšćak, Karolina. "The Recruiting and Sending of Yugoslav 'Gastarbeiter' to Germany: Between Socialist Demands and Economic Needs." In *Transnational Societies*, ed. Ulf Brunnbauer. Munich, 2009.

Perica, Vjekoslav. *Balkan Idols: Religion and Nationalism in Yugoslav States*. Oxford, 2002.

Portes, Alejandro, William Haller, and Luis E. Guarnizo. "Transnational Entrepreneurs: The Emergence and Determinants of an Alternative Form of Immigrant Economic Adaptation." *American Sociological Review* 67, no. 2 (2002): 278–98.

Repräsentativuntersuchung '72 über die Beschäftigung ausländischer Arbeitnehmer im Bundesgebiet und ihre Familien- und Wohnverhältnisse. Nuremberg, 1973.

Schiller, Nina Glick, Linda G. Basch, and Cristina Szanton-Blanc. "Transnationalism: A New Analytic Framework for Understanding Migration." In *Towards a Transnational Perspective on Migration: Race, Class, Ethnicity, and Nationalism Reconsidered*, ed. Nina Glick Schiller, Linda G. Basch, and Cristina Szanton-Blanc. New York, 1992.

Schönwälder, Karen. "Assigning the State its Rightful Place? Migration, Integration and the State in Germany." In *Paths of Integration: Migrants in Western Europe (1880–2004)*, ed. Leo Lucassen, David Feldman, and Jochen Oltmer. Amsterdam, 2006.

———. "The Difficult Task of Managing Migration: The 1973 Recruitment Stop." In *German History from the Margins*, ed. Neil Gregor, Nils Roemer, and Mark Roseman. Bloomington, IN, 2006.

Shonick, Kaja. "Émigrés, Guest Workers, and Refugees: Yugoslav Migrants in the Federal Republic of Germany, 1945–1995." PhD diss., University of Washington, 2008.

———. "Politics, Culture, and Economics: Reassessing the West German Guest Worker Agreement with Yugoslavia." *Journal of Contemporary History* 44, no. 4 (October 2009): 719–36.

Swain, Geoffrey. *Tito: A Biography*. London, 2011.

Tokić, Mate Nikola. "Landscapes of Conflict: Unity and Disunity in post-Second World War Croatian Émigré Separatism." *European Review of History* 16, no. 5 (October 2009): 739–53.

Ugrešić, Dubravka "A Requiem for the Yugoslav Guest Worker." In *Nobody's Home: Essays*, trans. Ellen Elias-Bursać. Rochester, NY, 2008.

"Urlaub and der Front." *Der Spiegel*, 18 November 1991.

Venema, Mathias, and Claus Grimm. *Situation der ausländischen Arbeitnehmer und ihrer Familienangehörigen in der Bundesrepublik Deutschland: Repräsentativuntersuchung 2001: Teil A, Tabellenband*. Bonn, 1981.

Vertovec, Steven. *Transnationalism*. London, 2009.

Zimmerman, William. *Open Borders, Nonalignment, and the Political Evolution of Yugoslavia*. Princeton, NJ, 1987.

Žmegač, Jasna Čapo. "Family Dispersal Across National Borders: A Strategy for Betterment." In *Transnational Societies*, ed. Ulf Brunnbauer. Munich, 2009.

CHAPTER TEN

~:~

Sifting Germans from Yugoslavs
Co-ethnic Selection, Danube Swabian Migrants, and the Contestation of Aussiedler Immigration in West Germany in the 1950s and 1960s

JANNIS PANAGIOTIDIS

Readers of *Der Donauschwabe*, a weekly newspaper for German expellees from Yugoslavia, were presented in December 1959 with the following statement on the newspaper's front page:

> On every working day, there is a motley crew of people queuing in front of a noble three-storey building in the busy Kneza Miloša Street of Belgrade. Peasants with fur caps wait next to elegant ladies and men in dirty working gear. Even though there is a big sign announcing that the door of the building will not open until ten o'clock, the first contenders take their spots already before dawn, sometimes even at three o'clock at night. . . . There is something that distinguishes the people in the queue from the Yugoslav passers-by: they speak only German among each other. They are ethnic Germans [*Volksdeutsche*] who have been released from Yugoslav citizenship, and the building belongs to the embassy of the Federal Republic of Germany. There they receive their immigration permit, which allows them to say goodbye to the dull everyday life of Yugoslav people's democracy.[1]

The scene described here evokes images that are commonly associated with Moscow in the late 1980s: members of an ethnic minority are queuing outside the embassy of their "kin country" in order to leave their socialist home country and start a new life in the West. Yet this scene took place in Belgrade, not Moscow, and the year was 1959 not 1989. Ethnic Germans from Yugoslavia were the first *Volksdeutsche* (or *folksdojčeri*, as they were called in Serbo-Croatian) from a socialist country who could freely emigrate to the West, and they did so in large numbers. At the time that the *Donauschwabe* article appeared in late 1959, over 57,000 former Yugoslav citizens had already been received in the Federal Republic of Germany (FRG) as so-called *Aussiedler*. Another 20,000 followed during the 1960s.[2]

Aussiedler ("resettler" or literally "out-settler") migration from Eastern Europe to West Germany was a consistent phenomenon throughout the period of the Cold War and beyond. It became the object of political and public controversy with the massive migration wave from the collapsing Eastern bloc during the late 1980s and early 1990s. The large numbers of supposedly German newcomers with little knowledge of the German language resulted in calls to end their preferential treatment and led to a tightening of the criteria used to identify these "co-ethnic" immigrants, who were admitted to the Federal Republic of Germany on the basis of their purported German ethnicity.[3] Most scholars have argued, however, that the resettlement of co-ethnic *Aussiedler* immigrants was uncontroversial before the 1980s.[4] As to the ethnic screening of the immigrants, the most comprehensive study of *Aussiedler* immigration so far has claimed that the administrative implementation of the related law was "rather lax" and resulted in "an open-door policy for anyone from Eastern Europe and the Soviet Union who could claim, however remotely, German origin."[5]

This chapter challenges these views. It will show that the relatively large influx of *Aussiedler* from Yugoslavia to West Germany led to a significant contestation of co-ethnic immigration already in the 1950s and 1960s within the state apparatus. On a practical level, German authorities struggled to identify *Volksdeutsche* among the mass of applicants for an immigration visa. They found that many candidates did not fulfill the criteria set by German law to define an ethnic German, especially if they lived in mixed marriages. In the absence of Cold War pressures in the relations to non-aligned Yugoslavia, and given that the Yugoslav emigration regime posed no real obstacle for most would-be migrants, the West German authorities had both the possibility and felt the necessity to erect higher obstacles themselves to control the flow of immigrants. On a more general level, the continuous flow of *Aussiedler* from Yugoslavia with increasingly dubious "German credentials" triggered doubts among these same authorities about the co-ethnic resettlement campaign as a whole. The West German representation in Belgrade even went so far as to suggest stopping *Aussiedler* immigration from Yugoslavia altogether. With the "German" newcomers appearing less and less German and against the backdrop of perceived signs of normalization in the socialist East, some actors extended the restrictive approach of the FRG toward immigration in general to co-ethnic immigration as well.

The method of controlling *Aussiedler* influx was to check candidates' eligibility under the main criterion provided for by the expellee law: German ethnicity (*Volkszugehörigkeit*). For the historian this provides a rare window into the process of administrative ethnic screening and thus an opportunity to see—beyond the letter of the law that defined the criteria for recognition—who West German officials in the 1950s and 1960s deemed to be a part of the German nation and on what grounds. As this chapter will demonstrate, the selecting institutions—diplomatic representations, the Federal Administrative Office (*Bundesverwaltungsamt*, BVA), and local expellee authorities—did not accept *Aussiedler* from Yugoslavia as German merely based on their German "origin" or "descent." Both cultural (especially linguistic) and political arguments were used to include or exclude applicants, while social criteria only played a marginal role. At the same time, the structure of the immigration procedure allowed for a flexible handling of doubtful cases if so desired.

Co-ethnic Migration to West Germany

The resettlement (*Aussiedlung*) of German citizens and ethnic Germans from socialist Eastern Europe started in the early 1950s, following the expulsion of German populations from Poland, Czechoslovakia, and Hungary that had been sanctioned by the Potsdam Agreement of 1945. With the passing of the Federal Expellee Law (*Bundesvertriebenengesetz* or BVFG) of 1953, the category of *Aussiedler* came to encompass Germans from all the countries of socialist Eastern Europe, including Yugoslavia. The initial intention was to reunite families that had been separated in the course of the expulsions. Over time this limited family reunification program developed into an established migration channel from Eastern to Western Europe. Until the beginning of mass emigration from the Soviet Union during *perestroika* in 1987, some 1.4 million *Aussiedler* came to the FRG through this channel, most from Poland and Romania. After 1987, approximately 3 million more migrants followed, most from the Soviet Union and its successor states.[6]

Both the expulsion and the *Aussiedlung* of Germans from Yugoslavia differed in significant ways from the developments in other affected countries. Yugoslavia was not included in the Potsdam agreement and hence could not rid itself of its German minority—mainly so-called Danube Swabians from the Vojvodina and adjacent Slavonia—with allied blessing. Direct expulsions only took place in Slovenia and parts of Slavonia.[7] In the Vojvodina, the new Yugoslav government dispossessed and interned those remaining Germans who had not been evacuated by the retreating *Wehrmacht* toward the end of the war.[8] As many as forty thousand internees fled from the camps until 1947 with the implicit approval of the authorities, a process that Hans-Ulrich Wehler has called "indirect deportation."[9] In 1948, the remaining Germans were released from the camps but were forced to work on state farms for another three years. From 1950, family reunification became possible under a special agreement between the Yugoslav and German Red Cross societies.[10] After 1951, Yugoslav Germans could emigrate within a standardized and fairly reliable procedure.[11]

The consistency and relatively liberal implementation of this procedure distinguished *Aussiedlung* from Yugoslavia from other socialist states. The country did not limit exit to cases of family reunification and in general posed few obstacles for people hoping to leave. Any ethnic German living in the country could apply for resettlement in West Germany, which since 1951 maintained diplomatic relations with Tito's socialist but non-aligned Yugoslavia. In order to migrate, the applicant needed both the permission to leave Yugoslavia, combined with the release from Yugoslav citizenship, and the approval to immigrate to the FRG with the guarantee of receiving German citizenship upon arrival (the "certificate of equalization" or *Gleichstellungsbescheinigung*).[12] The latter two were awarded after the applicant's eligibility had been positively assessed by the German authorities in the "takeover procedure" (*Übernahmeverfahren*). This procedure could be launched by relatives already living in West Germany, or by the applicants themselves at the embassy in Belgrade or the consulate general in Zagreb. The resulting migration channel was kept open even after the breaking of diplomatic ties between the FRG and Yugoslavia in 1957, when the French embassy in Belgrade took over the representation of West German interests.

Framing Ethnicity in Law and Reality

German authorities applied much tighter screening criteria on applications from Yugoslavia compared to *Aussiedler* from other socialist states. In those other cases the assumption prevailed in the administration that co-ethnic migration across the East-West divide was exceptional. The West German authorities did not dare jeopardize this exceptional movement by possibly rejecting candidates. At the same time, the strict exit regulations of countries like Poland (at least before 1956) and in particular the Soviet Union served as a type of "pre-selection" of candidates for co-ethnic immigration, the assumption being that those countries would only let people go that were "really" German. For Yugoslavia no such assumption could be made, and therefore the German authorities felt compelled to engage in a more thorough investigation of the eligibility of the applicants. In addition, it is important to consider in this context that ethnic Germans were seeking permanent residence and citizenship in the Federal Republic of Germany, unlike *Gastarbeiter* from Yugoslavia, who (as Christopher Molnar shows in his contribution to this volume) engaged in a high degree of transnational mobility between Yugoslavia and West Germany and, at least in theory, did not come to stay.

The decisive criterion for the eligibility of an applicant for *Aussiedlung* was German ethnicity (*Volkszugehörigkeit*) as defined by the Federal Expellee Law. Section Six stipulated that a German *Volkszugehöriger* was someone who had publicly identified in his country of origin as belonging to German *Volkstum* (*wer sich in seiner Heimat zum deutschen Volkstum bekannt hat*), provided that this self-identification (*Bekenntnis*) was backed up by certain characteristics like descent, language, upbringing, and culture (*sofern dieses Bekenntnis durch bestimmte Merkmale wie Abstammung, Sprache, Erziehung, Kultur bestätigt wird*).[13] In their assessment of an applicant, the local authorities had to rely mainly on information that relatives provided in special forms that asked for the applicant's *Volkszugehörigkeit*, native language, participation in German organizations or institutions in Yugoslavia, postwar internment, and membership in the German *Wehrmacht*.[14] In case of doubt, the German embassy in Belgrade or the consulate general in Zagreb could be asked by the internal authorities to invite the potential immigrants for a personal interview to check their credentials. The ultimate decision about admittance then lay with the BVA, based on the—possibly contradictory—input from the local expellee authorities and the diplomatic representations.

The single cases analyzed here will show how the legal criteria defining *Volkszugehörigkeit* were interpreted in bureaucratic practice, both on paper and in personal interviews. As will be seen, the complex definition given in the law with its strong emphasis on subjective *Bekenntnis* was in practice often reduced to one comparatively easy to handle and "objective" criterion: language. In mixed families, where the issue of *Volkszugehörigkeit* was generally most contentious, use of the German language was taken as evidence for the prevalence of German *Volkstum* as a precondition for immigration—but only after the practice of generally rejecting mixed families had ceased. In addition, there was a significant political aspect to *Volkszugehörigkeit*, which gained importance in the case of ethnic Germans who had sided with the Yugoslav partisans against the Nazi occupiers. Social criteria, on the other hand, only played a complementary role.

Volkszugehörigkeit and "Mixed" Families

In April 1960, the *Donauschwabe* reported from the transit camp of Piding in Bavaria: "More than before the repatriation of members of so-called mixed marriages became noticeable. Among them there are people who do not speak a word of German."[15] Already during the preceding years, the authorities had been grappling with the question of whether to allow the immigration of ethnically mixed families or not, and if so, based on which criteria. The approach changed over time, shifting from outright rejection to a flexible handling of cases that focused on the "prevailing of German *Volkstum*"—which usually meant speaking the German language—in the family.

Before 1959 there were several documented cases of mixed families that were not allowed into West Germany. In each case it was the woman who claimed to be German. The fact that she had "intermarried" was taken as a renunciation of German *Volkstum*. For example, a mother and her son were rejected by the authorities in 1956 because she had been married to a presumable non-German, despite the fact that she had relatives already living in the Federal Republic. The husband's non-German ethnicity was deduced from the fact that he had not served in the *Wehrmacht*, that she had not been interned despite her German ethnicity, and that their son did not bear a German first name.[16] In 1957, three other women were only granted an immigration visa following divorce from their non-German husbands.[17] In March 1959, another German woman, Elisabeth B., who had married a non-German was granted an immigration visa "on purely humanitarian grounds" after somebody intervened at the Committee of Petitions of the German *Bundestag*. As it turned out, she and her mother, who already lived in West Germany, had made "exceptionally heavy sacrifices" (*außergewöhnlich schwere Opfer*) because of their German *Volkstum*, which eventually made them worthy of being admitted to the FRG as citizens.[18]

The fact that in the available documentation only German women married to non-German men were denied recognition as ethnically German indicates a likely gender bias in the authorities' assessment of German *Volkszugehörigkeit*. The officials might have assumed that the husband's *Volkstum* would automatically dominate over that of his wife, analogous to the long-standing rules of German citizenship law. This law dictated that a woman automatically lost her German citizenship if she married a foreigner, while a foreign woman acquired the German citizenship of her husband—a rule that had only recently been abolished in 1953. This intention does not become explicit in the sources, but against the legal background it seems probable.

The practice of rejecting applications of families simply because of the fact that they were "mixed" ceased with an instruction by the Federal Interior Ministry in July 1959. The instruction stated that

> [j]ust because an ethnic German (*deutscher Volkszugehöriger*), no matter if man or woman, has married a foreigner of non-German ethnicity, does not mean he or she can be denied recognition of German *Volkszugehörigkeit* . . . In mixed marriages, one partner usually has an ethnically dominating influence (*einen volkstumsmäßig bestimmenden Einfluss*) on the other partner. . . . Evidence for the prevalence of the *Bekenntnis* to German *Volkstum* can be found in the use of the German language within the family, in the choice of typically German names for the children, in the German upbringing of the children and in the acquaintance of family members with German citizens or ethnic Germans. In

mixed marriages it should be thoroughly checked whether German *Volkstum* prevails in the family.[19]

True to the letter of this instruction, post-July 1959 screenings attempted to ensure that in the numerous cases of mixed marriages, the German partner at least managed to impose his or her German *Volkstum* on the non-German members of the family. In several documented cases families were not accepted into West Germany because the German *Volkstum* of the one partner was not dominant. In practice, this was assessed by checking whether the family spoke German at home or used another language, usually Serbo-Croatian or Hungarian. For example, in 1965 the family of Josef K., according to the BVA an ethnic German born in 1927 to two German parents, was not granted an entry visa because his non-German wife Djurdja did not speak any German and the children had "typically Slavic first names."[20] The fact that past applicants from their hometown Sokolovac in Croatia had had a good knowledge of the German language was held against this particular candidate. In a similar case in 1964, Emil S. and his wife Jelka from Vukovar were denied entry despite the "typically German" first names of their three children—Josef, Emmerich, and Karl—given that Jelka's Croatian *Volkstum* was judged to be dominant in the family.[21] In contrast, Stefan V., a Hungarian-German man from Czerwenka (Crvenka) in Serbia was allowed in, even though he had the typically Hungarian surname of his father and was registered as "Hungarian" in his Yugoslav identification. His son bore the equally Hungarian first name of Tibor. Yet he and his children spoke excellent German and, according to the embassy in Belgrade, "made a very good impression." Therefore, their application was granted without further ado.[22]

Contrary to the idea that anyone with even remotely German descent would be recognized as ethnically German, German ancestry at times counted for very little compared to language skills in the family. This can be seen in the case of Barbara and Marko K. from Komletinci in Croatian Syrmia, who wanted to relocate to West Germany with their four children Marko, Stefan, Adam, and Andreas. Their first application, filed in 1963, was rejected even though *both* partners had German mothers and Barbara even spoke quite good German. Over a year after the family had filed their application for the second time in 1968, they received a letter from the BVA that explained to them that they were in fact not German *Volkszugehörige*, since this presupposed a *Bekenntnis*. And the "most reliable evidence" for this *Bekenntnis*—according to the BVA—was the use of the German language in the family. Since the consulate in Zagreb had found out that they spoke Croatian at home, they had to be considered ethnically Croatian and were therefore denied the permission to immigrate.[23] This outright identification of language and *Bekenntnis*, which was not covered by Section Six of the BVFG, had become common administrative practice in the case of Germans from Yugoslavia. In the overall system of co-ethnic immigration to the FRG, it was not until the large-scale Russian-German immigration of the 1990s that language skills obtained such an important status.

However, there were other cases that indicate that there was no clear policy of keeping out mixed families, even if the personal interview revealed that German *Volkstum* did not prevail in the family. In some instances, applicants were given a second chance. This worked for example for a Hungarian-German family whose application had been rejected in April 1959. When they were reexamined by the embassy in Belgrade in June 1961, it turned out that

> the German *Volkstum* of [the mother] by now prevails in the family. The husband, who is of Hungarian descent and spoke little German in early 1959, has apparently made an effort to assimilate to German *Volkstum* (*im deutschen Volkstum aufzugehen*) and now speaks German. The daughter also speaks German— apparently she is raised the German way (*offenbar wird sie deutsch erzogen*).[24]

This "dynamic" approach to *Volkstum* was taken even further in a case in 1962, when Anton P. and his family were granted an immigration permit based on the embassy's judgment that "German *Volkstum* will soon prevail in the family."[25] One local office took this approach to its logical consequence when it supported the application of Johann and Katharina M., arguing that the husband's German *Volkstum* could only prevail over that of his Hungarian wife if they came to live with his relatives in Germany.[26] In yet other instances, families were taken in with a "special permit" issued by the local authorities at the place of residence of the applicants' relatives, despite a negative ruling by the embassy.[27]

Even so, applicants with doubtful credentials did not automatically receive the benefit of the doubt. A lot depended on the goodwill of the responsible authorities at their prospective destination.[28] Social considerations, while not the core piece of the screening process, could tip the scale for or against a candidate. The availability of sufficient housing was one of the relevant criteria in the takeover procedure. In 1964, for example, Roman and Maria T. were taken in despite their lacking German *Bekenntnis* and their "mixed Romanian-German-Hungarian-Serbian" *Volkstum*. Apart from the fact that they both spoke German, it was held in their favor that Maria's mother was already in West Germany and that their accommodation was secured.[29] In contrast, in 1961 two other families who did not fulfill the *Volkszugehörigkeit* criteria were also denied a special permit, given that, among other things, they had not secured accommodation.[30] In the case of Ferdinand and Maria T. and their children Slavia and Dezider, the authorities in Baden-Württemberg only agreed to take them in on the condition that the *Land* would receive adequate funding for housing construction.[31] In general, it seems that the local institutions tended to be more generous in their immigration decisions if they incurred no additional cost, or if this cost was covered by additional funding.

Political Criteria

While social screening among *Aussiedler* remained marginal and largely implicit, the assessment of *Volkszugehörigkeit* could obtain an explicitly political character. This is demonstrated by the case of Blagorodovac, a small Croatian village located between Zagreb and Osijek. In late 1959, the Federal Office for Administrative Matters (the precursor to the Federal Office) reported that the consulate general in Zagreb had been tipped off by anonymous letters about certain applicants from this village who had fought for the communist partisans during World War II.[32] Unlike other Germans they had not suffered internment or persecution after the war. The Office contacted the Federal Interior Ministry to clarify whether this engagement with the partisans allowed for a positive judgment of their *Bekenntnis*—their "objective" Germanness according to the law was not doubted.

After inquiring deeper into the matter and hearing different witnesses, the consulate general in Zagreb reported in March 1961 that the inhabitants of Blagorodovac, 99 percent of whom were German, had indeed served with the partisans.[33] Whether this happened under coercion was deemed irrelevant, since

> given the support for the partisans, for whatever reason and of whatever kind, we certainly cannot assume a *Bekenntnis* to German *Volkstum* anymore. For this reason, we suggest to reject all applicants from Blagorodovac unless it is proved that the individual applicant has *not* collaborated with the partisans.[34]

While it is not clear if this ban was ever enforced, it is remarkable that such a measure was even suggested. While in principle pro-Nazi engagement was not supposed to constitute a *Bekenntnis* to German *Volkstum*, fighting the German occupying army in Yugoslavia was considered a renunciation of one's Germanness—despite the fact that the people in question had at no point denied that they were German and were still registered as Germans in their passports. In fact, Blagorodovac was the symbol of a specifically *German* resistance to Nazi occupation and supposedly the place where the banner of the German-manned *Thälmann* battalion of the partisan army had first been raised.[35] At this point, the meaning of *Bekenntnis* turns into a strong political statement. This testifies to a politicized view of what and who was supposed to be "German" that neatly combined an apologetic view of the Nazi past with the anticommunist *raison d'État* of the West German state. An ethnic German after 1945 was supposed to have been a victim of communism, not a communist.

Yet the initiative by the Zagreb consulate to halt immigration from Blago-rodovac must also be seen in the context of the wider contestation of ethnic German resettlement from Yugoslavia at the time. The consulate closed its report with the supposition that German emigration from Yugoslavia by then was primarily economically motivated, which should lead to stricter standards in the assessment of the *Volkszugehörigkeit* of applicants or even to the end of the resettlement campaign.[36] It is this general contestation of the resettlement campaign to which we will next turn.

Contesting Co-ethnic Immigration

Ethnic German immigration from Yugoslavia caused irritation on several occasions after the late 1950s. Apart from the politically motivated case of Blagorodovac, there were also recurring instances of corruption in the emi-gration procedure, which even led to suspended sentences for some of the immigrants charged for using fraudulent documentation to prove their Ger-manness.[37] In March 1963, the *Donauschwabe* claimed that 75 percent of the newcomers at the time had doubtful German credentials.[38] As it turned out, this was only the prelude for a more general internal contestation of resettle-ment from Yugoslavia.

The challenge against Yugoslav German *Aussiedlung* started with a letter from the West German interests section (*Schutzmachtvertretung*) in the French embassy in Belgrade to the Foreign Office in Bonn in July 1963.[39] The interests section admonished the Foreign Office to "reconsider the foundation and the motivation of the resettlement." It suspected that the increase in applications was due to the fact that more mixed families were taken into consideration and the criterion of "prevailing German *Volkstum*" in the family was not rigor-ously applied. The author of the letter also criticized the common practice of letting people reapply after acquiring only a modest knowledge of German. He concluded that "the inevitable result of this generous practice is that even such categories of former ethnic Germans (*ehemalige Volksdeutsche*) who had long ago adapted to Yugoslav society and had no intention to emigrate before are now virtually encouraged to emigrate." With this latter statement, the West German mission in Belgrade anticipated Rogers Brubaker's observation about the "non-Euclidean demography" of co-ethnic migration, i.e., the phenomenon that with increased co-ethnic emigration to an attractive country, the pool of potential migrants does not decrease but increases as more people "redis-cover" their origins.[40] The concern was clear: while the initial purpose of the resettlement campaign had been to allow for the emigration of the "rearguard" of the former German minorities in eastern and southeastern Europe, the embassy understood that the current practice tended to attract more people with increasingly tenuous links to German *Volkstum*.

In another report in January 1965, the West German delegation in Belgrade was even more explicit in its criticism of the application of immigration policies regarding Yugoslav *Volksdeutsche*.[41] It complained that the percentage of "real" Germans among the *Aussiedler* was down to only 10 percent, while most of the families were of mixed ethnic background with the foreign element predominant. The criteria set by law were hardly applicable under the given conditions. A former *Bekenntnis* was hard to prove for lack of documentation, as was German descent in cases of mixed families, especially if they no longer carried German names. Crucially, given the predominant recognition practice, the author of the report argued that language could not be considered a valid criterion to identify a German, as many *Volksdeutsche* hardly spoke German anymore, while many non-Germans did. With this last manageable criterion for identification gone, the embassy representative proposed to set a deadline after which a resettlement from Yugoslavia to the FRG should no longer be possible.

As a reaction to this outright challenge of Yugoslav *Aussiedlung*, representatives of the Foreign Office, the Federal Administrative Office, and the Federal Expellee Ministry met in March 1965.[42] The Foreign Office officials supported the embassy's recent report. They regretted that the resettlement campaign could not be terminated any time soon and criticized the BVA's extensive definition of *Volksdeutsch*. The BVA representatives in turn rejected the charges in particular cases. Instead, they blamed the *Länder* authorities and local expellee offices for not being strict enough in rejecting applications.[43] The general discussion reached the following conclusions: a deadline for new applications could not be set, as this was against the Federal Expellee Law. There was no majority in parliament to change the law, as the general political line was to keep the door open for ethnic Germans from abroad. However, it was suggested to advise the Interior Ministry to limit the certificates of equalization to two years, a measure that was eventually implemented in August 1966.[44] Furthermore, the *Länder* should be encouraged to use stricter standards in the context of family reunification. But other than that, the forceful contestation started by the Interests Section in Belgrade and supported by the Foreign Office yielded no tangible results.

This discussion is important for two reasons. It provides clear evidence that the politically imposed "open door" for ethnic Germans was not as uncontested during the 1960s as it would seem on the surface. Both the West German interests section at the French embassy in Belgrade and the Foreign Office were in fact in favor of closing this very door to Germans from Yugoslavia. However, as this was a political rather than a bureaucratic decision, they could not act against the majority in parliament that wanted to keep the gates open. This discussion also resulted in a game of "passing the buck" between different institutions on different levels. The embassy blamed the BVA for being too generous. The BVA rejected this charge. But rather than defending its purported generosity—which, after all, could have been justified with the plight of ethnic Germans in Yugoslavia and the danger of their assimilation—its representatives pointed to their own restrictive record and indicated that the origin of the problem was to be found in the generosity of the *Länder* and expellee authorities.

This episode shows that by the mid-1960s, restrictiveness had become a virtue among the higher authorities involved in co-ethnic immigration procedures from Yugoslavia. The liberal Yugoslav emigration regime and the apparent normalization of living conditions in the country made the exceptionally generous co-ethnic immigration regime appear unnecessary to some West German institutions. This impression, as Christopher Molnar showed in his contribution, was presumably reinforced by the hundreds of visa applications from Yugoslav citizens to become guest workers in West Germany that had been flooding the German delegations in Yugoslavia since the early 1960s.[45] Hence, a restrictive immigration regime more akin to the general credo that "Germany is not a country of immigration" was suggested. But for political reasons this restrictive standpoint was not fully implemented. In 1969, the embassy in Belgrade complained once again that the BVA was too generous in granting immigration permits.[46] Unlike 1965, no controversial discussion followed. This time, not even a departmental meeting was scheduled to consider the issues.

*   *   *   *   *

This chapter has examined how West German authorities during the 1950s and 1960s sifted Germans from non-Germans among the candidates for co-ethnic resettlement from Yugoslavia. This screening process was neither as lax nor as uncontested as it has been claimed in the literature on the subject. In administrative practice, neither subjective identification with German *Volkstum* nor the German descent of a person alone were decisive in the determination of the ethnic belonging of potential *Aussiedler* from Yugoslavia. A significant part of the screening focused on German language skills, ethnic endogamy, and political convictions. These criteria were fluid, subject to change, and handled rather flexibly. Also, they contradicted each other in part. Linguistic skills did not necessarily have to be preexisting but could be acquired and improved. "Ethnic intermarriage" ceased to be a reason to automatically exclude applicants in 1959, but it remained an important issue that could make cases contentious. Acceptance then often depended on whether or not German was spoken in the family home. In other instances, however, the language criterion was ignored and mixed families were taken in with a special permit, especially if their accommodation was secured. The wrong political convictions, in turn, could cancel out the other two criteria. At that point political considerations trumped ethno-cultural concerns.

To put these findings into perspective it is instructive to subject them to a cross-temporal comparison. Different German authorities engaged in ethnic screening both before and after the period investigated here. In fact, the definition of *Volkszugehörigkeit* included in the Federal Expellee Law dated back to a circular of the Nazi Reich Interior Ministry from March 1939, stripped, however, of the racist provision that excluded from the definition "people of foreign blood, especially Jews."[47] It survived unchanged until the revision of the BVFG in 1992. While this immutable legal definition suggests a high level of continuity, it is necessary here, too, to look at administrative practice rather than just legal definitions to assess how much continuity there actually was between pre- and post-1945 ethnic screening.

Recent and older studies have shed light on the screening and selection that Nazi institutions like the *Volksdeutsche Mittelstelle* (*VoMi*) and the *Einwandererzentralstelle* (EWZ) conducted among ethnic Germans in Eastern Europe before and during the war.[48] In his pioneering study of the *VoMi*, Valdis O. Lumans spoke of "a bewildering series of physical, racial, occupational, and political examinations" that were implemented by these institutions to determine the "degree of Germanness" of candidates for *Heim ins Reich* resettlement.[49] As we have seen, the practice of *Aussiedler* screening was markedly different. Race, which was the central—if notoriously ill-defined—category of Nazi thinking and screening, was a non-category after the war. In addition, the German authorities involved in examining the potential immigrants displayed none of the preoccupation that the Nazi institutions had with health, biology, and with social criteria.[50] Despite the continuity in vocabulary and legal categories, the ethnic selectivity of postwar West Germany therefore needs to be clearly distinguished from Nazi practices.

The more salient continuity across the rupture of 1945 was the political (i.e., anticommunist) rather than the ethnic component of *Volkszugehörigkeit*. As the Blagorodovac case showed, the association with communist partisans was a reason to be excluded from recognition as German, even if in this case the partisan struggle had been explicitly coded as German. In the past, *VoMi* and EWZ, too, were concerned with the "Bolshevik contamination" of Russian Germans.[51] And still in 1992 the new version of the Federal Expellee Law contained a provision under Section Five that excluded from recognition as *Aussiedler* people who had held an "elevated political or professional position" in their country of origin or had shown "considerable support of the system."[52] The construction of Germanness in opposition to communism was thus the main element that connected the co-ethnic recognition practices of the Nazis, of West Germany, and of the reunited Federal Republic.

Yet the most striking similarity in the cross-temporal comparison of Yugoslav German *Aussiedlung* was with Russian German *Aussiedlung* in the 1990s, despite a difference in scale. In both instances, language turned into the critical point of difference that served to distinguish Germans from non-Germans. In the case of Russian Germans this even became official practice with the introduction of compulsory language tests in 1996. The other significant similarity lies in the contestation of these groups' immigration privileges in light of their supposed lack of Germanness and assumed economic migration motives. In both instances, "co-ethnics" were thus perceived as more akin to "regular" immigrants, who in the Federal Republic of Germany were not supposed to exist beyond the supposedly temporary *Gastarbeiter*, which eventually delegitimized their immigration privileges. Yugoslav German *Aussiedlung* thus had little in common with previous Nazi policies. Instead, it displayed many similarities with later policies toward Russian German *Spätaussiedler*. Based on this observation it can be argued that German *Aussiedler* policy, rather than being a case of a latter-day *Heim in Reich* campaign, was a genuinely and distinctive postwar West German phenomenon.

Jannis Panagiotidis is Junior Professor of Migration and Integration of Russian Germans at the University of Osnabrück Institute for Migration Research and Intercultural Studies (IMIS). He earned his PhD from the European University Institute in Florence in 2012 with a dissertation on co-ethnic immigration to West Germany and Israel after the Second World War. He is the author of several articles on issues of contemporary migration history, including: "Germanizing Germans: Co-ethnic Immigration and Name Change in West Germany, 1953–93," in *Journal of Contemporary History* 50, 4 (2015), 854-874, and "A Policy for the Future: German-Jewish Remigrants, Their Children, and the Politics of Israeli Nation-Building," in *Leo Baeck Institute Year Book* 60, 1 (2015), 191-206.

Notes

1. Franz Xaver Engelbert, "Pankow 'entdeckt' die Volksdeutschen," *Der Donauschwabe* no. 47 (22 November 1959): 1.
2. These numbers are taken from the official statistics as documented in Archiv für Christlich-Demokratische Politik (ACDP), Nachlass Waffenschmidt, 01-346-129/2. Gerhard Reichling argues that the number for the 1950s did not exceed forty thousand. He explains the difference with the fact that the official statistics incorrectly also counted former German POWs who had stayed in Yugoslavia after the war and

returned to Germany during the 1950s. See Gerhard Reichling, *Die deutschen Vertriebenen in Zahlen, Teil 1: Umsiedler, Verschleppte, Vertriebene, Aussiedler, 1940–1985* (Bonn 1986), 41–43.

3. For a brief overview see Douglas B. Klusmeyer and Demetrios G. Papademetriou, *Immigration Policy in the Federal Republic of Germany: Negotiating Membership and Remaking the Nation* (New York/Oxford 2009), 181–87. For a more extensive treatment see Daniel Levy, "Remembering the Nation: Ethnic Germans and the Transformation of National Identity in the Federal Republic of Germany" (PhD Diss., Columbia University, 1999).

4. See most recently Rogers Brubaker/Jaeeun Kim, "Transborder Membership Politics in Germany and Korea," *Archives européennes de sociologie/European Journal of Sociology* 52 (2011): 51.

5. Christian Joppke, *Selecting by Origin: Ethnic Migration in the Liberal State* (Cambridge, MA, 2005), 174.

6. For a brief historical overview of *Aussiedler* migration, see Rainer Münz and Rainer Ohliger, "Long Distance Citizens: Ethnic Germans and Their Immigration to Germany," in *Paths to Inclusion: The Integration of Migrants in the United States and Germany*, ed. Peter H. Schuck and Rainer Münz (Providence, RI, 1998), 155–210.

7. Hans-Ulrich Wehler, *Nationalitätenpolitik in Jugoslawien: die deutsche Minderheit 1918–1978* (Göttingen, 1980), 85. The expellees included ethnic Germans from the Gottschee region and Bosnia, who had already been displaced by the Nazi occupiers during the war.

8. In addition to Wehler's classic study see the more recent works on the topic by Michael Portmann, *Die kommunistische Revolution in der Vojvodina 1944–1952: Politik, Gesellschaft, Wirtschaft, Kultur* (Vienna, 2008), and Zoran Janjetovic, *Between Hitler and Tito: The Disappearance of the Vojvodina Germans*, 2nd ed. (Belgrade, 2005).

9. Wehler, *Nationalitätenpolitik*, 92.

10. Ibid., 93.

11. Ibid., 93–94; and Portmann, *Kommunistische Revolution*, 266–67.

12. Wehler, *Nationalitätenpolitik*, 93; and Regierungspräsidium Südbaden an die Kreisverwaltungen, Kreisämter für Umsiedlung, 9 January 1954, in Hauptstaatsarchiv (HStA) Stuttgart EA 12/201, Az. 2250, 32.

13. *Bundesgesetzblatt* I, 201, 22 May 1953.

14. Bundesministerium für Vertriebene (BMVt) an das Ministerium für Vertriebene, Flüchtlinge und Kriegsgeschädigte Baden-Württemberg (MVFK BW), 23 July 1954, in HStA Stuttgart EA 12/201, Az. 2257, 22.

15. "Pforte zu einem neuen, besseren Leben: Interessante Zahlen aus dem Grenzdurchgangslager Piding Obb.," 13.

16. HStA Stuttgart EA12/201, Az. 2257, No. 81.

17. HStA Stuttgart EA12/201, Az. 2257, Nos. 108, 111, and 114.

18. Bundesstelle für Verwaltungsangelegenheiten des Bundesministers des Innern (BSVA) an das Auswärtige Amt (AA), 23 February 1959, quoted in BMVt an MVFK BW, 23 March 1959, in HStA Stuttgart EA12/201, Az. 2257, No. 116.

19. Bundesinnenministerium (BMI) an BSVA, 11 July 1959, in Politisches Archiv des Auswärtigen Amts (PAAA) B 85 938.

20. Bundesverwaltungsamt (BVA) an AA (13 February 1964), and BVA an Inneministerium Baden-Württemberg (IM BW), 20 September 1965, both in HStA Stuttgart EA12/201, Az. 2257, No. 299.

21. HStA Stuttgart EA12/201, Az. 2257, No. 294.
22. HStA Stuttgart EA12/201, Az. 2257, No. 306.
23. HStA Stuttgart EA12/201, Az. 2257, No. 286.
24. BVA an AA, 3 May 1962, in HStA Stuttgart EA12/201, Az. 2257, No. 228.
25. HStA Stuttgart EA12/201, Az. 2257, No. 256.
26. HStA Stuttgart EA12/201, Az. 2257, No. 316.
27. Such cases from the 1960s are documented in HStA Stuttgart EA12/201, Az. 2257, Nos. 175, 214, 296, 306, and 310.
28. Cases from 1963–1964 in which a local office (the district council of Tettnang) denied the special permits are documented in HStA Stuttgart EA12/201, Az. 2257, Nos. 266 and 283.
29. BVA an AA, 5 March 1964, in HStA Stuttgart EA12/201, Az. 2257, No. 285 (also the protocol sheet of their interview at the interests section in Belgrade on 23 January 1964).
30. BVA an IM BW, 28 September 1961, in HStA Stuttgart EA12/201, Az. 2257, No. 220.
31. Case documented in HStA Stuttgart EA12/201, Az. 2257, No. 201.
32. BSVA an BMI, 30 November 1959, in PAAA B 85 938.
33. Generalkonsulat (GK) der Bundesrepublik Deutschland in Zagreb an AA, 16 March 1961, in PAAA B 85 938.
34. GK Zagreb an AA, 16 March 1961, in PAAA B 85 938 (emphasis added).
35. Heinz Kühnrich/Franz-Karl Hitze, *Deutsche bei Titos Partisanen 1941–1945: auf dem Balkan in Augenzeugenberichten und Dokumenten*, Schkeuditz, 1997.
36. GK Zagreb an AA, 16 March 1961, in PAAA B 85 938.
37. Those are documented in Bundesarchiv (BArch) B 106/39940.
38. "Missbrauchte Sozialgesetzgebung: Aussiedler ohne Ende aus Jugoslawien," *Der Donauschwabe* no. 9 (3 March 1963): 1–2.
39. Ambassade de France, Schutzmachtvertretung für deutsche Interessen, Belgrad (SMV) an AA, 10 July 1963, in BArch B 106/39940.
40. Rogers Brubaker, "Migrations of Ethnic Unmixing in the New Europe," *International Migration Review*.
41. See SMV Belgrad an AA, 21 January 1965, BArch B 106/39940.
42. Vermerk Ressortbesprechung, 19 March 1965, in PAAA B 85 938.
43. Already in January the BVA had rejected the charge of "frivolous generosity," arguing that it rejected more than one-third of the applications from Yugoslavia. BVA an BMI, 8 January 1965, in BArch B 106/39940.
44. AA an SMV Belgrad und GK Zagreb, 3 August 1966, in PAAA B 85 938.
45. Kaja Shonick mentions 150–200 visa applications per day in the consulate general in Zagreb in 1962. In 1963, two thousand Yugoslav citizens arrived in Germany each month. From 1961 to 1968 the overall number of Yugoslav guest workers reached 100,000. See Kaja Shonick, "Politics, Culture, and Economics: Reassessing the West German Guest Worker Agreement with Yugoslavia," *Journal of Contemporary History* 44 (2009): 727.
46. Botschaft der Bundesrepublik Deutschland, Belgrad an das AA, 17 May 1969, in PAAA B 85 812.
47. *Ministerialblatt des Reichsministers des Innern* (1939), 783.
48. Valdis O. Lumans, *Himmler's Auxiliaries: The Volksdeutsche Mittelstelle and the German National Minorities of Europe, 1933–1945* (Chapel Hill, NC; London, 1993);

Markus Leniger, *Nationalsozialistische "Volkstumsarbeit" und Umsiedlungspolitik 1933–1945: von der Minderheitenbetreuung zur Siedlerauslese* (Berlin, 2006); Andreas Strippel, *NS-Volkstumspolitik und die Neuordnung Europas: Rassenpolitische Selektion der Einwandererzentralstelle des Chefs der Sicherheitspolizei und des SD (1939–1945)* (Paderborn, 2011).
49. Lumans, *Himmler's Auxiliaries*, 184.
50. These practices are discussed in detail by Leniger, *Volkstumsarbeit*.
51. Ibid., 134f.
52. This provision is explained in detail in the provisional guidelines to the law, published in *Info-Dienst Deutsche Aussiedler* no. 41 (May 1993): 13–15.

Bibliography

Anonymous. "Missbrauchte Sozialgesetzgebung: Aussiedler ohne Ende aus Jugoslawien." *Der Donauschwabe* no. 9, 3 March 1963.

———. "Pforte zu einem neuen, besseren Leben: Interessante Zahlen aus dem Grenzdurchgangslager Piding Obb." *Der Donauschwabe* no. 16, 17 April 1960.

Archiv für Christlich-Demokratische Politik (ACDP), Nachlass Waffenschmidt, 01-346-129/2.

Brubaker, Rogers. "Migrations of Ethnic Unmixing in the New Europe." *International Migration Review* 32 (1998): 1047–65.

Brubaker, Rogers and Jaeeun Kim. "Transborder Membership Politics in Germany and Korea." *European Journal of Sociology* 52 (2011): 21–75.

Engelbert, Franz Xaver. "Pankow 'entdeckt' die Volksdeutschen." *Der Donauschwabe* no. 47, 22 November 1959.

Info-Dienst Deutsche Aussiedler no. 41, May 1993.

Janjetovic, Zoran. *Between Hitler and Tito: The Disappearance of the Vojvodina Germans.* 2nd edition. Belgrade, 2005.

Joppke, Christian. *Selecting by Origin: Ethnic Migration in the Liberal State.* Cambridge, MA, 2005.

Klusmeyer, Douglas B. and Demetrios G. Papademetriou. *Immigration Policy in the Federal Republic of Germany: Negotiating Membership and Remaking the Nation.* New York, 2009.

Kühnrich, Heinz and Franz-Karl Hitze. *Deutsche bei Titos Partisanen 1941–1945: Kriegsschicksale auf dem Balkan in Augenzeugenberichten und Dokumenten.* Schkeuditz, 1997.

Leniger, Markus. *Nationalsozialistische 'Volkstumsarbeit' und Umsiedlungspolitik 1933–1945: von der Minderheitenbetreuung zur Siedlerauslese.* Berlin, 2006.

Levy, Daniel. "Remembering the Nation: Ethnic Germans and the Transformation of National Identity in the Federal Republic of Germany." PhD diss., Columbia University, 1999.

Lumans, Valdis O. *Himmler's Auxiliaries: The Volksdeutsche Mittelstelle and the German National Minorities of Europe, 1933–1945.* Chapel Hill, NC; London, 1993.

Münz, Rainer, and Rainer Ohliger. "Long Distance Citizens: Ethnic Germans and Their Immigration to Germany." In *Paths to Inclusion: The Integration of Migrants in the United States and Germany*, ed. Peter H. Schuck and Rainer Münz. Providence, RI, 1998.

Portmann, Michael. *Die kommunistische Revolution in der Vojvodina 1944–1952: Politik, Gesellschaft, Wirtschaft, Kultur.* Vienna, 2008.

Reichling, Gerhard. *Die deutschen Vertriebenen in Zahlen, Teil 1: Umsiedler, Verschleppte, Vertriebene, Aussiedler, 1940–1985.* Bonn, 1986.

Shonick, Kaja. "Politics, Culture, and Economics: Reassessing the West German Guest Worker Agreement with Yugoslavia." *Journal of Contemporary History* 44, no. 4 (2009): 719–36.

Strippel, Andreas. *NS-Volkstumspolitik und die Neuordnung Europas: Rassenpolitische Selektion der Einwandererzentralstelle des Chefs der Sicherheitspolizei und des SD (1939–1945).* Paderborn, 2011.

Wehler, Hans-Ulrich. *Nationalitätenpolitik in Jugoslawien: die deutsche Minderheit 1918–1978.* Göttingen, 1980.

CHAPTER ELEVEN

~:~

Staging Immigration History as Urban History
A New *"Lieu de Mémoire"?*

BETTINA SEVERIN-BARBOUTIE

The commemoration of immigration history in museums and exhibitions has proliferated in Germany over the past fifteen years. The topic has diversified into a range of "sub-genres," addressing various issues, groups, and periods. Museums have started to incorporate immigration history into their permanent exhibitions, and special exhibitions have multiplied significantly over the past decades, with a major increase since the turn of the twenty-first century. The idea of a national museum dedicated to Germany's migration history has been launched by various institutions, among them DOMiT (Dokumentationszentrum und Museum über die Migration aus der Türkei e.V.).[1]

Neither the historical exhibitions nor the concept of a national migration museum are completely new phenomena in Germany, though. Indeed, the intersection of immigration history and public history was on display in a number of exhibitions long before the year 2000. After the 1970s, most of these exhibitions commemorated issues of immigration in German cities since the 1950s, addressing the topic from different perspectives and through a variety of objects.[2] However, it is only since the beginning of the twenty-first century that the incorporation of immigration history in museums has developed and is now emerging as a distinct field in Germany. The commemoration of immigration history as urban history opens interesting perspectives for the investigation of migration history and memory practices in the second half of the twentieth century. On the one hand, it sheds light on new techniques of representing people on the move. On the other, it reveals changing patterns in the reflection upon and the interpretation of immigration in Germany since the 1970s. Besides, it illustrates the changing self-perception and self-definition of German society alongside political, social, and economic evolution. Apart from that, urban exhibitions about migration, which preceded national and regional exhibition projects by several years, raise interesting questions about the link between immigration history, memory, and space in contemporary Germany.

None of these issues has been researched thus far, even though significant studies on memory cultures and identity building in Germany have been done in the past decades. This lack of academic attention may be related to the novelty of the named exhibitions, but it is more likely explained by the fact that, unlike immigration museums, historical exhibitions on immigration history have not received much attention from historians altogether. Apart from two ongoing research projects about "Migration on Display. A study on knowledge productions on migration in history and city museums"[3] and "Remembering, Narrating, and Representing Immigration: Immigration Museums and Exhibitions in Germany, France, and the UK,"[4] there is little evidence of broader research in this field. This situation is mirrored by a limited number of rather descriptive publications mainly written by exhibition makers themselves. Moreover, historical research on the immigration history of German cities after 1945 is still in its early stages. Interestingly enough, the number of studies investigating immigration on the national level has increased substantially in the last twenty years, whereas there is little evidence of similar historical research done on the local level. Hence the urban exhibition projects also preceded academic research on immigration history in urban space.[5] This chapter seeks to take a first step toward a better understanding of the increased commemoration of immigration history as an urban phenomenon. Based on the empirical data provided by exhibition curators on websites or in articles, and volumes or catalogues published along with the events,[6] it will analyze the triangular relationship of immigration, remembrance, and the city in both historical and comparative perspectives by focusing on three aspects: the emergence and changing patterns of representation since the 1970s; the function and pattern of memory; and the actors and places shaping the history of immigration exhibition.

* * * * *

It has already been mentioned that urban exhibitions about immigration in Germany preceded national and regional exhibitions by several years. While exhibition projects about immigration history as national or regional history only slowly emerged in reunified Germany at the end of the 1990s, displays on immigration history as urban history developed in the 1970s. In the aftermath of the cessation of labor recruitment, a growing number of families from abroad settled throughout the country, challenging the widespread assumption that the presence of foreign-born workers would only be temporary.[7] In cooperation with the *Berliner Festwochen*, the Cultural Office Kreuzberg set up a photo exhibition on Turkish immigrants in the Kreuzberg district in 1975 called *Mehmet Berlin'de Mehmet kam aus Anatolien.*[8] In the following year, Hamburg University's Seminar for Ethnology, Hamburg's Museum for Ethnology, and the German Orient Institute displayed two exhibitions on the local Turkish community. One shed light on Turkey as the homeland of one part of Hamburg's inhabitants, and the other one dealt with the living conditions of Turkish immigrants in the city.[9]

Taking place in a rapidly-changing demographic, social, and economic landscape, these early exhibitions from the 1970s were set in place by local institutions in Berlin and Hamburg—two cities with large immigrant populations—in order to make immigration history visible, foster knowledge about each other, and funnel mutual understanding in urban society. However, by focusing on the immigration of "guest workers" from Turkey, they singled out one particular national group, not only simplifying the heterogeneity of gender and age groups of Turkish immigrants, but also limiting immigration history to labor immigration from the Bosporus since the 1960s.[10] Furthermore, these exhibitions were hampered by a fundamental methodical contradiction, since they represented the receiving society from an urban perspective and the sending society from a national point of view. Despite these limitations, the exhibits from that period succeeded in bringing the history of immigrants in Germany to the broader public.

The first exhibitions in the mid-1970s served as a prelude to the commemoration of urban immigration history that began in the 1980s. Between 1980 and 1993, exhibitions launched during this second phase still focused mostly on labor immigration, but also integrated new actors and contents and put forward hidden aspects, persons, and places of immigration contributing to a more complex and less standardized understanding of immigration history. Building upon the exhibits from the 1970s, a group of female immigrants from Yugoslavia staged *Der Weg—Jugoslawische Frauen in Berlin*, an exhibition pulling women out of the shadow of their male counterparts and presenting the active role they played in historical immigration processes. This exhibit was the second one set up by immigrants themselves and the first and only one ever staged by and about foreign women exclusively.[11] *Der Weg* was followed in 1988 by another exhibition, set up by a group of foreign workers and entitled *Einwanderer—Einwohner—Einheimische? Ausländer und Inländer in Wilhelmsburg*. Like *Mehmet Berlin'de Mehmet kam aus Anatolien*, it concentrated on immigrants in a particular neighborhood of Hamburg by shedding light on both foreigners and Germans.[12]

The third (and still ongoing) phase, the beginnings of which go back to the early 1990s, has been characterized by a proliferation of the remembrance of urban immigration history—more than twenty-five exhibitions took place in less than two decades, compared to only five exhibitions in the previous twenty years. Since 2000, an exhibition has been organized almost every year.[13] The increase has been primarily an urban phenomenon; Rheine and Görlitz are the only smaller towns where a local exhibition has been staged so far. At the same time, the commemoration of immigration history was no longer exclusively urban, but was paralleled by a growing number of exhibitions on the national and regional level.

Amid growing tensions and xenophobia closely linked to the post-Wende integration of East Germany into a new unified state, this third period in the remembrance of immigration history as urban history was influenced by political controversies about the nature of citizenship and immigration. *Die türkische Einwanderung in Rheine: Stationen der türkischen Einwanderung* was the first exhibition to take place in this context, in a region where tensions and conflicts between German and Turkish inhabitants had occurred.[14] This event was followed by a series of exhibitions in various cities. On the fortieth anniversary of the labor recruitment agreement between Germany and Italy, Munich's cultural department displayed *"Für 50 Mark einen Italiener": Zur Geschichte der Gastarbeiter in München* at Munich's central train station in the spring of 2000.[15] In the same period, the Märkisches Museum Berlin organized *Durch Europa: In Berlin*, a collaborative project with Berlin's Institute of European Ethnology, the University for Arts and the Foundation for a city museum. Between 2000 and 2002, the Kreuzberg Museum presented a project on Turkish immigrants called *Wir waren die ersten . . . Türkiye' den Berlin'e*, dealing with the first generation of Turkish immigrants. Due to remarks from exhibition visitors, this first project was complemented by *Wir waren die nächsten . . .* portraying the second generation by the means of photographs and personal accounts.[16] In 2001, DOMiT marked the German-Turkish recruitment treaty's fortieth anniversary by presenting a bilingual project on immigration from Turkey to Cologne. In 2003–04 the Museum for European Cultures in Berlin and the Labor Museum in Hamburg displayed urban immigration history within the framework of the European project *Migration, Work and Identity: A History of People in Europe, Told in Museums*—a partnership of six European labor museums that was underwritten by the European Union. *MigrationsGeschichte(n) in Berlin*, an exhibition displayed in Berlin in 2003 and 2004, emphasized the possibility of several stories about immigration, whereas *Geteilte Welten: Einwanderer in Hamburg* played upon different facets of memory.[17] In 2005, the city of Munich observed the fiftieth anniversary of the German-Italian recruitment treaty by presenting *Xenopolis: Von der Faszination und Ausgrenzung des Fremden*, an exhibition on the treatment and exclusion of foreign-born inhabitants in the Bavarian capital since 1800. In 2006, the cultural center of Stuttgart-Nord, an urban neighborhood with a long tradition of immigration and a high percentage of inhabitants from abroad, organized *Meine Stuttgarter Geschichte: Interkulturelle Lebensverläufe in der Stadt.*[18] A year later, the District Museum Friedrichshain-Kreuzberg, a descendant of the former Kreuzberg Museum, set up *Gesichter der Migration.*[19] Since then, exhibitions have kept proliferating both in localities that had already organized exhibitions in previous years, such as Berlin, Frankfurt am Main, Munich, and Stuttgart, but also in cities that had not done so before like Aachen, Hanover, and Göttingen. In this third phase, some exhibitions remained closely linked to the nation-state, in that they were initiated on the occasion of the anniversary of one of the labor recruitment treaties or they continued to represent immigration history through national categories. Those that concentrated on the history of Turkish immigration maintained the focus on a nationally defined group of immigrants, which had become a target group for resentment and hostilities and were (and still are to a certain extent) stereotyped as culturally different and difficult to integrate into German society. Thus, they implicitly reinforced the image of Turks as the prototypical *Ausländer* in Germany—a role they inherited from the Italian labor migrants in the 1970s.[20] Nonetheless, the exhibitions on Turkish immigration organized from the 1990s onward opened new perspectives on the field. Not only did they shift the focus from men to women and subsequently proposed a more complex view of the immigration population, but they also took into account both the host society's as well as the immigrants' point of view. Hence, they not only enabled Turkish migrants to participate, but they also revealed previously unknown memories, experiences, and actions of these immigrants. The exhibitions subsequently shed light on the complexity and diversity of the immigration process.

Some exhibitions from this period offered a broader perspective on people on the move across time and space. Displaying women from Turkey in Berlin and female immigrants from Germany in Istanbul, *Erinnerungen an eine neue Heimat* for instance not only dealt with immigration to but also with emigration from Germany and thus took into account a form of mobility far less researched in German contemporary history than immigration into the country.[21] *Durch Europa: In Berlin* just as *Geteilte Welten* opened European perspectives. It portrayed contemporary immigration from all over Europe. Other exhibits took into account immigrants disregarding their national and geographic origins, some of them in a long term perspective. *Xenopolis* for instance reflected upon the exclusion and long-term resentment against foreigners in Munich over two centuries, *Schmelztiegel Duisburg: 500 Jahre Zuwanderung* offered an even longer retrospection. Exhibitions such as *Lebenswege ins Ungewisse—Migration in Görlitz-Zgorzelec von 1933 bis heute* displayed different forms of mobility, including forced migration during and in the aftermath of World War II. Besides, the exhibition in Görlitz was the first and so far the only one that displayed population movements in a city at the geographical margins of the

Federal Republic that had been divided into two different parts in 1945, one side in Poland and the other in the German Democratic Republic. More recent events, such as *crossing munich*, proposed a completely different narrative on immigration, underlining the long-lasting and fierce discussions on Germany's self-perception as an immigration country. They presented immigration as a central, daily occurrence in urban life in the past, present, and future, thereby as a *Normalfall* of urban development rather than as a threat or gain.[22]

The growing visualization and remembrance of immigration history since the 1990s not only reveal that the exhibition planners considered postwar immigration as primarily urban and defined German cities as immigration cities, but also highlight that exhibitions increasingly resulted from partnerships among museums, artists, and research institutes. Some even formed part of multilocal projects across national borders. Besides, they illustrate that exhibition concepts and representation techniques started to influence each other in the course of the horizontal and vertical expansion of commemorative practices, especially when the same actors participated in different events.[23] The project *crossing munich: orte, bilder und debatten der migration* is probably one of the most telling examples for the exchange of ideas and concepts along the expansion of exhibitions which had been impossible before. Approaching migration history from below without classifying people on the move it also avoids the methodological nationalism inherent in other projects and thus will certainly be a prescriptive vantage point for future projects itself.[24]

*   *   *   *   *

All the exhibitions meant active and sustainable memory work. First they typically assembled and preserved remains of the past. Ahead of historical research, the collection of memory items was all the more important, but all the more difficult for the early forerunners in the 1970s and 1980s. Recent events and ongoing projects point out that this has remained an important task even today.[25] Initially limited to the "first generation," the collection of memory items about immigration was slowly extended to the second and third generations, whose members were often born in Germany and had not experienced immigration personally. As a consequence, the collected memories extended to the period after the actual immigration had taken place, in other words, to processes of settlement. The first exhibitions concentrated exclusively on photographs, whereas subsequent ones included a growing variety of items and personal accounts that unfolded different dimensions and facets of immigration history and its actors.[26] The exhibition *Movements of Migration: Neue Perspektiven auf Migration* was even more ambitious. It aimed at integrating the gathered material into a digital "knowledge-archive" extending beyond the time of the exhibition.[27] Apart from collection and preservation, the exhibitions fostered active memory in two other ways. Trying to mobilize a growing range of memories, exhibits stimulated a process of self-reflection, especially among immigrants and their descendants. [28] By the way collected objects and accounts were displayed, they also offered different patterns of memory and a specific reading of the past.

Most exhibitions assessed the story from below rather than from above. A number of projects took over the immigrant perspective. *Drago Trumbetaš: Gastarbeiter in Frankfurt* even displayed memories of a single person—a male artist from Yugoslavia who had lived and worked in Frankfurt in the 1960s before moving back to Yugoslavia. Other events displayed memories of second and/or third generations. The participatory project in the Stuttgart-Nord neighborhood for instance traced the immigration history in the lives of third generation immigrants and in the place they had lived since birth. This was achieved first through the legacy of family memories, and second, by examining the interactions between urban and family memories. Third, the exhibit explored the historical memory of the city itself. The exhibition therefore intended to display the hybrid and interwoven character of memories in urban space and focused on both individual and collective memories.[29]

Several exhibitions presented local immigration history as shared but nonetheless divided memories. Organized in Cologne in 2003 *40 Jahre Fremde Heimat*, for instance, presented Turkish immigration in Cologne as a shared experience of the host society and first generation immigrants but pointed out that both sides had different memories linked to it.[30] *Die türkische Einwanderung in Rheine: Stationen der türkischen Einwanderung* highlighted the history of Turkish immigrants and their descendants both in Rheine and in Germany, but also explained Turkish culture and habits. The historical perspective on local immigration, together with the explanation of the Turkish way of living, had a didactic component. It was meant to acquaint Germans with the daily life of Turks, to alleviate misunderstandings, and to foster mutual understanding so as to improve the Turks' relationship with urban society.[31] Apart from that, the Turkish immigrants used their project to claim political rights for themselves. They were deeply convinced that their relationship with German citizens would be improved had they received the right to vote on the local level.[32]

In other cities, the display of different memories illustrated the contribution of immigrants to urban development in order to foster their recognition and create community cohesion on the local level, too. *Wir waren die ersten . . . Türkiye'den Berlin'e*, for instance, presented the numerous influences and marks of immigration from Turkey in the townscape and life in the Kreuzberg district.[33] *Xenopolis* und *"Für 50 Mark einen Italiener,"* on the other hand, remembered the biographies of male and female immigrants in order to put forward hidden memories, reveal an unknown chapter of urban history, and confront its visitors with representations of others.[34]

Regardless of the role of individual or collective memories in the named exhibitions, the narrative was always the same. All of them represented immigration as a constituent element of and a necessity for urban development. Therefore, remembering its history not only revealed unknown or unraveled entangled parts of urban history, but was also meant to unfold meaning both in the present and in the future, especially the acknowledgement of immigration as beneficial for urban life.

Influenced by new scientific, artistic, and museal approaches more recent displays such as *Geteilte Welten*, *crossing munich*, *Erinnerungen an eine neue Heimat*, and *Spurensuche: Die Griechen von Kettwig* diverged from previous exhibitions by looking upon immigration history as a story of both shared and individual memories. *Erinnerungen an eine neue Heimat* probably went the furthest in this direction by combining memories of people on the move in two different cities of two different countries. Approaching immigration through shared and individual memories made it possible to display mobility as a common experience of urban society at the same that it allowed to approach the plurality and diversity of experiences emerging from it. These experiences could hardly be combined, classified, graded or reduced, but constituted in their totality as well as variety an important part of the city's mnemoscape and identity. It was even one of the most important goals of *Geteilte Welten* to give "urban memory on immigration as many faces and voices as possible."[35]

*　　*　　*　　*　　*

In the exhibitions organized on local immigration history, the city played a crucial role both as a place and as an actor. It was the place where different memories were generated and coexisted, and at the same time, it was *a* place, if not *the* place, where memories on immigration were visualized and remembered. The events displayed in urban places recalling postwar immigration history into the city even recalled concrete physical places. *Meine Stuttgarter Geschichte: Interkulturelle Lebensverläufe in der Stadt*, for instance, took place in *Haus Nr. 49*, a social meeting point for the immigrants' descendants in the neighborhood that provided social events and free time activities. *Spurensuche* was organized in a cotton factory in Essen-Kettwig where male and female employees from Greece had worked together with people of various origins and backgrounds day after day, and *"Für 50 Mark einen Italiener": Zur Geschichte der Gastarbeiter in München* was displayed in Munich's central station, a place charged with memories of postwar labor immigration. The station not only represented an important communication and social meeting point but also a point of contact with the host society and a point of arrival, departure, and transit for immigrants. In fact, the immigrants from Italy, Yugoslavia, Greece, Turkey, and Tunisia all had to transit through the station. Hence, the station represented a *lieu de mémoire* for urban as well as national immigration history.[36] Inscribed into urban landscape at different locations and conceived as a "Walk of Migration," *Movements of Migration* even recalled a variety of sense-making places within the city.[37] Exhibitions on urban immigration history concerned individual or collective, shared or divided, generational or intergenerational, male or female, local, national or transnational memories. Despite these differences, they always had a threefold meaning: writing immigration history in the "spatial framework" of the city, anchoring it as a focal point in the cities' mnemoscape, and placing immigrants and their descendants at the heart of urban society. Thus, memory work cannot only be understood as a major attempt to reshape and reinterpret urban history. It also established (postwar) immigration history as a new *lieu de mémoire* the way Pierre Nora and other historians conceived it.[38] However, in contrast with Nora's original concept it is grounded on the local level and does not pretend unambiguity but relies on a highly fragmented and hybrid mnemoscape.

In the staging of immigration history, the urban exhibitions certainly represent a specific form of commemoration. One of their characteristics may be that they offered much more room for immigrant entrepreneurship than the events on the regional and national level. Thus, they were not limited to representation, but also functioned as places for negotiating the past, present, and future as well as for fostering both social inclusion and social cohesion. Furthermore, as in Rheine, they sometimes reversed accustomed roles of hospitality, as immigrants acquired the role of hosts and transformed the hosts into guests.[39] A second characteristic might be that they turned the relationship between the local, national, and transnational upside down by writing national and transnational memories into urban narratives and thereby "locating migration."[40] However, none of them undermined or refuted nationally or transnationally coined memories. Hence they complemented—rather than competed with—national and/or transnational representations in the ongoing struggle for an adequate narrative of Germany's immigration history in the second half of the twentieth century. A third characteristic may be the combination of new approaches and multiple perspectives. *Spurensuche* for instance followed people on the move instead of assessing them at their arrival point and thus chose a perspective commonly used by scholars in the emerging field of mobility studies.[41] Methodologically, urban exhibitions are therefore very much ahead of historical research on immigration issues. While there is no doubt about the pioneering character of the exhibitions on immigration history as urban history, it remains difficult to evaluate their actual impact on the mnemoscape of urban society, no matter how extensive they were. It is true that media coverage of these exhibitions varied, according to the financial, personal and technical support they enjoyed. *Crossing munich*, for example, utilized significantly more resources than other projects, allowing it to make itself much more visible than other exhibitions. It is also true that certain events received large public attention in the city or the respective neighborhood, even among immigrants who were not part of the venue's ordinary visitors.[42] However, neither the publicity nor the number of visitors really inform us about the question of whether the exhibitions provoked any change in the perception of Germany's immigration history and tell us even less about the question of how the mediated memories and interpretations were appropriated by the public and whether the exhibitions succeeded in implementing local immigration history in the mnemoscape of urban society. Two things seem to be certain, though. Immigration history as urban history has reached a privileged place in urban identity building,[43] and it may even be considered the "decentralized" answer to the request of a national site for immigration history in Germany, as the journalist Manuel Gogos suggested a few years ago.[44]

List of Exhibitions

Table 11.1. Urban Exhibitions in Chronological Order (1975–2016)

Title	Place	Date	Organized by
Mehmet kam aus Anatolien	Haus am Mariannenplatz 2	6 Sept–9 Nov 1975	Cultural Office Kreuzberg, Berliner Festspiele
Türkei—Heimat von Menschen in unserer Stadt	Museum for Ethnology Hamburg	June 1976 (Turkish Week)	Working group "Turkey" at the Seminar for Ethnology of Hamburg University, Hamburg's Museum for Ethnology, the German Orient Institute
Türkische Mitbürger in Hamburg	Museum for Ethnology Hamburg	June 1976 (Turkish Week)	Working group "Turkey" at the Seminar for Ethnology of Hamburg University, Hamburg's Museum for Ethnology, the German Orient Institute
Der Weg—Jugoslawische Frauen in Berlin	Berlin	Beginning of the 1980s	Female immigrants
Einwanderer—Einwohner—Einheimische? Ausländer und Inländer in Wilhelmsburg	Bürgerhaus Hamburg-Wilhelmsburg	23 Feb–15 Apr 1988	Bürgerinitiatve ausländische Arbeitnehmer e.V., Hamburg
Eingewandert—WIR in Braunschweig	Braunschweig	1993	Horst Weber
Die türkische Einwanderung in Rheine: Stationen der türkischen Einwanderung	Turkish School, Parents, Sports, and Cultural association, Rheine	1998	Turkish School, Parents, Sports, and Cultural association, Rheine
"Für 50 Mark einen Italiener": Zur Geschichte der Gastarbeiter in München	Munich, Rathausgalerie	10 Mar–7 May 2000	Munich's Cultural Department

Title	Place	Date	Organized by
Durch Europa: In Berlin	Berlin	24 Aug–26 Nov 2000	Institute for European Ethnology, Institute for Art of Berlin's University for Arts, Foundation City Museum Berlin
Wir waren die ersten . . . Türkiye'den Berlin'e	Kreuzberg Museum Berlin	26 Nov 2000–17 Mar 2002	Kreuzberg Museum, Meeting Centre of the Arbeiterwohlfahrt, Kotti-Nachbarschafts- and Gemeinwesenverein
40 Jahre Fremde Heimat— Einwanderung aus der Türkei in Köln	Historical Town Hall Cologne	27 Oct–23 Nov 2001	DOMiT
Wir waren die nächsten . . .	Kreuzberg Museum, Berlin	2001–02	Kreuzberg Museum, Berlin
MigrationsGeschichte(n) in Berlin	Museum for European Cultures—State Museums Berlin	11 July 2003 –01 Feb 2004	Museum for European Cultures—State Museums, Berlin
Geteilte Welten. Einwanderer in Hamburg	Labor Museum Hamburg	31 Oct 2003–20 June 2004	Museum for European Cultures—State Museums, Berlin
Von Fremden zu Frankfurtern—Zuwanderung und Zusammenleben	Historical Museum, Frankfurt am Main	19 May 2004 –27 Mar 2011	Historical Museum, Frankfurt am Main
Jeder nach seiner Façon: 300 Jahre Zuwanderung nach Friedrichshain-Kreuzberg	Museum of the Friedrichshain-Kreuzberg district	13 Apr 2005 –17 Oct 2010	Museum of the Friedrichshain-Kreuzberg district
Xenopolis: Von der Faszination und Ausgrenzung des Fremden	Rathausgalerie Munich	27 Apr–12 June 2005	Munich's Cultural Department
Meine Stuttgarter Geschichte: Interkulturelle Lebensverläufe in der Stadt	Haus 49 Stuttgart-Nord, Townhall Stuttgart	15 Mar–28 Apr 2006	Social Neighborhood Center, Stuttgart-Nord
Gesichter der Migration	Museum of the district Friedrichshain Kreuzberg	29 Apr–10 Jul 2007	Museum of the district Friedrichshain-Kreuzberg
crossing munich: orte, bilder und debatten der migration	Rathausgalerie Munich	10 July–15 Sept 2009	Munich's Cultural Department
Spurensuche: Die Griechen von Kettwig	J.W. Scheidt Manufacturing Plant, Essen-Kettwig	1 May–1 June 2010	Manuel Gogos (exhibition curator)
Erinnerungen an eine neue Heimat: Aus dem Leben deutscher Istanbulerinnen und türkischer Berlinerinnen— Yeni Memleketten Anılar; İstanbullu Alman, Berlinli Türk kadınların hayatından	First in Turkish cities, afterwards in German cities	Travelling exhibition since May 2010	KulturForum TürkeiDeutschland

Title	Place	Date	Organized by
'Liebe auf den zweiten Blick': 50 Jahre Anwerbeabkommen mit Griechenland	Municipal Museum of Stuttgart	16 Nov–28 Dec 2010	Municipal Museum of Stuttgart
'Der ausländische Mitbürger': ArbeitsmigrantInnen in Fotografien der Berliner Verwaltung	Museum Mitte, Berlin	25 Nov 2010–30 June 2011	Museum Mitte, Berlin
'Gastarbeit' in Hannover: Geschichte vom Kommen, Gehen und Bleiben	Historical Museum, Hanover	2 Feb–27 Mar 2011	Historical Museum, Hanover
Bochum: Das fremde und das eigene	Municipal Archives, Bochum	31 Mar–24 Apr 2011	Municipal Archives, Bochum
Lebenswege ins Ungewisse—Migration in Görlitz-Zgorzelec von 1933 bis heute	Schlesisches Museum, Görlitz	21 May 2011–25 Mar 2012	Schlesisches Museum, Görlitz
'Merhaba Stuttgart' . . . oder die Geschichte von Simit und Brezel	Linden-Museum, Stuttgart	5 June–18 Dec 2011	Stuttgart's Linden-Museum, Municipal Museum, German-Turkish Forum, Wirtschaftsgymnasium West and Schillerschule
Schmelztiegel Duisburg: 500 Jahre Zuwanderung	Kultur- und Stadthistorisches Museum, Duisburg	25 Sept 2011 –8 Jan 2012	Kultur- und Stadthistorisches Museum, Duisburg
Bewegung: Migration in Aachen seit 1945	Adult education center, Aachen, and other places in the city of Aachen	30 Oct 2011 –Dec 2013	Adult education center, Aachen
Angeworben—Gekommen—Geblieben 1961 bis 1975	Municipal Archives, Bochum	Since 4 Nov 2011	Municipal Archives, Bochum
Movements of Migration: Neue Perspektiven auf Migration	Künstlerhaus, Göttingen, and other places in the city	Mar 2013	University of Göttingen, the Kunstverein, and the Integration Council of the City of Göttingen
I primi Italiani—Italienische Premieren	Municipal Museum, Wolfsburg	15 Dec 2012 –1 Apr 2013	Municipal Museum, Wolfsburg
Drago Trumbetaš: Gastarbeiter in Frankfurt	Historical Museum, Frankfurt am Main	3 May–15 Sept 2013	Historical Museum, Frankfurt am Main
ortsgespräche. stadt—migration—geschichte: vom halleschen zum frankfurter tor	Friedrichshain-Kreuzberg-Museum	Jan 2013–31 Dec 2016	Friedrichshain-Kreuzberg-Museum

Table 11.2. Regional Exhibitions in Chronological Order (2000–2015)

Title	Place	Date	Organized by
So nah—so fern	Westphalian State Museum of Industrial Heritage, The Hannover Colliery, Bochum	2000	Westphalian State Museum of Industrial Heritage, The Hannover Colliery, Bochum
Gezwungenermaßen: Zwangsarbeit in der Region Rhein-Erft-Rur	More than 15 municipalities	Traveling exhibition since 3 May 2002	Working group of archivists of the district Rhein-Erft
hier geblieben—Zuwanderung und Integration in Niedersachsen 1945 bis heute	Hanover, Osnabrück, Oldenburg, Wolfsburg, Braunschweig, Syke, Peine, Göttingen	23 Oct 2002– 12 Sept 2004	Regional Center for Political Education, Historical Museum Hanover
Westfalczycy—Ruhrpolen Zuwanderer aus Polen im Ruhrgebiet 1871 bis heute	Westphalian State Museum of Industrial Heritage, The Hannover Colliery, Bochum	18 Aug–28 Oct 2007	Westphalian State Museum of Industrial Heritage, The Hannover Colliery, Bochum
Angekommen: Zuwanderung ins Oberbergische nach 1945	Municipalities in the region, Museum	Traveling exhibition 19 May 2008– 13 Feb 2009	Museum Schloss Homburg
Hauptsach se schaffet	Uhrenindustriemuseum, Villingen-Schwenningen	5 July–30 Aug 2008	Uhrenindustriemuseum, Villingen-Schwenningen
Eiskalte Leidenschaft: Italienische Eismacher im Ruhrgebiet	Westphalian State Museum of Industrial Heritage, The Hannover Colliery, Bochum	14 June–11 Oct 2009	Westphalian State Museum of Industrial Heritage, The Hannover Colliery, Bochum
Ihr und Wir: Integration der Heimatvertriebenen in Baden-Württemberg	Haus der Geschichte Baden-Württemberg	13 Nov 2009– 22 Aug 2010	Haus der Geschichte Baden-Württemberg
Nach Westen: Zuwanderung aus Osteuropa ins Revier	Westphalian State Museum of Industrial Heritage, The Hannover Colliery	10 June–28 Oct 2012	Westphalian State Museum of Industrial Heritage, The Hannover Colliery
Nicht von hier? Migration und Integration im Celler Land	Bomann-Museum Celle, Museum für Kunstgeschichte	Permanent exhibition since 2013	Bomann-Museum Celle, Museum für Kunstgeschichte
Glückauf und Uğur ola. Türkische Kumpel zwischen Zonguldak und Ruhrgebiet	Deutsches Bergbau-Museum Bochum (DBM)	31 Oct 2014– 12 Apr 2015	Deutsches Bergbau-Museum Bochum (DBM)
Von Kuzorra bis Özil. Die Geschichte von Fußball und Migration im Ruhrgebiet	Westphalian State Museum of Industrial Heritage, The Hannover Colliery, Bochum	21 Aug 2015– 22 Nov 2015	Westphalian State Museum of Industrial Heritage, The Hannover Colliery, Bochum

Table 11.3. National Exhibitions in Chronological Order (1981–2009)

Title	Place	Date	Organized by
Morgens Deutsch-land—abends Türkei	Kreuzberg district Berlin	26 May–23 Aug 1981	Cultural Office Kreuzberg
Griechen und Deutsche—Bilder von Anderen	Wurttemberg's Regional Museum Stuttgart	Beginning of the 1980s	Wurttemberg's Regional Museum, Stuttgart
Fremde Heimat: Eine Geschichte der Einwan-derung aus der Türkei	Ruhrlandmuseum Essen	15 Feb–2 Aug 1998	Ruhrlandmuseum Essen, DOMiT
Fremde in Deutsch-land—Deutschland in der Fremde	Cloppenburg	1999	Museumsdorf Cloppenburg, Wurttemberg's Regional Museum, Stuttgart, Altona's Museum, Regional Museum for the North of Germany, Museum of the History of Leipzig, Magdeburg's Museum for Cultural History
Neapel Bochum, Rimini—Arbeiten in Deutschland	Westphalian Museum for Industry Hanover Mine	12 July–26 Oct 2003	Westphalian Museum for Industry Hanover Mine
Unerwünscht: Eine Reise wie keine andere	Labor Museum, Hamburg	8 Nov–19 Dec 1999	Hamburg's working group Asyl e.V., Labor Museum, Hamburg
Blicke auf die Einwan-derungsgesellschaft Deutschland	Internetpresentation, Malakoffturm in Bottrop	2003, 2004	Network Migration in Europe
Zuwanderungsland Deutschland: Migra-tionen 1500–2005	German Historical Museum Berlin	22 Oct 2005– 12 Feb 2006	German Historical Museum, Berlin
Zwischen Kommen und Gehen . . . und doch Bleiben— 'Gastarbeiter in Deutschland 1955–1973'	40 different municipali-ties in Germany, among them Mainz, Nurnberg, Stuttgart, Mannheim, Ravensburg, Waiblingen, Ulm, Koblenz, Lörrach, Biberach and Offenburg	Since Feb 2005	Editorial board of the radio station SWR International
Aufbau West: Neubeginn zwischen Vertreibung und Wirtschaftswunder	Westphalian State Museum of Industrial Heritage, The Zollern Colliery, Dortmund	18 Sept 2005 –26 Mar 2006	Westphalian State Museum of Industrial Heritage, The Zollern Colliery, Dortmund
Projekt Migration: Zwei, drei Jahre Alemanya . . .	Cologne	1 Oct 2005– 15 Jan 2006	DOMiT, Cologne's Art Association, Institute for Cultural Anthropology and European Ethnology at Frankfurt University

Title	Place	Date	Organized by
Döner, Dienste und Design: Eine Werkausstellung zur Migrantenökonomie	Museum Dahlem, Berlin	21 Nov 2009 –28 Feb 2010	Museum Dahlem, Berlin
A chacun ses étrangers? France-Allemagne de 1871 à aujourd'hui Fremde?	Cité nationale de l'histoire de l'immigration, Paris	Dec 2008– Apr 2009	Cité nationale de l'histoire de l'immigration, Paris
Bilder von den 'Anderen' in Deutschland und Frankreich seit 1871	German Historical Museum, Berlin	Oct 2009 –Jan 2010	German Historical Museum, Berlin
Angekommen: Russlanddeutsches Leben	Ausstellungsscheune Westendorf	1 Apr–31 Oct 2009	LWL-Freilichtmuseum Detmold

Bettina Severin-Barboutie is professor of modern and contemporary history at the Justus-Liebig-Universität in Giessen (Germany) and a research fellow within the Research Group *Sirice* at the University Paris I Panthéon-Sorbonne. Her current research focuses on flight, migration and mobility, on visual media and on epistemological questions such as the study of the undocumented past. She is the author of *Französische Herrschaftspolitik und Modernisierung. Verfassungs- und Verwaltungsreformen im Großherzogtum Berg (1806–1813)*, editor of *Stadt in Bewegung. Wanderungsprozesse in pluridisziplinärer Perspektive* (2014), and co-editor of *Flucht als Handlungszusammenhang* (2018) as well as of *Verflochtene Vergangenheiten. Geschichtscomics in Europa, Asien und Amerika. Perspektiven auf ein Forschungsfeld* (2014). She has recently finished a project on *Migration als Bewegung am Beispiel von Stuttgart und Lyon nach 1945*.

Notes

To Marie E. Smith, in fond memory.

1. Jan Motte and Rainer Ohliger, "Men and Women With(out) History? Looking for 'Lieux de Mémoire' in Germany's Immigration Society," in *Enlarging European Memory: Migration Movements in Historical Perspective*, ed. Mareike König, Rainer Ohliger (Ostfildern, 2006), 154–56; Michael Stephan, "Archive und Migration," in *Archive und Migration*, ed. Roland Deigendesch and Peter Müller (Stuttgart, 2014), 25–27.
2. See the exhibition list at the end of this article as well as the regularly updated list of former and ongoing exhibitions on the following website: www.lwl.org/industriemuseum/standorte/zeche-hannover/migration-ausstellen. Retrieved 16 April 2016.

3. See URL: http://www.tokki.cc/index.php?/information/contact/. Retrieved 16 April 2016.
4. See URL: http://www.zeus.phil-fak.uni-koeln.de/fileadmin/zeus/pdfs/Promotionsprojekt _-_Sandra_Vacca.pdf. Retrieved 31 July 2016.
5. For an overview of historiography on migration in the second half of the twentieth century see Bettina Severin-Barboutie, "Historische Migrationsforschung auf dem Prüfstand," in *Archive und Migration*, ed. Roland Deigendesch and Peter Müller (Stuttgart, 2014), 10–17.
6. Articles: Martin Düspohl, "'In jeder Generation tauscht sich die Bevölkerung einmal aus . . .' Migrationsgeschichte in der Konzeption des Kruzberg Museums (Berlin)," in *Geschichte und Gedächtnis in der Einwanderungsgesellschaft: Migration zwischen historischer Rekonstruktion und Erinnerungspolitik*, ed. Jan Motte and Ranier Ohliger (Essen, 2004), 159–79; Jürgen Ellermeyer, "Geteilte Welten. Hamburg und Migration: Ein Projekt des Museums der Arbeit," in *"Wir sind auch da!" Über das Leben von und mit Migranten in europäischen Großstädten*, ed. Angelika Eder (Hamburg, 2003), 375–84; Caroline Gritschke, "Stadt und Biographiegeschichte: Migrationserfahrungen in transnationalen Räumen. Das Ausstellungsprojekt: 'Meine Stuttgarter Geschichte'," in *Migrationserfahrungen—Migrationsstrukturen*, ed. Alexander Schunka, Eckart Olshausen (Stuttgart, 2010), 175–96; Natalie Bayer, "'Crossing Munich': Eine Migrationsausstellung aus den Positionen Wissenschaft und Kunst," in *Das partizipative Museum: Zwischen Teilhabe und User Generated Content. Neue Anforderungen an kulturhistorische Ausstellungen*, ed. Susanne Gesser, Martin Handschin, Angela Jannell, Sybille Lichtensteiger, (Bielefeld, 2012), 257–61. Volumes or catalogues: Kunstamt Kreuzberg, ed., *Mehmet Berlin'de Mehmet kam aus Anatolien. Ausstellung im Haus am Mariannenplatz* (Berlin, 1975); Horst Weber, *Eingewandert: Geschichte und Lebenssituation von ArbeitsmigrantInnen in Braunschweig* (Braunschweig, 1993); Dursun Ceylan, *Die türkische Einwanderung in Rheine: Stationen der türkischen Einwanderung. Rheine'deki Türk Göçu. Kesitleriyle Almanya'yadaki Türk Göçu* (Rheine, 1998); Franziska Dunkel, Gabrielle Stramglia-Faggion, *"Für 50 Mark einen Italiener": Zur Geschichte der Gastarbeiter in München* (Munich, 2000); Institut für Europäische Ethnologie, ed., *Durch Europa: In Berlin; Porträts und Erkundungen* (Berlin, 2001); Dokumentationszentrum und Museum über die Migration aus der Türkei e.V. (DOMiT), ed., *40 Jahre Fremde Heimat—Einwanderung aus der Türkei in Köln* (Cologne, 2001); Angela Koch, *Xenopolis: Von der Faszination und Ausgrenzung des Fremden in München* (Berlin, 2005); Natalie Bayer et al, eds., *crossing munich: beiträge zur migration aus kunst, wissenschaft und aktivismus* (Munich, 2009); Haus der Geschichte Baden-Württemberg, ed. *Ihr und Wir: Integration der Heimatvertriebenen in Baden-Württemberg* (Stuttgart, 2009); Klaus Wisotzky, Ingrid Wölk, eds., *Fremd(e) im Revier!?, Zuwanderung und Fremdsein im Ruhrgebiet* (Essen, 2010); Schlesisches Museum zu Görlitz, ed., *Lebenswege ins Ungewisse: Görlitz—Zgorzelec 1933–2011* (Görlitz, 2011); LWL-Industriemuseum, ed., *Nach Westen: Zuwanderung aus Osteuropa ins Ruhrgebiet* (Essen, 2012). Websites: http://www.lwl.org/LWL/Kultur/wim/portal/S/hannover/ort/migration/exponat/ausstellungen/sonderausstellungen/2010/GriechenKettwig/. Retrieved 27 October 2014; http://mittemuseum.de/deutsch/ausstellung/vergangene-ausstellung/der-auslaendische-mitbuerger/der-auslaendische-mitbuerger.html. Retrieved 27 October 2014; http://www.archive.nrw.de/kommunalarchive/kommunalarchive_a-d/b/Bochum/Veranstaltungen/index.php Retrieved 27 October 2014; http://www.

movements-of-migration.org/cms/ausstellung/. Retrieved 30 October 2014; http://www.historisches-museum.frankfurt.de/index.php?article_id=748. Retrieved 28 October 2014; http://www.fhxb-museum.de/index.php?id=267. Retrieved 30 October 2014.

7. See Abdelmalek Sayad's general reflections on the link between this assumption and the state, Abdelmalek Sayad, *L'immigration ou les paradoxes de l'altérité*, 2 vols. (Paris, 2006), vol. 1, 161ff.

8. Kunstamt Kreuzberg, *Mehmet*; Düspohl, "Generation," 159.

9. Aytaç Eryilmaz, "Deutschland braucht ein Migrationsmuseum: Plädoyer für einen Paradigmenwechsel in der Kulturpolitik," in *Geschichte und Gedächtnis in der Einwanderungsgesellschaft: Migration zwischen historischer Rekonstruktion und Erinnerungspolitik*, ed. Jan Motte and Rainer Ohliger (Essen, 2004), 305–19, 312; Ellermeyer, "Welten," 375.

10. It needs to be pointed out though that the Cultural Office Kreuzberg had organized another exhibition on immigration from Silesia beforehand. See Düspohl, "Generation," 160–61.

11. Motte and Ohliger, "Men," 154.

12. Ellermeyer, "Welten," 375; Düspohl, "Generation," 159.

13. See the already mentioned list of former and ongoing exhibitions on the following website: http://www.lwl.org/LWL/Kultur/wim/portal/S/hannover/ort/migration/exponat/ausstellungen/. Retrieved 10 September 2013.

14. Ceylan, *Rheine*.

15. Dunkel and Stramglia-Faggion, *Italiener*.

16. Düspohl, "Generation".

17. Ellermeyer, "Welten"; URL: http://www.museum-der-arbeit.de/Sonder/GeteilteWelten/. Retrieved 11 July 2012.

18. Gritschke, "Stadt".

19. See URL: http://www.kreuzbergmuseum.de/index.php?id=51. Retrieved 2 July 2012.

20. Bettina Severin-Barboutie, "Die Fremdwahrnehmung von Italienern und Türken in der Bundesrepublik," in *Dolce Vita? Das Bild der italienischen Migranten in Deutschland*, ed. Oliver Janz and Roberto Sala (Frankfurt am Main, 2011), 125–27.

21. The most recent study is Jan Philipp Sternberg, *Auswanderungsland Bundesrepublik: Denkmuster und Debatten in Politik und Medien 1945–2000* (Paderborn, 2012).

22. Andrea Engl and Sabine Hess, "crossing munich ein Ausstellungsprojekt aus der perspektive der migration," in *crossing munich*, 14.

23. This was the case for instance for Necati Gürbaca who participated in *Morgens Deutschland—abends Türkei* as well as in *Wir waren die ersten . . . Türkiye'den Berlin'e.* See Düspohl, "Generation," 169f.

24. Engl and Hess, "crossing," 11–13.

25. See Anja Dauschek, "Meine Stadt—meine Geschichte," in *Archive und Migration*, ed. Roland Deigendesch and Peter Müller, (Stuttgart, 2014); the volume *NeuZugänge: Museen, Sammlungen und Migration; Eine Laborausstellung*, ed. Lorraine Bluche, Christine Gerbich, Susan Kamel, Susanne Lanwerd, Frauke Miera (Bielefeld, 2013); 78–92; DOMiD-Dokumentationszentrum und Museum über die Migration in Deutschland e.V., ed., *Stand der Dinge: Sammlung und Darstellung der Migrationsgeschichte.* Symposium am 25 April 2012 im Rautenstrauch-Joest-Museum, Köln (Tagungsdokumentation), retrieved 16 July 2012 from URL: http://www.domid.org/pdf/Stand_der_Dinge_Symposiumsdokumentation.pdf.

26. For collection strategies, see Dauschek, "Stadt", 91–90.

27. URL: http://english.kunstvereingoettingen.de/ausstellungen/movements-of-migration/. Retrieved 29 October 2014.
28. Düspohl, "Generation," 166.
29. Gritschke, "Stadt," 3f.
30. Dokumentationszentrum, *40 Jahre*, 8.
31. Ceylan, *Rheine*, 12.
32. Ibid.
33. Düspohl, "Generation," 162–174; URL: http://www.kreuzbergmuseum.de/index.php?id=98/. Retrieved 12 July 2012.
34. Dunkel, Stramglia-Faggion, *Italiener*, 10–12.
35. "Dem Einwanderungsgedächtnis der Stadt möglichst viele Gesichter und Stimmen . . . geben." Ellermeyer, "Welten," 382.
36. For the symbolic meanings of stations, see Wolfgang Kaschuba, *Die Überwindung der Distanz: Zeit und Raum in der europäischen Moderne* (Frankfurt am Main, 2004), 140.
37. URL: http://www.movements-of-migration.org/cms/ausstellung/. Retrieved 30 October 2014.
38. See the overview in Tillmann Robbe, *Historische Forschung und Geschichtsvermittlung: Erinnerungsorte in der deutschsprachigen Geschichtswissenschaft* (Göttingen, 2009), 81–112. The exhibition curators in Göttingen even used this term explicitly for the digital knowledge-archive in construction. Retrieved 30 October 2014 from URL: http://www.movements-of-migration.org/cms/ausstellung/.
39. The role of hospitality was also reversed during holidays, see for example the following article: Gast beim Gastarbeiter, in *Die Zeit*, 7 September 1962, p. 30, URL: http://www.zeit.de/1962/49/gast-beim-gastarbeiter. Retrieved 22 March 2016.
40. Nina Glick Schiller and Ayse Çağlar, "Introduction: 'Migrants and Cities,'" in *Locating Migration: Rescaling Cities and Migrants*, ed. Nina Glick Schiller and Ayse Çağlar (Ithaca, NY; London, 2011), 1–4.
41. See, for instance, Tim Cresswell, *On the Move* (London, 2006); John Urry, *Mobilities* (Cambridge, 2007).
42. Düspohl, "Generation," 162; see also the remarks about the feedback of the exhibition in Hanover, URL: http://www.lwl.org/LWL/Kultur/wim/portal/S/hannover/ort/migration/exponat/ausstellungen/sonderausstellungen/2011/Gastarbeit_Hannover/. Retrieved 28 October 2014.
43. Ongoing museum projects in different German cities leave no doubt about this. See, for instance, the exhibition in the District Museum Friedrichshain-Kreuzberg: *ortsgespräche. stadt—migration—geschichte: vom halleschen zum frankfurter tor*. URL: http://www.kreuzbergmuseum.de/index.php?id=20. Retrieved 17 February 2012.
44. Manuel Gogos, "Schaut! Uns! An!" *Der Tagesspiegel*, 10 January 2011. Retrieved 27 October 2014 from URL: http://www.tagesspiegel.de/kultur/ausstellungen-zum-thema-migration-schaut-uns-an/3694136.html.

Bibliography

Bayer, Natalie. "'Crossing Munich': Eine Migrationsausstellung aus den Positionen Wissenschaft und Kunst." In *Das partizipative Museum: Zwischen Teilhabe und User Generated Content. Neue Anforderungen an kulturhistorische Ausstellungen,* ed. Susanne Gesser, Martin Handschin, Angela Jannell, Sybille Lichtensteiger. Bielefeld, 2012.

Bayer, Natalie, et al., eds. *crossing munich: beiträge zur migration aus kunst, wissenschaft und aktivismus*. Munich, 2009.

Bluche, Lorraine, Christine Gerbich, Susan Kamel, Susanne Lanwerd, Frauke Miera, eds. *NeuZugänge: Museen, Sammlungen und Migration. Eine Laborausstellung* Bielefeld, 2013.

Ceylan, Dursun. *Die türkische Einwanderung in Rheine: Stationen der türkischen Einwanderung. Rheine'deki Türk Göçu. Kesitleriyle Almanya'yadaki Türk Göçu.* Rheine, 1998.

Cresswell, Tim. *On the Move*. London, 2006.

Dauschek, Anja. "Meine Stadt—meine Geschichte." In *Archive und Migration*, ed. Roland Deigendesch, Peter Müller. Stuttgart, 2014.

DOMiD-Dokumentationszentrum und Museum über die Migration in Deutschland e.V., ed. *Stand der Dinge: Sammlung und Darstellung der Migrationsgeschichte*. Symposium am 25 April 2012 im Rautenstrauch-Joest-Museum, Köln (Tagungsdokumentation). URL: http://www.domid.org/pdf/Stand_der_Dinge_ Symposiumsdokumentation.pdf. Retrieved 16 July 2012.

Dokumentationszentrum und Museum über die Migration aus der Türkei e.V. (DOMiT), ed. *40 Jahre Fremde Heimat—Einwanderung aus der Türkei in Köln*. Cologne, 2001.

Düspohl, Martin. "'In jeder Generation tauscht sich die Bevölkerung einmal aus . . .' Migrationsgeschichte in der Konzeption des Kreuzberg Museums (Berlin)." In *Geschichte und Gedächtnis in der Einwanderungsgesellschaft: Migration zwischen historischer Rekonstruktion und Erinnerungspolitik*, ed. Jan Motte and Ranier Ohliger. Essen, 2004.

Dunkel, Franziska, Gabrielle Stramglia-Faggion. *"Für 50 Mark einen Italiener": Zur Geschichte der Gastarbeiter in München*. Munich, 2000.

Ellermeyer, Jürgen. "Geteilte Welten. Hamburg und Migration: Ein Projekt des Museums der Arbeit." In *"Wir sind auch da!" Über das Leben von und mit Migranten in europäischen Großstädten*, ed. Angelika Eder. Hamburg, 2003.

Engl, Andrea and Sabine Hess, "crossing munich ein Ausstellungsprojekt aus der perspektive der migration." In *crossing munich*, ed. Natalie Bayer et al. Munich, 2009.

Eryilmaz, Aytaç. "Deutschland braucht ein Migrationsmuseum: Plädoyer für einen Paradigmenwechsel in der Kulturpolitik." In *Geschichte und Gedächtnis in der Einwanderungsgesellschaft: Migration zwischen historischer Rekonstruktion und Erinnerungspolitik*, ed. Jan Motte and Ranier Ohliger. Essen, 2004.

Gogos, Manuel. "Schaut! Uns! An!" *Der Tagesspiegel*, 10 January 2011. URL: http:// www.tagesspiegel.de/kultur/ausstellungen-zum-thema-migration-schaut-uns- an/3694136.html. Retrieved 27 October 2014.

Gritschke, Caroline. "Stadt und Biographiegeschichte: Migrationserfahrungen in transnationalen Räumen. Das Ausstellungsprojekt: 'Meine Stuttgarter Geschichte'." In *Migrationserfahrungen—Migrationsstrukturen*, ed. Alexander Schunka, Eckart Olshausen. Stuttgart, 2010.

Haus der Geschichte Baden-Württemberg, ed. *Ihr und Wir: Integration der Heimatvertriebenen in Baden-Württemberg.* Stuttgart, 2009.

Institut für Europäische Ethnologie, ed. *Durch Europa: In Berlin; Porträts und Erkundungen.* Berlin, 2001.

Kaschuba, Wolfgang. *Die Überwindung der Distanz: Zeit und Raum in der europäischen Moderne.* Frankfurt am Main, 2004.

Koch, Angela. *Xenopolis: Von der Faszination und Ausgrenzung des Fremden in München.* Berlin, 2005.

Kunstamt Kreuzberg, ed. *Mehmet Berlin'de Mehmet kam aus Anatolien.* Ausstellung im Haus am Mariannenplatz. Berlin, 1975.

LWL-Industriemuseum, ed. *Nach Westen: Zuwanderung aus Osteuropa ins Ruhrgebiet.* Essen, 2012.

Motte, Jan, and Rainer Ohliger. "Geschichte und Gedächtnis in der Einwanderungsgesellschaft: Einführende Betrachtungen." In *Geschichte und Gedächtnis in der Einwanderungsgesellschaft: Migration zwischen historischer Rekonstruktion und Erinnerungspolitik,* ed. Jan Motte and Rainer Ohliger. Essen, 2004.

Robbe, Tillmann. *Historische Forschung und Geschichtsvermittlung: Erinnerungsorte in der deutschsprachigen Geschichtswissenschaft.* Göttingen, 2009.

Sayad, Abdelmalek. *L'immigration ou les paradoxes de l'altérité.* 2 volumes. Paris, 2006.

Schiller, Nina Glick, Linda Basch, and Cristina Szanton Blanc. "From Immigrant to Transmigrant: Theorizing Transnational Migration." In *Transnationale Migration,* ed. Ludger Pries. Baden-Baden, 1997.

Schiller, Nina Glick, and Ayse Çağlar, "Introduction: 'Migrants and Cities'." In *Locating Migration: Rescaling Cities and Migrants,* ed. Nina Glick Schiller and Ayse Çağlar (Ithaca, NY; London, 2011).

Schlesisches Museum zu Görlitz, ed. *Lebenswege ins Ungewisse: Görlitz—Zgorzelec 1933–2011.* Görlitz, 2011.

Severin-Barboutie, Bettina. "Die Fremdwahrnehmung von Italienern und Türken in der Bundesrepublik." In *Dolce Vita? Das Bild der italienischen Migranten in Deutschland,* ed. Oliver Janz, Roberto Sala. Frankfurt am Main, 2011.

———. "Historische Migrationsforschung auf dem Prüfstand." In *Archive und Migration,* ed. Roland Deigendesch and Peter Müller. Stuttgart, 2014.

Stephan, Michael. "Archive und Migration." In *Archive und Migration,* ed. Roland Deigendesch and Peter Müller. Stuttgart, 2014.

Sternberg, Jan Philipp. *Auswanderungsland Bundesrepublik: Denkmuster und Debatten in Politik und Medien 1945–2000.* Paderborn, 2012.

Urry, John. *Mobilities.* Cambridge, 2007.

Weber, Horst. *Eingewandert: Geschichte und Lebenssituation von ArbeitsmigrantInnen in Braunschweig.* Braunschweig, 1993.

Wisotzky, Klaus and Ingid Wölk, eds. *Fremd(e) im Revier!? Zuwanderung und Fremdsein im Ruhrgebiet.* Essen, 2010.

Afterword

JARED POLEY

Prussia's Great Elector Frederick William declared in the Edict of Potsdam of 29 October 1685 that his "Lands and Provinces" were officially to be a "secure and free refuge" for French Protestants suddenly experiencing a new climate of religious intolerance after King Louis XIV revoked the Edict of Nantes.[1] Frederick William's stunning invitation not only opened the door of Prussia to fleeing Huguenots, but it also sharply delineated a new understanding of the importance of immigrants to the economic, cultural, and even religious life of the territory. Almost three hundred years later, Chancellor Helmut Kohl of the Federal Republic of Germany made an equally stunning remark. In a private conversation with Prime Minister Margaret Thatcher that took place on 28 October 1982, Kohl expressed his opinion that "over the next four years, it would be necessary to reduce the number of Turks in [West] Germany by 50 percent." He went on to explain that relations between West German citizens and Turkish immigrants were strained. As Kohl put it, "a clash of two different cultures" stemmed from the fact that "the Turks came from a very distinctive culture and did not integrate well."[2]

There is an entire history of migration to Germany that crosses this three-hundred-year gulf and the very different valuations of migrants to Germany that are contained in these two statements. This volume has helped us see the history of migration to Germany in new ways and in wider perspective. The essays in the volume cohere as a fresh expression of what might be called "Global German Studies," in that these authors are less interested in "Germany in the world" than they are in an analysis of the "world in Germany." As such, the essays contained here represent cutting-edge scholarship: the sounding of new voices and emerging scholars as well as the introduction of German academics to a wider English-language audience.

The approach of the volume as a whole reflects a fusion of world history and German studies, what Joanne Miyang Cho, Eric Kurlander, and Douglas T. McGetchin usefully identify as part of the "transcultural turn" in historical studies.[3] The authors of that volume assert that "truly global, transnational history demands . . . the broadening of parameter from nation or region to the world and acknowledges cultural hybridity."[4] The contributions to this volume exhibit a similar mindset. While world history has long been engaged in the production of knowledge about human migration, the focus of much of that scholarship has been on what might be called European outmigration, processes that Alfred Crosby has identified as the products of Europe's "ecological imperialism"[5] and the lasting implications of the Columbian exchange.[6] Taking a view of migration (and of world history) as a process lacking consistent direction, historian Patrick Manning identifies world history as the "story of past connections in the human community."[7] Indeed, cross-cultural contacts and trade have been central areas of research in world history, and the heuristic devices of "culture," "encounter," and "trade" have generated landmark interpretations of the past.[8] This volume explores these issues in historically specific and contextual ways.

The present volume falls at the intersection of German History and World History (with its disciplinary emphasis on migration, exchange, and cross-cultural interactions), and it is at its heart concerned with understanding how the experience of mobility and migration—both within and to the German-speaking lands—has affected German society, culture, and economy. The chapters, which cover the large chronological period of the sixteenth to the twentieth centuries, are grouped around three central thematic points: religion and exile; flux and the politics of immigration; and cultures of exile and the formation of exilic identities. No single volume will ever cover all the aspects of migration in Germany. Gaps and caesurae indicate opportunities for further research and underline the dynamism of the questions animating the field as a whole.

The essays in the first section demonstrate how religion and religious identities shaped how exile was "felt" by different groups over a period spanning the sixteenth to the twentieth centuries. Martyrdom, assimilation and autonomy, and the return of religious minorities wrestling with the enormity of genocide are but three ways to see better how exilic and migratory communities explored Germany. The essays together indicate how religion played a prominent role in shaping the experience of exile in both the early modern and modern periods. The second theme animating the essays in the volume—flux and the politics of immigration—produces a parallax view of the political stakes involved with in-migration over the span of time covered by the book. Finally, the historical production of "cultures of exile" and of "exilic identities" in the German-speaking lands reveals the importance of transcultural studies as a way to see the ramifications of cross-cultural exchange more clearly. Each of these themes is explicitly historical in its orientation. By including works that together transcend long historical periods and cross the most obvious dividing lines in German history (1517, 1648, 1740, 1806, 1871, 1918, 1945, 1968, 1989) the volume allows us to take the long view of migration and mobility. And by considering the social, political, economic, and cultural effects of these practices, the volume provides an exciting range of interventions that allow us to see not only historical changes and continuities, but also to place Germany amid larger global processes.

Chancellor Kohl was surely serious when he articulated his dream of a Germany with fewer Turkish immigrants in 1982. The Great Elector was equally serious when he made it possible for a Prussia with even more Protestants— even if they were French—in 1685. Between those points we see the history of migration within and to the German lands develop in tangled and complex ways. The contributions to this volume—detailing as they do the importance of religion to migration, the shifting politics of migration, and the transformations adhering to the cultures of migration over the last five hundred years—contribute a new way to view Germany as the product of a history of heterogeneous populations constituting and responding to forces with both a long temporal span and of a strong global character.

Jared Poley is Professor of History at Georgia State University. He is the author of *Decolonization in Germany: Weimar Narratives of Colonial Loss and Foreign Occupation* (2005) and *The Devil's Riches: A Modern History of Greed* (2016), and co-editor of *Conversion and the Politics of Religion in Early Modern Germany* (2012) and *Kinship, Community and Self: Essays in Honor of David Warren Sabean* (2014).

Notes

1. C.A. Macartney, ed., *The Habsburg and Hohenzollern Dynasties in the Seventeenth and Eighteenth Centuries* (New York, 1970), 270.
2. Claus Hecking, "Secret Minutes: Chancellor Kohl Wanted Half of Turks Out of Germany," *Spiegel Online*, 1 August 2013, retrieved 17 January 2014 from http://www.spiegel.de/international/germany/secret-minutes-chancellor-kohl-wanted-half-of-turks-out-of-germany-a-914376.html. The language comes from recently declassified files housed in the British National Archive (PREM 19/1036). Kohl's remarks were included in the notes of the meeting recorded by Thatcher's personal assistant, A.J. Coles.
3. Joanne Miyang Cho, Eric Kurlander, and Douglas T. McGetchin, eds., *Transcultural Encounters between Germany and India: Kindred Spirits in the 19th and 20th Centuries*, Routledge Studies in the Modern History of Asia (New York, 2013), 2–4.
4. Ibid., 4.
5. Alfred W. Crosby, *Ecological Imperialism: The Biological Expansion of Europe, 900–1900*, 2nd ed. (Cambridge, 2004).
6. Alfred W. Crosby, *The Columbian Exchange: Biological and Cultural Consequences of 1492 30th Anniversary Edition* (Westport, CT, 2003).

7. Patrick Manning, *Navigating World History: Historians Create a Global Past* (New York, 2003).
8. Philip D. Curtin, *Cross-Cultural Trade in World History*, Studies in Comparative World History (Cambridge, 1984); Jerry H. Bentley, *Old World Encounters: Cross-Cultural Contacts and Exchanges in Pre-Modern Times* (New York, 1993).

Bibliography

Bentley, Jerry H. *Old World Encounters: Cross-Cultural Contacts and Exchanges in Pre-Modern Times.* New York, 1993.

Cho, Joanne Miyang, Eric Kurlander, and Douglas T. McGetchin, eds. *Transcultural Encounters between Germany and India: Kindred Spirits in the 19th and 20th Centuries.* Routledge Studies in the Modern History of Asia. New York, 2013.

Crosby, Alfred W. *The Columbian Exchange: Biological and Cultural Consequences of 1492: 30th Anniversary Edition.* Westport, CT, 2003.

———. *Ecological Imperialism: The Biological Expansion of Europe, 900–1900.* 2nd ed. Cambridge, 2004.

Curtin, Philip D. *Cross-Cultural Trade in World History.* Studies in Comparative World History. Cambridge, 1984.

Hecking, Claus. "Secret Minutes: Chancellor Kohl Wanted Half of Turks Out of Germany." *Spiegel Online*, 1 August 2013. Retrieved 17 January 2014 from http://www.spiegel.de/international/germany/secret-minutes-chancellor-kohl-wanted-half-of-turks-out-of-germany-a-914376.html.

Macartney, C.A., ed. *The Habsburg and Hohenzollern Dynasties in the Seventeenth and Eighteenth Centuries.* New York, 1970.

Manning, Patrick. *Navigating World History: Historians Create a Global Past.* New York, 2003.

❦ Index ❧

www.ingramcontent.com/pod-product-compliance
Lightning Source LLC
Chambersburg PA
CBHW070916030426
42336CB00014BA/2435